MW01130311

ANCESTRAL TALES

STANFORD STUDIES IN JEWISH HISTORY AND CULTURE

Edited by David Biale and Sarah Abrevaya Stein

ANCESTRAL TALES

Reading the Buczacz Stories of S.Y. Agnon

Alan Mintz

STANFORD UNIVERSITY PRESS
STANFORD, CALIFORNIA

Stanford University Press
Stanford, California

©2017 by the Board of Trustees of the Leland Stanford Junior University. All rights reserved.

This book has been published with the assistance of a contribution from
the Publication Fund of The Jewish Theological Seminary.

No part of this book may be reproduced or transmitted in any form or by any means, electronic
or mechanical, including photocopying and recording, or in any information storage or retrieval
system without the prior written permission of Stanford University Press.

Printed in the United States of America on acid-free, archival-quality paper

Library of Congress Cataloging-in-Publication Data

Names: Mintz, Alan, author.

Title: Ancestral tales : reading the Buczacz stories of S.Y. Agnon /
Alan Mintz.

Other titles: Stanford studies in Jewish history and culture.

Description: Stanford, California : Stanford University Press, 2017. |
Series: Stanford studies in Jewish history and culture | Includes
bibliographical references and index.

Identifiers: LCCN 2016049624 (print) | LCCN 2016050555 (ebook) |
ISBN 9781503601161 (cloth : alk. paper) | ISBN 9781503601864 (e-book)

Subjects: LCSH: Agnon, Shmuel Yosef, 1887-1970. City in its fullness. |
Buchach (Ukraine)--In literature. | Jews in literature.

Classification: LCC PJ5053.A4 C536 2017 (print) | LCC PJ5053.A4 (ebook) |
DDC 892.43/5--dc23

LC record available at https://lccn.loc.gov/2016049624

Cover photo: Buczacz, Ukraine, 2006. Wikimedia Commons

Typeset by Bruce Lundquist in 11/16 Bembo

To Avraham Holtz and Arnold Band
Who ushered me into the world of the Master

Table of Contents

Acknowledgments

I am deeply grateful to Jeffrey Saks, Michal Arbell, Ariel Hirschfeld, and Omer Bartov for their warm collegiality in all matters Agnon and for their reading chapters in manuscript and making important suggestions. I recall with affection and loss my close collaboration with the late James S. Diamond. Emunah Yaron graciously talked with me about the editing of her father's works. I am grateful for advice and feedback from Rachel Manekin, Avraham Holtz, Raymond Scheindlin, Menahem Schmelzer, Gershon Hundert, Marcin Wodzinski, Roman Katsman, and Hillel Weiss. Anne G. Hoffman, David Stern, and David Roskies have been unstinting sources of encouragement. The participants in the research group on "Galicia: Literary and Historical Approaches to a Jewish Place" at the Israel Institute of Advanced Studies provided stimulation and expertise in the latter stages of this project; I am grateful to the Institute for enlightenment and hospitality. My thanks to Beit Agnon in Jerusalem for its sponsorship of a trip to Buczacz under the erudite leadership of David Assaf and Haim Be'er. A fellowship from the Guggenheim Foundation underwrote an important phase of the work. I am grateful to Alan Cooper, Provost of the Jewish Theological Seminary (JTS), and to JTS as a whole for its encouragement of scholarship and the acknowledgment of its importance. The staff members of the JTS Library were always genial and helpful. Finally, I owe an unending debt to my wife, Susanna Morgenthau, and my daughters, Amira and Avital, for their ready support and affection.

ANCESTRAL TALES

An undated view of Buczacz. With permission of Beit Agnon, Jerusalem.

Introduction

"I Am Building a City"

In the spring of 1956, the critic Baruch Kurzweil wrote to S. Y. Agnon to ask what the writer was currently working on. Agnon, in the midst of launching an extensive cycle of stories about the Galician town in which he grew up, responded by saying: "I am building a city—Buczacz."[1] The present book is a study of those stories, which appeared under the title *A City in Its Fullness* [*'Ir umelo'ah*] in 1973, three years after Agnon's death. Agnon's pithy response to Kurzweil provides a revealing snapshot of the writer's aspirations. A brief meditation on Agnon's choice of words can provide us with an entrée into this most extraordinary undertaking.

Today Buczacz is a small city in western Ukraine, eighty-three miles southeast of Lviv. Before 1772, it was located on the southern frontier of the Polish-Lithuanian Commonwealth; after the partitions of Poland, it became part of Galicia, a province of the Austrian Empire. Buczacz had a populous and vibrant Jewish community until the destruction visited on Galician Jewry during World War One; during World War Two, the city's Jews were liquidated by the Nazis. Precisely because the Jewish community of Buczacz no longer existed, Agnon's statement that he is *building* a city is curious. We would have expected him to say that he is *re*building or to use other language that would indicate an act of restoring, reconstructing, or recollecting. Yet there is nothing that implies that the result of his work is a simulacrum of the Buczacz that once existed. It is a new building that stands on its own.

To be sure, Agnon's ebullient reply to Kurzweil at the beginning of his new project should not be taken as a considered programmatic statement. Nevertheless, there is something revealing in Agnon's insistence on the originality of the Buczacz stories, originality in the sense of something primary that is not a nostalgic tribute to the past. The image is distinctly one of new creation; this is not the work of a craftsman who is restoring a damaged painting or an architect/builder who is reconstructing a model, however true to the original, of a destroyed city. Cannot the difference between the historical Buczacz and the Buczacz that Agnon is building be accounted for by the fact that the latter is a literary endeavor? The city has been destroyed, and now Agnon is reimagining it in words. True, but Agnon's assertion would seem to go beyond the distinction between history and the imagination. When he writes, "I am building a city," the "I" is not simply a marker of agency but a proprietary stamp of a veteran writer who writes using an established repertoire of modernist techniques. Reimagining Buczacz through the filter of *this* imagination that abandons nothing from the toolkit of modernism must of necessity mean creating something new, a new city. The bricks and mortar may be taken from the historical record, but the building will be a new creation.

No other writer in modern Jewish culture has attempted a project of similar scope or ambition. In the sequence of 140 stories in *A City in Its Fullness*, Agnon endeavors to do nothing less than to reimagine the life of Polish Jewry in the period of its classical flowering and to do so, moreover, through the resources and energies of the modern literary imagination. By classical I mean what historians today call the early modern period; and, indeed, all of the stories are set in a two-hundred-year period between the last half of the seventeenth century and the middle of the nineteenth century. This is a time before modern memory, either the memory of Agnon as a boy or the recollections he heard directly from his parents and grandparents, or the flood of images that has come to us after the Holocaust of East European Jewish life in the twentieth century. This is Agnon's great presumption: to fashion memories of life beyond the range of memory and to bring back a vanished world through the power of modern writing.

The vast enterprise of building the city of Buczacz was the great calling of Agnon's later years. It was a demanding calling because to achieve it he could not simply adapt or extend the modes of writing he had cultivated over the previous half-century of literary production. Agnon's greatest work depends for its success upon the ironic deployment of an autobiographical persona, a narrator who very much resembles Agnon himself in life circumstances and religious allegiances. When it came to reimagining the life of Polish Jewry hundreds of years ago, there could be no pretense of personal observation or recollection. So Agnon looked for useable pre-modern models of storytelling and found one in the voice of the chronicler, the curator of the *pinkas*—the communal minute book and registry maintained by all Jewish communities in Eastern Europe. Agnon fused this voice of impersonal authority with the garrulousness of other traditional storytelling figures to fashion the narrator of the stories in *A City in Its Fullness*. The invention of this new narrator and the development of a unique late style are the subject of the second chapter of this study.

The Consecration Story

What brought a great master with so many great works to his credit to undertake so daunting and ambitious a challenge in the last phase of his life? We are fortunate to have a story that comes very close to providing the answer. It therefore makes sense to begin this inquiry into Agnon's Buczacz stories with a look at this text. The story is called "The Sign" ["Hasiman"], and it has an unusual publishing history. The kernel of the story, only one page in length, appeared in a journal in 1944, and then the story in its full length as we have it now—fifty-two pages in length—appeared in 1962 in the last volume of Agnon's collected stories.[2] We do not know when between these years that Agnon grew the germ of the idea into the full story. These are the years when Agnon was consolidating his plans for the great enterprise that would eventually become *A City in Its Fullness*. The story describes a fundamental experience which, when read together with another key text, identifies the catalyst for the new project.

"The Sign" is set in Jerusalem in the mid-1940s, and at its center is an autobiographical narrator much like Agnon himself. The precipitating event is the arrival of the terrible news that the Jews of the narrator's Galician hometown have been murdered by the Nazis. The time is afternoon on the eve of the holiday of Shavuot, and, as an observant Jew, the narrator knows that mourning is forbidden after the midpoint of the day, when thoughts are to be turned to the joy of the holiday. He dutifully puts his grief away. Around the festive dinner table that evening, he tells his family stories from his childhood about the customs connected to preparations for the Shavuot holiday that were practiced in his town, the town whose destruction has just been announced to him. He is alone later that night when he is vouchsafed a mystical experience. He has come to the shack that serves as the neighborhood synagogue to observe the *tikkun leil* Shavuot, the custom of remaining awake and studying Torah on the night that marks the giving of the Torah. Instead of reading the selection of classical sources that forms the standard liturgy for the occasion, the narrator tells us that it is his longstanding custom to recite a sacred poem, versifying the commandments, composed by Solomon Ibn Gabirol, the great eleventh-century Spanish Hebrew poet. But his concentration is marred by memories of his hometown and when his eyes close, he is visited by nightmarish images of the town in its decimated condition after World War One.

It is at this moment that Ibn Gabirol is revealed in all his regal poetic glory between the doors of the Holy Ark. Through a kind of mystical telepathy, the august and ghostly poet discovers that the poem the narrator is reciting is one of Ibn Gabirol's own creations; and the narrator in turn remembers the electrifying effect of the first sacred poem of Ibn Gabirol's that he heard as a child, intoned by the old *ḥazzan* (synagogue cantor) of this town. That memory collapses the barriers he has constructed against his grief, and he breaks down in tears. After determining the reason for the narrator's anguish, Ibn Gabirol announces that he will fashion a sign, a *siman* that will enable the name of the town to be remembered. The sign takes the form of the alphabetic acrostic of the poem he is composing in which the first letter of each line spells out the name of the town. "If my town has been expunged from the world," the narrator says gratefully, "its name survives in the sign made for it by the poet in his poem."

When Emunah Yaron compiled *A City in Its Fullness* after her father's death, she took this stunning and evocative story and made it the conclusion of the volume. This was an intuitive act that was not part of her father's editorial guidelines. She must have seen in the story—with its news of the final destruction of Buczacz—a tragic but fitting ending to this epic account of the city in its fullness. Emunah Yaron's thorough and thoughtful editorial work generally proceeds from a deeply informed understanding of her father's mentality. In this instance, however, I believe the choice she made was wrong. "The Sign" should appear at the beginning of *A City in Its Fullness* and not at its end, and I make an argument why this should be so, and why this issue of placement matters a great deal.

"The Sign," I propose, is a narrative of consecration. The Agnon-like narrator undergoes a transformative mystical experience in which he is called upon to memorialize the lost community of Buczacz and to do so through the medium of his narrative art. The story presents the revelation of Ibn Gabirol as a profound event that actually took place rather than a dream or a reverie or a literary conceit. The assertion is strengthened by the fact that this revelation appears in the one-page text published in 1944, the kernel from which the full story grew. As modern readers, we are well practiced in naturalizing the supernatural events we encounter in poems and novels by recourse to the fact that they are manifestations of the literary imagination. But the events in "The Sign" make a truth claim of a different sort. Agnon is saying to us, "With all due regard to the literary imagination, *this* really happened."

Even if we accept that claim, there remains a gap between the enigmatic ending of the story and the writing of *A City in Its Fullness* as the harkening to a call that issued from the mystical experience. "The Sign" ends with Ibn Gabirol modeling an act of remembrance by fashioning a poetic sign for the city; but in his disorientation, the narrator cannot remember the poem and remains dejected by the finality of the destruction. If there is a call and it is answered, it is not, explicitly, within the bounds of the story. I say "explicitly" because there exists a hermeneutic key that can bridge this gap and explain why the narrator would experience Ibn Gabirol's actions as a prompting to undertake a project of creative memorialization.

That key is to be found in another story. As so often is the case in the Agnonian world, one text is parsed and opened up by another. The story is called "A Sense of Smell" ["Ḥush hareaḥ," 1937], and in it the Agnon-like narrator makes explicit his connection to the writing of sacred poetry. He bases the connection upon the fact that Agnon was born into a Levitical family. The Bible mandates that the tribe of Levi be separated from the rest of Israel and dedicated to the service of the Temple. This distinction of birth became largely inoperative and restricted to minor roles played by Levites in the synagogue service after the destruction of the Temple.

Yet the narrator of "A Sense of Smell" takes his identity as a Levite very seriously in a very specific way. The narrator declares that

> [i]f the Temple were still standing, I would be up there on the platform among my singing brothers, reciting each day the song that the Levites sang in the Temple. Since the Temple remains destroyed and we have no priests at service or Levites at song, instead I study Torah, the Prophets and the Writings, Mishnah, laws and legends, supplementary treatises and fine points of Torah and the works of the scribes. When I look at their words and see that of all the delights we possessed in ancient times there remains only this memory, my heart fills up with grief. That grief makes my heart tremble, and it is out of that trembling that I write these stories, like one exiled from his father's palace who makes himself a little hut and sits there telling of the glory of his father's house.[3]

The tradition of sacred song (*piyyut*) has its origins in the psalms sung by the Levites as an accompaniment to the Temple service. Although this practice was silenced by the Destruction, the inspiration of sacred poetry and song survived in the work of the synagogue poets (*payyetanim*), who composed a vast and varied body of *piyyutim* beginning in Late Antiquity and continuing into modern times, together with the *hazzanim* (the synagogue cantors), who realized their work in musical settings and transmitted it to the people. This is the path of transmission described in "The Sign" but not in the passage above. Here the narrator presents himself as a kind of laid-off Levite who turns to the study of Torah as an alternative to his former employment. Despite its great prestige, Torah learning is considered here—rather surprisingly—as second best. The gap between it and "all the delights we possessed in ancient times," namely, the sacred service in the Temple, generates a grief that causes a trembling of the heart, and that trembling, in turn, results in the narrator's writing stories (*sippurei ma'asiyot*).

Why stories and not poems? The parable that ends the passage explains the reason. Exile from the palace means living in a little hut. The majestic and sublime modes of expression are no longer available to us, and now the only medium available for narrating the glories of the palace is storytelling. In a post-exilic age of prose, stories are the successors to sacred poetry; and if they are fallen as a form, nonetheless the greatness of their success underwrites their authority.

We are now very close to putting the pieces together and appreciating the full import of Ibn Gabirol's revelation. Earlier in "The Sign," the narrator's deep connections to piyyut and *ḥazzanut* are underscored at several key junctures. Perusing his grandfather's prayer book, he discovers that the author of a hymn that moved him greatly is Solomon Ibn Gabirol; and, in a memory recovered during the revelatory experience, the narrator recalls hearing (as a young child) another sacred poem of Ibn Gabirol's rendered by the old ḥazzan of Buczacz. He further recalls the circumstances of imprisonment that led the ḥazzan to compose the melody. These experiences and affiliations help us to grasp the larger resonance of what the Agnon-like narrator undergoes on that Shavuot night.

This image of the writer's lineage and mission can help us better understand the situation of the narrator in "The Sign" as he sits dumbfounded and entranced before the ghostly presence of Solomon Ibn Gabirol. The narrator sits abashed and humbled in the presence of the great poet, and we realize that the very fact that he is made the recipient of this extraordinary visitation is not accidental. He has been chosen to play a role in this drama because in an essential sense he belongs to the chain of sacred creativity of which Ibn Gabirol is an apotheosis. That is why he was especially attuned as a child to the piyyutim and the spiritual drama they enacted, and that is why it was the memory of the old ḥazzan singing those poems that opened the floodgates of grief over the loss of Buczacz. When we construct Agnon's autobiographical myth by reading "The Sign" together with "A Sense of Smell," we see two things. First, Agnon is not simply a consumer or a beneficiary of the tradition of sacred song that goes back to the Temple; he is an actor who is himself a belated link in that chain. Second, precisely because of his belated status, his role in the tradition takes the form of telling stories rather than composing poems.

Seen from this angle, the exchange between Ibn Gabirol and the narrator of "The Sign" takes on a far more portentous and even exhilarating aspect. The great poet is not merely offering a memorial lamentation for Buczacz and its Jews, although that is no small gift. Rather he is modeling, in *his* own classical medium, an act of creative memorialization that he expects the narrator to imitate in *his* own—belated—creative medium. Ibn Gabirol is at the same time demonstrating a way out of the cul-de-sac of grief and loss while summoning the narrator to activate himself and apply his creative gifts to perpetuating the memory of his town. "The Sign" is a consecration story that resonates with the scenes from classical prophecy in the Hebrew Bible in which the prophet is called by God to undertake a high mission that transforms his life and from which he is not free to desist.

Let us return, finally, to the question of placement. There can be no doubt that "The Sign" is an extraordinary story that is essential to understanding Agnon's Buczacz project. Does it belong at the end or at the beginning? Placing the story at the end—the choice of Emunah Yaron when she edited the stories—gives Ibn Gabirol's lament a funereal finality and suggests that the function of the book as a whole is to provide an epitaph for the community of Buczacz. Placing the story at the beginning—as I have done in a selection of the stories in English translation—makes the composition of the lament into an invitation to be emulated in the narrator's belated prosaic mode of creativity. It makes the book as a whole into an imaginative construction that possesses its own reality separate from, though of course dependent upon, the destroyed world of Buczacz. Both placements are interventions and interpretive choices. I argue that making "The Sign" a gateway honors Agnon's ambition in *A City in Its Fullness* to build the city anew through the resources of his own imagination rather than merely performing a memorial gesture.

Under the Sign of the Holocaust

To understand the dilemma that faced Agnon in taking up this fraught, monumental task, I first set the aperture as wide as possible. In Agnon's situation we can see the plight of all writers and intellectuals who survive the destruction of their native civilizations and take it upon themselves to convey what vanished to contemporaries who know little about what was lost. When a whole culture vanishes—whether by genocide, cultural domination, or modernization—how does the work of remembrance proceed? What elements of the lost culture does a writer who is a survivor or an exile select for representation? How do the literary means chosen—the very question of mode and style—differ from the choices made before the fact of loss becomes final? Thus, the Holocaust, despite its uniqueness, is only the most terrible and absolute example of a phenomenon that is an indelible part of our world, and the ethical and aesthetic choices made by a great master like Agnon warrant our attention.

Agnon's case—and that of many other Hebrew writers—is complicated by the fact that his survival was the result of his having voluntarily exiled himself from a world that was later destroyed. Agnon emigrated from Galicia and came to Palestine in 1907 and, after a twelve-year sojourn in Germany, returned there permanently in 1924. He returned to Buczacz only twice, for a week following his father's death in 1913 and for five days in 1930. Agnon, then, put Buczacz behind him and rejected it as a place where he could live, and he did so long before the city's Jews were murdered. The fact of the rejection remains even if we exempt Agnon from the vulgar manifestations of *shelilat hagolah*, the negation of the Diaspora, that were integral to Zionist ideology of the time. Yet, at the same time

Buczacz and Galician Jewry are a major axis of Agnon's fiction and stand at the center of three of the four novels published in his lifetime, as well as the center of dozens of short stories. *The Bridal Canopy* [*Hakhnasat kalah*, 1931] is set in the heartland of traditional Jewish life in Galicia during the time of the Napoleonic Wars. *A Simple Story* [*Sippur pashut*, 1935] presents Buczacz as a town of shopkeepers in the first years of the twentieth century. And *A Guest for the Night*, [*Ore'aḥ natah lalun*, 1938] describes a year-long visit by an Agnon-like narrator to a Buczacz decimated by the ravages of World War One. Having given so much of his creative attention to Buczacz during the major phase of his career, what more was there to say, or what different things were there to say, once the loss of the town and Galician Jewry as a whole had become utterly final?

Apparently so, and *A City in Its Fullness* is the evidence. Although not evident to Israeli readers at the time, Agnon embarked on a vast new project that dominated his energies from the middle of the 1950s until his death in 1970 at the age of 82. This was not, to be sure, his only creative outlet in the post-war period, but it was the only one that constituted a major new direction for his work. Agnon published other important works during this period, but they were largely continuations or refinements of the modes of writing he had developed earlier. What was new about *A City in Its Fullness*, in addition to its vast scale, is a set of solutions that Agnon developed to deal with the great task he had taken on. Like the narrator at the conclusion of "The Sign," Agnon must have felt the solemn duty to overmaster his grief and convert it into imaginative constructions capable of effectively memorializing the lost city and its culture. But how? If the duty and the desire were clear and profoundly felt, the literary means for discharging such an exigent mission were hardly self-evident or ready-made.

Characteristically, Agnon said little about what was on his mind regarding the project either in his correspondence or his public statements. But it is not difficult to infer from the final product some of the key choices that were made at the outset, especially when it comes to the options Agnon sought to avoid. The early 1950s, for example, was a time when many memorial volumes for destroyed European communities were being assembled.

These *sifrei zikaron* (in Hebrew) or *yizker bikher* (in Yiddish) were collaborative efforts that depended on the contributions—both in the sense of money and articles—of emigrants from a given town scattered around the world. These volumes aspired to cover all aspects of a town's life: the history of the community, famous rabbis and scholars, synagogues, schools and other institutions, important communal leaders, clubs and organizations, economic life, and, of course, documentation of the liquidation of the community by the Germans and their local helpers, with eye-witness reports by survivors.

Buczacz was no exception to this surge of memorialization. The writer and editor Yisrael Cohen worked for ten years on compiling *Sefer Buczacz*, which appeared in 1957.[4] From the inception of the project, Cohen tried unceasingly to cajole his friend Agnon into taking a major role in compiling the volume. Yet, although Agnon encouraged Cohen and endorsed his efforts, he remained aloof. He declined to attach his name to the initial announcement soliciting material and contributions, and he rebuffed Cohen's invitation to join him as coeditor. In the end, Agnon contributed several short stories, a bibliography of books published in Buczacz, and a brief list of places where the town is mentioned in responsa literature; these are ornaments to the book but far less than had been hoped.[5]

Agnon's reluctance to take a more central role in this worthy undertaking undoubtedly had something to do with the fact that it was precisely during these years that he was formulating his plans for his own, very different, book on Buczacz. Agnon kept his own counsel, and concerning this new project, no word was said by Agnon to Cohen over the many years of their published correspondence, even as Cohen reported on the material he was gathering for the memorial book. One can imagine that the variegated collaboration involved in such a project was not congenial to Agnon's temperament. But more serious limitations to the genre of memorial books as a whole, and not just that of Buczacz, would have made it unsuitable for Agnon's purposes. The accounts of Jewish communal life in these books generally focus on the several decades before the war in accordance with the personal recollections of the writers, whereas Agnon was after a classical past that was beyond the range of such reminiscences. Further, a memorial book explicitly saw as its function to become a *matseivah*, a gravestone in words for a lost community, whereas Agnon sought imaginatively to recreate a spiritual vigor it once possessed. Finally, Agnon saw storytelling as the only vehicle for accomplishing his goals, and the assemblage of documentation and testimony in the memorial-volume genre was something else entirely.

The other model from which Agnon distances himself is the kind of writing that came to be called Holocaust literature. This kind of writing is not much in evidence in the Israel of the 1950s except for a writer such as Ka-Tsetnik (Yehiel Dinur), whose *House of Dolls* [*Beit habubot,* 1953], often served as the first exposure of young readers to the graphic horrors of the camps.[6] At the center of this growing literature was the problem of the representability of the Holocaust. How can an event of such negative transcendence with no precedence in human history be rendered intelligible? What are the literary means by which atrocity can be conveyed? Is language capable of sustaining this burden?

Of all of these serious and legitimate questions Agnon wanted to have no part. Finding effective ways to convey the horror of the death throes of European Jewry was not the goal to which he wished to commit his considerable artistic resources. The narrator of the stories in *A City in Its Fullness* never hesitates to register the reality of the horrible deaths of the Jews of Buczacz and to excoriate the perpetrators. But it is not their deaths that are the object of the work of memorialization that Agnon is undertaking, and not even their lives, that is, not the lives of the generation that died in the Holocaust, but rather the lives of their distant ancestors. Agnon wants to go back even further. Not because he is seeking to escape from a brutal confrontation with the gentile world—there is ample brutality in these earlier periods—but rather, as will be discussed shortly, the fabric of traditional Jewish culture had not yet been torn asunder.

So, in the final analysis, is Agnon's Buczacz project part of Holocaust literature? To consider this question I briefly rehearse a chapter in my own intellectual biography. When earlier in my career I was undertaking the research that resulted in *Ḥurban: Responses to Catastrophe in Hebrew Literature,* I examined Agnon's oeuvre to see whether this figure, considered by many to be the greatest Hebrew writer of the twentieth century, had mounted a major response to the murder of European Jewry.[7] My determination was negative.[8] There were indeed several stories that obliquely related to the Holocaust, but I concluded that by the time of World War Two, Agnon's career, like a vast ocean liner whose direction could not be easily changed, had been formed in its major phases and could not be brought around to undertake a major engagement with the tremendum of the Holocaust.

I was wrong, as the present study makes abundantly clear. The source of my error was in what I assumed at the time were the established markers of Holocaust literature: ghettos, camps, victims, perpetrators, survivors, traumatic memory, and so on. Based on those criteria, Agnon indeed came up short. What I did not see was that during the last twenty years of his life, Agnon had in fact reoriented his career and redeployed his formidable imaginative resources in the service of a major project of memorialization. Yet rather than turning to the appurtenances of the "concentrationary universe," he set upon the idea of conjuring—in his own imaginative terms— the lost world of Polish Jewry, viewed not in its fallen, belated aspect but in the vigor of its golden age. This was not inevitable. Agnon could have surely rested on his laurels. Having written so much about East European Jewry in general and Buczacz in particular, he could easily have anthologized his own work and produced a stirring tribute to this vanished world. Instead, during the last phase of his career he undertook a vast project that was entirely new and remarkably different from his earlier work. It is important to note that, with the exception of "The Sign," not one of the 150 texts in the 730 pages of *A City in Its Fullness* was written earlier or published previously in book form. To present these stories, Agnon developed a new mode of storytelling and fashioned a new kind of narrator to tell them.

Agnon's way of dealing with the Holocaust, in sum, was *not* to deal with it—at least not directly. He chose instead to reanimate, in his own terms and under the sign of the Holocaust, what was most valuable in the civilization that had been destroyed. In a narrow and conventional sense, then, *A City in Its Fullness* may not fall into the category of Holocaust literature, but it is most certainly a major response to the Holocaust. (It is ironic and

significant that it took the emergence of the construct of "Holocaust consciousness" to make it possible for us to look back at what Agnon was doing
during those years and realize its enormity and innovation.) Agnon's project
points to a new, alternative path to Holocaust memorialization. It is a path,
moreover, that shares more with responses to catastrophe in earlier periods
of Jewish history than do the familiar classics of Holocaust literature. In
the responses to the destruction of the two temples and to the catastrophic
massacres of the Middle Ages, emphasis was always placed on the reconstruction of the paradigms of meaning that had been stressed or broken by
the calamities.[9] There is something, then, deeply continuous with the classical tradition in Agnon's undertaking to restore, if only through the medium
of the storyteller's art, the world of Jews and Judaism that had been brought
to its final extermination.

Fundamental Choices

I now turn from the options Agnon rejected to the new principles he fashioned for himself. I present these under five headings framed as a series
of critical choices Agnon made concerning the conception of his project.
In speaking of these as choices, I am aware that I am inferring them from
Agnon's praxis—*A City in Its Fullness* as a finished product—and dramatizing them as conscious interventions. It should be evident by now that
Agnon was not the kind of writer who was given to discussing motives
and intentions. But it is productive and legitimate to argue backward from
the text if it helps us to provide a foreground for the distinctive departures
embodied in the text.

First was the choice of historical parameters. *A City in Its Fullness* begins with the generation following the Khmelnytskyi massacres of 1648
and ends around 1867, the year the Jews of Galicia were emancipated and
given the vote. The starting point is explained, I believe, by the scarcity of
historical materials about Buczacz before this time and by Agnon's desire to
underscore the fortitude of the Jews of Buczacz, and their collective will in
rebuilding the community, after those massacres and the ones visited upon
the city by the Tartars and the Turks in the following decades. The end

point is explained by the great changes that swept over Buczacz and all of Galician Jewry in the second half of the nineteenth century: pauperization, emigration to the West (Vienna, Warsaw, and America), and the influx of socialism, Zionism, and territorialism as ideological and social movements. These changes spelled the end of rabbinic authority and the intense culture of lay Torah scholarship that Agnon saw as the hallmarks of his city.

The next phases in the history of the city had been abundantly documented in the novels *A Simple Story* and *A Guest for the Night*; and, as discussed above, Agnon wanted the horrific fate of Buczacz's Jews in the 1940s to be registered and recalled frequently and unequivocally, but not to be made the subject of literary representation. All this was not avoidance but principled choice. What Agnon wanted to convey to future readers about his town was located in the centuries when, as often repeated in the book, "Buczacz was Buczacz," by which he meant when the town and its Jewish inhabitants lived under the sway of the Torah before the full effects of modernization.

Second is the decision to write about a single town. Holding in one's hands this heavy tome with its encyclopedic store of lore about Buczacz, this fait accompli, it is hard to imagine that it could be otherwise. But the choice represents a more complex calculation. To be sure, Agnon was a man of Buczacz, he had a deep loyalty to the place in which he grew up, and he had spent a lifetime collecting documents and materials about his town. Yet he was also a great Hebrew writer—undoubtedly the greatest in his own eyes—with a felt responsibility to the whole of the Jewish people. Sentimentality and convenience could not be the paramount motives of a figure of such eminence as he poised to undertake a great project memorializing the murder of European Jewry. If Polish Jewry as a whole was too wide a focus, then certainly a narrower aperture focused on Galician Jewry would have been coherent and appropriate, especially in light of the fact that, despite the endearing attention invested in its depiction, Buczacz was not among the first rank of towns in the province. Yet Agnon insisted on Buczacz and Buczacz alone. This insistence, I would argue, can best be understood as an aesthetic choice. What James Joyce had done with Dublin and what William Faulkner had done with Yoknapatawpha County, Agnon intended to accomplish with Buczacz. The choice is much more than making a place serve as a representative function or become a microcosm. This approach proceeds from the modernist premise that the deepest and most universal truths can be grasped only through the radical particularity and specificity of the one instance. It is a guard against the blunting of concreteness, which can turn remembrance into nostalgia. Agnon's identification with Buczacz and the stock of lore in his possession surely paved the way, but the choice itself was a modernist move.

Third is the selection of those aspects of life in Buczacz to foreground. Again, we must make an effort to suspend our experience of *A City in Its Fullness* in its monumental givenness to consider how it could have been otherwise. To get a sense of just how fungible was the representation of small-town Jewish life in Eastern Europe, one needs only to look at the variety of versions extant in Hebrew and Yiddish literature: the shtetl as a cradle of folly and superstition (Sh. Abramovitch/Mendele), the shtetl as a harmonious human organism (Shalom Asch), the shtetl as the stage for the dark comedy of the human condition (Sholem Aleichem), the shtetl as a scene of social and class conflict (I. M. Weissenberg), the shtetl as a container for the lives of women and families (Devorah Baron), the shtetl as the ground of a life-denying religious fundamentalism (Mordecai Ze'ev Feierberg), the shtetl as an educational regime that damages the inner life of the child (Sh. Benzion, Yosef Haim Brenner).[10] And this is only a partial catalogue, to which one should add Agnon's own important earlier contributions. So, when belatedly Agnon revisited this busy field of representation—all the literature just referred to was written before the war—how did he shape the portrait of Buczacz?

The answer is that Agnon self-consciously chose two related categories around which to constellate the reimagined world of Buczacz: Torah study and synagogue worship, or, in the traditional formulation, *'al hatorah ve'al ha'avodah*. Torah study includes the chronicles of the great scholars who were brought to Buczacz to serve as the town's rabbinic authorities, as well as those, sometimes greater, scholars whom the town could not succeed in attracting or retaining. Yet what Agnon places at the center is not the remunerated position of community rabbi but rather the *batei midrash* (*beit midrash,* singular), the study houses, which were the greatest and most characteristic glory of Buczacz. The beit midrash, as presented in *A City in Its Fullness,* is filled from morning to night with full-time scholars, bridegrooms devoting themselves to study, shopkeepers meeting their study partners after work in the evenings, and tradesmen popping in for an hour to read Psalms or recite *mishnayot*. Adjacent to the beit midrash is the *beit keneset,* the synagogue, which is the other focus. Agnon devotes considerable attention to how the prayer houses of Buczacz were financed and built; to the lives of the salaried (*shamashim,* sextons; [*shamash,* singular]) and non-salaried (*gabaiim,* treasurers; [*gabai,* singular]) personnel who maintained them; and to the zealous loyalty to the particular customs of prayer that had been inherited from the town's founders, who had come—according to Agnon's historically questionable assertion—from the Rhineland Valley in medieval Germany. Crucial to this picture are the lives of the great ḥazzanim, who served as both the custodians of the collective tradition of piyyutim and men of individual talent who originated new musical settings for old texts.

Yet, ironically, despite Agnon's manifest intention to organize his account of Buczacz under the sign of these two norms, the strongest texts, that is to say the greatest stories of *A City in Its Fullness,* are about deviations from these norms. These are stories of class conflict and human fallibility written in modes of social critique and satire. This is the productive inner duality of Agnon's project: the desire to conjure Buczacz as a *kehilah kedoshah,* a holy community, built on study and worship, and the fact that a truly good story qua story cannot be based or sustained on the wholly normative. The "best self" of Buczacz as expressed and fulfilled in these collective norms is the proper subject matter for a chronicle but not for fiction as Agnon practiced it. The deviations are of all kinds. There is cupidity, cruelty, pride and sensuality, and other divagations of the individual human heart. There is hypocrisy, oppression, and high-handedness in the communal realm. There are ordeals that challenge God's righteousness and justice. And then there are exaggerations of the norms in the form of excessive piety and self-sacrifice. The complex dialectic between the ideal and the real is at the heart of the book's power.

Fourth was the choice to compose *A City in Its Fullness* not as a novel but as cycle of texts that alternates between ethnography and story. The modernist novella and the sprawling novel, forms Agnon had mastered between the two world wars, were not suitable vehicles for this endeavor. Agnon chose instead an ostensibly pre-modern version of the story as a literary form. This was not the short story perfected and aestheticized by Chekov, Maupassant, and Joyce, but rather the kind of tale told by a storyteller in a world before the institutionalization of literature. It is these stories—there are about twenty of them, some quite long, depending how one counts—that are embedded in the historical account the narrator provides of the customs, institutions, and personalities of Buczacz. The story had of course been Agnon's métier since "Agunot," his first published story in 1908; the kind of story Agnon fashioned for *A City in Its Fullness* is different because of the workings of a new kind of narrator, as I discuss below. The insistence on story should be understood in the context of Agnon's quarrel with memorial books and other forms of memorialization that treated the past as dead and lost. Agnon saw the special kind of imaginative means he was working with as possessing the capacity to do just the opposite: to bring the past back to life. He knew that this was a virtual life, a fiction. But as a modernist and a storyteller, he also knew that this was no small thing. Finally, there is the large, architectonic form in which the individual units are arrayed. This form properly should be called a story sequence, a form of epic dimensions comprised of linked but individual units organized along purposeful principles of composition. In its mode of organization, *A City in Its Fullness* also represents an innovation in Agnon's corpus. To be sure, there are other collections of stories, such as *Eilu ve'eilu*, but all of these are just that: collections that have been assembled after the fact and put together to be published as a volume. *A City in Its Fullness* was a new departure for Agnon because the individual stories were conceived from the outset as part of a coherent project with a unique epic trajectory.

Fifth, and most important, was the fashioning of a new narrative persona. Open up *A City in Its Fullness* at any point and read a few pages and you will immediately sense that the words on the page are not simply there but they are *told*, and they are told by a narrator with a characteristic voice who frequently lets his presence be known. Who is this narrator? With reference to Agnon's earlier work, it is easier to say who he is *not*. He is not the narcissistic, self-ironic *moyen homme sensuel religieux*, the autobiographical persona that is a fixture of much of the author's best work, especially the novel *A Guest for the Night*, in which the narrator is actually named Shmuel Yosef.

To do the work of narration in *A City in Its Fullness*, Agnon needed a more impersonal narrator who was attached to the pre-modern centuries when "Buczacz was Buczacz." He found a model for some elements of this narrator in the *pinkasim*, the communal registers kept by Jewish communities in Eastern Europe. His narrator could be presented as a kind of *ba'al hapinkas*, a traditional chronicler who possesses authoritative knowledge of the affairs of the community. Indeed, Agnon's narrator is an apotheosis of such a figure. His knowledge is not just authoritative but also omniscient, and it ranges over the centuries. He knows the innermost thoughts of rabbis and thieves and can report their intimate conversations with their wives.

To demonstrate his reliability as a reporter, he frequently stipulates his uncertainty about trivial matters, admitting, for instance, that he is not certain whether a wagon journey undertaken at the beginning of the eighteenth century cost fourteen coins or eighteen. One thing is certain: the narrator is a man of Buczacz whose worldview is close to the worldview of believing Jews in the early modern period. That a deceased scholar might descend from the Other World to teach his orphaned son Torah, or that it is possible to find an entryway to Gehinnom, the netherworld, near Buczacz, or even that the soul of a tsaddik might be reborn in the body of a fish—all these occurrences are noted as remarkable and uncommon but entirely plausible. Yet simultaneously and inexplicably, this narrator possesses full knowledge of the fate of Buczacz's Jews during the Holocaust, and he often observes that various customs and family lines persisted until the coming of the "obscene and polluted murderers." The Holocaust—just the fact of it, not its substance—forms the outer horizon of the narrator's historical knowledge.

Finally, the self-referential voice of the narrator as an "I" directly addressing the reader is busily heard throughout the pages of *A City in Its Fullness*.

The narrator explains why he has presented events out of order, apologizes for digressions, defends the accuracy of his sources, states moral principles as aphorisms, and does not hesitate to draw simple moral lessons from complex human entanglements. By allowing his narrator such frequent, garrulous interventions, Agnon has negotiated a creative deal with the pinkas model, appropriating its austere and impersonal authority while at the same time retaining something of the arch playfulness of his previous, narcissistic personae.

Pangs of Reception

Now, if *A City in Its Fullness* is such an innovative and important work, one would have expected its publication in 1973 to have been a major event in Israeli culture. Yet this was hardly the case. A survey of the literary supplements and journals of the time yields only a handful of critical notices. Substantial and adulatory reviews of the book were written by Yehudah Friedlander in *Haaretz*, Hillel Barzel in *Yedi'ot Aharonot*, Yisrael Cohen in *Moznayim*, Yaakov Rabi in *Al Hamishmar*, and A. Y. Brawer in *Ha'umah*.[11] But all of these reviewers were either life-long friends of Agnon (Cohen and Brawer) or part of the Bar-Ilan University literary circle, which included Friedlander and Barzel, and which was presided over by Baruch Kurzweil, the foremost interpreter of Agnon's work. They were all already persuaded of Agnon's genius and already disposed to welcome a major work that grappled with the inheritance of East European Jewish culture. In addition to the general paucity of critical reaction, conspicuous is the absence of response from the younger, secular generation of intellectuals and writers, especially the members of what was called *Hador ba'arets*, the State Generation.

This tepid reception should not surprise us. What we might view today as a crucial artistic encounter with the lost Jewish past seemed in the climate of the times merely to be elegiac at best and nostalgic at worst. The world of Galician Jewry in the eighteenth century seemed, to understate the matter, very remote from public consciousness in Israel during the two decades after independence. While Agnon was deeply involved in building the city of Buczacz, David Ben-Gurion was busy building a state. The enormous energies required to build the institutions of the new country, settle the vast numbers of refugees, and defend the state against it enemies left little room for thinking about the past. The publication of the book, it should be recalled, coincided with the outbreak of the Yom Kippur War.

In the eyes of Zionist ideology, moreover, that exilic past had become identified with inner corruption, powerlessness, and victimization. Agnon's stories about the Old World, as they appeared on the pages of *Haaretz* in the 1950s and 1960s, evoked little interest. They appeared there, in the first place, because Agnon was under obligation to the Schocken family, the publishers of *Haaretz*, to supply the newspaper with material regularly although the editors would have much preferred to have been supplied with writing closer to the interests of their readers. One gets the sense that *A City in Its Fullness* was generally regarded as a huge and intimidating tome full of recondite lore about the lost exilic past. Charitably, Agnon was seen as erecting a headstone over the grave of his ancestors; less charitably, he was seen as having abandoned himself to sentimentality and nostalgia and given up the high road of modernism to become an amateur ethnographer.

Ironically it was Agnon himself who played a role in the marginalization of *A City in Its Fullness*. The book was actually the second of the posthumous works to be published. A year after Agnon's death, the novel *Shira* appeared, and the Israeli literary community exploded. The novel tells the story of Manfred Herbst, a married, German-born professor at Hebrew University who has a romantic relationship with Shira, a nurse who later contracts leprosy. The story is set in the late 1930s in a Jerusalem deluged by destitute, forlorn, and over-educated refugees from Austria and Germany. Not only was Agnon returning to the setting of Erets Yisrael and not only was he describing a time closer to the present than the Second Aliyah of *Only Yesterday*, but he was also dealing directly with love between a man and woman, and adulterous love at that. It was all Israeli readers could want. Agnon had been working on the novel since the 1940s—why he did not complete it is a matter unto itself—and had published chapters of it along the way. The appetite and curiosity of the reading public were whetted in anticipation of the publication. *Shira* had the additional asset of being a roman à clef set in the university circles of Jerusalem, and the gossipy curiosity it generated was not a small factor in its immediate success.

A City in Its Fullness would have to wait several decades to begin to garner the attention it deserves. Even for the passionate aficionados of the master's writing among general readers, this imposing volume—whose subject was familiar but whose structure seemed blurry and abstruse—had a place on the shelf but remained largely unread. Yet recently there has been awakening interest in Agnon's Buczacz stories. This new openness is the result of a series of changes in public consciousness both in Israel and in America. The Holocaust first had to be "admitted" into the realm of active discussion and exploration; this brought a change in attitude toward the victims and the survivors, and this in turn led to a greater curiosity about the life they led in Europe, and, finally by extension, to the history of European Jewry before the twentieth century.[12] Hillel Weiss and the late Shmuel Werses are veteran scholars who took an interest in *A City in Its Fullness*.[13] More recently, a younger generation of scholars has been drawn to Agnon.

What's striking in this new work is the range of critical approaches *A City in Its Fullness* has stimulated. Roman Katsman has devoted two books to the Buczacz stories, each of which develops a body of literary theory and then applies it to the Agnon text. The first, in Hebrew, emphasizes the revival of interest in rhetoric in recent theory and explores the relationship between the presumption of sincerity and the reality of rhetoric.[14] These ideas are applied to a reading of book 1 of *A City in Its Fullness* and foreground the communal voice of the narrator. The second, in English, is titled *Literature, History, Choice: The Principle of Alternative History in Literature (S. Y. Agnon, The City with All That is Therein, book 2).*[15] The concept of alternative history describes works of literature that explain what life would have been like if the course of history had taken a different turn from the one we recognize as factually true. Katsman sees Agnon's depiction of Buczacz as a recreation of Buczacz after it has been erased by the Nazis, a reimagining that is not limited by historical constraints.

A very different angle of approach is adopted by Shulamit Almog, a professor of law at Haifa University, in *'Ir, mishpat, sippur* [City, law, story], which examines the surprisingly many instances in the stories of *A City in Its Fullness* in which communal conflict is resolved by, or at least submitted to, the processes of legal deliberation.[16] Ariel Hirschfeld has recently taught graduate seminars on *A City in Its Fullness* focusing on the concept of tragedy. The Agnon scholar Michal Arbell has continued her interest in figures of artistic creation in the Buczacz stories.[17] Avidov Lipsker has taken an anthropological approach by examining the major story "Pisces" in light of the experience of the grotesque.[18]

Standing alongside these literary studies and occupying its own category, is Omer Bartov's *The Voice of Your Brother's Blood: Buczacz, Biography of a Town.*[19] A historian of the Holocaust and twentieth-century German history, Bartov is also the son of a mother who was born in Buczcacz and later emigrated to Palestine/Israel. His study tells the story of the interaction among the three main religious–ethnic groups in Buczacz (Poles, Jews, and Ruthenians/Ukrainians), each with its own narrative, from the founding of the town in the Middle Ages until the liquidation of Buczacz's Jews in the Holocaust. (I elaborate on his perspective in Chapter 1.) Bartov makes extensive use of *A City in Its Fullness* for understanding the experience of the Jews—as it is refracted through the unique prism of Agnon's mind—from the seventeenth century through the nineteenth century. Our books complement each other in method. Whereas I make use of the historical record to chart how Agnon has remolded his received materials, Bartov uses Agnon's fictional account to grasp both the historical reality as well as the narrative that the Jews of Buczacz constructed of their own history.

The status of *A City in Its Fullness* within the Agnon corpus has been affected by two related questions. What was the role of his daughter in producing the volume? And, given the absence of citations, how reliable is the book as a historical source? Regarding the first issue, most of what we know comes from the testimony of Emunah Yaron herself in the afterword to the volume, aptly titled "Ma'aseh hasefer" [The making of the book, pp. 717–20].[20] She reports that in a public reading in Jerusalem in 1965, her father introduced the story he read by saying that it was part of a book called *'Ir umelo'ah* that would contain three books or large sections and tell the story of Buczacz over six centuries from its founding until its destruction. Agnon was also clear about the general structure of the book. In the early generations, the rabbi-scholar would be primary and the city secondary, and in the later generations it would be the reverse.[21]

After her father's death, Emunah Yaron unpacked the box labeled 'Ir umelo'ah; she found there about a hundred pages of text, several outlines listing the titles of stories and the order in which they should appear, and many slips of paper with the names of stories and instructions about where they should be inserted. These guided her as to the placement of many of the major stories that had appeared in newspapers and journals. Internal references within stories about other stories provided another guideline. There were points where she was forced to extrapolate. So, for example, her father provided titles for book 1 ("Sippur shel 'ir" [The story of a city]) and book 2 ("Raboteinu hari'shonim shebeBuczacz" [The early rabbis of Buczacz]) but not for book 3, to which she gave the title "Dorot aḥaronim" [Later generations] and signified her intervention by placing the words in square brackets. She created a short book 4 to accommodate stories about Buczacz that were obviously part of the enterprise but did not have a home elsewhere. And, as I noted previously, she placed the story "Hasiman" as a conclusion to the entire volume.

Approximately 60 percent of the texts were published in Agnon's lifetime—these are signified by an asterisk in the table of contents—and the remainder transcribed from manuscript or typescript. Fortunately, Emunah Yaron had long experience in deciphering her father's difficult handwriting. Still, there are some unreadable lines, and there are a number of stories whose endings are not complete or that have multiple endings that Agnon had not yet resolved. Aged and not well, Agnon was clearly working against time to close open loops, organize the corpus of texts, catch inconsistencies, and polish rough passages. Any scholar who has worked with the canon of works Agnon published in his lifetime knows full well that the man was a writer who unceasingly revised his earlier works. So when we take his collected stories in hand and read, for example, "Agunot," his first published story, or *The Bridal Canopy*, his first published novel, we are reading the last version of a text that went through many changes—some, major transformations and some, minor alterations. Emunah Yaron is honest in acknowledging that *A City in Its Fullness* did not benefit from that process. The undertaking was too vast and her father's allotted time too limited. For readers and scholars alike, this situation is both bad and good. We are deprived of the perfection that adequate time for revision would have provided; however, at the same time we are granted access to the writing as it flowed from Agnon's pen, and we feel the master's imagination in the process of origination.

In the final analysis, then, where does this leave the scholar-critic in working with *A City in Its Fullness* and the reader in reading it? Generally, I would say, in a confident but cautious position. To begin with, we can be assured that, aside from some titles, every word is Agnon's and every text appears as he intended, even if he might have wished to revisit and revise it. We can also be assured that the organization of the volume has been realized in accordance with his general instructions. We can never know had he been alive for the final editing whether he would have "deselected" certain stories or arranged them in a slightly different order. But we do know that the person who made these final decisions understood her father's implied intentions better than anyone else and acted in all instances with exquisite care and responsibility. Nonetheless, the final structure of the book remains something of a speculative construction; and it makes a difference which parts of the book we scrutinize. Book 1, perhaps because it proceeds on the explicit model of a guided tour of Buczacz, seems like it is closest to the intent of the master. In practical terms, then, we are on firm ground when we make statements about the wording, style, or structure of an individual text. The ground is less firm when we seek to make inferences from the subtleties of the juxtaposition of the texts one to another. The question of juxtaposition deserves to be a caution but not a constraint.

Another question: Can *A City in Its Fullness* be trusted as history? The answer, unsurprisingly, depends on what we mean by this term. If by history we mean the collection and evaluation of sources and documents to produce an objective account of past events, then *A City in Its Fullness* cannot qualify given the fact that Agnon does not disclose his sources. *A City in Its Fullness*, in any case, does not present itself as that kind of history. With his well-known disdain for the adequacy of *Wissenschaft des Judentums* (the science of Judaism) as a mode of understanding the experience of the Jewish people, Agnon sought a mode of presentation that freed him from conventions and constraints of academic history. He found what he was looking for in pre-modern models of recounting the past, such as the chronicle and the pinkas.

It would not be out of place to evoke Herodotus and notions of history writing that are hospitable to custom, legend, story, and myth. Yet this may not be enough to get Agnon off the hook. For as modern, post-Enlightenment readers, we expect to be served our history straight, and the mélange of fact and story—with some of the fantasy of magic realism mixed in for good measure—does not put us at ease. Not all the historical facts Agnon presents, moreover, stand up to scrutiny. For example, Yisrael Cohen, who also grew up in Buczacz, states that he never heard of the story of the founding of the town according to which Jews from the Rhineland Valley on their way to Erets Yisrael suspended their journey and built Buczacz.[22] (This is the first story in *A City in Its Fullness*.) The geographer A. Y. Brawer, who himself grew up close to Buczacz, finds it extremely curious that through his narrator Agnon asserts that the antinomian messianic pretender Jacob Frank was born in Buczacz, where the ruins of his house could still be seen, whereas historians agree that Frank was born in Korolivka, a town on the Eastern boarder of Galicia.[23] Both men were lifelong friends of Agnon's, and their demurrals are voiced with respectful understatement.

There is no doubt that *A City in Its Fullness* remains an extraordinary repository of information about Buczacz and Galician Jewry. Over decades Agnon was indefatigable in his efforts to debrief Buczacz natives who found their way to Palestine/Israel about what they remembered of his town. He scoured the responsa literature (*she'eilot uteshuvot*) written by the rabbinical authorities of Buczacz for clues to the texture of everyday life as well as well as communal conflicts. His bibliography of books published in Buczacz, which appeared in *Sefer Buczacz*, ran to over seventy items. And then there is the store of first-hand memories of the author himself during his first nineteen years of life, memories of the lad who spent his days in the beit midrash of Buczacz and pressed the old timers for their recollections. In the end, however, the vast miscellany of information and imagination that is *A City in Its Fullness* remains Agnon's proprietary kingdom. On the one hand, we are not invited to ask niggling and fastidious questions about where the master found his building materials and whether he used them correctly. On the other, we are positively invited to enjoy the feast that has been laid out for us in this capacious palace of memory. The reductive question of historical truth fades as we settle in to the embrace of a broad imagination that is historically grounded but possessed of its own freedom.

The absence of sources also throws up a challenge to the literary scholar who seeks to interpret the stories in *A City in Its Fullness.* Consider the story about a rabbi and his assistant who descend into Gehinnom, or the daughter of a ḥazzan who dies of melancholy, or a rabbi who goes into hiding because of an impolitic legal ruling, or a demobilized Jewish soldier who is locked up by a Polish noblewoman, or a teenage scholar who volunteers on the spot to marry a bride whose bridegroom has just abandoned her. One hungers to know about the folk stories, the legends, the incidents inscribed in the communal pinkas, and the hearsay that Agnon used as an armature for creating the stories we have before us. For which tales did he have preexisting materials, and which stories were made up out of whole cloth?

The question of sources is different for the literary scholar than for the historian. A historian might focus on the usefulness of the stories as historical sources and measure them against what is known of the historical record. Valorizing the stories as works of art, the literary scholar is less concerned with establishing their reliability as representations than with assessing the degree of imaginative transformation that has been worked upon the sources. The literary scholar not only expects that gap to be large but delights in documenting the degree and kind of transformation and then taking it as a tribute to the writer's imaginative powers. In Chapter 5, I explore this issue further and propose that Agnon, while basing himself rigorously on the way life was lived in a particular historical period, took upon himself to conceive plots that sometimes "corrected," that is, improved, the treatment of the Jews and sometimes portrayed their behavior to one another as crueler than it may have been.

Agnon does not make it easy. It is exceedingly difficult and often impossible to discover the materials Agnon had at hand; and when it is possible, it is only through dedicated and erudite detection work. It is just this kind of work that Avraham Holtz did in his extraordinarily annotated and illustrated edition of Agnon's first novel, *Hakhnasat kalah*.[24] Integrating this kind of source criticism with thematic interpretation has been the goal of the Agnon scholar Hillel Weiss. Very little of this sort of work, unfortunately, has been done on the texts of *A City in Its Fullness*, and, the current study, due in part to my temperament as a scholar, will make only a partial and inconstant contribution to that goal. I have proceeded on the basis that the stories in *A City in Its Fullness*, to the degree that they are strong works of art (as I believe many of them to be), can be read on their own terms. Historical contextualization is obviously very important, as of course are the references to classic biblical and rabbinic sources. When lucky, it is possible to find the old bottle into which Agnon is pouring new wine. So, for example, when the compartments of Gehinnom are described in "The Parable and Its Lesson" ["Hamashal vehanimshal"], it is possible to examine the templates Agnon borrowed from medieval treatises on the afterlife and then discover the radically new content he is filling them with. But, again, Agnon, the wily Galitsianer that he is, has not made it easy to be lucky often. I offer this study as an open matrix to be supplemented and enriched by future discoveries.

The Plan of this Study

Such a variegated, complex, and epic work as *A City in Its Fullness* creates challenges for readers and critics alike. The new studies mentioned above each consider the work from a different point of departure. My own approach has been to focus on the longer, more "literary" stories. Of these I count about twenty out of the 140 separate texts in the volume. All the stories in *A City in Its Fullness* are an amalgam of storytelling, on the one hand, and a conveyance to the reader of ethnographic information about the history and customs of Buczacz on the other. I favor the texts in which the storytelling impulse dominates and takes the form of sustained, complex narrative. I do so out of a certain polemical enthusiasm. For the many decades since its publication, *A City in Its Fullness* has been regarded as something other, a work that is not exactly literature but more resembles a repository of proprietary nostalgia, historical arcana, and familial anthropology. My wish is to make a case for the work containing some of the greatest fiction Agnon ever wrote, fiction that deserves not only to be given a place in the Agnon canon but to reshape it.

Yet I well understand that the way to make this case is not by demanding recompense for the unwarranted years of misunderstanding and neglect. Rather, the only way to gain acknowledgement for the greatness of a literary text is to demonstrate *why* it is great, and the only way to do that is through the hard work of analysis and exposition—hence my decision to submit a limited number of stories to close inspection rather than to attempt a survey or taxonomy of the multiplicity of units that comprise the book. In most cases I endeavor to relate the central story under discussion to other related but shorter texts; however, for a major story, in general, I prefer to offer a thorough account.

This approach surely would not be responsible or sustainable if the reader could not have access to the stories in translation. For that reason, this study was conceived from the very beginning as being twinned with a substantial selection of the stories in English translation. That project was begun in collaboration with the scholar and translator James S. Diamond, and it was continued in collaboration with a number of other translators after his untimely death. All the texts analyzed in this study can be found in that collection, and the two books are meant to be used in tandem. The citations in the following chapters refer to both the original Hebrew and to the stories as they appear in *A City in Its Fullness* (Toby Press, 2016), which contains the major stories from the 1973 Hebrew volume of that name.

The study contains eight chapters in addition to this introduction. Chapter 1 presents the historical background of the Jewish community of Buczacz and then proceeds to describe the "grand tour" of the key institu-

tions of that community as they unfold in book 1 of *A City in Its Fullness*.
Chapter 2 is devoted to the signal innovation of the Buczacz stories: the
invention and deployment of a new kind of narrative mechanism. Because
Agnon was reimagining events from the distant past, he had to give up the
autobiographical persona that had served him for so long and instead adopt
more classical modes of storytelling. These narrators, who proclaim their
authority and omniscience while manifesting their unreliability, give these
stories their intriguing and canny power.

The subsequent chapters are devoted to the two norms that organize
Agnon's reimagining of Buczacz: worship and study. Chapter 3 focuses on
a set of stories concerning the ḥazzanim, the professional prayer leaders
whose vocation required close—and ultimately dangerous—proximity to
the holy. Stories that deal with the more rarefied world of elite Torah scholars are the subject of Chapter 4. There is no more greatly exalted ideal in
the world Agnon has imagined than a rabbi whose prodigious learning
allows him not only to perpetuate the great tradition of scholarship but
to augment it and alter it by the force of his mental acuity. Yet the rabbi is
an employee of the community, which operates under the constraints and
interventions of the Polish magnates. The great, sprawling novella at the
center of the chapter, "In Search of a Rabbi, or The Governor's Whim,"
explores the complex knot of these tensions.

Buczacz was first owned outright by the Potockis, a Polish noble family;
but after the first partition of Poland in 1772, it was governed by officials of
the Austrian Empire as part of the province of Galicia. Chapter 5 discusses
a set of stories that stage fateful interactions between Jews and high-born
Poles. Chapter 6 and Chapter 7 deal with the effects of the "enlightened"
absolutism of the Austrian Empire on the Jews of Buczacz. In the stories
set both before and after the Partition, Agnon positions his tales against a
background of historically accurate circumstances even as he exercises his
artistic freedom to imagine alternate outcomes and to focus on the responsibility of the Jews for their own fate. The stories set in the Austrian period
are particularly severe in their judgment of the behavior of the communal
leadership of Buczacz.

If in the earlier sections of *A City in Its Fullness* the city is presented brightly under the sign of worship and learning, in the later sections its luster is significantly tarnished. Chapter 8 is devoted to the countertheme of redemption, which is realized through individual acts of spiritual and ethical heroism. The Epilogue meditates on the place of Agnon's project in rethinking the imaginative construct of East European Jewry in the wake of its destruction.

A Baedeker to Buczacz

A Myth of Origins

When was our city founded and who founded it? Long have all the chroniclers labored to find this out in vain. But some few facts have been revealed to us, and I am herewith setting down a faithful record of all I know.[1]

With this simple and appealing declaration, Agnon's narrator begins the first story in *A City in Its Fullness*, which is an account of Buczacz's origins. Yet despite this profession of modesty and truthfulness, any historically informed reader soon realizes that the account rendered in the pages that follow is a fabrication. We should already be alerted to this fact by the implied contrast between "us" and the chroniclers, who are referred to not as historians but, in the antique locution *dorshei korot ha 'itim*, as investigators of the events of the past. Whereas their arduous labors have born meager fruit, the narrator, who begins speaking as "we" and then goes over to "I," has been vouchsafed his knowledge about Buczacz's origins, however slight it may be, by a different means. It has been revealed (*nitgalah lanu*) rather than gathered through investigation and inquiry. The narrator is thus in possession of a truth which, given as an act of grace, is superior to the hard-won results of the chroniclers' exertions.

This superior alternative truth that Agnon presents at the beginning of his grand project is a version of what anthropologists call a myth of origins: a story told by a community about how it came into being that accords with its present identity. Yet whereas most myths of origin are products of the collective folk imagination, this one is Agnon's own. And it is self-consciously fashioned rather than spawned by the folk unconscious.

As a modern Jewish intellectual, Agnon knew full well that the Jews who settled Galicia came from neighboring Poland, that they were escaping the economic exclusion created by the assertiveness of guilds of Polish tradesmen, and that the brunt of the migration took place in the sixteenth century. The account of the origins of Buczacz placed in the mouth of the narrator at the beginning of *A City in Its Fullness* is woven out of different cloth: the settlers came directly from the ancient Jewish communities of the Rhineland Valley; their motives were spiritual, and the time of their arrival earlier by several centuries. What were Agnon's reasons for launching *A City in Its Fullness* with a narrative that is so starkly at odds with the historical record? And if it is indeed a myth of origins, what are the values it is intended to serve? Let us first attend to the story as he tells it.

The caravan of Jews who sold all their belongings and left their homes in Ashkenaz in Western Europe had only one aspiration: to "ascend" to the Land of Israel. They possessed no map and knew only that the Land of Israel was in the east, and so they pushed on eastward. Because of their holy purpose, God protected them from princes, brigands, and wild animals as they passed through distant gentile lands. They pass far beyond areas of human settlement and find themselves on the eve of the Days of Awe in the midst of trackless forests. There they make an encampment and observe the round of the holy days in joy and faith. But there in the land of the Slavs winter comes early, and it was barely possible to observe the commandment of dwelling in booths. They become reconciled to the necessity of remaining encamped there for the winter before continuing eastward.

As they shudder from cold in their hastily improvised cabins, a hunting party of Polish nobleman on horseback suddenly appears. Every year in early winter they come here to hunt, and they were astonished to find a group of Jews in a place that had been utterly devoid of human habitation. Through exchanges that take place in Latin, the nobles discover the wisdom and civility of the Jews, and, citing the difficulty of surviving the winter in the open, they invite the Jews to split up and take refuge by returning with them to their scattered estates. They are further invited to begin trading because there is no one in the area with commercial experience or ability. The Jews accept the offer, and their presence brings great benefit to their hosts. Each year the Jews gather together in the same place in the forest from Rosh Hashanah through Sukkot so that they pray and read the Torah as a community.

It is the dissatisfaction with this arrangement that provides the kernel from which Buczacz eventually grows. The Jews long to pray in a minyan and to hear the parts of the service, especially the reading of the Torah, which can be recited only in public gathering. First they build a synagogue on land granted to them by the local magnate, and individuals undertake to travel from their dispersed locations to be present on the days when the Torah is read. From a love of public prayer and study, some build homes adjacent to the synagogue; a mikveh, a ritual bath, is also built, and, rather than traveling the countryside to trade, shops are opened there as well, which in turn attract the peasants from the surrounding villages on market days. And so the kehilah kedoshah, the holy community of Buczacz came into being.

Looking at this introduction to Buczacz with the eyes of a modern reader, we are first struck by its indifference to chronology and geography. The gauze of biblical antiquity, even eternality, is spread over the story. We know that the band of Jews sets forth from the Rhine Valley and moves eastward, but their route and final stopping place remain dim and indeterminate. When it comes to time, we are at an even greater loss. For most of the story we are given the sense only that all this happened a very long time ago in the depth of the European exile. But toward the end, when Buczacz has already been established as a secure community, we are informed about the arrival of "Jews from other places, especially from Germany. Disaster had overtaken the people of God, the holy community of Worms, Mayence, Speyer . . . because of the filthy infidels whose arrogance moved them to go up to the Holy Land to fight the king of Ishmael and to conquer the Land" (p. *13*, *36*). The first round of the Crusader massacres in the Rhine Valley took place in 1096, and by this time, supposedly, Buczacz was sufficiently established to serve as a refuge for the survivors. Let us grant that precise time coordinates are not important in the mythic mode in which Agnon's introduction to Buczacz is written. Nonetheless, a discrepancy of five centuries between the hoary antiquity implied in this telling and the standard historical accounts of the town's settlement in the 1500s is far from trivial.

The depiction of the encounter between Jews and gentiles is notable for the amity that prevails in the relations with the Polish nobles and the complete absence of anyone else. The indigenous Slavic population, the Ruthenians, who are later called Ukrainians, who were ruled by the Polish magnates and in many cases owned by them, who were served by Jewish tavern keepers, who brought their grain to Jewish mills, and who bought their necessities in Jewish shops—of these there is no mention. The place of hills and streams and forests where the caravan of Jews makes its encampment is a virgin, uninhabited land. The Jews serve the Polish nobles as wise counselors and estate agents by invitation and not duress. These great land owners need the Jews because the commercial skill required to develop their estates is both beneath them and foreign to them. When the bloody massacres of the seventeenth century rage, it is not the Poles that are responsible for Jewish suffering but the Cossacks, the Tatars, and the Turks, who are the enemies of the Jews and the Poles alike.

Buczacz is a city and not a village—we deal with the relevant Hebrew and Yiddish terms below—and Agnon emphasizes how the Jewish families scattered throughout the countryside coalesced to form a Jewish city. In this account, there is only one driving force that matters, and it has little to do with the economic explanations put forward by historians for the great migrations of Jewish life in Europe. The Jews of Buczacz, to be sure, need to make a living, but their economic self-interest would dictate that they remain dispersed and close to the various lords whose estates they help to run. Their motive for moving to town is to be close to the synagogue, and it is only once they have taken that step, presumably at some material sacrifice, that they set up shops and enter into trade to make the best of their situation. Their inability to engage in communal prayer and hear the Torah read when they are dispersed in the countryside is depicted as if it were a painful deprivation and the suppression of a deep and essential longing.

Finally and most pointedly, the founding of Buczacz is presented as an arrested ascent to Zion. "There once was a band of Jews who were moved by their own pure hearts to go up to the Land of Israel, together with their wives and their sons and their daughters." So begins the story with no further explanation or elaboration. No persecution is mentioned, no economic hardship. The desire to overcome the Exile and return to Erets Yisrael is laid down as a truth that needs no further justification. Yet it is the very purity of their aspiration, however self-evident it may be, that ends in compromising their high errand. The other side of their innocence is their unworldliness. They sell all their belongings and move eastward with no practical notion of the route of the journey, and so they find themselves stranded in snowy forests deep in the land of the Slavs. The preservation of life dictates their acceptance of the offer to disperse and winter with the Polish nobles. What was a necessary improvisation, however, becomes an unspoken accommodation, and thus begin the many centuries of Buczacz's continuous life as a holy community "until the Enemy came and eradicated them all" (p. *13, 37*).[2]

As an introduction to the grand enterprise of *A City in Its Fullness*, the story "Buczacz" is at one and the same time an excellent entrée into Agnon's aspirations and a misleading guide to their realization. Little that follows has spread over it the veil of mythic totality that surrounds this telling of the founding of Buczacz. Although its inhabitants are frequently and variously praised for their virtues, the prevailing principle is ironic realism. This is not realism after the manner of the stylistic trend in nineteenth-century European fiction; this is moral realism in the more general sense of a commitment to represent the problems and shortcomings of a society as part of the larger enterprise of truth telling. The idyll of Jewish-Polish relations presented above, for example, contrasts pointedly with many stories about casual humiliation and violence meted out by Polish overlords. The image of Buczacz as a kehilah kedoshah acting in concert is undercut by numerous instances of divisiveness and sectarian strife. Its image as a caring community is similarly dispelled by accounts of oppression of the poor and the marginal. And even when it comes to study and worship, the needs of the self often confound sacred purposes.

This gap between what crudely might be called the idealization of Buczacz and its reality is not, I would argue, an expression of false consciousness. Rather, in this opening myth of origins, Agnon establishes the key signature in accordance with which, and against which, the rest of his large composition is played. The idealization of Buczacz as a kehilah kedoshah is not a mystification but a truth of its own. It represents a structure of values that may not have been fulfilled often, but whose existence makes sense of everything else. To put the matter in a helpfully tautological way: although deviations from the norm may have in fact been the norm, the deviations cannot be recognized as such without the existence of the norms themselves. Yet we have occasion later to savor the fact that, when it comes to writing stories, norms provide little nourishment. The great imaginative creations within *A City in Its Fullness*, the fully realized stories that stand out among all the rest, are all rooted in imperfection. For art, perhaps it cannot be otherwise.

Thus, this introduction to Buczacz should be understood as the presentation of a schema of normative truths that transcend historical facts. By charting a journey directly from the Rhine Valley to the forests of western Ukraine, for example, Agnon is establishing a spiritual genealogy that insists that those fabled Ashkenazic communities are the source for the liturgical practices of Buczacz and the authority of its scholarly traditions. By backdating the founding of the city by many centuries, Agnon is not only asserting its hoary antiquity but also declaring his intention to tell the story of Buczacz according to the cannons of chronicle time rather precise metrics of modern historians. By making the longing for public prayer rather than trade the motive for urban life, Agnon is signaling his plan to reframe the life of Buczacz under the twin signs of prayer and learning.

Agnon's boldest arrogation is to imagine the founding of the city as an indefinite hiatus on the return to Erets Yisrael. To say that this was a projection of Agnon's religious Zionism is true but insufficient. He was writing the stories of Buczacz in Israel after 1948 and during a time of intense state building. Attitudes toward traditional Jewish life in Eastern Europe, whose disappearance had been predicted by Zionism and whose destruction had just been carried out, were tortuous and complex. By framing the beginnings of the city as a compromised ascent to Zion, Agnon is able to draw Buczacz into the millennial dialectic Homeland/Exile/Return. Buczacz remains ever a station rather than a destination, even if the duration of the stay is many, many centuries.[3] And if that other-directed consciousness was not always present to the Jews of Buczacz, Agnon's re-evocation of their lives in *A City in Its Fullness* provides a retrospective correction. It is in fact the vocation of his writing to identify and disclose moments of potential redemption—together with the human complexities that lead to their tragically being squandered—within the flow of historical occurrence.

Buczacz in History

Buczacz (Buchach in Ukrainian) is a city in what is today the west of Ukraine, about sixty miles southeast of Lviv (Levov, Lemberg). It is located on the southernmost border of historical Poland and which later was part of the Austrian province of Galicia. Buczacz is located on the banks of the Strypa River, a tributary of the Dniester, in an area of hills, valleys, and lakes. In the early Middle Ages, Buczacz was ruled by the Orthodox principality of the Kievan Rus'. Beginning in the fourteenth century it came under Polish rule, and a Roman Catholic Church was established as a sign of Polish dominance. In 1569, the Union of Lublin established the Polish-Lithuanian Commonwealth and formalized the annexation of Volhynia and Rus'. It was during the sixteenth century that Jews began to settle in Buczacz; the oldest tombstone in the town cemetery is from 1587.

Jews were motivated to emigrate southeastward from Poland because of the economic competition that resulted from the rise of a Polish bourgeoisie. The Polish nobles possessed vast agricultural estates and ruled large numbers of Ruthenian serfs. Because the nobility lacked a managerial class that could make its estates profitable, the nobles welcomed the Jews into their lands and offered them the right of residence and internal rule in return for the Jews' leasing breweries, saw mills, and flour mills; money lending; marketing agricultural produce; and providing supplies to the peasantry.

Most cities and towns were owned wholly and outright by the nobles, often called magnates. Buczacz was one such city. At first it belonged to the Buczacki clan and, through marriage and inheritance, passed to the Potocki family, in whose hands it remained until the period of Austrian rule. Already in 1539 the Polish Crown had placed the jurisdiction of the Jews residing on the lands of the nobility directly in the hands of the magnates. Jews were not owned by a magnate, as were the serfs, but they lived as a kind of estate or corporate entity within towns owned by him in which his word was the ultimate law. The Jews proved their usefulness and prospered.

The second half of the seventeenth century, however, turned into a time of carnage and destruction. Because the region surrounding Buczacz represented the farthest assertion of Polish power, it was exposed to hostility on all sides. To the west was the Austrian Kingdom and to the east was the increasingly powerful Moscovite sphere of power, together with the Cossack Hetmanate and Zaporozhia. Most provoked by the Polish expansion was the Ottoman Empire, whose northern reaches extended to Moravia, Bessarabia, and the Black Sea. Each side used proxies to defend or contest this southern frontier. The Polish nobles engaged the services of the Cossacks to repel the Ottomans, who in turn used the Crimean Tatars to harry the Poles.

The situation changed dramatically when the Cossacks, under the charismatic leadership of Bohdan Khmelnytskyi, defected from the service of the Polish lords, made an alliance with the Tatars, and cast themselves as the liberators of the oppressed Ruthenian peasantry. Although the Poles were the target of the rebellion, the Jews, who served their interests, ended up faring the worst. A significant number of Jews—somewhere in the many tens of thousands—were killed and their homes, shops, and synagogues destroyed. The brutal and gruesome ways in which the Jews met their deaths, recorded in such chronicles as Natan Nata Hanover's *Yeven Metsulah* [The abyss of despair, 1653], remained inscribed in the collected memory of East European Jewry for many centuries to come. What was an unremitting calamity for

Jewry was remembered in Ukrainian history as the great rebellion against the Polish overlords; the simultaneous existence of distinct and contradictory national narratives was to become a permanent feature of this region.

It was the special fate of Buczacz to be spared the worst during the Cossack uprising of 1648 but then to suffer more than other cities and towns twenty-five years later. Because of its geographical situation and its castle and fortifications and because of collaboration between Poles and Jews in defense of the city, Buczacz succeeded in withstanding the siege placed upon it, although many died from famine and epidemics. But that same location along the southern flank of Polish territory exposed it to ongoing attacks from the Ottoman sphere of influence. Khmelnytskyi proved to be a mercurial leader, and soon after they had unleashed so much slaughter and devastation, the Cossacks returned to the eastern bank of the Dnieper and ceased to be a military threat. Incursions by Tatar raiding parties were common during these years. In 1672 Buczacz was besieged by a vast Ottoman army. Jan Potocki, the lord of the city, was off fighting the Ottomans elsewhere; and with only his wife and children left in the castle, the city soon capitulated and was spared extensive damage. Later, Potocki returned to Buczacz, and elaborate plans were made for Jews and Poles to take responsibility for the defense of different quarters in the case of a future attack.

An attack came soon enough. The Ottoman army laid siege to Buczacz again in 1675, and this time encountered considerable concerted resistance. But the defenses of the city could not prevail against massive military force; the ramparts were breached, and the Turks rushed inside and put the city to torch. The great synagogue and almost all Jewish shops and dwellings were destroyed, and a great many Jews—we do not know the exact numbers— were slaughtered. The Ottoman threat was eventually neutralized by Sobieski, who was elected as King Jan III of Poland in 1674. His success in repelling the Ottoman siege of Vienna eleven year later was a turning point that ushered into the region two centuries of relative stability. These are the years that are covered in *A City in Its Fullness*, the great classical period of the city as a Jewish community, a kehilah kedoshah, when, as Agnon repeatedly avers, Buczacz was Buczacz.

Under Stephan Potocki, the lord of the city from 1675 to 1733, Buczacz undertook a program of reconstruction. A new synagogue was built—at first a wooden structure and then a massive stone edifice in 1728—as well as a beit midrash, and the Jews were granted expanded privileges and commercial advantages. Under a broad policy of toleration, the Jewish community enjoyed internal autonomy. Jews paid taxes and were represented in municipal life, and they were expected to participate in the defense of the city when necessary. But within the community, disputes were adjudicated by rabbinic judges (*dayanim*; *dayan*, singular) and communal affairs generally governed and enforced by *parnasim* (*parnas*, singular), well-to-do leaders appointed by the community. Buczacz came under the rabbinic umbrella of Lviv, and together they were represented in the Council of Four Lands, which set internal policy for all of Polish Jewry until its abolishment in 1764.

Stephan was succeeded by Mikołaj Potocki, who ruled Buczacz until the Austrian annexation.[4] Mikołaj Potocki was both pious and dissolute, and he embodied the figure of the capricious, all-powerful magnate in his feudal relationship to his subjects. He contributed generously to all the branches of Christianity and converted from Roman Catholicism to the Greek Catholic faith and spent the last years of his life in a monastery. (Greek Catholicism, also called the Uniate Church, combined the practice of the Orthodox rite with loyalty to the Pope.) He built the Basilian Monastery in 1753, which was one of the great edifices of Buczacz; it was a school for priests and regular students and the first institution of formal education in the city. (The students from this school were also responsible for destructive and vicious pranks played on the Jews of Buczacz over the course of many decades. In one story, it is related that while the Jews were in the synagogue, all the sukkot of the town were vandalized and rendered unfit for use during the holiday.)

The most imposing architectural achievement of the city was the town hall, completed in 1751, a lavish building that distinguished Buczacz from other even larger Galician cities. It was adorned with sixteen sculptures, representing the Twelve Labors of Hercules, and biblical figures and was topped by a 115-foot tower. The town hall was the work of the architect

Bernard Meretyn and the sculptor Johann Georg Pinsel. Yet in Agnon's tell-ing, an Italian architect named Theodore is brought to Buczacz for the job. Theodore turns out to be a Jew who was forcibly converted to Christian-ity as a child, and the features of the biblical figures he sculpts are drawn both from early recollections of attending synagogue on Yom Kippur and from the Jewish faces he sees during his stay in Buczacz. After completing the town hall, Theodore is locked away in a tower in the castle by Count Potocki so that he will be unable to design more beautiful buildings else-where. To escape starvation, he fashions a set of wings and, Icarus-like, flies out of his cell only to crash and die on a nearby hill. To this day, we are told, the spot is called the Fedor Hill, after the Ruthenian pronunciation of his name. Agnon concludes the story by writing that later, it was on that same hill that the Germans and their local helpers buried alive five hundred Jews.

Galicia was created as a province of the Habsburg Monarch as a product of negotiations with Russia and Prussia that led to the partition of Poland in 1772. And it ceased to exist as a political entity in 1918 with the defeat and dissolution of the Dual Monarchy of Austria-Hungary. Rather than being a land with a longstanding identity of its own, Galicia was an in-vented land, an artificial entity that acquired meaning over the course of its historical experience.[5] Yet for the Jews, Poles, and Ruthenians who lived in the borderlands north of the Carpathians between the Dniester and Vistula rivers, the experience of Austrian rule for a century and a half left a pro-found imprint.

In the case of Buczacz, some effects were drastic and immediate. The city ceased to be owned by the Potocki family in the sense that its autocratic judicial authority was abrogated. Buczacz was now a city within an admin-istrative region within a province of the Austrian Empire whose affairs were administered by civil servants appointed in Vienna. The great Polish nobles maintained their titles, but they were no longer the law of the land. For the Jews of Galicia generally, the annexation presented a complex new reality. On the one hand, the Jews were made to bear special financial burdens: a toleration tax, a tax on kosher meat, and, as a special insult, a tax on the can-dles so necessary for the observance of Shabbat and holidays. On the other, the Jews were treated like other minorities in the Empire. Perhaps ironically, it was these more general measures, with their origins in the "enlightened" reforms of the new centralized state that turned out to have the most corrosive effects on traditional life and communal organization. Nevertheless, under the Austrians Buczacz grew considerably. The Jewish population was 1,464 in 1814 and 6,077 in 1870, which represented well over half the population of the city.

Rabbinic courts lost their authority over civil matters involving Jews. The kahal as a structure of communal leadership that could impose its will on the community was weakened. The imperial army was now open to Jews, and each city was required to produce its quota of young men, whose long years of service in remote locations made religious observance impossible. (The moral corruption this led to as communities handed over to the authorities the poor and unlettered is the theme of the story "Disappeared," discussed in Chapter 7. In the hope of turning Jews toward "productive" occupations such as agriculture, Vienna, among other measures, prohibited Jews from operating taverns in the countryside. But instead of producing Jewish farmers, the law created a class of uprooted and destitute men who were forced to wander widely in search of subsistence, often abandoning their wives and families in the process.

The introduction of German culture brought by Austrian rule had consequences that were less material but farther reaching. Jews were required to take German names. A gymnasium was eventually established in Buczacz, which presented an educational track separate from the Basilian monastery school. German as a language of enlightenment and modernity was in the air in Buczacz, along with Polish as the banner of Polish nationalism.

Yet despite these exposures and constraints, Jewish practice and learning remained strongly established in Buczacz during the first seventy-five years under the Austrians. This was exactly the time of the explosion of Hasidism in Eastern Europe, and nowhere more so than in Galicia. As town after town came under the sway of this movement of religious enthusiasm and revivalism, Buczacz stood apart. The mitnagdic lay and rabbinic leadership of the town closed ranks to prevent Hasidic rabbis or tsaddikim from taking up residence in Buczacz. The existence of a number of Hasidic prayer houses (*kloyzn*) was tolerated, but Hasidic leaders themselves were allowed only to visit but not to stay overnight. The boundaries, however, were not entirely impermeable. One of the important figures of this period, Avraham David Wahrman—he served as rabbi of Buczacz between 1814 and his death in 1841—was a follower of the Hasidic master Moshe Leib of Sassov, and although he was an imposing scholar in the mitnagdic mold, his Hasidic tendencies were a source of contention for the learned elite of the town. (Agnon's own grandparents were Chertkov Hasidism; by the late nineteenth century the sectarian struggles had waned.)

This antagonism can be understood in part as a reaction to the memory of Shabetai Tsevi, the messianic figure who, during the Turkish wars a hundred years earlier, had a not insignificant number of followers in Buczacz. His conversion to Islam and the bitter end to the millennial expectations he had aroused made the faithful of Buczacz vigilant against the least signs of antinomianism. Yet separate from this historical memory, the resistance to Hasidism can be read as a sign of the robustness of traditional Talmud study in Buczacz, which remained dynamic and prestigious.[6] The hallowed norms of learning and public worship apparently were not experienced as so desiccated and remote as to require radically new forms of religious experience and leadership. Finally, the other transformative tendency in East European and Galicia in particular, the Haskalah (Enlightenment) established a tentative hold in Buczacz during the first half of the nineteenth century. Never a mass movement, the Haskalah in Buczacz was rarely militant; it engaged the sympathies of select individuals, often among the commercial elite, who combined their interest in wider Jewish affairs with traditional observance.

The Jews of Galicia were emancipated in 1867 and given the right to vote. In Buczacz, Jews formed a plurality on the municipal council, and Bernard Stein, a Jew, served as mayor from 1879 until 1921. Buczacz was combined with Kolomea and Sniatyn to form a single parliamentary district for electing representatives to the Galician Seym and the Austrian parliament. Orthodox parties vied with more nationalist parties for the Jewish votes, and various and changing alliances were made with the Ruthenian and Polish parties to form voting blocs. As time went on, members of the intelligentsia of Buczacz were drawn either to the Polish or the German sphere of culture and national identity.

Buczacz was an especially fertile ground for Zionist sentiment and organization. The Zion Society was founded in 1893, and by the eve of World War One, every Zionist party was represented in the town. Socialism in its Jewish and general manifestations also had a strong presence in Buczacz. Economic conditions in the region remained grim, and the greatest response to the situation was neither electoral nor ideological. Many Jews simply left Buczacz. Some left for the imperial capital of Vienna, where they could attend university and train for professional careers in marked contrast to Russian Jews, who were barred from Russian universities. (E.g., Sigmund Freud's parents, whose ancestors hailed from Buczacz and Tisminitz, settled in Vienna in 1865.) And many Buczacz Jews emigrated from Galicia to North America.

As did other Galician Jewish communities, Buczacz suffered horribly during World War One.[7] In midst of fighting both the Red and the White armies during the Russian civil war in 1919–20, Symon Perliura's Ukrainian troops perpetrated acts of pillaging, rape, and murder on the Jews of Galicia; the number of Jews killed in the pogroms is estimated to be between 35,000 and 50,000. Only 3,858 Jews, half of the pre-war population, were left in Buczacz when the city was conquered by Poland and became part of the restored Polish state; many had fled in anticipation of the violence and had become refugees elsewhere. Jewish life gradually reconstituted itself during the interwar period, and it is estimated that there were approximately 10,000 Jews in Buczacz at the outbreak of World War Two.

The final fate of the Jews of Buczacz during the Holocaust is grimly predictable, but the stages of arrival are complicated. The first action taken by the Germans when they occupied the city in July 1941 was to murder several hundred "intellectuals" on Fedor Hill. Sixteen hundred Jews were deported to Belzec in October and another 2,500 in November. Each *Aktion* was accompanied by the shootings of hundreds of Jews. A ghetto was established in Buczacz in which Jews from surrounding towns were concentrated. In

February 1942 approximately 2,000 Jews were shot to death and buried in mass graves on Fedor Hill. Those who were thought to be the last remaining Jews were shot in the cemetery in June 1943. But it turned out that over 800 Jews had survived in hiding, some presumably assisted by local gentiles. They came out of hiding when the city was liberated by the Red Army in March 1944. Tragically, the city was retaken by the Germans shortly afterward, and the survivors were slaughtered. Of the Jews of Buczacz and its environs only 100 were left after the Germans were finally driven out. No Jewish community was reestablished in Buczacz after the war.

The Grand Tour

How does Agnon's Buczacz in *A City in Its Fullness* compare with the historical Buczacz? In answering this question we have the good luck to be able to consult *The Voice of Your Brother's Blood: Buczacz, Biography of a Town* by the historian Omer Bartov. Much of the historical account of Buczacz in the previous section was in fact drawn from this study. Bartov's "biography" of Buczacz is founded on a commitment to historical comprehensiveness. He tells the story, with an artful interwoven simultaneity, not only of the Jews but also of the Poles and of the Ruthenians/Ukrainians. It is a challenging task because each narrative, understandably but unhelpfully, tends to devalue, dismiss, or exclude the other two. Bartov's comprehensiveness extends also to the time frame of these narratives. He begins with the earliest records before the arrival of the Poles and the Jews and then takes the story through the centuries of Polish rule, the 150 years under Austria, the return of Polish rule between the two world wars, the Holocaust, Soviet rule, and then the Ukrainian state.

The rich multi-dimensionality of Bartov's study provides a valuable control for grasping the radically delimited nature of the choices made by Agnon and their rationale, as well as the ambitious achievements he aspired to by virtue of these delimitations. From within the broad historical arc, Agnon chose to focus on roughly two centuries: from the Khmelnytskyi massacres of 1648 to the emancipation of Galician Jewry in 1867.[8] Although the murder of Buczacz Jewry in the 1940s is mentioned throughout, the

Holocaust serves only as a horizon of knowledge that remains outside the frame of the main narrative. When it comes to the multiplicity of national narratives, it goes without saying that Agnon is interested in telling the story of the Jews of Buczacz and from their point of view although there is constant reference to the gentile rulers, be they Polish or Austrian, because of their generally baleful effects on the life of the community.

Even within the Jewish milieu Agnon's exclusions are far-reaching. To be sure, many aspects of Jewish life in the city are touched on, including commerce, class relations, crime, and communal conflict. Yet the author repeatedly declares his intention to concentrate on matters relating to pubic worship and Torah study, even if the deviations from these norms is what energizes the stories themselves.

Now it may seem incongruous, even absurd, to compare the work of a historian writing within the canons of the academy in English in America to the fiction of a Hebrew writer in Israel some sixty years earlier. But the juxtaposition serves to delineate what is distinctive about Agnon's project. There is a striking duality, to begin with, when it comes to the amplitude of focus. On the one hand, the parameters are tightly restricted in terms of themes and time period. On the other, within those restricted categories the sheer amount of story and lore is enormous. Agnon truly gives us, literally, the city and the fullness thereof.

The status of *A City in Its Fullness* as history writing displays a similar duality. Agnon expressly seeks to do what the best historians do, especially more recent historians who, freed from writing about the succession of political elites, attempt to render the deep material culture of a time and a place. But instead of a commitment to historical method however broadly construed, Agnon wants to write history through the medium of fiction. Yet this is not the historical fiction we are familiar with from nineteenth-century Europe such as Walter Scott's *Waverly* or Alessendro Mazoni's *I Promessi Spousi* or George Eliot's *Middlemarch*. After his own very different fashion, Agnon wrote a historical novel, *The Bridal Canopy* (1931), which undertook an epic recreation of Jewish life in Galicia in the beginning of the eighteenth century. But the novel form itself would not answer for the new task at hand. For even if *The Bridal Canopy* is episodic, picaresque, and digressive to the point of often devolving into aggregations of tales, it must track the adventures of Reb Yudl, its central character within a single historical moment. In *A City in Its Fullness*, Agnon needed to range over a period of two hundred years, and to do so without the constraints of a plot. Furthermore, although he aspired to the epic totality of the historical novel, he sought a form of composition that was more heterogeneous and multi-vocal. *A City in Its Fullness* mixes up long texts with short texts and conventional stories with ethnographic essays; its narrator selectively invites other narrators to share the stage; and it ranges freely between illustrious historical figures and those whose reality may be wholly imaginative.

This is a book, in short, that manifestly refuses to slip into the berth of any conventional genre. With that stipulation stated, I wish to propose a rubric for reading *A City in Its Fullness* that views the work as organized along two axes: an axis of space and an axis of time. The spatial axis takes the form a guided grand tour of Buczacz. The narrator introduces us to the key institutions and customs of the town by taking us in hand and walking with us from site to site. We the readers are construed as belated tourists who have enough curiosity to bestir ourselves to join a long and demanding tour but who are ignorant of the local manners and mores. Even with that provisional good will, the guide feels the constant burden to make the information he is purveying as piquant and lively as possible. Therefore at each station of the tour, whether it is the town well or the candelabrum of the synagogue, the guide accompanies his explanations with vignettes about the history of the site and the personalities associated with it, and often he has his listeners sit down and sit back in order to take in a full-fledged story.

The guided grand tour, to which book 1 of *A City in Its Fullness* is devoted, rests upon a rather startling assumption: Buczacz exists! Within the reality of the walking tour the narrator takes us on, the city exits in the here and now. This is not a tour of the ruins of Buczacz with each stop along the way introduced with some versions of "Here once was. . . ." But was not Buczacz destroyed, substantially in World War One and totally in World

War Two? The narrator of *A City in Its Fullness* is supremely aware of this grim finality, but he makes an aesthetic and existential choice to behave otherwise.

> Because of the last calamity Buczacz was destroyed together with all the places where Jews had lived. Later on I shall tell of the calamity. For the time being, I proceed as if the world is orderly and intact and Buczacz is Buczacz and the Great Synagogue stands in its glory and the Old Study House is full of Torah. I continue to recount the praise of Torah and the majesty of prayer. (pp. *212–13*)

The promise "to tell of the calamity" is never fulfilled in *A City in Its Fullness*, whether Agnon's death deprived him of the chance, or, as I would assert, he declined to do so. Mention of the Holocaust is liberally scattered throughout the volume, serving often as the notation that closes the history of a family or the account of a custom. But the Holocaust is not dramatized within the volume and instead remains its outer horizon. The main business of the book itself takes place in the "time being" [*le'et 'atah*], the great "meanwhile" that expands to encompass the account of the city. Within the medium of that indefinite present, Buczacz stands whole and complete, and the institutions that represent the two chosen pillars of the city's best self operate at full tilt and full power.

The tense structure of the narration is the progressive present, which the narrator instantiates when he avers at the close of the passage that he continues to recount the praises of the city. The Hebrew is *ve'ani mesapper veholekh*, literally "I recount as I go." When the narrator explains "I proceed as if the world is orderly and intact" [*'oseh ani ke'ilu ha'olam sadur 'al siduro*], he is making two statements. First, treating Buczacz as present and undestroyed is a considered choice, even a willful one. Second, he is fully aware that doing so means proceeding on an "as if" footing. The knowledge of the later fate of Buczacz Jewry is neither suppressed nor denied but willfully suspended in favor of the more constructive undertaking of presenting the city in its fullness.

In the Introduction, we remarked on Agnon's report to Baruch Kurzweil in 1956:"I am building a city, Buczacz."[9] In this context, underscoring the present progressive tense of the verb (*boneh*) in this simple statement helps us to understand a contradiction about the "presentness" of Agnon's description of Buczacz. In the passage above, on the one hand, Buczacz already exists in its fullness, and the author-narrator need only take us on a tour to point out its features. On the other, Agnon's statement to Kurzweil, written during the years he was at work on the stories, implies that the city is in the process of being built; it is a construction site in which the infrastructure, armatures, and facades are being progressively fitted into place.

The difference, to my mind, has little to do with one being the process and the other the completion. Rather, the contradiction lies between Agnon's desire to see Buczacz present and whole and the fact that that state of wholeness can be achieved only through the step-by-step, story-by-story labor of narration. The two positions can coexist because, for better and for worse, the Buczacz of *A City in Its Fullness* is a literary creation. The true historical Buczacz was destroyed by the Nazis and before that by the Ukrainians, and its classical greatness was degraded even before that by the forces of modernization. That greatness exists now only and wholly in the imaginative simulacrum Agnon has created. As a world made only from words, it is a poor thing compared to the Buczacz of flesh and bone, brick and mortar. But at the same time, as a world made only from words, it is a brilliant thing that brings back a glory that was lost in a form that can never perish.

But even the wonder of Buczacz redivus, presented in the totality of its presence and presentness, can only be part of the story. Having chosen to take responsibility for a period of two hundred years in the life of the city, Agnon can hardly relate to it solely within the "as if" of its classical distillation. And in fact he does not. The spatial axis of *A City in Its Fullness* is intersected by a historical axis. The book divides between the "early generations" and the "later generations," which roughly correspond to the shift in the late eighteenth century from Polish rule to Austrian rule. (The ratio of pages devoted to each is approximately 5:4 in favor of the earlier period.) Not only was the Polish period farther away in time but it was feudal in nature and seemed to belong to an unchanging, pre-modern world.[10] The Polish magnates, moreover, left internal communal and religious authority relatively intact and related to the Jews of Buczacz as a self-governing corporate entity. Within this period, then, Agnon was freer to relate to the city as existing all at once in a classical configuration that could be laid out and approached spatially. For him this was the time when "Buczacz was Buczacz." When it came to the Austrian regime, the proximity to the present, with its abundant documentation, actually modernized the very experience of time. The affairs of the Jews were now in the hands of a modern bureaucratic apparatus that allowed much less room for communal inner-directedness. The Jews of Buczacz were thus forced to be much more aware of and connected to the sweeping changes in European society.

Now the time has finally come to join the tour and to catch up with Agnon's narrator as he introduces his audience to the layout of Buczacz. The tour proceeds in two loops. The first is tightly wound around the Great Synagogue and the New Beit Midrash, the sacred objects they contain, and the people who manage them, both lay and professional. The second moves outward to the marketplace, where Jews and gentiles encounter each others in commercial exchanges, and then to the ornate and monumental town hall and other civic buildings built by the Potocki family, the owners of Buczacz.

The banks of the Strypa are a liminal area inhabited by the Jewish outliers of various sorts; this space is home to a kosher slaughtering house and the Basilian Monastery. Beyond the Strypa are the fields and woods of the Ruthenian peasant farmers, and even further beyond are the estates of the Polish magnates. There is a scattering of small villages that form a hinterland for which Buczacz serves as the market center. And even in these villages there are Jews who cannot afford to live in the city, or who find their livelihoods in operating rural taverns. Even though Buczacz is not a large town, the tour on offer is long and detailed because of the boundless esteem and affection the guide feels toward this place, of which he is a native. He has made it part of his life's work to gather historical material and legends about the town, and it is of ultimate importance to him to communicate this knowledge to us. Because the tour is so extensive, we are able to sample only a few of its stops, but they give a sense of the whole.

The sacred core of Buczacz is a cluster of three buildings—the Old Beit Midrash, the Great Synagogue, and the New Beit Midrash—and each has its story. The Old Beit Midrash was the first of the three buildings to be built in the aftermath of the massacres of the seventeenth century, and the site on which it was constructed was determined providentially. A fabric Torah mantel that had been ripped and desecrated in the massacres was caught by a sudden burst of wind and buffeted in the air until it landed on a certain spot. Buczacz is built on a series of hills, and this spot turned out to be the only location in the town from which crosses and Christian statues were not visible. A beit midrash is a house of study, but at first the building had to serve also as a house of prayer. This arrangement was not suitable for long, and this was not only because of the increasing number of Jews who were returning to Buczacz after the massacres but also because of a fundamental divergence in the needs of two classes of worshippers.

For the generality of the town—shopkeepers, tradesmen, artisans, ped-dlers, and laborers—daily public worship in the morning and the eve-ning was their central religious exercise and they were in no hurry to rush through it, despite the demands of the workaday world. The other class was the *benei torah*, men who spent their days in the beit midrash studying the Talmud and its commentaries and codes. This included adolescents who had finished ḥeder, bridegrooms of well-to-do families, older men who were no longer working, and scholars who devoted their days to learning, sup-ported by their working wives or their own wealth. It was ironically the *benei torah* who wanted prayers to be conducted at a fast pace and be com-pleted quickly because, even though they did not have to rush off to the marketplace, they were zealous to continue their studies as soon as possible. And so the elders of Buczacz, assessing and collecting the contributions each member of the community could make, erected the Great Synagogue, the *beit hakeneset hagadol*. It was built as a fortress synagogue, a structure of large proportions, thick walls, and a sunken floor so that it could serve as a refuge in the event of Tatar incursions.

As we are ushered inside the synagogue to be shown the special objects it contains, the guide's method becomes apparent to us. At each stop along the way, the guide describes the physical properties of the object or the place and its function in the religious or communal life of Buczacz. But the guide does more: he attaches to the object or place a story. Sometimes the story is a brief vignette [ma'aseh] about how a sacred object came to be contributed to the synagogue or how a place got its name. Yet at other times, the object or place serves as the impetus for a full-fledged story, one that we as modern readers recognize as an instance of "fiction" because it has an independent set of characters and a realized plot, or, to put it simply, it tells a finished story. (Whether Agnon would have owned to these distinctions is doubtful; in his own mind it was likely all part of the act of telling stories.) Two examples of the shorter, anecdotal exposition concern the synagogue's grand chandelier ("The Brilliant Chandelier," pp. 25–27, 40–43), the gift of an apostate from Trieste, and a glass-enclosed board inscribed with the blessing for the new moon ("The Blessing of the Moon," pp. 228–30, 185–87), which was connected to the cure of a sleep-walking young woman.

In both of these instances—and this is the general case throughout—the narrator pauses to provide us with an extended explanation only when the object in question is not a typical synagogue appurtenance but an object unique to Buczacz or at least one with an unusual provenance. The explanation itself can be delivered only in the form of a story. The guide in whose hands we place ourselves is not an eager docent or an amateur anthropologist. He is a storyteller and although he acquits himself of the conventional requirements to give physical descriptions of places and things, the truth of the matter can be conveyed only via the ma'aseh.

Telling the ma'aseh typically takes us far away from the object and its sacred use before it brings us back. In the case of the chandelier, it is Trieste and the history of a Jewish family forced to convert to Christianity. In the case of the board with the blessing for the new moon, it is a rare case of "sleep walking" that can be cured only by faithful adherence to ritual rather than by recourse to charms and wonder working. Not only are we taken back to the past in each instance but we are taken to an exotic place, whether it is in a foreign clime or in the human heart. With the conclusion of the vignette we are brought back to the present and the object before us, but we are not left there. There is a fast forward to the Holocaust in which the Jews and the objects sacred to them came to a final, violent end. This sudden and wrenching turn pole-vaults over all the complex intervening history of the Jews of Buczacz to make contact, if only momentarily, with its final horizon.

If the ma'aseh takes us to exotic places, it is not for long and it is only to bring us back to the object with an enlarged understanding of its origins. The sippur, the story, is another matter. It is a term that is so common and so fungible in Agnon's world that it is futile to try to tie it down. But in the context of *A City in Its Fullness* and even more specifically in the descriptions of Buczacz in book 1, a characterization may be attempted. In the ma'aseh, the vignette directly serves the purpose of our better grasping the object or place at hand. In the story, the object or place is not so much an excuse as an occasion for the telling of the story; and although this anchor in the realia of Buczacz remains important, the story itself occupies an independent aesthetic field. The greater length is also a significant difference, not so much as a quantitative measure but as indication of the existence of conflicts and mysteries that must be submitted to a process of emplotment before they can be resolved.

The greatest difference is the freedom the story arrogates to itself to expose the workings of the human heart. A good example of the more exfoliated story is "Ad sheyavo Eliyahu" [Until Elijah Comes, pp. 57–70, 58–77], which I discuss in detail in Chapter 8 in the context of the theme of redemption. The impetus for the story is, again, a unique object in the synagogue precincts that requires explanation. The story involves a life-changing encounter between a harried and discontented shamash and an Elijah figure in the form of a cheerful vagrant. The psychological examination the story undertakes and the entry it provides into the thoughts and feelings of the characters are not possible within the mode of the ma'aseh and its more traditional storytelling means.

As the grand tour continues, the narrator-guide takes particular pains to point out not only places and things but practices as well. This is the wide realm of *minhag* (*minhagim*, plural) in which the narrator aspires to be an expert curator.[11] One aspect of minhag simply refers to the text and performance of the liturgy, which existed in variations as Jewish communities developed in different parts of the world. Our narrator-guide takes every opportunity to aver that the Jews of Buczacz were unswerving in their loyalty to the minhag of Ashkenaz as it solidified by the eleventh century in the Rhine Valley (in such famous communities as Worms, Speyer, and Mayence).

This insistence goes hand-in-hand with the narrator's assertion that Buczacz is the direct lineal descendent or extension of those ancient communities and their spiritual and scholarly authority although we know, despite the myth of origins with which Agnon opens his book, that this was hardly the historical record. What's at stake is not so much the text of the statutory prayers as much as the poetic supplements, the piyyutim, which could indeed vary considerably from region to region. Even if the texts themselves were fixed, their musical realization offered only limited scope for innovation. We learn in the story "Haḥazzanim" (pp. *70–84, 78–97*) that although there were some ḥazzanim who succeeded in having their new melodies accepted into the tradition, many never departed from the melodies they received from their predecessors.

The narrator's insistent rhetoric of continuity, in fact, diverts attention from the evidence of major liturgical innovations that swept through Buczacz and other Polish communities, all the result of the export of Lurianic Kabbalah from Safed and its domestication within Eastern Europe. The Kabbalat Shabbat service on Friday evenings, the Simhat Torah ceremony, the all-night vigil on Shavuot—all these inventions of the kabbalists took root in Galicia not earlier than the beginning of the seventeenth century. Nonetheless, the narrator speaks of them as if they had almost always been part of the hoary rite of the Buczacz community.

Book 3 of *A City in Its Fullness* touches on the greater disruption that took place in the late eighteenth century, namely, ecstatic behavior during prayer and alterations in the times for prayer that arrived with the ascent of Hasidism. There, too, while acknowledging these challenges, the narrator exercises his right to refrain from giving them much attention to buttress and burnish the image of Buczacz's loyalty to minhag.

In its non-liturgical sense, minhag can designate the practices that are unique to a particular community. Our narrator-guides takes particular pleasure, not only in pointing out the unique minhagim of Buczacz but, also, in knowing their origins.[12] And when he cannot provide an explanation, he is aggrieved and abashed. Such is the case, for example, with the custom on the first Shabbat after a wedding of the bride being accompanied on the way to the synagogue by her mother on her right side and her mother-in-law on her left. "There must certainly be a source for this," the narrator opines, "but I for my sins have not merited finding the source" (p. 53).

The importance of minhag is illustrated by the case of the man whose observance of the statutory commandments was weak but whose practice of the minhagim was fastidious. In the divine judgment after his death he could not avoid being sent to Gehinnom, but a decree was issued that Hell should be cooled off for him (p. 55).

A special concern surrounded the appointment of a new rabbi, who almost always came to Buczacz from another community with its own practices. Buczacz was therefore careful to make sure that one of the contractual provisions in the rabbinic letter of appointment addressed this issue: "The rabbi will be required scrupulously to observe the ancient minhagim of Buczacz, whether it is the recitation of piyyutim or any positive minhag has long been practiced, and he should not exchange them for new minhagim that have no writ from halakhic authorities" (p. 312, 258).

Some minhagim were lofty expressions of communal spiritual will. This was the case with the 20th of Sivan, a fast day that commemorated the onset of the Khmelnytskyi massacres with the attack on the city of Nemirov. (There is an extraordinary description of observances of this solemn day, complete with the dirges composed for the occasion, in the story "The Parable and Its Lesson" [pp. 419–31].)[13] The observance of the fast was not unique to Buczacz, but the community took special measures to combat the attenuation of this historical memory.[14] In the same letter of rabbinic appointment, it enjoined the rabbi not to provide exemptions for newcomers to the city from German or Ottoman lands who might argue that the fast did not pertain to them and their ancestors (p. 312, 258).

In a similar but less funereal vein, there are minhagim whose goal is to help the community be its best self, especially when it comes to the challenging task of synagogue decorum. Over and over again the narrator-guide declares that chatting during the sacred service, especially during the reading of the Torah, was something that simply was not done in Buczacz, or if such a violation did perchance occur, one could be certain it was accountable to a visitor to the city, not a native. In the story "The Parable and Its Lesson," an aged shamash astounds his listeners with an account of a journey to Gehinnom taken decades earlier in which he witnessed great scholars enduring horrendous suffering for the sin of having spoken, even about exegetical matters, during the Torah reading. Buczacz boasted a special *Mi Shebeirakh* prayer, a prayer recited by the leader of the service on behalf of all those who "keep their mouths from utterance during prayer in the synagogue" from the time the prayer leader calls the congregation to order (the *barekhu*) until the conclusion (p. *21*).[15] In the untoward case of any audible murmuring in the midst of the congregation, the shamash also had at his disposal another instrument. This was a bunch of empty pages bound together like a book, called *sefer haperlnik*, which sat on the reader's table and upon which the shamash would bang "with the same vigor a woman beats her laundry to get out the water" (p. *436*).[16]

The last station on the first loop of the tour is the New Beit Midrash. Here, as opposed to the grand synagogue, the structure and its appurtenances hold no special wonder. Yet despite the absence of visual interest, it is abundantly clear that the batei midrash, both old and new, form the core of the narrator's loyalties. As a guide to Buczacz, he is responsible for the whole of the Jewish life of the city; but he himself is a creation of the beit midrash and its values, and he cannot help lavishing upon it special attention. This comes in the form of an extended account of its origins (pp. *43–57*), a monitory story of Torah study as hubris and obsession, which takes place in the aftermath of the Tatar incursions when the community of Buczacz was recovering and expanding.

Despite the narrator's preoccupation with liturgical practices and matters pertaining to the synagogue, there is no doubt that his allegiance lies with the beit midrash, whether old or new. It is the axis mundi of his worldview, the sacred center of Buczacz. It is a space that is constantly in danger of being encroached upon by other, legitimate needs of the community (circumcision ceremonies and meetings of the rabbinic court) or being polluted by mendacity. Parties to lawsuits are sometimes required by the court to render solemn oaths, and often only one can be truthful. The prospect of the beit midrash being violated by perpetration of deceit in its precincts was so disturbing that even though the court proceedings were held there, the administration of oaths took place elsewhere, sometimes outside the bounds of the city altogether. The narrator-guide concludes his remarks on the construction of the New Beit Midrash by jumping from a concrete sense of space to one far more sublime. The new building made provision for forty additional places or study stations, and to this precise notation is added the citation of a famous statement in the Talmud (*Berakhot* 8a):

> It is said in the Gemara: "From the day that the Temple was destroyed, the only room left for the Holy One is the four cubits of halakhah." Happy is he who builds houses for Torah for, as it were, he expands God's world.

In the local context of the story, this statement has a congratulatory, homiletic ring that calls down blessing on R. Yosef, the man whose initiative is to be credited with the successful construction of the new building. In the broader context of the grand tour of Buczacz, the statement has a much larger resonance. The passage is conventionally understood to describe the way in which observance of commandments and study of Torah replaced the Temple ritual as vehicles for the divine; in other words, the holiness that inhered in a specific edifice and its protocols has now been transferred to forms of religious experience that are no longer dependent on a specific place. Agnon's exegesis of the passage makes it rotate back in the direction of valorizing space. Yes, houses for study can be built anywhere after the Destruction, but the very fact of their being built or expanded cannot be taken for granted. And it is within these special places that God dwells; he who builds them does nothing less than expand God's presence in the world. The entire project of *A City in Its Fullness* can be taken as an effort to re-spatialize Diaspora Judaism by making a single, concrete place come to life. In this sense Agnon is practicing a kind of inverted Diaspora Zionism. He espouses the need to reconnect soul to body and spirit to place, but he demonstrates that that unity, in its own way, was found in a place like Buczacz in its heyday well in anticipation of the later fulfillment in Erets Yisrael.

The Outer Loop

There is a break now in the grand tour. The loop of the sacred institutions is complete, and the tour continues shortly with a briefer circuit of the marketplace and the municipal buildings. Between them is a lengthy delineation of the communal functionaries and leaders of the beit midrash and the synagogue. If the trope of the guided tour can be extended even a little more, it is as if the group is taking a midday break from walking the town and viewing each site to sit down for a series of brief lectures on the part of the landscape of Buczacz that cannot be seen, the human landscape.

By means of anecdotes and individual profiles, the exposition lays out the hallmarks of the following groups: the shamashim, the sextons or beadles who are responsible for the day-to-day operations of the synagogue; the ḥazzanim, the cantors who lead services on Sabbath, holidays, and special occasions; the rabbis, who serve as halakhic authorities for the town and preach a number of times a year; the gabbaiim, the treasurers of the synagogue responsible for its maintenance; and the *lomdim*, scholars who spend the whole day or portions of it engaging in Torah learning for its own sake in the beit midrash. The shamashim, ḥazzanim, and rabbis are employees of the community. The gabbai is an unpaid officer selected by the community. The lomdim are self-selected and not appointed. It's worth pointing out in passing the positions that fail to merit substantive attention in *A City in Its Fullness*: parnasim, wealthy merchants who take turns serving as heads of the community, especially in relations with gentile rulers; *shoḥatim*, ritual slaughterers; and *melamdim*, teachers of elementary-age children who maintain private classrooms in their homes. Although these positions and occupations figure prominently in much Hebrew and Yiddish literature from Eastern Europe, they are not part of the cavalcade of types in Agnon's account. The reason, I would suggest, lies in the parameters Agnon has imposed by making worship and study the foundational categories for the re-creation of Buczacz.

In the case of the occupations and positions that Agnon has chosen to represent, three (ḥazzanim, gabbaiim, and lomdim) are presented—in that order—in the presentation of Buczacz that constitutes book 1 of *A City in Its Fullness*, which we have been calling the grand tour. The shamashim are not treated as a class under a separate heading, but they do figure as protagonists with rich inner lives in two stories "Until Elijah Comes" (pp. *57–70*, *58–77*)[17] and "The Parable and Its Lesson" (pp. *394–441*). The rabbis are the preoccupation of book 2 and many of the stories in book 3. I discuss the sequence of three stories that deal with the ḥazzanim in the chapter on worship (Chapter 3).

There is something curious about the presentation of the gabbaiim. Four are named, and each is given his own entry; together they form a substantial swath of material (pp. *123–50*). Yet we find out almost nothing about what they actually do as gabbaiim, the demands of the position, or their aspirations, successful or thwarted. Instead, the pages are filled with fascinating anecdotes and melodramatic events that impinged on their lives. But, again, there is little about the task in connection to which they presumably come into the picture in the first place. Has Agnon lost his way and given in to his congenital weakness for digression? Yes, in a sense, but in his giving in there is something creative and instructive. If Agnon had in fact focused his attention in a disciplined way on describing the work of the gabbaiim—the raising of funds, the supervision of the shamashim, the implementation of maintenance and repairs—he would have bored his readers and himself. As a form of creative denial, he therefore allows his narrator to be drawn to all manner of intriguing incidents and stories associated with the figure and with the times he lived in. The essence may be missing, but the piling up of secondary reports and curiosities teaches us much and keeps us, and apparently the narrator as well, engaged.[18]

R. Tsvi, the first of the gabbaiim mentioned, is one of many whose life story is more interesting than his—in this case, non-existent—achievements in office. He is a man whose life is marked by a great renunciation. As a brilliant student from a poor family, he is snapped up as a bridegroom by a wealthy merchant and set on course for a life devoted to scholarship. During the engagement, the merchant loses his capital, and his wealth is wiped out. The boy's family has every right to return the marriage contract, but, as a matter of honor, the boy insists on going ahead with the marriage. He gives up the life of a scholar and dedicates himself to restoring his father-in-law's fortunes, which over time he succeeds in doing. When he is in a position to devote himself to the affairs of the community and is appointed gabbai, he ends up performing the job poorly. Because of the sacrifice all those years ago, the desire for learning was suppressed and unfulfilled, and now all he wants to do is study. Each day on his way to manage the affairs of the synagogue, he pops into the beit midrash to look something up and never emerges. Eventually he gives up his office to someone better suited to the job. He is best remembered in Buczacz for his longevity; he merited participating in the Blessing of the Sun ceremony (*birkat haḥamah*), which takes place every twenty-eight years, three times in his life. At the first of these, when he was four, he was privileged to glimpse Ham, son of Noah, from the Bible who, according to legend, missed the first blessing of the sun ceremony because he was busy feeding the animals in the ark; therefore during each new cycle he is roused from heaven to be present at the ceremony in a different community each time.

So the pattern continues with the other gabbaiim. R. Moshe Aharon is a mead merchant with knowledge of worldly matters and political affairs outside the confines of Galicia. As a purveyor of mead, the honey-based alcoholic beverage, he comes in frequent contact with the Polish nobility. It is in fact the melodramatic account of one such powerful noble, whose quest for atonement for a great crime moves him from Poland to Egypt and then to Buczacz, that entirely overwhelms the story of R. Moshe Aharon himself, not to mention his work as gabbai. The next is R. David Shlomo, a substantial shopkeeper, whose effectiveness in office is diminished by an act of sentimental foolishness. On his way to a commercial fair to purchase merchandise for the season, he comes across two men who have acquired a cache of *etrogim* (*etrog*, singular), the citrus fruit essential to the celebration of the festival of Sukkot. It had been three years since an etrog had been seen in Buczacz, and his desire to have one is so great that he ends up parting with his entire bankroll and nearly impoverishing himself. His story, too, is overshadowed by his far stronger wife, Henegidah Marat Sarah, who in turn figures in the denouement of a ripping tale about the local Polish magnate, who brought back from Paris a lover disguised as a man servant.

In contrast, there are no colorful anecdotes that attach to the brief account of the life of the last-mentioned gabbai, R. Shalom. It turns out that retiring from business to devote himself to synagogue affairs, he is the only one who accomplishes something. The plaza in front of the synagogue is cleared of refuse and paved, the peeling walls of the synagogue are painted, and a sundial is installed on the tower. Having done his duty by describing R. Shalom's having done his duty, the narrator moves on.

There are similar challenges when it comes to describing the life of the lomdim. The lomdim of the Old Beit Midrash stand at the absolute center of the structure of values elaborated in *A City in Its Fullness*. Their devotion to the study of Torah is unmarred by all the factors that make a rabbi's life difficult and often compromised. They are not appointed to positions; they are not dependent on the community for their livelihood; they are not vulnerable to the whims of the gentile rulers; and because they do not issue legal determinations, they don't have a constituency to please or displease. Rather than simply reading and reviewing the Talmud and its commentaries as a reverential homage to the tradition, the lomdim actively reexamine, re-argue and re-stage the teachings and controversies that have been passed down to them and thereby become themselves part of the tradition as it moves forward.

Yet as important as this drama is and as close to the core norms of the book's worldview, it remains an experience difficult to represent to outsiders. Agnon attempts to suggest something of the dialectical confrontation—although not the scholarly substance—in the encounter between two scholars in his epic story "Hamevakshim lahem rav" ["In Search of a Rabbi," discussed in Chapter 4].[19] Here, in the section of *A City in Its Fullness* that deals with sacred occupations, Agnon decides not to bring us inside the beit midrash proper, and his reasons are likely the opposite from those that led him to steer the story away from the work of the gabbaiim. There the matter was tedious; here, the give and take among the scholars in the beit midrash is electric with excitement. But the problem is that this excitement is so heavily coded that it cannot be easily conveyed to the reader.

He gives us instead a miniature family saga—if not the scholarship of the scholars, then at least the lives of the scholars. "The Yerahmielites" (pp. *163–94*) is a cluster of anecdotal stories about a patriarch named Yerahmiel and the grandson born just after his death and given his name. Branching out through the potential stories of the children and grandchildren, "The Yerah mielites" could well have served as the outline for a whole novel. But those plot lines are unelaborated, and the story has about it a kind of episodic lightness that is not weighed down with the asides and obiter dicta we have come to expect in this volume. The mode is domestic, and despite our expectations for a glimpse into the scholarly wrangling within the beit midrash, Agnon instead takes us outside and renders the emotional life of one of its principle denizens. Yerahmiel is not a tsaddik or a rabbi of legendary repute whose every deed is wrapped in mystery and moral instruction. He is also not a simple everyman. By embodying a mixture of humanness and devotion to learning, Yerahmiel emerges as a certain kind of Agnonian hero.[20]

Now we are ready to embark on the second loop of the tour of Buczacz. This loop is structured as an outward spiral. It begins with the marketplace and its well and then moves to the town hall and from there to a marginal neighborhood formed by the Strypa and a canal that connects to it. On the other side of the Strypa there is a kosher slaughterhouse, a convent, and a monastery—and later the gymnasium. On one side is Fedor Hill, and on the other side are fields and forests leading to the surrounding villages, and beyond that are estates of the Polish magnates.[21] For the most part, this is the realm of gentiles, and the narrator-guide gives it much less attention, and that attention requires justification. At the beginning of this loop of the tour, he is constrained to offer the following rationale.

> I now turn from the synagogues and study houses to the marketplace. For as long as Jews are occupied with Torah and worship and trade in good faith, the Holy One Blessed Be He gives them livelihood from the marketplace.

They receive livelihood so that they can occupy themselves with Torah; and they study Torah so that they should merit livelihood. It therefore follows that the marketplace is an extension (*snif*) of the realm of Torah. (p. *230*)

The interdependence between Torah study and commerce is an idea well established both in Jewish sources and in Jewish historiography. The narrator-guide takes the idea one step further by making it into a syllogism that proves that the marketplace is subsumed by Torah. To apply the syllogism to the work of narration means that dealing with gentile spaces such as the marketplace can also, potentially, be construed as occupying oneself with Torah. Whether or not the argument is convincing, it attests to the narrator's conviction that the description of gentile space is justified only if it can be understood as Jewish space as well.

This is not so much an apologia for exploring gentile space as a description of the narrator-guide's practice. The most magnificent building in Buczacz, with its high tower and its sculptures, is the town hall commissioned by Mikołaj Potocki. As mentioned in the historical section earlier in this chapter, Agnon chose to disregard the fact that the architect and sculptor came from German lands and instead gave us Theodore, the Italian artist and master craftsman, who was converted as a child and whose early Jewish memories are rekindled by his time spent among the visibly Jewish Jews of Buczacz in "The Great Town Hall" (pp. *233–39*, 192–200). It is not only the fact of his origins that turns the town hall into a Jewish space; Jewishness is encoded in the faces of the sculptures themselves that look out over the city, and which are modeled on a combination of present-day Buczacz types and the now-recurrent memories of the Yom Kippur of his childhood. Locked away in the tower and facing starvation, Theodore's fate, in its heroic last moments, connects with the martyrdom of other artists in *A City in Its Fullness*, especially the ḥazzanim. It is no surprise, then, when the town hall at the city's civic center becomes linked to the hill on its outskirts, named for the Jewish Icarus who crashed and died there, where the Jews of Buczacz were buried alive some two hundred years later.[22] The penetration and appropriation of gentile space reach their apotheosis in the important story that follows: "The Partners" (pp. *239–55*, 201–23), which I examine in Chapter 5. The story begins with a fateful encounter between the feared Count Potocki and a humble Jewish charcoal maker in the eighteenth century and manages, in its final pages, to refer Agnon's own parents and their family connection to Emanuel Ringleblum, the murdered historian of the Warsaw Ghetto.

Next to the great town hall is a building called the little town hall. The story of that title, "The Little Town Hall" (pp. 255–69), provides the exact inverse of the situation described in the story just discussed. If in the case of the great town hall it is the Jews who take up a small part of a gentile space, in the case of the little town hall, it is a gentile who (once) occupied one unit of a building otherwise occupied by Jewish families. The building was originally built to serve a municipal function, but the steep ransom that had to be paid to the Tatar raiders meant that a proper roof was never built. An improvised roof was fabricated and the building sold to Jews.

The story is an amalgam of two vastly different but ultimately related narratives. One is an account of internal Jewish economic competition. The gentile peasants entering Buczacz to buy goods come across this building before they get to the marketplace; and so those Jewish families that could buy apartments in the little town hall and also use them as shops had the advantage over the Jews who maintained stalls and stands in the marketplace proper. Buczacz divided into two warring factions over this issue; but the conflict was put aside when Mikołaj Potocki, frustrated by having found no game on a hunting day, made a Jewish woman climb a tree and shot her and shot two Jewish men shortly thereafter.

The second narrative concerns a gentile knife grinder, who has rented a space in the building because the Jewish tenants do not want the competition from an additional Jewish merchant. The knife grinder is a foreigner who is said to have escaped the hangman's noose in another country. In a city in which everyone loves to gossip and to haggle about prices, the knife grinder is an alien figure because he refuses to do either. When a headstrong young peasant abuses him for not lowering the price to sharpen a scythe, the knife grinder ominously tells him that the instrument will be so sharp that it will take off the head of his wife and his mother-in-law. The young man is unmarried but he does have his heart set on a young maiden. Yet instead of respecting the village mores and approaching the council of elders to ask for her hand, he rushes ahead recklessly, and through a con-catenation of circumstances ends up killing the woman he wished to marry and her mother and in getting killed himself, all via the selfsame scythe. The knife sharpener takes his wheel and disappears and the shop in the little town hall is boarded up and never again occupied.

It is natural for us as readers to take the lurid melodrama surround-ing the wheel and scythe as confirming a stereotype about the potential for murderousness at the heart of peasant life. This identification places us squarely and reassuringly on one side of a divide between the commanded civility of Jewish life and the unpredictability of gentile violence, which includes not just peasants but also a capriciously homicidal Polish mag-nate. But a second reading of the story goes some distance in blurring that border. On the economic ladder of Jewish life in Buczacz, the shopkeepers who take space in the little town hall are already a rung or two above the keepers of stalls and stands in the marketplace, yet they seek to gain even more advantage by preempting the peasant foot traffic and cutting off the flow to the marketplace.

Within the framework of Jewish values and behaviors, this is certainly a kind of violence, even if heads are not being sliced off by agricultural implements or being shot at by hunting rifles. This economic oppression has a hardness precisely because it is pervasive and unrelenting and goes unmarked as a clear offense under the law. The single boarded-up storefront among the Jewish shops of the little town hall becomes a symbolic wound or vacancy. It hints not only at the vulnerability of Jewish space to penetra-tion from the outside but also at a source of infection within.

The penultimate stop on the tour provides another example of a very specific site to which, through the resourceful collective memory of the guide-narrator, a vivid story is attached. Again, the directions are precise: "Moving uphill to the left from the town hall, you will find seven or eight shops. . . ." (p. *272*). Before the great fires and before the shops were built, the peculiarity of this spot was that *kohanim*, Jews of priestly lineage, would not walk there because of a long-held tradition that it was the site of the grave of a young woman. Her headstone had been inscribed with the verse from Deut. 22:27: "Although the betrothed girl cried for help, there was no one to rescue her." The story that explains the unusual inscription and the singular location of the grave could not be more chilling. A pious, widowed merchant who imports spices and dried fruit form Turkey settles with his only daughter in Buczacz. The girl, who becomes engaged to a young scholar, has a gift for preparing sweet desserts, and she is engaged to do so for a large celebration to be held in the local palace. During the preparations, a pet bear breaks free of his chains. The lord's son, who has been observing the girl and desiring her, exploits the ensuing confusion to grope her. The girl runs away from him but falls and dies; not knowing she is dead, he rapes her. Her distraught father insists on burying her at the spot where she fell and emblazoning on her stone a reproach to the bystanders who did not save her.

This grim little tale illustrates a dimension of space that is especially important to the guide-narrator: what lies underneath rather than just what lies on the surface. This is Buczacz as *tel* and the narrator-guide as archeologist. The shops standing on the site were built after the great fires; beneath them were the grave and the gravestone, and, in a figurative sense, beneath them are the girl and her story, as well the feudal milieu of spice merchants from the East and autocratic nobles with their pet bears and wayward sons. What gives us access to these buried layers, it should be noted, is a memory cultivated by the kohanim of Buczacz in their vigilant attention to the sacred geography of their town.

Agnon brings to a close the grand tour of Buczacz—and book 1 of *A City in Its Fullness*—with the most powerful and disorienting instantiation of the paradigm of place plus story. We are directed to take the road that leads from the town hall and the marketplace, cross the bridge, and arrive at the land on the other side of the Strypa, an area formed by the bend in the river and a canal dug to power water mills (pp. *274–79*). To the right is the kosher slaughtering house, and to the left is the gymnasium built by the Austrians in the nineteenth century. There was once a Jewish neighborhood there with a well of bubbling fresh water; the houses were torn down to build the gymnasium, and the well was fenced in and placed off limits. Somewhat beyond is the great Basilian Monastery. Beyond that in the shadow of Fedor Hill, is a secluded section, which centuries ago, was the place of the first Jewish settlement in Buczacz and probably a cemetery. The fortress that overlooks the area lies in ruins because the people of Buczacz were forced to demolish it themselves when they were conquered by the Turks. The synagogue was destroyed in the 1648 massacres and a church built in its place. It is the place where the kabbalistic holy man, the Good Jew, described in some detail in the story "The Ḥazzanim" (pp. 77–78, 87–88), once lived. When the narrator was a boy, aside from a few gentiles who worked in the city, only one or two Jews lived there, and they chose to do so "either because they were eager for the clean air, or because of the low rents, or because they were negligent about observance of the commandments and wished to escape scrutiny by their neighbors" (p. 275). The area, on the other side of the Strypa, is truly a liminal space, a space "in between" Jews and gentiles, the city and the countryside, the river and its man-made canal.

Is this a fitting end to a grand tour? Have we been accompanied to sites of compelling interest only to be left in this no-man's land? Agnon, in fact, organized this last stop with great care and gave us an ending to book 1 that is a bang rather than a whimper. This big effect derives precisely from the connection of this strange space to the story it anchors. The story is "Feivush Gazlan" (pp. 280–97, 227–252), and it concerns the implementation of the hated candle tax. After annexing Galicia, the Austrian government sought ways to extract income from its new Jewish subjects, and, in addition to taxing the sale of kosher meat, it put into effect a tax on candles. Because candles were an important part of Sabbath observances and wedding celebrations, Jews were constrained to put up with the tax.

The implementation of the tax was put in the hands of Jewish tax farmers, who were chosen for the concession because they promised the largest yield. They in turn placed the enforcement of the tax in the hands of Jewish thugs who, accompanied by gentile helpers, would march into people's homes on Friday evenings and extinguish all their candles—it was the gentiles who did the actual extinguishing—if the tax hadn't been paid.

The enforcer in Buczacz is Feivush the thug, and his portrayal is surprisingly sympathetic. Rather than being a screed against gentile oppression, the story makes a point of asserting the complicity of Jews in their own persecution and presents the community, even the denizens of the beit midrash, as hypocritical and morally flawed. Feivush, too, is culpable, but he is also exploited, and he and his wife end up paying a dear price.

It is with this strong, de-idealizing gesture that Agnon brings the first great section of his book to a close. The analysis of the story proper belongs to the discussion of social injustice in Chapter 6.

It is, again, the physical place where we are left that retains a troubling resonance. The beginning of the story adds a subversive detail to the already disorienting list of strange features of the little valley on the other side of the Strypa.

> There, at the far end of the courtyard valley, facing the street where the synagogue destroyed by Khmelnytskyi once stood, Feivush made a home for himself. Wood and stone debris from the demolished house of Jacob Frank lay there, untouched by human hands. Feivush collected it and built his home out of it. (p. *280, 250*)

We already know that for the Jews this is a place of destruction that has been abandoned as a place of settlement. What is new and shocking is the mention of the name of Jacob Frank, the infamous Polish Jew who considered himself the reincarnation of Shabetai Tsevi and led his followers in a mass conversion to Christianity in 1759. In contrast to most historians, who identify Frank's birthplace as Korolivka in Podolia, Agnon held that he was born in Buczacz and returned there to live for a time later in his life (p. *221*). The fact that Feivush, knowingly or unknowingly, built his home with the detritus of a great heretic points to a darkness that comes from within—even if it is from the margins and not the center, of the holy community of Buczacz.

2

Inventing a Narrator

The unprecedented nature of *A City in Its Fullness* as a composition challenged Agnon to come up with a new narrative scheme. The various narrative personae—the vessels into which Agnon had poured himself over the vast corpus of his previous stories and novels—would not serve for executing and managing this new form, a grand cycle of short stories set in earlier centuries. The invention of a new narrator is one of the great discoveries of Agnon's late style. And lest you think that this is merely a technical matter, know that in truth *everything* depends upon it. How we as readers know what we know comes to us through the grace of what the narrator shows us and how he shows it to us and the attitude he takes toward what he has shown. The new narrator of *A City in Its Fullness* is a complex and composite creation. We can begin to understand the materials from which Agnon fashioned this new creation by examining the passage that concludes "The Parable and Its Lesson."

The story concerns a journey in the netherworld taken by the rabbi of Buczacz accompanied by his assistant, the shamash. When the shamash tells the tale for the first time many decades later, it has such a stunning impact on the holy community of Buczacz that the community officially decides to record the tale and its lesson for posterity in the pinkas, the communal register. A fresh page of the pinkas is allotted to the account so that it would not get lost amid other, lesser matters. The community summons a scribe who struggles mightily to find the correct and true exalted Hebrew words in which to tell the tale. Finally, he inscribes the text in a calligraphic hand.

> After he had made his corrections the scribe sat down and copied everything out in a handsome script, the letters written the way they were written back when Buczacz was Buczacz, each letter distinct unto itself and each one in its place on the line, like people standing for the silent devotion, where the tall ones stick up like a *lamed* and the short ones are small as a *yod*, and all of them are directed to the same place. Had the pinkas not been consumed in the flames, we could have read the entire story just as it was set down in its true and original form, with the unique blend of wisdom and faith that marked all that our ancestors wrote and did and thought and said. But now that book is no more, and Buczacz is destroyed, and many thousands of Jews have been slain, the least of them the equal of the eminent of the Gentiles, who watched the loathsome monsters destroy the world and did nothing. From our town there were those who were buried alive in graves they dug for themselves; there were those who were never buried; there were those upon whom the murderers poured kerosene and were immolated one by one, limb by limb.

> So now, since that pinkas went up in flames and Buczacz has been destroyed and the deeds of the former generations have been forgotten in the recent suffering, I pondered the possibility that the Gehinnom of our time would make us forget the Gehinnom that the shamash saw, and the story about it, and all we can learn from that story. So I said to myself, let me put it all down in a book and thus create a memorial to a holy community that sanctified its life in its death as its ancestors sanctified their lives with Torah, which is our life. (p. 437–38)[1]

The shamash's tale of the journey to Gehinnom is already full of amazements, and here on the last page of this lengthy story we are given one more jolt. The story we have just read, we are informed, is not only a substitute for the original account but a poor substitute at that. The original was a document whose very materiality, expressed in the exquisite rectitude of its hand lettering, reflected a fusion of wisdom and faith that existed only in the years when "Buczacz was Buczacz." That account was burnt completely in the flames that engulfed the holy community of Buczacz and its great pinkas. Yet despite the pathos and the imprecation evoked by that horror, the narrator hastens to declare his intention not to allow the moral teaching of the story to be overshadowed; he will not allow the "Gehinnom that the shamash saw" to be lost in the enormity of the "Gehinnom of our time."

What a provocative statement! Let us pause to make sure we understand it correctly. Put in plain terms, the narrator is acutely concerned that in the fulsomeness of our outrage and pathos over the Holocaust, we will lose sight of the moral lessons brought back from Gehinnom by the shamash. When it comes to the destruction of the pinkas in the flames that consumed Buczacz, the narrator endeavors to shift our attention from the burnt-alive bodies to the loss of the *story* that pinkas contained, a story that had been recorded there almost three centuries earlier. It is that loss that the narrator seeks to repair when he takes up pen and paper to retell the story after his own manner. Yet how can a story and its moral make a greater claim on us than the tragedy of real Jewish bodies incinerated by the enemy?

This seemingly perverse insistence helps us to understand how the narrator situates himself historically within *A City in Its Fullness* as a whole. The narrator, we learn, is fully aware of the Holocaust in general and of the gruesome manner in which the Jews of Buczacz died in particular. This provokes rage and execration, but the narrator does not allow these fierce emotions to become more than occasional ejaculations or bitter asides. (They often punctuate the end of the stories.) He refuses to embark upon the work of mourning or to explore the theological mystery thrown up by the Holocaust because these undertakings would divert him from the burden that has been thrust upon him by the very fact of the destruction: he must now devote himself to restoring something of what was lost. And this is the irony. Although his mission is activated by the destruction, he must work against the representational pull it exerts—the outrage and fascination—in order to clear and create a space for the story of the city in its fullness.

The task at hand is to compensate for the loss of the pinkas. The narrator has labored mightily to retell the story of the journey to Gehinnom and its lesson, and he has done so knowing all the while that his substitute version must of necessity be deemed makeshift and inferior compared to the beautifully executed and officially authorized original. But let us pause a moment to ask whether we the readers share the narrator's pious and self-deprecating judgment. We have just finished reading a hair-raising story of sustained dramatic and metaphysical tension, which features a fantastic monologue by a semi-reliable narrator, full of intriguing gaps of meaning. Would we easily trade this virtuoso performance, with all its ironies and nuances, for the guileless, straightforward, devout, and—yes, let it be said—boring account of the kind that would have been contained in the pinkas, even with the full purity of its style and transcription? We may of course be heartbroken by the conditions under which the pinkas was destroyed. But leaving that aside, if we were forced to choose between the official account that perished and the story the narrator has written to replace it, as modern readers there is little doubt we would opt for the latter. Yet at the same time if we had before us the story alone without knowing about the pinkas account it replaces, we would likely regard it as *only* a story, a piece of literature lacking the aura of true and real events.

The Pinkas as Sanction

Thus we encounter the dialectical interdependence at the heart of *A City in Its Fullness*. On the one hand, no matter how successfully camouflaged in traditional discourse, the stories in this volume remain modern literary artifacts, unthinkable without Kleist and Kafka and Agnon's own prewar writings and fully exploiting the toolkit of modernist narrative techniques. On the other hand, the authority and weight of the stories, which elevate them above being merely literature, derive from their being a substitute for the holy community of Buczacz and its written embodiment in its pinkas. It is from these two foundations that Agnon fashions the device of his narrator. He takes the traditional collective authority of the pinkas and combines it with modern, individual literary invention. It is the secret amalgam of the two that enables his project to be born aloft. Let us first look at each component of this amalgam separately before appreciating how they are joined together.

Pinkas, from the Greek *pinax* (writing tablet), is a term from rabbinic Hebrew that denotes a register in which accounts are kept. In the Middle Ages
the term was adopted to describe the official minute book of a Jewish community, especially in Eastern Europe. The keeping of a communal pinkas was
a phenomenon as widespread as it was multifarious. There was no standard
for the pinkas as a physical object as to its size or appearance; nor were there
general rules for what information was included or excluded. In principle,
the pinkas included everything that was important to the kehilah, the community as a whole. Certain to be included were the following: the *takkanot*,
the rulings and regulations issued by the kahal, the governing council of a
town or city; *piskei din*, legal determinations by the leading rabbinic authority and the local court; matters pertaining to the relations between the Jewish community and the gentile rulers, especially regarding taxes and levies;
decisions taken and sums paid for the ransoming of captives; details of the
appointment of communal officials, both salaried and volunteer; letters of
rabbinic appointment specifying duties and responsibilities; and the births,
weddings, and deaths of members of the community.

In addition to these communal protocols, there is a free-floating provision
for recording events that are startling or anomalous, and it was under just
such a heading that the holy community of Buczacz, according to the story
mentioned above, saw it a positive duty to record what the shamash saw
in Gehinnom and the astonishing lessons it taught. In many communities,
moreover, there was more than one pinkas. In the story "HaYeraḥamielim,"
the pinkas of the Ḥevra Kadisha, the burial society, of Buczacz is mentioned
in connection with the death of a ten-year old who had mastered all of
Talmud (p. *185*).[2] Pinkasim from burial societies in fact become increasingly important during the period of Austrian rule in Galicia because the
authority of the central community, the kahal, had been curtailed and the
burial societies remained a central registry for communal information and
demographics. Finally, the pinkasim as physical objects, usually imposingly
large registers, had their own mystique. They were kept under lock and key
by the parnas, the lay leader of the community, either in his home or in
the community's office or bureau, and taken out on special occasions for

the purposes of recording new enactments or checking the historical record. To ordinary folk, the pinkas was an object of wonderment and veneration.[3]

The figure of the narrator throughout *A City in Its Fullness* is linked to the institution of the pinkas in a variety of subtly shifting connections: he is the extension of the pinkas, its heir, its replacement, its belated voice. Above all he arrogates to himself the authority, in its many manifestations, that had been invested in the pinkas. The pinkas possesses an indisputable historicity; it is a guarantor of the fact that certain events assuredly took place. As an institution of the community, the pinkas is the expression of a collective will and a corporate identity. Even though the pinkas often contains evidence of conflict and deviance, the values implicitly conveyed in its entries reflect the views of the lay and rabbinic elite. And, just as its function is to document the life of the community, the pinkas is itself a venerated document and, in its special style and calligraphy, it is a graphic embodiment of the community's best self. All of these qualities are useful to Agnon in establishing the traditional authority with which his narrator speaks and in protecting the narrator from the imputation that he is simply a storyteller or an "author." He does not invent, he does not speak for himself, and his views and values are located squarely within the traditional worldview of Buczacz in its heyday.

Now all this rhetoric of traditional authority might seem to obligate the narrator to a straightjacket of formal constraints. Yet, in a certain regard, the opposite is true. For despite its traditionalism, the pinkas is by its nature a remarkably open format. The essence of a pinkas is a list (enactments, appointments, events, etc.), and the make up of that list is miscellaneous and its order additive. Nor is it a code or a commentary in which individual items are arranged in a rational order. It is not even a chronicle, in which historical eventualities are correlated with their causes and cast into large shapes and patterns. The only order is chronological; it is an agglomeration of events presented in the order of their occurrence.

This special quality of the pinkas—the piling up of events without shape or causation—provides Agnon the modernist with a kind of freedom that could be realized from no other form of traditional writing. It is a secondary gain that descends upon him unbidden but relished. It gives permission to the narrator Agnon has created to observe things and describe events without having to explain away the sometimes absurd juxtapositions, the "why" of one following the other. Gaps, unexplained connections, and troubling theological questions can be left to let their ironic surpluses of meaning simmer without the taint of irresponsibility attaching to the narrator. With this traditional sanction for unexpected juxtapositions in place, the narrator can be liberated from having to produce well-wrought tales that exhibit either the charm of the folktale or the artfulness of the European short story.

Miscellaneousness is a pinkas-derived principle that Agnon embraces in the construction of *A City in Its Fullness*. The relationship among items and events here is not sequence but appositeness. In his representation of Buczacz to the reader, as we saw in Chapter 1, the narrator continually mixes and matches narrative material within the same textual unit. A section, for example, about the well in the marketplace, may contain a physical description of the site and an account of its history and the customs associated with it before proceeding to furnish a story with its own self-contained plot. In the pinkas mode of exposition there is no privilege or preferment given to a decorous separation of modes. It is this miscellaneous quality that in all likelihood is responsible for the resistance or bewilderment that some readers have experienced in approaching *A City in Its Fullness*. Is this a collection of customs and historical anecdotes, a kind of traditional ethnography? Or is it literature containing the kind of modernist tales to which we are accustomed from the canon of stories published during Agnon's lifetime?

The fact that it may be both means that we must allow ourselves to be reeducated by Agnon as to how to read his late works. The case for the existence of a late style in Agnon does not depend solely on the evidence of the Buczacz stories. In an elegant discussion of a number of other later works, Ariel Hirschfeld has demonstrated how in his last years Agnon was in the process of sloughing off some of the narrative strictures that hitherto had bound together his way of writing. What might be dismissed as haste or incompletion reveals itself instead as a renunciation of closure and causality and a freedom to entertain more open forms of the imagination.[4] The appeal to the pinkas in *A City in Its Fullness* is the largest and most explicit use made of this freedom. But the entire landscape of the master's late work deserves to be looked at anew.

The Unexpungable "I"

But the pinkas can take Agnon only so far. Open up any story in *A City in Its Fullness*, and you will discover a presence that would be unthinkable in any true pinkas: the first person singular. Even if some events chronicled in a pinkas bear on the lives of individuals and even if it is the hand of a single scribe who sets them down, the entries are made on behalf and from the point of view of the collective, of the kahal. The pinkas is a register of corporate existence. Yet the stories of *'Ir umelo'ah* are told by a narrator who speaks in his own voice and never hesitates to say "I." This "I" is busy and ubiquitous. It proclaims the truthfulness of its reporting, admits small lapses in memory or historical knowledge, abjures the reader not to lose interest, gives assurances that a story will be brought to its conclusion expeditiously, protects the honor of certain families by withholding mention of their names, and continually lets us know that it/he is releasing only a portion of the information about Buczacz in his possession.

Who is this "I"? It would be the most natural thing in the world to answer: Why, of course, it is Agnon himself, the native son of Buczacz, who is telling its story. But such a reader, heedless of the cautions of literary criticism or oblivious to them, would in fact not find much support in the stories for identifying their narrator with the author. This is a complex matter upon which I say more below. It is enough to point out at this juncture that there are innumerable instances in Agnon's major fiction, especially the novel *A Guest for the Night*, in which he makes his narrators powerfully resemble himself—middle-age men with imperfectly realized religious aspirations—but this is not one of them. Fashioning an ironic version of his own persona is perhaps Agnon's greatest stock-in-trade. But, again, here Agnon does not employ a persona that reflects back on himself and for a simple and objective reason. The very project of *A City in Its Fullness* requires writing stories about events that took place in the centuries before Agnon was born and, moreover, writing about them as if they were happening in the present.

So we are returned to the question: if this is not the persona of Agnon the writer as we know it, then who is it? The answer I propose is that the narrator created by Agnon is a function *with* an identity—of a sort—but *without* a personality. The narrator who speaks in the "I" is identifiable in a generic way: he is a man of Buczacz, he is a devoted chronicler of the city, and he shares the traditional faith and values of the scholarly elite of the city in its heyday. Yet, although he has his tics and peccadilloes and often speaks in an identifiable voice, he does not possess a personality in the sense of being an individuated person or the persona of such a figure.

This is undoubtedly the great act of renunciation and a constitutive moment in the making of *A City in Its Fullness*. A fair swath of Agnon's greatest work, especially the high modernist stories in *The Book of Deeds* [*Sefer hama'asim*] are wholly dependent on what Arnold Band has called the "dramatization of the ego,"[5] a process whereby Agnon uses the persona of a man very much like himself and exploits it as an ironic foil for exploring the dilemmas of the self in a world after faith. *A Guest for the Night*, one of Agnon's greatest novels, describes the year-long sojourn in Buczacz (called Shibush in the novel) on the part of a native of the town who now lives in Palestine; the play with Agnon's own autobiographical figure is so close that he goes so far as to call the protagonist Shmuel Yosef. To give this up, one of the principle strategies of his success as an artist, is to give up a great deal; and this is a further sign of risk and resolve Agnon was willing to undertake in the last decades of this life.

The viewpoint of the child was another mode of approach to Buczacz that Agnon relinquished. Even though it was used less frequently in his work than the adult persona, it might have recommended itself as a natural means for reevoking the city of his childhood. In the extraordinary story "The Kerchief" ["Hamitpaḥat"], for example, the adult narrator imitates the first-person consciousness of a boy, very much like Agnon himself, on the eve of his bar mitzvah. In recognizing the existence of evil in the world, the boy also comes to terms with the contradictions of his town, a holy community of charitable people that at times denies the existence of suffering. One could imagine a whole approach to the representation of Buczacz productively based on the dualities of the childhood viewpoint. But that would have limited Agnon to the Buczacz of his childhood when he was endeavoring to comprehend the sweep of earlier centuries. Again, he was constrained to take upon himself an act of *tsimtsum*, a contraction of self, and work toward a narrative persona whose hallmark is impersonality.[6]

Of the many tasks performed by the narrator's "I," none is as fundamental as the function of reminding us again and again that we are reading stories that are told by someone. Lest this seems trivial or taken for granted, it is worth thinking about the ways it could have been otherwise. The authority of traditional chronicles, for example, is often established and maintained by creating the illusion that historical events are simply telling themselves and that pieces of history are being directly converted into writing without the handling or manipulation of the chronicler. Similarly, folk tales usually present themselves as generated by the folk and seek to conceal the fact that they have been fashioned or refashioned by a teller. The pinkas partakes of this quality as well. Even though it is patent that the entries in the pinkas are written by a scribe at the behest of the community, once written down they attain the status of statements whose truth is given and guaranteed by the corporate entity that inscribed them.

In contrast to the implied effacement of the agency behind the writing in all these instances, the narrator of *A City in Its Fullness* rarely lets us forget the narrated quality of these stories. The narrator's "I" keeps us aware that what we are reading is constructed rather than given and that the form in which it comes to us is the result of a myriad of decisions being made as to what to include and what to exclude and how to shape it for our consumption. And even though the agent behind the agency is not a person with a name or a defined historical existence, it is also not anonymous and collective. This is an "I" that is feisty, idiosyncratic, justificatory, and assertive. Most of all it is busy, busy working to produce the narratives we are reading. And we are not allowed to forget it.

Where does this busy but impersonal "I" come from? I propose a triple provenance. One source is nothing less than the entire aggadic, storytelling tradition of post-biblical Jewish literature. This begins with the stories in the

Palestinian midrash collections and the *aggadot* in the Babylonian Talmud and continues in the Middle Ages in the tales of R. Nissim of Kairouan and the rhymed prose of the poets of Andalus and comes into the modern period in the tales of the Hasidim and the parody of those tales by Galician *maskilim* (*maskil*, singular) and in the performances of itinerant *maggidim* (preachers) and *badḥanim* (wedding entertainers). Mixing reverence with wit, Agnon's narrator is the heir to these tellers and these traditions.

The second source is the most speculative: the eighteenth-century English novel as mediated through translation into German. (Agnon did not read English but he was at home in German.) Integral to the rise of the novel in England, as practiced by Richardson, Fielding, and Sterne, was the convention of direct address to the reader on the part of the narrator-novelist and the cultivation of the illusion of an easy, conversational channel of communication between the two. This channel was also the means by which the novelist could moralize and declare his sentiments and sympathies. This enabled the narrator-novelist to bare the device of the making of the novel to his readers and to render its writing a consciously exposed process. From these practices, as they spilled over into the literature of the European Enlightenment, Agnon took the liberty he gave his narrator to address the reader and expatiate on the deliberations and decisions that occupied him in executing the book.

Finally—and most assuredly—there is Agnon himself. Much of his genius as a writer, as has already been proposed, is manifest in his ability to render an ironic treatment of his own, autobiographical persona. Undertaking the great project of telling the story of Buczacz in its golden age, Agnon steeled himself to make a sacrifice of his signature literary ego. At the same time, however, Agnon could not let go altogether, and he contrived to retain that part of the self that could be decoupled from concrete historical embodiment. What he was left with was the rhetoric of the "I" as a locutionary device that could express intentions and frustrations and a degree of wry playfulness but not serve as a window onto the soul.

The time has come both to summarize and to take account of exceptions. The narrator of *A City in Its Fullness* is a construction that essentially is new but draws on modes Agnon had experimented with in the past. Agnon put this device in place for the special task of telling the story of Buczacz. He—for convenience we will use the personal pronoun in referring to the narrator—is an amalgam of two principles. One is the official, corporate authority that derives from the model of the pinkas and requires the divestiture of individualized personality. The other is the busy, executive "I" of the narrator that addresses the reader and reflects aloud on the production of the narrative. Now this configuration, especially the norm of impersonality, is not a set of laws but a construct that has been generalized from observing the way in which the stories of *A City in Its Fullness* are told. As such, it explains most but not all of the phenomena of the text. There are some major and minor exceptions that must be accounted for. If the norm of impersonality calls for Agnon to decline dramatizing himself, then there are two major instances where he does not desist.

The first is "The Sign," the story that was placed at the end of *A City in Its Fullness* by Emunah Yaron in her editing of the volume but that I place at the beginning in the English translation. Recall from the opening of this study that the first-person narrator of the story is identical in his life circumstances to those of Agnon's: a native of Buczacz living in the Talpiyot neighborhood of Jerusalem. The story dramatizes a key autobiographical moment when the news of the murder of the Jews of Buczacz reaches the narrator and he is vouchsafed a mystical visitation from the great medieval Hebrew poet Solomon ibn Gabirol. Whether placed at the end or the beginning, the very inclusion of "The Sign" is the product of an editorial decision that was not Agnon's. It crosses several boundaries: it appeared previously in book form, it occurs in the near present, it takes place in the Land of Israel, and its narrator is more than implicitly identified with the person of Agnon. Nevertheless, there is a case to be made that, because the story is supremely relevant to the project of the Buczacz tales, it is of practical use to the reader to connect it to the volume.

A second major exception is the story "A Book That Was Lost" [*Sefer she'avad*, pp. *207–12*].[7] The story, which, again, is told in the first person by a figure very much like Agnon, begins when the narrator was still a youth studying in the beit midrash of Buczacz. In the attic of the great synagogue, the narrator discovers the unbound leaves of a treatise by a scholar who had lived four or five generations earlier. The scholar, one R. Shemaryah, labored twelve years on a work that elucidated the obscurities in a commentary (*Magen Avraham*) on the *Shulhan Arukh*. When he brought his manuscript for binding, he found on the bookbinder's work table another manuscript (*Maḥatsit Hashekel*), which covered, and covered adequately, the same subject. He withdrew his own and never sought to publish it. Having read the put-aside work, the narrator believes its author prematurely undersold its originality, and he is determined to deposit the manuscript for posterity in a newly established national library in Jerusalem. He underwrites the cost of the shipment to Palestine by surreptitiously diverting the lunch money his mother gave him. A number of years later, when he himself had immigrated to Palestine, he goes in search of the manuscript at the library, but the book cannot be found. It has been lost.

Now, this is a wholly canny and beguiling story; and Anne G. Hoffman and I chose it as the title story for our anthology of Agnon's short stories. But it is out of place in *A City in Its Fullness* both because of its explicit autobiographical armature and its being set—at the turn of the twentieth century and partially in Erets Yisrael—after the temporal and spatial frame of the narrative of *A City in Its Fullness* has been brought to a close. The temptation to include it is understandable, and it did not appear elsewhere in book form, having appeared only in *Haaretz* in 1956. We don't know whether Agnon would have included it had he lived. It is, together with "The Sign," an exception that proves the rule.

There are other instances which, though fleeting and mentioned in passing, are more interesting because, rather than deriving from editorial decisions, they are indisputably organic to the enterprise itself. One example comes from the story "Haḥazzanim" [pp. *70–84, 78–97*], which tells the story of Miriam Devorah, the wife of a ḥazzan who is herself a gifted musician and composer, who dies of melancholy. After her death, her husband R. Elya makes a successful third marriage but soon begins to display signs of ascetic withdrawal from the world. He spends all day absorbed in the study

of a single book of kabbalistic wisdom called *Ḥemdat Yamim*.[8] Regarding
the particular volume R. Elya held in his hands, the narrator remarks: "That
was the only copy that existed in our town, and it was the one I read in my
youth" (p. *82*, 94).

The second example comes from the story "Hashutafim" ["The Partners," pp. *239–55*, 201–23], which tells the story of how a Jewish family came
into possession of a permanent leasehold on the basement of the ornate
town hall of Buczacz and how its descendents lived there continuously
until World War One. After relating the foundational event from the days of
Count Potoki, which was responsible for this unlikely occurrence, the narrator finishes the story by introducing us to the last of the line of the family,
one Naḥum Ber. In regard to his younger daughter the narrator mentions,
"I knew her when I was a child because my mother, peace be upon her,
served as a kind of patron for her; her mother had died and she had no relations in the town" (p. *254*, 222).[9]

Do these cases—there are others scattered here and there in the volume—require us to revise the conception of an impersonal narrator?[10] Are
these instances in which Agnon "bares the device" and owns up to the fact
that his narrator is really he himself tricked out as a pinkas-like chronicler?
To begin with, in constructing his narrator, I don't believe that Agnon ever
intended to sustain an illusion or pull the wool over his readers' eyes. He
understood full well that when his readers picked up a volume of stories
by him about Buczacz that their natural point of departure would be to
identify the first-person narrator with Agnon the author. Agnon therefore
needed to neutralize this assumption and foster the credibility of an unbound narrative persona capable of presiding over a grand cavalcade of
historical memory. For what was at stake was making *A City in Its Fullness*
a book about Buczacz and not about himself. Given the scale of the project
as well as the scale of renunciation it demanded, Agnon was remarkably
successful in sustaining the operative credibility of the narrative device. The
occasional instances in which he puts himself in the picture are not failures
to prop up this artifice but reminders of the proprietary connection between the author and the city that undergirds the whole endeavor, a con-

nection about whose existence we were never in doubt from the outset. We know that Agnon is writing this book because Buczacz is his town; yet we grant him the freedom to decouple himself from the burdens of his self-myth to do the work of collective portraiture.

What Does the Narrator Believe?

So let us say for the moment that we know what Agnon wishes us to believe, for the purposes of this undertaking, his narrator is *not*. But what in fact *is* he? How does he view the world? What does he believe? Where in time does he exist relative to the more than two centuries covered in the volume? Whom is he addressing when he turns toward his readers? How does he know what he knows, especially the inner thoughts of the characters he writes about? These are, to be sure, technical questions that bear on the poetics of any serious work of narrative prose. But they are also questions that matter a great deal to the larger issue of what it means to recover the lost past through the imagination. This is the "how" of Agnon's approach to that challenge, and it shows us that there can be nothing naïve or uncalculated about how that project is undertaken. The construction of his narrator is the major strategy, and it will therefore behoove us to clarify three issues: What does the narrator believe? Who is the audience for his storytelling? And, what functions does the narrator perform in the managing of the narrative?

A caveat before proceeding. *A City in Its Fullness* is not a novel but a story cycle comprising nearly 150 separate texts. The voices that narrate these units are not identical throughout although they are all variations and inflections of a general paradigm. It is this general pattern that I describe in the discussion that follows. In fact when referring to the "narrator," I intend to describe a repertoire of characteristics from which Agnon draws when he sets the narrative signature for the performance of each story. On the one hand, it is in Agnon's interests to locate each of these realizations within a recognizable family resemblance to make *A City in Its Fullness* a coherent work. On the other, he reserves the right to fit the voice of the teller—as well as the mode in which the story is told—to the particular event or practice that is the business of the story at hand to relate. It is the common repertoire I am trying to elucidate in this discussion. Examples of how these options are configured in different combinations are presented as I analyze the individual stories in the thematic chapters that follow.[11]

The best way to understand the narrator's mental world—and to answer the question "What does he believe?"—is to see it as a back formation of the city that is his subject. "When Buczacz was Buczacz" is the way Agnon repeatedly hypostatizes the city he memorializes and recreates in *A City in Its Fullness*. By this tautology he means to indicate the centuries during which the community existed under the sway of rabbinic law and leadership and the ideal of Torah study before those norms were challenged by modernity and the prerogatives of the centralized state.

The narrator is a man of *that* Buczacz, and he believes what would have been believed by a member of the learned elite of that time and place. He takes for granted, for example, that reality is inscribed within the Torah, that observance of the commandments is incumbent upon all Jews, both humble and learned, that Talmud study for its own sake is the Jew's highest vocation, and that, despite a respect for great merchants and their power, the true shepherds of the community are its scholars. The narrator has a profound investment in the received practices of Buczacz, its minhagim, with its hoary origins in the famous centers of piety and learning in the Rhineland Valley. His hostility to Hasidism, which leads to a general avoidance of the subject, derives from the way in which Hasidim disregarded the fixed times for prayer, altered the received liturgy, and bypassed the authority of great scholars. Of their miracles he wants no part. After describing what is an ostensibly amazingly fortuitous coincidence, the narrator remarks: "As for us, who have no desire to take advantage of miracles even in a story, we will reveal things as they really were in fact" (p. *344*).

In contrast to Hasidism, the narrator's attitude to Kabbalah is more open if still circumspect. He is, after all, describing a period of extraordinary cultural transfer during which the theological revolution fomented in sixteenth-century Safed by Isaac Luria is being exported to the distant sphere of Polish Jewry through the propagandizing energies of talented disciples and by the powerful impact of the *Shnei Luḥot Habrit*, the treatise by Isaiah Horowitz. Certain ritual innovations, such as the Kabbalat Shabbat service Friday evenings and *tikkun leil Shavuot*, the all-night study vigil on Shavuot, are quickly absorbed into synagogue practice. The more esoteric and theosophical ideas of Kabbalah become an attractive, albeit elective, pursuit of the learned elite. Consider, for example, as mentioned above, R. Elya's absorption in the kabbalistic book *Ḥemdat Yamim*. His attention to the book is in no way transgressive; a problem arises only when his immersion draws him away from his family responsibilities. Reflecting the norms of his time and place, the narrator admits that it is legitimate to interpret *'al derekh hasod*, based on mystical understanding, even if this way of viewing things does not fit his own temperament.

Yet when it comes to the afterlife, the narrator is no skeptic. He unreservedly believes that there is a *gan eden* for the righteous and that great scholars continue their studies there in a heavenly beit midrash. He further believes that under extraordinary circumstances a departed sage can visit the world of the living. R. Meir ben Jacob Hakohen Schiff, called Maharam Schiff, was a towering scholar from Frankfurt who died in Prague in 1644. To find him 150 years later sitting at a gathering of scholars who are debating his insights is, in the mind of the narrator, a surprising occurrence because of the honor it confers on the occasion, but it is hardly an incredible one (p. *315*). Another departed scholar, R. Aryeh Leibush Auerbach, secretly visits his son to teach him Torah until he is ready to marry (p. *305*).

The most elaborated representation of postmortem reality can be found in the "tour of Gehinnom" undertaken by Rabbi Moshe and his shamash in "The Parable and Its Lesson," [pp. *394–438*],[12] one of the greatest stories in *A City in Its Fullness*. The rabbi embarks on this perilous visit to free a young relation from the bonds of being an agunah, and he indeed succeeds in finding her dead husband and, in a scene that seems borrowed from Dante, listening to his tragic story. It is what else is observed in Gehinnom that proves astonishing. The rabbi and his assistant observe several compartments in which great scholars are being subjected to tantalizing tortures, a sight that confounds the conviction that the World to Come is precisely where the righteous will receive their just rewards. It turns out that there is crucial but hidden deficiency in the righteousness of these scholars that has led to their punishment, and when the Jews of Buczacz make this discovery many years later, it requires them to make a significant revision of their notions of the afterlife.[13]

Now, even though the afterlife is very real for the narrator, the boundary between it and our world is crossed only infrequently. The journey of the rabbi and his assistant is singular and never repeated, and the visitations of scholars from the heavenly beit midrash are rare and reserved only for the select few. The boundary between here and there, in either direction, is not porous. The world of *A City in Its Fullness*, as presented by the narrator, is decidedly empty of the kind of demons encountered either in the Babylonian Talmud, in Hasidic stories in general, or in the stories of Isaac Bashevis Singer. The narrator's origins in the beit midrash of Buczacz and his identification with its values insulate his imagination from the kind of folk knowledge that abounds in dybbuks and revenants. Yet make no mistake. The rarity of visitations from the other world makes them no less real. They are organically part of reality for the narrator rather than marking off a separate world of the fantastic.

The narrator's mind is similarly conservative and traditional when it comes to sensitive questions of divine justice. He acknowledges the challenges to faith presented by the catastrophic persecutions, but he has a reservoir of rationales from which he can draw to neutralize the threat. The following example is spoken by the shamash in "The Parable and Its Lesson," but it is offered with the endorsement of the overall narrator of the story, who has provided us with the shamash's monologue.

> One inquiry leads to another, like one mouse that squeals out to another until very soon a whole horde of them come and chew up all the clothing and household goods. Because of His love for us, God encumbers us with suffering in order to purge us of the *kelipot* we have acquired in the lands of the goyim and thereby prepare us for the day of His Redemption. But this young man reached the false conclusion that God had withdrawn his love from Israel. (pp. *398–99*)[14]

At issue is the question of why God allowed the Cossacks to destroy hundreds of Jewish communities in the Ukraine and slaughter many tens of thousands of Jews. This is the classic problem of theodicy, and it will give no peace to Aaron, the prize student of Rabbi Moshe and the husband of the only member of his family to survive the massacres. The traditional answers don't satisfy him, and he careers down a slippery slope of doubt until he meets a sad end. The shamash, however, is secure in his faith, although the rationale he offers is not necessarily the one we would have expected. If he had carried over the standard rabbinic lines of argument, he would have sought to position the persecutions as punishments for sin or as an opportunity given to the righteous to demonstrate their piety. Instead he gives us a more contemporary theological argument that has been influenced by the recent influx of kabbalistic thought.

Living in the lands of the gentiles unavoidably incurs impurity; these are the kelipot, the husks left over from the primal "breaking of the vessels." The persecutions purge the impurities and bring the Jewish nation that much closer to bringing the exile to an end. Yet even if the shamash's rationale is of recent theological provenance, it performs the same function of shielding God from the appearance of either powerlessness or gratuitous cruelty. Elsewhere in *A City in Its Fullness*, when the narrator proper confronts similar instances of seemingly inexplicable suffering, he is more likely than not to avoid taking on the contradiction altogether. He adopts the traditionally pious gesture of regarding God's ways as a mystery and often avails himself of the radical understatement *ketsat kasheh*, "it is a little difficult," a phrase appropriated from the Tosaphist commentators on the Talmud when confronting gross contradictions.

Now, if the narrator were only a vessel of traditional beliefs, *A City in Its Fullness* would be a much less interesting book than it is, or it might not exist at all. The fascinating, animating, and triumphant drama in this work is the tension between the traditionalism of his worldview and the insatiability of his imagination as a storyteller. The narrator's allegiance to the norms of custom, worship, and learning are unwavering over time; yet the sights and spectacles that come before him in the chronicle he has taken upon himself to narrate are invariably deviations from these norms. One might therefore expect that his accounts would be freighted with judgment and censorious editorializing. But this is far from the case. Consider, for example, the case of Aaron, the heretical student quoted above. Although the narrator—in this case the shamash—notes his faith in God's justice, his attention is compelled by and lavished upon the affecting tale of the young scholar whose desperate quest to understand God's ways led him to shame and early death. (In fact, his story is told twice, once briefly before the encounter in Gehinnom [pp. *398–99*] and, then later, at greater length in his own words in chapter 7.) The judgment that issues from the narrator's beliefs is far outstripped by his curiosity about all things and people connected to Buczacz and his self-ascribed duty to render a true and comprehensive account of the life of his town. In *A City in Its Fullness*, story unquestionably trumps belief, yet belief serves as a normative frame that contains the ungovernable abundance of people and their deeds.

What the narrator believes, in the final analysis, is less important than what he knows. And he knows a great deal. He is as privy to the private conversations between the mightiest Polish nobles and the mightiest Jewish businessmen in Galicia ("In Search of a Rabbi") as he is to the inner thoughts of a humble shamash ("Until Elijah Comes"). He knows as much about the whims of the early Polish magnates as he does about the procedural niceties of the later Austrian administrators. He boasts an encyclopedic knowledge of the minhagim special to Buczacz and vents his embarrassment and frustration when he cannot pin down the origin of one of them. In short, whether it is high or low or early or late, our narrator's knowledge approaches omniscience. Although this principle is laid down as a root assumption of the entire enterprise, the narrator is sensitive to its presumption, and he frequently explains his sources and avers an unwavering commitment to truth. His chief strategy for establishing his control of the facts is his willingness to admit his ignorance over small matters. Consider one such admission at the opening of "The Parable and Its Lesson":

> There was in our old beit midrash an elderly shamash named Reb Yeruḥam ben Tanḥum. Some insist that his name was Reb Tanḥum ben Yeruḥam and

that the Great Synagogue was where he served. In any case, it is of him
that this story is told. If there are those who claim that it is about a certain
shamash named such-and-such, it is not for me to say. I know only the names
of the men who served as shamash in the ten generations before I left my
hometown, so I cannot make this determination and can only tell the story.
(p. 394)[15]

What is the purpose of cranking up this noisy apologetic machinery? Not
only does it make no material difference what the shamash is called, but
throughout the long story that follows his proper name, in any combination, is never once used. He is everywhere and always simply "the shamash."
Yet by stipulating his fallibility in trivial matters, the narrator can position
himself as a chronicler of impeccable integrity who will utter no statement
of fact, minor or momentous, without complete assurance of its truth. After
all, his is a memory that can reach back *only* ten generations.

For modern readers, the narrator's omniscience, despite its antic implau-
sibility at times, presents no great problem. We are used to encountering
and accepting many varieties of conventions, especially when we read far
afield in periods and cultures distant from the here and now. The narrator's
greatest presumption, his knowledge of the unvoiced thoughts of his characters, is in fact familiar to us from much closer to home. It is the creative
freedom that we grant as a matter of course to all modern novelists. For
example, in the case of Flaubert, one of Agnon's favorite writers, we take it
utterly for granted that the novelist explores the inner thoughts of Emma
Bovary or Félicité, the servant girl in *Un coeur simple*. Yet for the narrator of
A City in Its Fullness, that man who belongs to the time when Buczacz was
Buczacz, there is nothing easily self-evident about this assumption. Flaubert's freedom is predicated upon the imaginative liberty granted to artists;
great art may be the vehicle for great truth, but, as fiction, it is not held up
to a standard of factual, documentary veracity.

Although our narrator is a storyteller and his medium is stories, he
would bridle at the imputation that he was taking advantage of the conventions of modern literature. What he writes, sippurim, are neither naïve folk
tales nor the aestheticized "short stories" of Joyce or Maupassant.[16] Because
the narrator views his activity as a chronicler/storyteller as located within

the epistemic world of Jewish tradition, he is stuck with a problem. He (the narrator) is not prepared to regard what he writes as fiction, and he therefore does not avail himself of the prerogative in invention.[17]

How, then, within the traditional framework within which he works, can the narrator justify representing the inner thoughts of characters who lived long ago? The problem obviously does not bother him enough to impose any constraints on his practice; this is his stock-in-trade, this is what he does, and he goes about his business *as if* he were a pious Jewish Flaubert. The problem is the rationale, not the practice. The closest thing to a rationale is placed in the mouth of one of the narrator's guest monologists Gavriel, the linen merchant with the beautiful voice who is prevailed upon to lead services on Yom Kippur when he visits Buczacz. So moving is his leadership of the prayers that on the spot he is offered the vacant position of ḥazzan. He declines the offer, and to explain his refusal to the notables of Buczacz who are gathered in the rabbi's house, he embarks on a long monologue that tells the story of his martyred grandfather. His story meticulously reconstructs the thoughts and deeds of that tsaddik, whom he did not know having been born after his death. To justify this practice, he explains at some length:

> For, after all, I was not with them. I never met either R. Eliezer Simḥa or, it goes without saying, my sainted grandfather, after whom I am named. How then can I offer such abundant details of their lives? In this, I tell you, I follow the example of my sainted grandmother. When she recounted the events that took place in his life, she related not only the events themselves but also the thoughts in the recesses of his heart. The old-timers from that generation who knew my sainted grandfather used to say that when she would speak of her husband we would hear not only his voice but the thoughts of his heart, as well, as if those thoughts had found articulation and were speaking from his throat. To the words of my sainted grandmother I add what I heard in the name of R. Eliezer Simḥa of blessed memory, who would always talk about what had happened to my sainted grandfather on a given day. Now that I have dispelled your astonishment I return to the story. ("The Linen Man," p. *102*, 123)

Because his speech is a monologue, we don't know whether the astonishment he feels called upon to dispel has arisen from his distinguished listeners or from within his own scrupulous soul. Gavriel would no more dream of making up his grandfather's words or deeds than would a Torah sage advance an idea because he had invented it rather than having drawn it out of the tradition. The authority invested in his grandmother derives less from the fidelity of her memory than from the excellence of the imagination with which she had been graced. Based on her intimate knowledge of her husband, she has the capacity to give voice to his thoughts and feelings—after his death—in such a way that, to the ears of those who knew him in his life, as if they had come from his own voice. They are not fooled but rather consoled by this accomplishment. It would not be too much to say that in *A City in Its Fullness*, Agnon positions his narrator to partake of the model provided jointly by Gavriel and his grandmother. Like the grandson, the narrator is separated in time from events and persons that are dear to him, and, like the grandmother, he is gifted with the faculty of a faithful and accurate imagination, so much so that what he imagines and puts down in writing becomes historical truth. And like Gavriel, he feels confident that he has dispelled our astonishment.

Who Is the Narrator's Audience?

It was one of the signal accomplishments of literary criticism in the middle of the twentieth century to foreground the importance of the narrator in prose fictional texts and to catalogue the permutations of reliability and unreliability and the configurations of point of view. Semiotics went on to explore the implicit or explicit recipients of the meaning the narrator sought to convey; it did so given the assumption that all messages that have a sender must also have a receiver. The receiver is variously called the addressee, the audience, or the narratee. This is not merely a technical issue, because we cannot understand why a message is shaped the way it is unless we grasp the target toward which the narrator is dispatching it. Applying this to Agnon's practice in *A City in Its Fullness* turns out to be both necessary and challenging. The fact that the narrator often speaks as "I" and often directly addresses the reader makes the existence of an implied audience inescapable and crucial to understanding the narrator's motives. But pinning down the identity of this audience is difficult because of the unusual nature of the book's narrator. Does the narrator exist—understanding, of course, that this is a virtual existence—at the time of the writing, the 1950s and 1960s, or does he speak from a time—or a series of different times—that are coincident with the historical existence of Buczacz in the seventeenth through nineteenth centuries? He frequently reminds us of the fate of the Jews of Buczacz in the 1940s, yet at the same time he displays a more-than-intimate knowledge of the town at various stages in its classical, early modern existence.

This is, to be sure, a complex landscape, and we can map it most effectively by thinking in terms of three sets of narrative relations that fit inside each other like Chinese boxes: (1) the historical author and the historical audience; (2) the implied author and the authorial audience; and (3) the narrator and the narratorial audience. In common parlance about fiction, these relations are often confused or rendered synonymous. But it is important to make these distinctions, again, not for the sake of theoretical nicety but for the help they give us in understanding how Agnon was able to create an epic narrative project with multiple lines of sight.

The historical author is, simply, S. Y. Agnon, the man who lived in the Talpiyot section of Jerusalem, had a wife and two children, and wrote in the decades after the war, among other writings, a cycle of stories about the town in Galicia in which he grew up. The historical audience were real people who read the stories about Buczacz as most of them were published in the periodical press, especially *Haaretz*, during the author's lifetime and then after his death as collected in *A City in It Fullness*. For reasons explained in the Introduction, there were many fewer of these real readers than Agnon might have wished. Beyond the religious Zionist cultural camp, in which the lost traditional world of East European Jewry remained a hallowed realm, the interest was nil during these years of state building and the "ingathering of the exiles." For the republic of Hebrew letters, which conducted its business in the weekend literary supplements and the cafes of Tel Aviv, Agnon's turn toward Buczacz made little stir.

Yet, when this relation is transposed into the work of fiction, new possibilities are opened up. For here, within the work itself, the implied author can construct the readers with whom he wishes to communicate, because it is he, after all, who has created this world in the first place. In *A City in Its Fullness* the narrator is similarly the creation of the implied author. Yet whereas the narrator belongs to—or is an outgrowth of—the world of Buczacz in its various historical removes, the implied author lives in the present of the writing even if he, too, is a son of Buczacz. The implied readers whom he addresses are his contemporaries, cultured Hebrew readers of the 1950s and 1960s. But rather than being historical persons, who retain the freedom to ignore his work and in fact exercised that right, these are readers who are called into being by the text itself. They are ideal readers both in the sense that they do not exist in reality and that they are the readers the author desires. They are the suitable consumers of his stories because they are open to being persuaded of the importance of the subject and because they possess the literacy necessary to understand them.[18] These readers are the authorial audience.

Yet it is not to these readers whom the garrulous narrator of *A City in Its Fullness* turns when he tells his stories. *His* readers are inscribed with him within a more intimate and pre-modern hermeneutical circle. When he speaks of the shamash's journey into Gehinnom or the piety of R. Gavriel, he does so without embarrassment or apology. These are not primitive or quaint practices that must be domesticated for an enlightened audience because his audience is contemporary in time to his various historical embodiments. As was pointed out in the previous chapter, Agnon made the fundamental decision to have his narrator describe Buczacz in the present tense as if its study houses were full of learners and its marketplace still bustled with buyers and sellers, that is to say, when Buczacz was Buczacz, before the collapse of religious authority, the decimation of the Great War, and the finality of the "Second Destruction." As in the case of the implied author, the narrator's audience comes into being by virtue of being addressed by him. They may be unfamiliar with Buczacz—this is the reason, after all, he undertakes this project of description—but they share his assumptions about the world. They comprise the narratorial audience.[19]

The interplay between the authorial and narratorial audiences in *A City in Its Fullness* is not simple. Most of the time we, who are belated members of the authorial audience, are in the position of eavesdropping on the narrator's discourse with his audience. And there may be times when we shed our modernity and meld into the historical audience who make up the narrator's interlocutors. There are, however, moments of stark differentiation such as when at the end of a story, the narrator states that such-and-such a situation obtained in Buczacz until the vicious and polluted enemy slaughtered and destroyed. Then the veil is torn, and we are left alone with our belatedness. Yet much of the time the interplay is more subtle and canny. A good example is the story "Haḥazzanim" (pp. 70–84, 78–97).[20]

At the center of the story is a woman named Miriam Devorah, who is the daughter of a ḥazzan and the wife of a ḥazzan. She herself is graced with substantial musical endowments; she composes folk melodies that are sung by the womenfolk of Buczacz as they attend to their chores and settings for the prayers of the synagogue service that are sung by her husband, although these, her sacred music, are rejected by the community because they are composed by a woman. All of a sudden Miriam Devorah falls into the throes of melancholia, and although many steps are taken to cure her, she dies of her illness three years later, leaving her husband and six young children. Five diagnoses for the origins of her condition are offered in the story, and they are presented in the following order. First, her father the ḥazzan comes from a neighboring village to amuse her with tricks of his voice; and when that fails, he tells her rudely that she must grow up and stop expecting the world to make her happy. He assumes that her problem is a delay in maturity. The second diagnosis comes from a *ba'al shem*, a wonder worker, who has been summoned to offer healing; he states that she has been set upon by female evils spirits, which are known to be crueler and more unrelenting than male spirits. The third comes from an ascetic kabbalist who, in addition to prescribing a very peculiar kind of therapy, locates the source of her trouble in the evil eye of women who are envious of Miriam Devorah's musical gifts. The fourth comes from Miriam Devorah herself relayed to us by a confidant after her death. At the onset of her illness, she had a dream in which she was wearing a robe and leading the congregation in prayer on Yom Kippur. She was struck with the tragic awareness that she must have been born a man in a previous life and condemned to return as a woman because of some grievous but unknown sin. Finally, the narrator himself informs us that Miriam Devorah was married at such a young age that she resisted living with her husband and ran home as often as she could. It was only after several years that she resigned herself to her domestic role and gave birth to her children in quick succession.

Now, although this is the order in which the five explanations for Miriam Devorah's melancholia are presented in the story, it is not the order of their occurrence within the history of her life.[21] The visits of the holy men (2 and 3) take place at the very end of the three-year period of her illness. The father's visit (1) happens at an indeterminate point in the duration. Miriam Devorah's dream (4) is explicitly defined as being close to the onset of her depression. And the background provided by the narrator about the trauma of being married as a young girl (5) obviously relates to the earliest period of her life in relation to the others. Leaving aside the father's visit that does not carry the same weight as the other episodes, we have a structure in which the earliest are presented last and the latest first.

Why does Agnon have his narrator tell the story in this inverted order? I would argue that this arrangement is an instance in which the differentiation between the narratorial audience and the authorial audience comes into play. The descriptions of the visits from the wonder worker and the kabbalist are presented first, even though they occur last, because they belong to an ancestral world in which bedevilment by demons and the evil eye are credible notions. True, there are satiric elements in both episodes. The obsession R. Mikhl the ba'al shem has with his beard is ridiculed by Miriam Devorah herself; and the mystical speculations of R. Manly the kabbalist lead him to offer a cure centered around a fish fin. Nevertheless, in each case the narrator takes seriously the theological reasoning behind the nostrums of each practitioner. Although they may be located along the margins of his mitnagdic worldview, the discourse that underlies them is very much part of his world. Just in the same way as they assuredly are *not* part of the world of twentieth-century Hebrew readers. For these readers, the authorial audience, the gender confusion and guilt expressed in Miriam Devorah's dream are very much part of the by-now familiar world of modernity. This is true as well for the psychologically oriented explanation offered by the narrator concerning the costs exacted by being married at puberty.

Does the later placement of these two modern, psychological explanations give them priority over the earlier, more traditional explanations? Or are both sets persuasive in their own spheres? I would answer yes and yes. It is only common sense that Agnon, as both the historical author and the implied author, would make his first priority to connect with the readers of his own time, whether real or hypostasized. The unusual quality of *A City in Its Fullness* as a text is the constituting of an audience significantly removed in time from the present of the writing, and the making of it coexistent with contemporary readers. *A City in Its Fullness* thus becomes a work that operates on at least two frequencies; two channels of communications are broadcasted either simultaneously or in tandem. The implicit tensions and convergences between the two create a rich and busy grid of interpretive possibility.

What Does the Narrator Do?

The main job of the narrator, it goes without saying, is to tell the story. There are many stories in *A City in Its Fullness* and a number of different narrative modes in which Agnon activates his narrator, ranging from hagiography and folk tale to realism and satire. By writing a story cycle rather than a novel, Agnon can avail himself of a kind of narrative pluralism. I explore this variety when I discuss individual stories in the body of this study. For now, we continue the focus on characteristics of the narrator that are present—in varying degrees, of course, throughout *A City in Its Fullness*. We've asked what the narrator believes and to whom does he speak, and now we shall ask what, in addition to the telling itself, does he do.

It's helpful to remember that the narrator sees himself not as a modern writer but as a chronicler who is reshaping and conveying received materials. He resembles a major domo busy handling many portfolios. He is busy controlling the release of information to the reader, regulating the pace of the stories, apologizing for missing information and attesting to the truthfulness of what is known, guiding the reader to the correct moral of each story, defending the legitimacy of storytelling as a proper endeavor, hosting guest narrators, and translating the learned discourse of sages into language we can understand. Although not all of these functions are explicitly at play in all of the stories, it is nevertheless possible and useful to put together a general profile of what keeps our narrator so busy.

Not a small portion of the narrator's energies are consumed by the executive management of the narrative. The narrator often infers that he is in possession of an enormous reservoir of stories and information about Buczacz. Even though we may occasionally feel saturated with the lore of this town, the narrator has an endless love for Buczacziana. What does he tell and what does he withhold? Sometimes the impetus is attributed to the readers, as in the story about the origins of the glass sign with the blessing for the new moon etched on it, when he declares, "If you want to hear [the story], I would like to tell it" (p. 229, 185). Sometimes a state of mystery and anticipation is created such that it would be cruel not to tell the story. Regarding a chest that has lain for generations in the passage between the old beit midrash and the new one, the narrator asks, "Who does it belong to? Who placed it there? The matter is worth recounting," (p. 57, 58).

The narrator is not only a high-minded custodian of communal lore but also something of a gossip. In accounting for the behavior of a deviant orphaned teenager named Yekele, he admits that "Because it was long ago, we are not apprised of the reasons that led Yekele to provoke the parnas. On the other hand, we are in a position to relate what we heard from the elders of the city who heard it from their ancestors," (p. 508, 439). The narrator sits on a vast repository of rumor that he tends and dispenses as he sees fit. There are times when he even teases us by bruiting a juicy piece of scandal, but when it comes to revealing the name of the concerned party, he primly states, "Because of the honor of their families I will withhold it" (p. 592, 503).

In a more serious vein, the narrator exercises discretion in esoteric matters. In regard to the spiritual mysteries a holy man disclosed to a rabbi, the narrator remarks circumspectly: "I know only the smallest amount of the awesome secrets the hidden one revealed in his learned discourse. Out of respect for God's mysteries, I keep them hidden in my heart" (p. 225).

The narrator is frequently embroiled in a contest between his natural tendency to be forthcoming and the very constraints he has placed upon himself in order to give coherence to his enterprise. The story "Haḥazzanim," as was mentioned above, concerns the sad fate of the musically gifted Miriam Devorah. After her death, eventually her husband, R. Elya, marries his niece Rivkah Henyah, who turns out to be an excellent mother to his children, but she insists that none of his sons or her sons become professional ḥazzanim, so they will not be beholden to the community. After the narrator embarks upon informing us about the paths in life these boys chose as an alternative to the cantorate, he catches himself and says, "Because my intention has been to tell about the ḥazzanim that served in our city and because they were not ḥazzanim, I put them aside and I concern myself solely with matters relating to ḥazzanim" (p. *84*, 97). The narrator has fashioned a plan that calls for dealing first with the ḥazzanim and then with the gabbaim. He catches himself in the act of following the story whither it leads and reins himself in.

A similar, self-imposed constraint comes into play when the narrator feels himself tempted to stray from the principle of organization he has set down for himself. He feels called upon to offer a justification for including stories about the marketplace—and about affairs bearing on trade in general—because they are ostensibly not germane to the norm of Torah study to which his project is devoted (p. 230). After concluding a brief tale about a mysterious old man and the well in the marketplace, he proceeds to inform us about the fate of huge barrels that were once used by the pious for storing water over Passover because of fears of the well's purity. When that practice ceased, the town elders decided to distribute the barrels around the city and to "repurpose" them for fighting fires. But before they could be filled with water, they were consumed in the great fire that overtook Buczacz. Rather than going ahead with the narrative, the narrator ends the story by explaining, perhaps ironically, "Because a fire is a calamity, I do not dwell on it" (p. *232*, 191). The narrator reaffirms a principle he has enunciated elsewhere: he will tell the story of Buczacz under the sign of its achievements in learning and worship and not under the sign of destruction (*pura'nut*).

These inclusions and exclusions materially affect the pace at which a story is told, and this is an issue much on the mind of the narrator. His stories are not just told but told to an audience, and the narrator expresses recurrent anxiety about whether his detailed expatiations on the customs of Buczacz, a matter of endless and ever-fresh curiosity on his part, will be experienced as alienating longueurs on the part of his readers. The standard to which he holds himself in all of his discursive practices is, unsurprisingly, one of disciplined utility: what is said should only be what needs to be said. As unexceptionable as this principle is, it remains a high road to travel for a chronicler/storyteller who is bursting with information and displays a conspicuous penchant for digression. The whole texture of reading *A City in Its Fullness* is taut with the tension between a self-declared allegiance to concision and an expository practice drawn toward the accumulation of detail and the exploration of ramifying side paths. There is a wonderful moment in the story "In a Single Moment," [pp. *558–88, 455–497*] in which the narrator congratulates himself on his restraint.

> Mikhl Ber took the rabbi's walking stick and put it in the hand of the rabbi. This is the walking stick our Master received from his grandfather R. Jacob of Lissa. I have much to tell about our Master's walking stick. But just in the same way that our Master would not get diverted by matters that did not pertain to halakhah, so I too will not get diverted. (p. *587, 495*)

The master in question is Avraham Teomin (1814–68), the rabbi of Buczacz from 1853 until his death. That there should be many tales to tell about a rabbi's walking stick (*makel*) is not surprising; from the Baal Shemtov onward there was many a tsaddik whose staff was imbued with magical powers. The rabbi of Buczacz, however, was not a ḥasid, and therefore it is something of a tease for the narrator to dangle before us a purported cache of stories about his walking stick and its distinguished lineage. The fact that these stories will be withheld from us, according to the narrator's asseveration, is a sign of his discipline and integrity. But the real connection to the great rabbi turns out not to be his walking stick but the way he studied and taught Jewish law, which brooked no departures from his sacred goal. This analogy, in which the narrator's determination to decline the temptation to digress is modeled on the rabbi's unwavering focus, has the unmistakable effect of ennobling the ethics of storytelling. Yet as any reader of *A City in Its Fullness* knows, this is a high road that is not lacking in its unacknowledged side paths.

Among the narrator's tasks, the greatest gravity attaches to his self-ascribed responsibility to guide the reader to the correct construal of events he has narrated. In this work, there is a profound duality in the narrator's vocation. On the one hand, his task is to tell the story of the city *in its fullness* with an allegiance to the unvarnished truth. On the other, he is impelled to help the reader discern within this plenum of human behaviors the right moral perspective on what has been described. It is our great good fortune as readers that the narrator is much better at the first task than at the second. But *our* good fortune is *his* moral turmoil. We are often spectators to a frantic discomfort at the end of a story as the narrator realizes that unruly lines of thought have been opened up by the disturbing behaviors depicted hitherto. The narrator must then labor with redoubled earnestness and expostulation to prevent the reader from drawing the wrong conclusions. Two examples suggest the workings of this fundamental tension. One is drawn from "The Parable and Its Lesson" and illuminates the urgent desire to bring the reader back from the brink of theological extremity. I take the other from the grotesque satire "Pisces," and it illuminates the mock urgency—and futility—of trying to put the genie back in the bottle once the chaos of human appetites has been released.

The overt theme of "The Parable and Its Lesson" is the encroachment of human grandiosity on divine speech, as embodied in the public reading of the Torah. Scholars, who should know better, often cannot restrain their self-importance and are impelled to whisper their exegetical insights to worshipers seated next to them during the reading of the Torah in the synagogue. What would seem to be a peccadillo is revealed to be a major transgression when, in a daring journey to Gehinnom, a rabbi and his assistant discover that great scholars are suffering hideous tortures for the commission of this very act. The covert theme of the story is the emotional and theological aftermath of the massacres of 1648. Although Buczacz itself was not destroyed, everyone suffered the loss of family, institutional life was decimated, and masses orphaned and left homeless. These losses haunt the community as it simultaneously attempts to rebuild its religious and commercial life and to engage in ceremonious public mourning for the dead. It is in the nature of trauma that it is ungovernable and that its effects cannot be forestalled or foreseen. And this is what differentiates it so starkly from matters of law and value. Whether an individual scholar overcomes his urge to hawk his latest ingenuity and whether a community tolerates or censures this behavior are matters that are susceptible to will and the aspiration toward virtue. But the same cannot be said when a scholar becomes consumed by doubts about God's justice after the massacres and descends into madness and apostasy, as is the case with the rabbi's chief student Aaron, whom he has given in marriage to a girl who is his only surviving relation. (Confirming Aaron's death, to free his widow from being an agunah, is the object of the journey into Gehinnom.) By describing the spiritual vulnerability that followed the massacres—this, after all is the "truth" about Buczacz in those difficult years—the narrator has opened up a passel of theological questions whose troubling implications cannot then easily be reined in. Hence the need for the narrator to mobilize his energies on behalf of a religious goal whose attainment, even if challenging, lies within reach. And indeed, the ending of the story chronicles—quite literally so, by inscribing events in the pinkas, the communal register—the resolve of the good people of Buczacz to uproot any untoward competition with God's word as read aloud in the synagogue. The narrator has worked hard to steer us away from stormy waters toward a moral message that is congruent with the ideal of Buczacz as a holy community.[22]

"Pisces" is as antic and satiric as "The Parable and Its Lesson" is serious and trauma laden. Nevertheless, both stories evince a similar structure in which a pious moral is imposed on ramifying complexities. "Pisces" tells the story of three characters: a wealthy glutton named Fishl Karp, an enormous, regal fish that comes to its end in the waters of the Strypa and is purchased by Fishl Karp, and a penniless orphan named Bezalel Moshe, who draws fish and other creatures to adorn ritual objects but who has never seen a real fish. The end of the story finds both Fishl and the fish dead whereas

Bezalel Moshe's artistic urge has been fulfilled by having drawn a fish from life. Through this satiric fable, which is one of the creative pinnacles of *A City in Its Fullness*, Agnon manages to meditate on such weighty themes as greed and the hunger for absolute power, religion as camouflage for insatiable indulgence, hunger and extremity as the engines of thought and moral speculation, art as the transcendence of misfortune, and reality as a structure of doubles and analogies. And yet, when it comes to distilling the moral of this tale, the narrator has this to tell us:

> What does the story of Fishl Karp teach? That if you are going to pray, do not set your eyes upon meat and fish and other delicacies, but let your path be holy. Lest you say that Fishl is one matter and you are another, know that if you are not avid in the pursuit of meat and fish, you are avid for other things. (p. *631, 559*)[23]

The layered complexity of this moral fable is thus flattened into a few items of practical advice about how to avoid temptation on your way to the synagogue. The narrator's self-confident intervention on the last page of the story is, truth be told, of a piece with his noisy declaration in the story's first paragraph: "I have taken it upon myself to recount things exactly as they happened" (p. *602, 518*). Yet despite the narrator's braggadocio, the need to rein things in remains acutely felt.

Remarkably, there are key moments in *A City in Its Fullness* in which the narrator is willing to let go of the reins of the narrative altogether. There is no disputing the narrator's proprietary relationship to the narrative project as a whole; yet at the same time, his authority is based in part on the fact that he is a chronicler who is continuing the work of the pinkas, and that makes him a custodian of a memory that is collective rather than a possession of one person. It therefore behooves the narrator on occasion to hand his role over to guests whose eye-witness proximity to events yields vividness and authenticity. As disingenuous readers, of course, we know that these guest narrators are created and controlled by the main narrator, who in turn is the product of the implied author, behind whom stands Agnon himself. Yet, in each case, the voice of the guest is so unique and fascinating that all we feel is wonderment, together, perhaps, with a twinge of guilty gratitude for a respite from some of the narrator's anxieties and mannerisms.

There are four major instances of guest narrators in four major stories. The first is the monologue of Gavriel concerning the martyrdom of his grandfather in "The Linen Man." The second is the chronicle offered by R. Avraham Moshe Abush, the rabbi of Zabno, concerning his relations with R. Mordekhai as an explanation for his decision to reject the offer of the rabbinic seat of Buczacz in the story "In Search of a Rabbi." The third is the tale the shamash tells in his defense concerning the journey to Gehinnom in "The Parable and Its Lesson." The fourth is the diary of the Polish noblewoman who imprisons and humiliates Dan, the Jewish conscript from Buczacz, in "Disappeared."

In the case of each of these guest narrators, there are urgent, extraordinary reasons for why the monologue comes into being, confessional and justificatory reasons that make the act of speaking an unprecedented and unrepeatable occasion. And what these narrators have to say to their listeners is totally unexpected. In the case of Gavriel, the notables of Buczacz ask him to accept the office of ḥazzan after having been uplifted by the way he led the High Holiday prayers. He declines the offer but uses the occasion to tell the story of his grandfather, an exemplary prayer leader who refused to accept compensation for his services and who, as the result of a seemingly absurd concatenation of circumstances, was gruesomely martyred. It is only after Gavriel returns to his village and dies—an apparently self-willed consummation—that we realize that his exit from this world was made possible by the unique and one-time chance afforded him to disburden himself of his grandfather's story.

In "In Search of a Rabbi," the lengthy narrative of R. Avraham Moshe is, similarly, an explanation offered to assuage a rejection. R. Avraham Moshe refuses the rabbinate of Buczacz because, unbeknownst to the representatives of the town who have traveled a great distance to make him the offer, there is a sage greater in learning than he named R. Mordekhai who lives and works as a modest tinsmith under their very noses in Buczacz. In telling the story of how he discovered R. Mordekhai and became his study partner, the rabbi of Zabno does much more than make a case for the worthiness of his younger colleague; he also reveals his own limitations and insecurities as well as the depths of his emotional connection to the other scholar. When, in a state of heightened expectation, the Buczacz notables expectantly return home to anoint this unacknowledged genius, they are astonished to discover that R. Mordekhai, now exposed by R. Avraham's confession, has secretly left the town.

The greatest monologist in *A City in Its Fullness* is undoubtedly the shamash in "The Parable and Its Lesson," the tale of the descent into Gehinnom. The story he tells is justificatory in a literal and statutory sense; he is brought up on charges of public humiliation, and his narrative is the defense he offers the court for his actions. Agnon has mastered the conventions of the dramatic monologue in nineteenth-century poetry—one thinks of Browning in "My Last Duchess"—in creating a rich character whose nature is progressively revealed by what he includes, suppresses, and inadvertently mentions in a protracted speech act. The trip to Gehinnom took place fifty-four years earlier, when the shamash was the young assistant to Rabbi Moshe, and the reader is left to imagine the kind of traumas that led him to suppress such extraordinary occurrences for so very long.

The shamash is such a beguiling monologist that the narrator at times seems to regret having handed over the floor to him, and he intervenes to make sure the reader can distinguish between the shamash's words and the discourse of the narrator who is hosting him. The narrator's ambivalence reveals something fundamental about the choices Agnon has made in his Buczacz project. The narrator he has constructed, so we have seen, cannot be a person, despite his tics and propensity for speaking in the first person. He cannot exist as a historical embodiment because he must be "on duty" over a period of more than two centuries. This is a renunciation *not* imposed upon the shamash, who, like the narrator, is a master storyteller and with whom he shares a similar religious outlook. Is it any wonder then that the narrator should not be entirely successful in disguising his jealousy for the prerogatives of embodiment given to his guest and denied him?

If the shamash is too close for comfort, it is impossible to imagine a figure more distant from the narrator than the Polish noblewoman whose diary is appended to the story "Disappeared." Not only is she formally the "other" in her nationality, her religion, and her class, not to mention the Polish language in which she writes, but she perpetrates an act of victimization that transcends all of those categories, or embodies them, depending on your point of view. Her diary, which "happened to find its way" into the possession of the narrator, is appended to the story rather than incorporated within it, as if to say that the direct speech of its mistress is a growth that could not be tolerated within the tissue of Jewish narrative. Whenever a writer of fiction gives us the speech of a character, he is engaging in an act of ventriloquism. In putting on the mask of a depraved and predatory Polish noblewoman and speaking in her voice, Agnon reaches the outer limits of the imaginative world of *A City in Its Fullness*.

Finally, there is one important aspect in which the narrator seeks to do nothing less than convert his listeners. He wants to make them into erstwhile Buczaczers. Consider the following passage from the story "In a Single Moment." A father is walking with his fifteen-year-old son on the return trip into the center of the town from a visit to a Ruthenian farmstead and telling stories about Buczacz. Although these are tales that Avraham David has told his son many times, neither the teller nor the listener seems to tire of them. But the repeating and recycling of stories causes the narrator some embarrassment in the presence of his readers, who are not natives of his town, and he feels called upon to defend the practice. In so doing, he presents an apologia that could serve for the entire project of *A City in Its Fullness*.

> The Buczaczers love nothing more than talking about Buczacz, and the essence of the town is its distinguished scholars, those who made Buczacz what it was, who made it world-famous, to the point where Buczacz even began to recognize its own worth. Consequently, do not be surprised if, when a Buczaczer mentions one of the town's great scholars, he goes on and on, saying things that everyone knows and yet is astonished to hear again. That is what makes us love beautiful things: they have a perennial appeal, and hearing about them a second and third time can be even better than the first. The first time you hear it but not all of it. When you hear it again you savor every detail. Thus, when Avraham David spoke about our Master, the distinguished Av Beit Din, he would go on and on about things we already knew, but both

the speaker and the listener felt as if they were only now hearing the real gist of it for the first time. (p. 565, 472)

Implied in this passage are two analogies, one local and one universal. Just a few pages earlier in the story, Avraham David had cited his father's achievement of completing many times over the study of the Talmud—and specifically its first tractate Berakhot—along with his claim that true comprehension comes only with repetition. This parallel has the effect of raising the activity of re-elaborating of tales about the great masters of Buczacz to a level of high canonicity. What is true within this parochial radius is true as well in a broader cultural sphere. The narrator mounts the argument that the Buczacz stories belong to the category of beautiful things whose attractiveness increases with each repeated exposure; so rich are they in detail that new aspects are revealed—and savored—with each retelling. This is the same language concerning the surplus of meaning that is used in the discourse of European culture to describe classic works of art. Although these analogies remain implicit, they serve to elevate to an exalted status artifacts that are homely and neither classic nor canonical. Yet it is impossible not to hear a plaintive tone in his argument. The opening of the passage already confesses to a radical limitation. The delight and pleasure in the recycling of these stories works its effect principally if not exclusively on *other* Buczaczers, for whom the fascination of the subject is taken for granted. But we are not they, and our position outside this intimate circuit means that Agnon, through his narrator, is constantly faced with the challenge of engaging us and, through the repeated and mounting delights of *A City in Its Fullness*, turning *us* into erstwhile Buczaczers.

Speaking through the voices of others is not so much a distinct activity for the narrator as simply a heightened expression of the nature of the job. His task is to bring others to life and to animate them with words that seem characteristically their own but are really of his own conveyance. It is both a great renunciation and a great achievement. It was important to Agnon to create a coherent story cycle rather than an assemblage of stories that had been gathered together. Had he lived longer he would have undoubtedly spun even more subtle filaments of connection among the stories. The thematic unity furnished by making Buczacz the center was a great stroke, but it could go only so far. Agnon sought to bring to his project something of the epistemological stability the classic novel inherited from its origins in the epic. Yet at the same time he wanted to preserve something of the irrepressible "I" that had been the spring of his earlier creativity. By inventing his non-personal but garrulous narrator, a figure whose voice and degree of intervention could be varied flexibly, Agnon succeeded in coming up with a way to handle the great and exigent storytelling challenge he took up at the end of his life.

3

Worship and Danger

A Cantorial Triptych

Together with Torah learning, public worship is the great norm upon which Agnon establishes his reimagining of Buczacz. There was no religious observance more pervasively and consistently practiced by males than daily communal prayer. The adult males who lived in town almost universally attended prayer services early in the morning and then again in the early evening. Village Jews and rural tavern operators who had no access to a prayer quorum of ten men accounted this a regrettable disability. The very founding of Buczacz is presented as being born of a heartfelt longing for communal prayer. Yet the pervasiveness of this practice—its very normativity—is not the same as its spiritual success or failure. On Sabbaths and holidays when the liturgy and its melodic signatures were more elaborate, sacred poems of great linguistic difficulty required proper recitation, and spiritual uplift was generally expected, the congregation relied upon the expertise of especially adept lay prayer leaders (*ba'alei tefilah*) or professional cantors (ḥazzanim). But the experience of the worshipers and the experience of the emissaries who represent them before God are not identical. At the same time as the hearts of the faithful may be uplifted, the individuals charged with leading them expose themselves to the dangers of trafficking in the holy.

This is the duality of worship in Agnon's reimagining of Buczacz: the routine of long-sanctioned communal practice alongside the radical instability of individual fates. Much of book 1 of *A City in Its Fullness*—as was surveyed in the reconstructed guided tour of chapter 2—is devoted to introducing the reader to the houses of worship of Buczacz and delineating the liturgical customs of the community. The narrator-guide places special emphasis on the real or imagined continuity in liturgical texts and practices between the ancient communities of the Rhineland Valley and his native town in Galicia. The detailed section on the particular order of the prayers in the Friday evening service ("Seder Kabbalat Shabbat," *40–42*) demonstrates how the liturgical innovations initiated by the kabbalistic revolution in sixteenth-century Safed were seamlessly integrated into the practice of Polish Jewry.

Pains are taken to present the appurtenances of the synagogue that were special to Buczacz, such as the Italian chandelier and the etched glass panel for the recitation of the blessing for the New Moon, as well as to tell us unique and astonishing stories attached to the origins of those objects (the menorah, Elijah's seat) that would have typically been found in other towns like Buczacz. In Agnon's reconstruction of Buczacz, it is the synagogue that stands for the town as a whole. It is little wonder that the narrator of the story "The Sign," having just heard about the final liquidation of the Jews of Buczacz, conjures up his native town in his mind's eye by placing each male head of family, together with his sons and sons-in-law, not at home but in his hereditary seat in the synagogue.[1] And it is in the synagogue that received and sanctioned practices, minhagim, hold sway, enforced by the careful eyes of the shamash and the gabbai and their successors throughout the generations.[2]

Yet for the ḥazzanim, the professional cantors employed by the community to lead the service on the holiest occasions, the synagogue was not always an unchanging realm. At these moments of heightened religious consequence, a ḥazzan functioned as a *sheliaḥ tsibbur*, a representative or emissary of the congregation before God, and the metaphor of an emissary sent on a high errand does not miss the mark. For the successful fulfillment of the mission in question, nothing less than the acceptance of the prayers of Israel before God is at stake, and the outcome is by no means taken for granted. That acceptance presupposes, of course, the sincerity and purity of heart of the worshipers that the ḥazzan is representing, but it also depends upon his own ability to acquit himself of a complex and fraught set of challenges. Although the Hebrew text of the ancient statutory liturgy was well known, the baroque sublimities of the ancient piyyutim, the sacred poems that formed a proud part of the rite in Galician communities, demanded enormous expertise to be articulated correctly.

A ḥazzan's musicianship came into play on several levels. Although the power, range, and beauty of his voice were endowments beyond his control, by training he could acquire mastery of *nusaḥ*, the corpus of traditional melodies used to perform the texts of the service, and, working within the tradition, he could even introduce original musical settings of his own. Success in creating a fulfilling experience for the ḥazzan's congregants also depended on their confidence in the quality of his piety in everyday life and on the performance of that piety as religious fervor when he represents them in the sacred service. He faced the daunting challenge of, at one and the same time, deploying the full resources of his virtuosity and remaining sufficiently invisible so that his own personality would not interfere with the responsibility to serve as a representative of the interests of others.

Now all this creates a high bar of professional accomplishment, but can it truly be said to be dangerous? The source of danger comes not from the demands and expectations of the congregation, positioned physically, behind the ḥazzan as he stands facing the Holy Ark, so much as from the numinous authority that emanates from the ark itself. This requires a brief excursus about the terminology connected to the synagogue service. In Talmudic literature, the container housing the Torah scrolls is called the *teivah*. The wall facing Jerusalem in ancient synagogues contained a niche in which the teivah was placed during the service after being carried in from an adjoining room. Over time, the teivah became a fixed installation within the main hall of the synagogue.

When an elder was asked to lead prayers, he was asked *likrav el hateivah*, to approach the teivah. The act of accepting that commission, stepping forward and taking up a position as the ba'al tefilah, the prayer leader—and later ḥazzan—is called one of two terms: la'avor lifnei hateivah (to pass before the teivah) or leired lifnei hateivah (to descend before the teivah). The distinction is not material and may have reflected differences in the construction of synagogues in Babylonia and Palestine in Late Antiquity.[3] What is key is the term teivah itself. In the ancient Jerusalem Temple, the ark containing the Tablets of the Law, on which were written the Ten Commandments, was called the aron haberit (Ark of the Covenant), and it was located in the Holy of Holies. After the Destruction in 70 C.E., synagogues and verbal prayer that took place within them, which had long existed parallel to the Jerusalem Temple, were recognized as authorized replacements for the Temple and the system of sacrificial offerings.

In this system of substitutions, the teivah took on the symbolic weight of the aron haberit; although it contained the words of the Torah written by human hand on parchment rather than the original tablets with their divine inscriptions, the teivah carried over some of the numinous potency of the object it replaced. Later on, in Ashkenazic synagogues the teivah was called the aron kodesh (the Holy Ark), and in Sephardic synagogues the heikhal (chamber).

Less clear are the origins of the office of the ḥazzan, of the one who descends or passes before the teivah. During the period of the Talmud, the duties of the ḥazzan seem to be closer to those of the shamash, the synagogue sexton or beadle, which are familiar to us from a later period. The ḥazzan is in charge of moving the teivah into position for public worship and supervising the care and placement of the Torah scrolls. The chanting of the liturgy on special Sabbaths and holidays was often handled by the payytan, the composer of sacred poems, texts of great complexity and erudition, which were integrated into the synagogue service.[4] It is not until the Middle Ages in Ashkenaz that we encounter the ḥazzan in a role more familiar to us as a singer employed by the community to lead public worship on important occasions. This professionalization of the role was likely necessitated by the consolidation in the Ashkenazic rite of both the canonical piyyutim and the melodies associated with them and with specific statutory prayers.

In Galicia of the period Agnon is writing about in *A City in Its Fullness*, the contracted responsibilities of the ḥazzan would have been generally codified. In the case of R. Yitshak Wernick, who was the ḥazzan of Buczacz in the years after the 1648 massacres—as his grandfather of the same name had been before those events—those duties are specified as follows: "R. Yitshak delighted the hearts of his brethren with his pleasant voice on the eves of Sabbaths when the new moon is blessed, Sabbaths on which *yotserot* are recited, the eves of holidays and during the holiday itself, the eve of Rosh Hashanah and on Rosh Hashanah itself, the eve of Yom Kippur, *musaf* and *ne'ilah*, and on the days on which *seliḥot* are recited" (p. *70, 78*). The ḥazzan also performed at weddings and "brought delight to the bridegroom and bride under the *ḥuppah*."

Alongside this professionalization and routinization, there remained the potent residue of the connection between the ḥazzan and the priests in the Jerusalem Temple. When sacrificial offerings were the main channel of divine worship, careful attention to prescribed protocols was a matter not just of proper procedure but of the life-and-death consequences of mishandling the holy materials. The instant death meted out to Aaron's sons Nadav and Abihu in Leviticus 10 for the "alien fire" brought on the altar is the foundational monitory tale of priestly recklessness. After the Destruction, the sacrificial cult had been abrogated and the priesthood effectively abolished and disbanded; nevertheless, the peril and uncertainty involved in representing the community of Israel before God did not wholly dissipate. The Rabbis worked vigorously to persuade the people that the "service of the heart," the oral recitation of a written liturgy, was every bit as acceptable to God as the smell of burnt animals sincerely offered.

The replacement of the one Temple by many synagogues was therefore not merely symbolic; holiness resides where it is allowed to be vested. The kehilah kedoshah, the holy community of Buczacz—or any other pious congregation in the diaspora—in the finest moments of its worship aspired to compel God's presence to dwell within it. It was now the ḥazzan—having inherited the priest's mantel—who was exposed most frontally to the holy as he represented the faithful.

The fusion of these two roles is most keenly experienced during the Avodah service on Yom Kippur, which describes the solemn preparations of the *kohen gadol*, the high priest, for entering the Holy of Holies and uttering the secret name of God. The liturgy for the service is taken from the text of one of several medieval piyyutim—the differences are according to rite and region—which are in turn based on Leviticus 16 and Mishnah Tractate *Yoma*. The Avodah stands apart from the rest of the liturgy on Yom Kippur or any other occasion. The prayers of the siddur are almost always cast as the worshiper's direct address to God that is transpiring in the present moment as it is being uttered.

The Avodah, however, is a historical reenactment of the divine service that took place in the Temple on Yom Kippur before it was destroyed. It is a kind of oratorio that tells the story of the high priest in which both the ḥazzan and the congregation play roles. The ḥazzan plays the role of the high priest and the congregants play the role of the Israelites who thronged the courtyard outside the Holy of Holies awaiting the priest's emergence after his ordeal. His safe emergence from the Holy of Holies was not a foregone conclusion. Pronouncing the four-letter name of God at the exact point on earth in which divine holiness was most powerfully concentrated exposed the high priest to great danger, and any flaws in his worthiness could result in disaster for his person and for the nation. This is the contingency that is discussed by community notables who gather in the home of the gabbai after the fast in the second of the stories about ḥazzanim. Referring to the text of the Avodah service, one of the guests makes a learned point:

> [The high priest] would make a holiday for his friends after emerging safely from the Holy. Because it states "when he emerged safely from the Holy," we learn that it was not every year that he emerged safely from the Holy. Either the soul of the high priest expired or the soul of the people. (p. *87*, 102)

The context of the discussion is an appreciation of the powerful performance of the Avodah turned in that day by R. Gavriel, a visitor who had come to Buczacz to do business and visit his grandfather's grave and had been prevailed upon to serve as prayer leader because of his beautiful and fervent voice. The point of the observation is that, despite the fact that the Avodah is merely a narrative of what took place long ago when the Temple still existed, its numinous power, and the threat it contains, are still felt today when the prayer leader hits the right spiritual pitch. In musing on the profound experience of the Avodah service that day, the same speaker of the passage above goes on to aver that "there are some narratives [*sippurei devarim*] that bring the listener to such powerful longings that the soul expires" (p. *87*, 102).[5]

It is this continuity of danger that Agnon's stories about ḥazzanim seek to convey. Something of the risks the priests exposed themselves to in handling the "fissionable" materials of the Sanctuary so very long ago was carried over into the lives of the ḥazzanim. Agnon's strategy for underscoring the connection is to make the teivah into a quasi-animate object, a portentous source of authority, which suffers the proximity of some prayer leaders and repels that of others, to their peril. The opening sentence of the second of the stories about ḥazzanim, "The Man Dressed in Linen" ["Ha'ish levush habadim"] tells us that after the death of the long-lived R. Elya, "the teivah stood with no permanent ḥazzan" (p. *84*, 98), and we assume as a matter of course that the phrase "the teivah stood" (*'amdah hateivah*) is simply a figure of speech. But a few sentence later, we are told: "Because passing before the teivah was permitted to anyone, people *whom the teivah would not countenance (sh'ein hateivah kolatetam)* began to storm the teivah, this one on the strength of his having a yahrzeit and that one because he believes that his voice is as pleasant to others as it is to himself" (my emphasis).

Another example comes from the third story in the triptych, which concerns a ḥazzan also named R. Gavriel who has withdrawn from serving as a ḥazzan in Buczacz but still enforces high standards when it comes to public worship. "So long as R. Gavriel was alive, even though he did not pass before the teivah, the *teivah did not complain (hateivah lo kavlah)* about the prayer leaders because no one without a voice dared approach the teivah" (p. *120*, 149; my emphasis). Endowing the teivah with agency and judgment is, so far as I can tell, Agnon's imaginative invention.[6] To be sure, the animation of the teivah does not bring it to the point of becoming a cartoon figure or pushing it over into the realm of the fantastic. But it is just enough to register the serious risks involved in drawing close to the teivah. These stories concern ḥazzanim who do just that.

As presented by Agnon, the vocation of ḥazzan exists at the intersection of three important traditions, and that lineage raises it above the other synagogue-related occupations and offices, such the shamash and the gabbai, with which it is grouped in *A City in Its Fullness*. The first tradition, as we saw above, derives from the connection to the service in the ancient Jerusalem Temple. If on Yom Kippur the ḥazzan reenacts the role of the high priest, for the great part of the liturgical year his role is closer to that of the Levites, who performed the Psalms in musical settings as well as tending to the holy objects. The Levites lost their role when the Temple was destroyed, and the function of beautifying the service, which was now an oral liturgy practiced in synagogues, fell to the payyetanim.[7] Their prodigious creativity in Late Antiquity and in the Middle Ages created a large corpus of sacred poems that circulated among many communities and, especially because of the printing press, became standardized according to region by the time Agnon takes up his chronicle of Buczacz in the seventeenth century. The ḥazzanim inherited the mantle of the payyetanim; but their focus was not on the creation of new texts but on musical settings for piyyutim that had already become part of the canon.

The romantic artist was the second tradition, a tradition, of course, of much more recent provenance, which was retrojected onto the figure of the ḥazzan of earlier times. A product of nineteenth-century European culture, this conception presents the artist as an individual endowed with a sensitive soul that resonates in tune with the anima mundi, the soul of the universe. In the creative process, the artist converts feeling into signs—images, sounds, or words—and creates an art object that participates in eternity. His achievement often comes at the expense of his own wellbeing because he has poured into the art object that which is most vital in his being; creation thus becomes a kind of self-annihilation, a sacrifice rendered on the altar of art. This is a notion that was intrinsic to Agnon's work from its very beginnings. His first major published story "Agunot" featured the figure of Ben Uri, a religious artist who invests so much of his soul in the Holy Ark that he is fashioning that he is eventually cast aside "like a violin whose strings have broken." Agnon sees a set of affinities between the romantic artist and the ḥazzan. Both are *kelei kodesh*, "holy vessels," a term that describes both the objects in the ancient temple and the persons responsible for handling them. Both have special access to the transcendent and take as their calling the effort to convey that transcendence to others. And because of that proximity both are at risk of being consumed.[8]

The third tradition is martyrology. The ḥazzan, like the artist, sacrifices himself on behalf of his congregants by drawing too close to the holy. His self-sacrifice has a special resonance within a religious culture that models itself, and not just in its enthusiasm for piyyutim, on the piety of medieval Ashkenaz. When at the end of the eleventh century the Jews of Worms, Speyer, and Mainz martyred themselves and their family members rather than be converted or killed by the Crusaders, they viewed themselves not as being victimized but as being given an opportunity for spiritual distinction. Because of the sincerity of their piety they were given the chance to reenact in their own bodies the sacrificial worship of God that had been in abeyance for a thousand years. (This pertains especially to the second story in the triptych.) The iconographic shaping of these extraordinary deeds in the chronicles and piyyutim of the following generation created a delicately balanced paradox. The gentiles who visited these persecutions upon the Jews could be vehemently excoriated while at the same time the acts of self-sacrifice undertaken in response to them could be extolled as *yisurin shel ahavah*, suffering bestowed by God upon those He loves. The martyrological background is the key to the gruesome consummation described in "The Man Dressed in Linen," and it gives a larger resonance to all the narratives about ḥazzanim.

The genealogy of the ḥazzan, moreover, was far from foreign to Agnon's conception of his own vocation. He seems to have been of two minds on the subject. On the one hand, the narrator of *A City in Its Fullness* confesses that he is not musical and lacks a memory for melodies. In one of those occasional moments in which he exposes his own childhood connection to Buczacz, a moment that takes place in the final sentences of the third story in the triptych, the narrator describes how the last ḥazzan of the town, who was a denizen of the beit midrash at the time the narrator spent his adolescence there, set some of his juvenile poems to music. "But because I am not expert in melody and I do not play, they [the musical settings] did not remain in my mouth, and the poems and their melodies were lost" (p. *122*, *97*).[9] The same incapacity to remember a melody afflicted the narrator at the conclusion of "The Sign." Solomon Ibn Gabirol has miraculously appeared and composed a poem to memorialize the destroyed Buczacz, yet, so overcome by the experience, the narrator cannot remember it, and he has to be consoled by the fact that "the poem sings itself in the heavens above, among the poems of the holy poets, the beloved of God."[10] Apart from his own lack of musical endowment, the narrator exudes a chronic skepticism as to whether, except in rare instances, ḥazzanim can free their selves from a grandiosity that detracts from the divine service rather than enhances it.

Yet when it comes to those rare ḥazzanim who transcend these limitations, Agnon sees intimations of true religious art. Agnon's family was descended from the tribe of Levi, whose members served as psalm singers in Temple, and it is this lineage that allows him, or at least his narrative persona in the story "A Sense of Smell," to insert himself into a genealogy that begins in the ancient Temple, passes through the library of rabbinic learning, and ends in his vocation as a writer of stories. (The passage is quoted in the Introduction in the section called "The Consecration Story." Although ḥazzanim do not appear in this genealogy, they play a key role in a complementary genealogy laid out in "The Sign." For the Agnon-like first-person narrator of that story, one of the foundational moments of childhood was discovering the stirring poems of Ibn Gabirol, first as a text in the prayer book given to him by his father, and then as sung in the synagogue by the old ḥazzan, and then again in the big prayer book in his grandfather's house.

The fantastic manifestation of Ibn Gabirol to the narrator as an adult during the nighttime Shavuot vigil is a confirmation of an essential affinity of vocation between the great payyetanim and the artistic work of the narrator. Although the figure of the old ḥazzan of Buczacz cannot attain to the supernal attainments of Ibn Gabirol, his role in actualizing these sacred poems through performance is a crucial, penultimate link in this chain.

The last link is the Agnon figure himself. He is the proxy for their tears (*hareini kaparat dim'atam*), and the one who, in story rather than in song, carries the mantel of their sacred vocation. In short, although he is no aficionado of cantorial singing, Agnon has written himself into the story of sacred song and thereby lifted the figure of the ḥazzan, in exceptional instances, to the level of religious artist.

The Voice of a Woman

> The first of the ḥazzanim who served in the Great Synagogue after it was erected was R. Yitsḥak Shats. He was a fourth-generation descendent of R. Yitsḥak Wernick who, eighty years before 1648, served as a loyal representative of his congregants in their prayers; he delighted brides and grooms underneath their canopies with his pleasant voice. (p. *70, 78*)[11]

The opening paragraph of "Haḥazzanim," the first story in the cantorial triptych, presents continuity and steadfastness as the qualities that undergird the office of ḥazzan. Rather than being an instance of nepotism or hegemony, the fact that the office has been in the hands of one family for so many generations guarantees that the minhag of the community, the sacred protocols of its worship, have been securely protected during the vicissitudes of historical change. Even the duplication and confusion of names is reassuring. Yitsḥak Shats is really Yitsḥak Wernick, *shats* simply being a contraction of the name of his office, sheliaḥ tsibbur, the emissary of the congregation before God. The fact that the great-grandson bears the name of the great-grandfather underscores the kind of continuity desired in the realm of the sacred service.

The brief sketch of the life of R. Yitsḥak Wernick (the great-grandson) presented at the opening of the story is absolutely essential to establishing the norm that almost immediately is violated. He is the paragon of a ḥazzan. He led the congregation in prayer on all the important Sabbaths and holidays according to the rites they had received from their forebears; he even composed an original melody for the memorial prayer recited on the 20th of Sivan.[12] He made a special contribution to the community's happiness by devoting himself to celebrating weddings and marking the presence of the groom and the bride with special melodies. On those special occasions he displayed his expertise in the complicated etiquette of distributing honors to relatives as part of the Torah reading. In the twenty-two years between the consecration of the Great Synagogue and his death, he was not absent from the synagogue even for a single day. This included when the students from the monastery school gathered to riot. When others told him that it was his own merit that had saved him from death, he protested and said "It was the teivah, which recognizing that all my days there has been no ulterior motive in my prayer, hid me from the eyes of the scoundrels" (p. 70, 79). He was succeeded by his eldest son R. Yekutiel, who honored the ancient musical traditions that had been practiced by his forefathers, who had received them "from the exiles of Ashkenaz upon whose piety Buczacz had been founded. R. Yekutiel made no alterations whatever in those melodies and made up no new ones of his own."

Yet just when the negotiation of a generational transition seems assured, everything begins to break down. After three years, the anointed successor R. Yekutiel loses his voice as a punishment for preening before gentile nobles who came to the synagogue to hear him sing. His youngest brother R. Elya takes over his post, but this R. Elya's wife Miriam Devorah, who is the most talented musician of them all, dies of depression, despite the efforts of the healers of the day. When R. Elya eventually makes a successful remarriage, his new wife vehemently insists that his sons never become professional ḥazzanim. And so the Wernick line of ḥazzanim, with so many generations of service to its credit, comes to an end.

But it is precisely from the termination of the line that the story is born. "Haḥazzanim," the first of the stories, is preoccupied with the tragic story of the brilliantly creative Miriam Devorah, whose death from mental anguish brings about the collapse of the Wernick cantorial dynasty. This is not a preoccupation that is telegraphed at the beginning of the story when the narrator lays out the exemplary life of R. Yitsḥak Wernick. In his guise as chronicler and master of the pinkas, the narrator embarks by informing us about synagogue-related occupations and offices and chooses to begin with the ḥazzanim. R. Yitsḥak is the fourth generation of his family to occupy that office, and the narrator is poised to continue with a narrative of succession when his project encounters unexpected obstacles and founders on rocks of anomaly and deviation.

Instead of registering shock and moving the story in a different direction, the narrator delves ever more deeply into the "deviant" instance of a pious woman who dies because her voice is suppressed. He is willing to follow the outcomes wherever they lead, which is far afield from his declared task. He pursues this line until he brings himself up short and declares in the last line of the story, disingenuously or not, that enough is enough: "Because my sole intention is to describe the ḥazzanim that served in our city, and these [the sons of Miriam Devorah] did not become ḥazzanim, I am taking my leave of all of them and returning to deal only with the affairs of ḥazzanim" (p. *84*, 96–97).

The narrator's willingness, even desire, to interrupt the narrative of succession and turn toward the anomalous instance enacts a moment that is not only crucial for the story at hand but paradigmatic for the entire enterprise of *A City in Its Fullness*. The narrator aspires to render a normative account of Buczacz and then quickly yields to the deviant and anomalous. Does this shift represent a commitment to truth-telling on the chronicler's part that compels him, despite his intended program, to follow the story wherever it leads? Or does it represent the narrator's unspoken intuition that when it comes to the telling of stories, the normative path is ultimately too constricting and unsatisfying? Both are true, I would argue, but the second is truer. Agnon sets up his narrator as a chronicler who is both a believer and an honest broker when it comes to acknowledging deviations from the norm.

Yet as an author, who is a modernist and an ironist, Agnon understands, profoundly, that the possibility of story arises *only* from the deviation of the norm and that it is stories that he wants—and has only ever wanted—to tell. *A City in Its Fullness* is constituted by an armature of chronicle to which stories are attached. The moment of turning from the normative to the deviant is the quintessential narrative act that is repeated endlessly in this work. Thus at the end of "Haḥazzanim" when the narrator expresses annoyance with himself for having wandered from his avowed focus, this is not necessarily disingenuous on his part. But the author who sets him up in this role knows full well that the events surrounding the life and death of Miriam Devorah are the real story.[13]

There can be few stories more affecting than that of Miriam Devorah, and it is little wonder that her fate, mentioned as a footnote to her husband's career, balloons in importance and takes over the story. She herself is the daughter of a ḥazzan and the sole survivor of siblings who died in childhood. She is preternaturally gifted in ways that wholly exceed the achievements of any ḥazzan mentioned in these stories. She inherited her father's voice, which is described as a bewitchingly flexible instrument that imitates the sounds of the changing seasons. But a good voice is where the accomplishments of most ḥazzanim begin and end. Her genius lies also in composition. "She composed new melodies for prayers and piyyutim and especially for a *kerovah* for Parashat Haḥodesh" (p. *71, 80*). A kerovah is an extremely complex genre of piyyut that versifies the Amidah on special occasions; composing musical settings for it is an ambitious undertaking.

She also writes words and music for use outside the synagogue service. She composes poems, which she puts to music, on the subject of the persecutions of 1648, and she composes songs to entertain children. In both cases, the narrator discloses a personal and intimate connection to these compositions. When he was a boy in the beit midrash reading a chronicle of those persecutions, an old man who identified himself as the grandson of Miriam Devorah sang one of those songs for him.[14] As for the children's songs, the narrator takes the unusual step of reproducing the full text of one of them, in both Yiddish and Hebrew, prefaced by the statement: "It seems to me that I am transmitting them according to their language" (p.*72, 81*). That these songs should be circulating so many generations later such that the narrator can quote one accurately by heart is extraordinary evidence of their staying power.

Quoting her song in full is also a measure of compensation the narrator supplies for the signal rejection Miriam Devorah has suffered. Her synagogue compositions were rebuffed in the sacred arena for which they were intended. The reason is laconically given by the narrator without comment: "Her melodies were not accepted in synagogues because it was said that the voice of a woman was recognizable in them" (p. *71*, *81*). "The voice of a woman" is the halakhic prohibition of *kol 'ishah*, which, for reasons of modesty, forbids a male to listen to a woman singing who is not a close relation.[15] But the prohibition manifestly does not apply here; Miriam Devorah's melodies are not sung by her but by male voices, presumably her husband's among other ḥazzanim. The male community of Buczacz has banned her melodies because of the taint of femininity or female origins that are presumably discoverable in the music itself. It is therefore with implicit sympathy—and perhaps with a mischievous smile—that the narrator informs us in the next sentence that these same sacred compositions achieved currency in a different venue: "However, when women were sitting together over their work, whether plucking feathers, sewing, knitting, or crocheting, they would sweeten their chores with her melodies." The circle of women at work provides a nice counterpoint to the male preserve of the synagogue, and there is some poetic justice in seeing these sacred songs being domesticated even as the domestic chores are being sanctified.

In the fashion of artists who die young, Miriam Devorah claims our attention for the manner in which her life came to an end. After giving birth to six children and composing much music, all this while still in her twenties, Miriam Devorah begins to suffer melancholia and dies three years later.[16] Clarifying and determining the etiology of her illness becomes the preoccupation of the narrator, who seems intent on belatedly supplying to this unfortunate young woman the attention she was denied during her lifetime.

The narrator adduces two approaches to the problem that involve traditional healers and two that provide psychological explanations, with considerably more attention and space given to the first group than to the second. This bifurcation can be illuminated in part by recourse to the notion of the two different audiences presented in Chapter 2. The ministrations of the healers make sense to the narratorial audience that is contemporary to the events described, whereas the psychological explanations make sense to the authorial audience contemporary to the time in which Agnon is writing the stories.

This notion helps us to understand the narrator's inner duality, but it does not shed much light on the question of the disposition of the narrative materials, namely, why one side is given so much more space than the other. Let us first meet these two healers and then try to answer this question.

The account of the first of these, R. Mikhl, is so replete with detail and incident that it nearly constitutes a story within a story. R. Mikhl is a *baʿal shem*, a spiritual healer who employs the names of God and the writing of amulets to counteract the work of demons. (The time of the story is the period shortly before the rise of modern Hasidism, whose founder, Israel Baal Shem Tov, belongs to this generic class of religious charismatics.) It was entirely natural as a first course of action for Miriam Devorah's father to summon a baʿal shem to deal with a disorder of the soul. Yet despite the gravity of the situation, the figure who presents himself ready to serve is utterly and totally ridiculous. He materializes from behind clouds of smoke that billow from the pipe he smokes, and he hushes the relatives of the patient when they try to describe her symptoms claiming that he is already in possession of all that needs to be known. It is precisely this arrogant claim to omniscience that provokes Miriam Devorah into taunting him rather than submitting to his authority. "You think you know the fate of every living creature," she says to his face, "but you do not even know what is in store for your beard!" (p. *74, 83*).

R. Mikhl's beard turns out to be a story unto itself. It is his pride and joy, the narrator tells us as he proceeds to put us in the know. The beard is legend, literally, for it is a butt of satire for the wags of the day. It is as broad as it is long with each strand perfectly straight and distinct. He achieves this effect through a technique of his own devising. Every Friday afternoon after he returns from the bath house he fills a receptacle with liquor and bathes his beard in it, partakes in a glass of brandy, and takes a nap. During one such ritual at a point in time soon after his unsuccessful visit to Miriam Devorah, his rest is disturbed by the depredations of bed bugs, and when he goes after them with a candle, his liquor-saturated beard is accidentally ignited and burnt up.[17] He accounts his humiliation to Miriam Devorah's curse, whereas she, having been told of his accusation, reasonably fires back that it is not she but the brandy he consumed that bears the blame.

Yet despite this buffo comedy, which contrasts so sharply in tone with Miriam Devorah's deteriorating mental condition, the narrator relates with utter gravity to the diagnosis R. Mikhl delivers. Adopting the high moral ground, R. Mikhl renounces taking revenge on her because the demons (*sheidin veruḥin*) have already done so. In undertaking to unpack this cryptic statement, the narrator once again shows himself to be a man of his time, if that time is an early modern age, in which mental illness is still understood in terms of possession of the soul by external hostile forces. There are both male and female demons, explains the narrator in a learned exposition, and the most incurable cases occur when female demons attach themselves to women. "It is in the nature of a man to pursue a woman," the narrator avers, "and it is not in the nature of a woman to pursue a man" (p. 76, 86). Having somehow transgressed these boundaries, Miriam Devorah has laid herself open to the fatal relentlessness of female possession.

R. Menele, the second healer, is ostensibly the opposite of the buffoon-ish ba'al shem. He is an ascetic kabbalist who has chosen to live among poor workingmen on the other side of the River Strypa. This is a community of outliers living beyond the sphere of the official prayer and study houses of the community. Although the real distance between this quarter and Buczacz proper is insignificant, it is a distance that is not easy for R. Elya, the ḥazzan of the main community, and his cantorial father-in-law to cross, and they do so only at the shrewish insistence of Miriam Devorah's mother Puah, who taunts them: "Is it the Sambatyon River that separates them? It's only the Strypa!" (p. 77, 87).

The narrator provides a detailed account of R. Menele's daily routine, which involves early-morning immersions in the river and the recitation of psalms and lengthy meditations (kavanot) even before morning prayers. He makes his living as a scribe, but he sells very little because each set of tefillin he writes requires the performance of extensive spiritual exercises, and he is willing to sell them only to the rare customer who meets a high bar of religious sincerity; moreover, he prefers not to detract from the livelihood of the city's other scribes, who are not as accustomed as he to a life of poverty and renunciation. In his role as a healer, R. Menele composes amulets for

people, Jews and Gentiles alike, who are suffering from disease and affliction. He does so free of charge because of his empathy for humanity, and he
writes the amulets only after carefully intuiting the nature of the affliction
to be healed.

From a holy man with such impeccable sensitivities, much is to be expected. The narrator encourages our hopes by treating the latticework of
his esoteric beliefs with great respect and by ventriloquizing these doctrines
as if they were his own. But the build-up, alas, leads to a greater letdown.
R. Menele does think deeply about Miriam Devorah's affliction, but his
diagnosis, rendered with great empathy and no sarcasm, turns out to be not
so different from R. Mikhl's. The problem, he determines, is the evil eye,
and its source is the jealousy of other women, which has been provoked
"because of her voice, which God gave her as a divine gift" (p. 78, 89).

R. Menele has a sure antidote to offer, but he knows in advance that it
will seem ludicrous. His advice is to take a fish fin and hang it around the
neck of the sufferer. In the face of the anticipated astonishment, he explains
that the numerical value of both *snapir* (fin) and *'ayin ra'* (evil eye) is four
hundred and that one will work to counteract the other. The people of
Miriam Devorah's household accept the prescription but delay several days,
proceeding on the assumption that the fin of a fish prepared for the Sabbath
will have more effectual power than one prepared for a weekday. But they
are wrong and in this short interval, Miriam Devorah's "wretchedness got
the better of her to the point where they feared for her life" (p. 79, 90). In
the final analysis, the ridiculousness of R. Mikhl's person is matched by the
ridiculousness of R. Menele's prescription for fish-fin therapy.

Both men concur that the roots of Miriam Devorah's affliction lie in
the ill will of other females, whether human or demon. And in this they
are both spectacularly wrong. The narrator has already informed us that,
after its rejection by synagogue culture, her music found a receptive home
only among other women as they knitted and plucked. Why then does the
narrator present the mistaken views of these two characters at such length,
especially when he is about to provide psychological explanations that
are much more compelling? The two healers are necessary to accomplish

Agnon's intention to convey to modern readers the nature of the cognitive matrix out of which Miriam Devorah's sense of self was formed. The unfortunate young woman lives in a time in which certain kinds of endowments and certain realms of spiritual creativity are marked as male. These boundaries are reinforced by an elaborate system of esoteric doctrine controlled by special adepts and practitioners, which in turn provides a new and radical theological overlay for the received, traditional devaluation of female religiosity outside the home.

The pathos of Miriam Devorah's situation is that she is both a rebel against this set of attitudes and its unwitting victim. By realizing her musical gifts, she inevitably crosses over into the preserve of male spirituality; yet, tragically, she remains prisoner to a chauvinist philosophy when it comes to her own perception of her actions. The only resources available for understanding herself are the very same ones drawn on by R. Mikhl and R. Menele. She must therefore draw the conclusion that her gift is a perversion or a displacement.

This is the inevitability that the narrator finally deigns to disclose to us when, after the lengthy depictions of the holy men, he informs us, briefly and almost in passing, that the "real" source of Miriam Devorah's melancholia lay in a dream three years before her death. She dreamt she was "dressed in a kittel and a large tallit as she led prayers [literally, passed before the teivah] in a synagogue filled with worshipers" (p. 79, 90). Her response upon awakening was happiness; yet as she passed the experience through the cognitive filters available to her, the happiness gave way to dread and self-accusation. Her interpretive efforts brought her to the conclusion that in a previous life she must have been born male and that her present embodiment as a woman must be a punishment for grievous sins she committed in that earlier life. It is the fruitless search to identify those sins that plunged her into the depression from which she never emerged.

The whole notion of the existence of previous lives, it should be noted, is not some stray folk belief but a doctrine called *gilgul neshamot*, the transmigration of souls, or metempsychosis. These notions are part and parcel of the theology of Lurianic kabbalah, which had been imported into Polish and

Galician Jewry in the previous century. It is this body of belief, the same one that undergirds R. Mikhl and R. Menele's worldviews, from which Miriam Devorah must draw to construct her guilt-ridden sense of self.

The last explanation, which is presented as an adjuvant explanation to the dream, is entirely free of theological content. Miriam Devorah, we are told, was married while she was still a minor (younger than twelve and a half); she was homesick for her parents and sought every opportunity to flee Buczacz for her parents' village of Monastritz. After several years she reconciled herself to her role as a wife and bore R. Elya six children in quick succession. Although the narrator states only these facts and draws no conclusion from them, we as modern readers are likely to construe her experience as one marked by the trauma of early marriage and premature and overwhelming motherhood, and all this on the shoulders of a girl born with the gifts of an artist.

As a story, "Haḥazzanim" begins by tracing the history of the Wernicks, the great cantorial dynasty of seventeenth-century Buczacz, then quickly turns its attention to the tragedy of Miriam Devorah. Is her story the deviation from the norm, the rock upon which the dynastic vocation of ḥazzanut founders? Or, as a kind of richly gifted, crypto-ḥazzan herself, does she lay claim to be rightfully included within the class of "holy vessels" connoted by the story's title? Or, finally, as a female artist, does her story mark the hidden beginnings of a new narrative, one that can be told only at some future time after the breakdown of tradition, a time when Buczacz has ceased to be Buczacz?

Agnon seems contented to leave the ambiguity in place, but he does take pains to finish the story of the Wernick clan, and he does so not simply to satisfy our curiosity. Overwhelmed by caring for his children after Miriam Devorah's death, R. Elya marries a woman who turns out to be entirely unsympathetic and unsuitable. After divorcing her, he makes a successful match with Rivkah Henyah, a woman a few years older than he who is the daughter of his older brother Yekutiel. She is a widow whose beloved husband died of wounds incurred when he tried to stop a fight between gentiles that broke out in his store. She is an excellent homemaker and parent who maintains control over this large blended family and practices a policy of equality among her own children and her stepchildren. Her strength compensates the children for R. Elya's absenteeism. He has fallen under the spell of the mystical asceticism of the book *Ḥemdat Yamim*, another outgrowth of the new spirituality that had been imported from abroad and threatened the immemorial minhagim of Buczacz.[18]

Rivkah Henyah's most consequential move is to forbid her sons and stepsons from becoming professional ḥazzanim and to make them swear to adhere to this prohibition after her death. She insists that they and their sisters marry into mercantile families and make their livings in ways that involve no dependence on the community. They may exercise their voices as prayer leaders so long as their service is voluntary and unpaid. Serving in a lay capacity as readers of Torah, they become agents of an important process of rectification.[19] "What Miriam Devorah failed to accomplish with her melodies for the liturgy and the piyyutim she succeeded in when it came to the reading of the Torah; for all the Torah readers in the city—and it goes without saying in regard to the Scroll of Esther—strove to model their chanting on what they had learned from Miriam Devorah's sons, who learned directly from her" (p. *83*, 96). This is Rivkah Henyah's negotiated settlement. Honor given posthumously to Miriam Devorah's musical creativity is a price willingly paid for permanently decoupling the family from the enterprise of ḥazzanut and repositioning it within the normal—and normally admirable—course of Jewish society. They will never have to worry about the dangers of drawing close to the teivah.

Holy Consummations

"Ha'ish levush habadim" [The Man Dressed in Linen, pp. *84–113*, 98–139], the middle panel of the cantorial triptych, is one of the most extraordinary stories in Agnon's late period. Both of the main characters, a grandfather and a grandson, each named Gavriel, embody an ideal of the ḥazzan that is found nowhere else in Agnon's works. The dramatic monologue at the center of the story, which is spoken by the grandson about the grandfather, is a marvel of narrative construction. And the act of victimization and self-sacrifice at the story's climax presents a provocative challenge both to the tale's contemporary and to its modern readership. It was challenging to its author as well. Agnon published the first sixteen pages of the story (through chapter 19) in *Haaretz* in 1965;[20] he left it to his daughter to add the remaining thirteen pages in manuscript and publish the whole story in *A City in Its Fullness*. Even so, the end is made up of three fragments that give the story's conclusion a provisional and unfinished quality.

The new story takes its point of departure from the ending of "Haḥazzanim." The worshipers of Buczacz had been spoiled by R. Elya's long, continuous service, and when he died at the age of ninety-seven, the teivah was left bereft. The community's resources are drained by the need to pay heavy taxes and levies, ransom prisoners, and pay bribes to governing officials; there are no funds to attract a new ḥazzan. The descendants of Miriam Devorah have heeded Rivkah Henyah's caution to avoid the professional cantorate. "Anyone who descends before the teivah, the teivah seizes hold of him and he seizes hold of the teivah," she declared. "In the end, he will lose his voice and the congregation will become disgusted with him, and yet he will not let go of the teivah and the teivah will not let go of him" (p. *84, 95*). In the meantime, the teivah is being abused by the assaults upon it on the part of congregants who like to hear the sound of their own voices.

The extent of the congregation's dissatisfaction is brought into sharp relief when it gets a taste of something better. On a Sabbath shortly before the High Holidays, a visiting fabric merchant is given the honor of reading the portion from the Prophets in the synagogue and then is asked to continue on by "descending before the teivah" and leading the congregation in the Musaf service. The worshipers are moved and astonished by his performance in a way unfamiliar to them. The fabric merchant has a way of erasing his own personality and facilitating the direct access of the worshipers to the prayers and, through the prayers, to God. "When R. Elya used to pray," says one of the worshipers, "I used to hear R. Elya," but through the agency of the visitor, "all I hear is the prayer itself" (pp. *85, 100*).[21] Realizing the depths of the deprivation his townsmen have been experiencing, the gabbai of the synagogue, who has been struggling to prevent the teivah from falling into chaos, prevails upon the visitor to return to Buczacz and lead services on Yom Kippur.

The visitor's name is Gavriel, as was his grandfather's after whom he was named, and the fabric he sells, and in which he is also attired, is linen. He is known in those parts as the linen man, *dos linen yidl,* in Yiddish, and ha'ish levush habadim (literally, the man dressed in linen) in Hebrew. For the literate Hebrew reader, the epithet is familiar from a number of contexts. In the book of Daniel, a "man clad in linen" functions as an angel who vouchsafes the vision of the end of days, and in Ezekiel's prophecies he is an avenging angel charged with executing God's will. In rabbinic literature, ha'ish levush habadim in the Bible is associated with the ministering angel Gavriel. And in the medieval piyyut concerning the ten sages martyred by Rome, which is read in synagogues on Yom Kippur mornings, this same figure is one who knows what is taking place in heavenly spheres.[22]

The name and the epithet, which identify the two Gavriels as superior, even other-worldly creatures, are just one example of a series of clues or markers that prepare the reader for the extraordinary events to come. For example, the reason the linen man comes to Buczacz every year before the High Holidays is not just to sell his wares, which he could do at any time, but because this is the season that Jews visit the graves of their ancestors, and "a part" of his grandfather is buried near Buczacz. Considering why only a part of the body and not the whole suggests ominous possibilities. The grandson consistently refers to his grandfather as *zekeni hakadosh,* which can mean either "my saintly grandfather" or "my sainted grandfather." On a first reading of the story, these markers lay down a subliminal film of unease and suspense; on a second reading, the reader has the satisfying sense of having seen what is coming.

The linen man's service as emissary of the congregation before the teivah over the course of Yom Kippur makes a profound impression on the leadership of Buczacz. When friends of the gabbai gather at his home after the fast, they compete in praising the services of the linen man as prayer leader and testifying to the powerful religious experiences he made possible. One says that his prayer "arouses the heart to repentance," while another goes further and claims his prayer is so persuasive that it engenders the conviction that God "has accepted our repentance, and it is not even worth mentioning the matter of sin" (p. *87*, 102). The gabbai and his party move on to the rabbi's house, where it is universally agreed that the linen man should be invited to become the permanent ḥazzan of Buczacz.

In the meantime, the linen man himself is carrying out the custom, rare even among the most pious, of observing a *second* day of Yom Kippur during which he recites the entire liturgy inaudibly to himself. After breaking his two-day fast with only a little apple wine and cake brought from home, he is ready to set out in the darkness on his several-hour walk back to his village. At that moment he is accosted by the shamash, who has been sent to bring him to the gabbai's home. There he is presented with a bag of gold coins as payment for his services, which he promptly refuses to accept.[23] His refusal is incomprehensible to the practical men who sit before him. Lest he be concerned that the money comes from charitable donations pledged in the synagogue, he is reassured that it comes from the gabbai's personal funds. Lest he be concerned that the money may have come from questionable business dealings, he is reassured of the gabbai's unassailable integrity in all commercial matters. In explanation of his refusal, all he can say is: "My name is Gavriel and I am named for my sainted grandfather R. Gavriel" (p. *89*, 106). His pragmatic-minded listeners fail to see the relevance of his statement and demand to be told precisely what it is about his grandfather that would contribute to his refusal.

This is a critical moment in the story that illuminates the nature of each party. The gabbai and his associates believe that they will humor the meek and inarticulate linen man by listening patiently to a sentimental anecdote about his grandfather; all the while they are eager to get on to the business of signing him up as the community's permanent ḥazzan. They do not have the least notion that their prodding will unleash a major narrative whose telling will last until the morning hours and leave them disturbed and confused. For his part, their prodding, wholly unbeknownst to them, sets the stage for the great moment of *his* life: the telling of his grandfather's story. This is an opportunity that has long eluded him; or, perhaps more accurately, he has eluded it. He is awed by the responsibility and utters a prayer for himself: "Let my words be acceptable to He who opens the mouth of the dumb" (p. *90*, 106). If the linen man is not dumb, he is diffident and unused to speaking, and it takes a great deal for him to screw up his courage and launch his story. To overcome his hesitation, his listeners piously observe that it is a religious duty to recount the praises of tsaddikim. The linen man responds with a qualification.

> It is indeed a religious duty to recount the praises of tsaddikim but only if the recounting of those praises results in deeds like those of the tsaddikim. I, for my sins, have no deeds to show. All I have is the story of the deeds of my sainted grandfather, for whom I am named. Many times I've told the story of his deeds, but only to myself. Now that you ask me to tell you the story of my sainted grandfather, the words rise up to my lips and seek to come out. (p. *90*, 107)

Despite the fact that its importance is likely lost on his listeners, the linen man is making a statement whose significance, like the markers mentioned above, can only be appreciated after hearing his story in full. He presents himself as existing in the shadow of his grandfather, who was a man of deeds (*ma'asim*). He himself has nothing to show *except* for the telling of his grandfather's story, the telling of his deeds, which he has not yet realized. The act of narration—in the grand, masterful and potent way he brings it off—represents his one chance to perform a deed and enter the realm of ma'aseh (which as a term, of course, also means a story!). Only later do we realize that this act is coterminous with his life and that, once it is completed, so is his existence.

It is worth pausing to appreciate the artistry of the great monologue that follows and takes up almost all of the remainder of this long story. The modest and laconic fabric seller turns out to be a master of exposition and scene setting and a man who knows how to retard the action to create interest and to return to the same scene from different angles. In the scope and ambition of his story, he compares to the shamash in "The Parable and Its Lesson," who narrates his journey to Gehinnom and back. The shamash, by contrast, is giving an account of events in which he himself participated, even if those events took place more than a half century earlier, and he has an ulterior motive for telling his story, which is to exonerate himself before a court assembled to judge him. The linen man addresses an audience that is more sympathetic but no less demanding that its curiosity be satisfied. His challenge is to overcome the fact that he never met his grandfather, and he presents a rationale derived from his grandmother's practice for empathically imagining thoughts and feelings and placing them within his characters. For both the shamash and the linen man, the biggest compliment paid them is the fact that the narrator of *A City in Its Fullness* is willing to hand over to them the baton of narration and is willing to share the stage with them.

The linen man is filled with trepidation because he knows that the story he will tell that night will be the most important performance of his life and that once he has delivered it, he will have discharged his purpose for living. The way Agnon has shrewdly structured the story makes it clear that it is the phenomenon of performance that underlies and connects the three central spheres of action. Within the context of a series of stories about ḥazzanim, the appearance of the ḥazzan before the audience and before the teivah is obviously the preeminent paradigm for performance. The second is the linen man's canny construction of his monologue, delivered as the performance of a lifetime.

Less evident but equally performative is the third: the martyrdom of R. Gavriel. What is most astonishing about his ordeal is not the gruesomeness of the tortures and execution visited upon him but his success in gaining control of his situation and using it to exhibit his faith. From Second Maccabees to the Roman executions of the Sages, the goal of martyrs has been to demonstrate the superiority of their convictions in the face of their dominators. The subversive truth of the story is that for both Gavriels, grandfather and grandson, there is something insufficient in the calling of the ḥazzan, and they succeed in finding the consummate performance of their lives elsewhere.

The story that the linen man tells of his grandfather is a narrative of a gifted and studious youth who grows into a paragon of righteousness until something happens to make him falter. Born with a voice that only comes

along once in a century, Gavriel is adopted by the old ḥazzan and asked to
serve in his place after his death. When a servant of the community—this
is not Buczacz but a considerably smaller town—attempts to pay him for
his services after his first cycle of holiday performances, he peremptorily
rejects the payment and says that he fortunately does need to depend on
the community. His refusal is supported by his young wife Rivkah Devorah
and his father-in-law, in whose home the couple lives according to the customary arrangement. Thus the pattern is set: Gavriel undertakes to lead the
community in prayer without payment; he rejects the title "ḥazzan," which
would imply a remunerated professional role, and prefers to be known simply as Gavriel ba'al tefilah, Gavriel the prayer leader. He and his wife start
a family and establish their own household, and Rivkah Devorah opens a
shop and proves herself an able businesswoman. Gavriel is given the freedom to pursue a life of holiness; he spends his days learning in the beit
midrash and teaching a daily public lesson on the Mishnah; on the Sabbath
and on holidays he leads the congregation in prayer. The only time he has
contact with money is Friday afternoons when he helps his wife set aside
their tithe for charity. Although the fame of his voice attracts lucrative proposals from larger communities, he declines all offers.

Into the perfection of this life inevitably come sources of instability. It
is only after his martyrdom that the bewildered elders of the generation
are forced to conclude that Gavriel had provoked Satan's envy because
the sincerity of his prayer led his congregants to thoughts of repentance
(p. *111*, 137). From first to last, the story of Gavriel's martyrdom unfolds
with the inevitability of tragedy.[24] The ostensible precipitant is a trivial accident. The wagon of a bookseller on his way to a major convocation of
sages loses a wheel on its journey through the small town; while he waits
for the repairs to be completed, he is prevailed upon to display his wares in
the beit midrash. Among the books is a handsome printing of *Torat ha'olah*
(published in Prague in 1570) by Moses Isserles, one of the greatest scholars
of his age. The treatise describes the dimensions of the various precincts
of the Temple and explicates the details of the sacrifices according to the
teachings of the Kabbalah. Gavriel experiences an overwhelming desire to

acquire this expensive volume, and all his troubles soon begin to unfold from his efforts to do so.[25]

The powerful connection to *Torat ha'olah* does not come from nowhere. In his own studies Gavriel had always adhered to the curriculum favored by the rabbinic elite that focused on the study of Talmud with the commentaries of Rashi and the Tosafists. He prepared studiously for the lessons in Mishnah that he gave as a communal service, and he studied the commentaries on the piyyutim in advance of each holiday. He avoided esoteric speculation, heeding the Talmud's advice (quoting Ben Sira): "Inquire not into what is marvelous and in what is hidden from you do not seek" (p. 97, 116).[26] Yet without seeking it, hidden knowledge is revealed to him in a series of dreams. In one he is shown the secret correspondence between the structure of the Jerusalem Temple and the structure of the cosmos; in another he is told that the seven-stringed harp of King David will have eight strings in the time of the Messiah and ten strings in the World to Come. Shortly afterwards he is vouchsafed a waking vision of R. Amnon of Mainz, the medieval martyr who, according to legend, composed the famous hymn "Unetaneh Tokef," a centerpiece of the High Holiday liturgy.[27]

When Gavriel peruses the bookseller's copy of *Torat ha'olah*, he is stunned to discover that some of the same secret insights that had come to him unbidden are found in a work by a great sage whose authority is accepted by almost all communities.[28] The confirmation of his private visions by such an august authority is an overwhelming feeling, and he realizes that the book before him would open up vastly more secret knowledge about the Temple and it rituals, knowledge that he was on his way to discovering on his own. He undergoes at that moment a life-changing experience: "He passionately desired the precious volume with which he could delight his holy soul" (p. 97, 116). The word for "desired" is *ḥashak*, a strong term with an erotic connotation, and the word for "delight" is *lesha'ashei'a*, a term similarly connected to notions of giving and taking pleasure. Gavriel experiences for the first time, in other words, the desire to possess something he does not have and until now did not know was missing in his life, and which, if acquired, will bring him joy. When he returns home, his wife observes that his demeanor has changed; and after she extracts from him the reason, she proposes to empty her cash reserves to buy the book. Gavriel, who has never held money in his hands except for purposes of charity, takes the coins the next day to the bookseller only to discover that the volume has been sold to someone else.

Gavriel gets a second chance, and its source tells a great deal about how his desire for the book is linked to the world of the synagogue. A worshiper approaches him on the night of Simḥat Torah and reports that Gavriel's chanting of the prayer for rain in the morning service had brought him much pleasure (*'oneg*); he identifies himself as the person who purchased *Torat ha'olah* and offers to sell it as thanks for the pleasure given him, that is, if he still desires (*mit'aveh*) it. When he approaches the teivah the next morning to lead the Musaf service, he is stricken by the thought that likely he cannot afford the purchase price of the book and he becomes physically weak. His changed behavior is immediately noticed by those who are used to saying that "R. Gavriel's prayer gives them Sabbath pleasure (*'oneg*) on the Sabbath and holiday joy (*simḥah*) on holidays" (p. *98*, 118). Some observers write off his weakness to the sustained pressure of performing during the holiday season. Others point to worries stemming from his bourgeoning family and their limited income in the aftermath of his father-in-law's death. Is it any wonder, they reason, that "if he has no pleasure (*ta'anug*)," he has none to give others?

Synagogue worship emerges here as a setting in which spiritual pleasure has become commodified. The worshipers rely upon the powers of the ḥazzan or the lay prayer leader to create a euphoric experience they are not capable of sustaining on their own; they long to be transported beyond themselves. The congregants realize how much they take their pleasure for granted only when Gavriel's powers momentarily falter; if Agnon's tales of the ḥazzanim tell us anything, it is that there are innumerable obstacles to this exchange succeeding and that the consumers of Gavriel's (the grandfather's) services are lucky indeed. In the frame story about Buczacz and the linen man, the gabbai deploys all his wiles to pursue the visitor because he knows too well the rude and contentious state of a congregation chronically deprived of pleasure.

If it is true that the ḥazzan must experience pleasure in order to give it to others, then what sources can he draw upon for his own happiness? In Gavriel's case, standing in the sacred space close to the teivah and serving as an emissary before God would seem to be satisfaction enough, that is, until his dreams and his discovery of a book give him a taste of something more profound and satisfying. *Torat ha'olah* opens up for him a trove of secret lore about the Temple and its sacrifices and promises an unmediated route to transcendence. The synagogue and its liturgy are the "service of the heart" that the Rabbis instituted after the Destruction to substitute for the sacrifices offered by the priests. To be sure, the Rabbis insisted that this priest-less oral worship found as much favor in God's eyes as what it replaced; nonetheless, the loss of a sense of direct proximity to God was never fully dispelled.

Gavriel, who craves service to God, is the apotheosis of the true ḥazzan, but his quest for holiness is circumscribed by the substitute nature of the very regime of synagogue worship. It is as if he has hit a wall and can go no farther. *Torat ha'olah* gives him the promise of unfettered access to the innermost secrets of the originary, prelapsarian site of divine worship. With such a prospect in view, why would he not be passionately desirous of obtaining this tome? Yet it is crucial to note that even such esoteric pleasures have their limits. The access offered to the world of the Temple is only speculative and theosophical. It allows for the luxuriating of the mystical imagination, but it does not—it goes without saying—bring back the act of sacrifice itself. But the absence of that possibility does not mean that one cannot long for it, and immersion in the lore of the Temple only stokes the desire to transcend even this barrier. When Gavriel's chance comes along, as we soon see, he is not insensible to its possibilities.[29]

Until this point, the story has been told with such brisk economy that it is easy to forget that it is a monologue being spoken before an audience. The teller calls little attention to himself, and the story flows. Beginning with chapter 19 (p. 99, 121), however, there is a palpable shift. Time dilates, and ten pages are devoted to three hours of real time. The linen man makes his role as narrator conspicuous as he announces and justifies his choices to lavish attention on some scenes and not on others. He indulges in a long apologia for the freedom he takes in dramatizing conversations and feelings whose only source is his empathic imagination (I discuss this passage [p. *102, 226*] in Chapter 2). He returns several times to the same touching picture of his grandfather replacing the water in which he is preserving a precious etrog. He gives us two renditions of the crucial meeting between Gavriel and R. Eliezer Simḥah, the gabbai of the synagogue. Interpolated digressions create suspense and retard the action. Taken together, all these effects have a distinctly cinematic quality. It is as if the narrator has finished with the exposition and now focuses his attention on setting up the climactic scene.

A Burnt Offering unto the Lord

The sudden introduction of R. Eliezer Simḥah is an important part of this shift. A story that has so far focused on the two Gavriels makes room in midcourse for another character. He is as exemplary in his own sphere as Gavriel is in his. A man of great intelligence who could have been an eminent scholar, R. Eliezer Simḥah chose instead to represent the interests of the Jewish communities of the region before the governing authorities and, within the community, to serve as a mediator in disputes among powerful rival mercantile families. Like Gavriel, he has often been invited to establish his residence in larger and more influential cities. He has refused because the Jews of their town, of which there are only two hundred, possess the highly uncommon quality of dwelling together in peace. It is he who explains to the wholly unworldly Gavriel the current interregnum in the governance of the Polish monarchy, which, in the absence of a monarch, has allowed Jewish communities to decline paying the Shpilowka, a tax that funds the queen's jewels. It is the existence of this unexpected windfall that he uses to breakdown Gavriel's resistance to accept a sum of money from the community for his services during the High Holiday period that has just ended. R. Eliezer Simḥah's purpose is not to corrupt Gavriel. He was witness to Gavriel's faltering performance in the synagogue the day before and took to heart the presumptions—mistaken, as it turns out—that it was due to anxieties about livelihood. Little does he know that the roll of coins that he places in Gavriel's hands will be used in the next few hours to buy a book. The substance of R. Eliezer Simḥah's own fortune soon will be depleted by the lavish bribes he offers, unsuccessfully, to persuade the Polish authorities to ameliorate the harsh conditions of Gavriel's incarceration and to avert his execution.

Gavriel takes the money and sets off to the house of Gershon Wolff, the wealthy manufacturer who had purchased *Torat ha'olah* and then offered to sell it to Gavriel in gratitude for the spiritual pleasure he had provided him. It is exactly at this point, at the beginning of chapter 25 and in the middle of page *107* (132) that the great monologue spoken by the grandson breaks off. Anticipating the first light of morning, the linen man announces a break in the narration for the purpose of morning prayers. That he does so an hour earlier than necessary, a fact pointed out by his listeners, is due either to his practice of spending an hour in private meditation before the arrival of the statutory time for communal prayer or to an uncertainty as to the resumption of the monologue.

It is now (p. *108*, 133) that the general narrator of the story returns to the stage—relinquished on page *91*, (107)—and takes over, and he offers a fascinating rationale for doing so. He begins by admitting that he does not know when the story was resumed, and he lists a number of reasons, mostly bearing on the requirements of the holiday of Sukkot, for why it is implausible that Gavriel continued telling the story after services that morning or any time soon after. Concerning this problem, the narrator can only throw up his hands and admit that "there are difficulties in the world that it is not in our power to resolve."[30] (When it comes to irresolvable difficulties, this one soon pales in comparison to the challenge presented by Gavriel's torture and execution, and the troubling persistence of unanswered questions will be raised again.) The narrator is constrained to explain that the monologue he has conveyed so far is based on a chain of transmission that goes back directly to the men who heard the linen man's account in the rabbi's house. In the concluding five pages of the story, however, his source of authority is less direct and derives from "those who were stirred by [the example of] the linen man to expound upon the events in the life of the sainted R. Gavriel."

Even though the voice telling the story has changed, the cinematic quality of the narrative remains vivid. This is the chronicle of a death foretold. Gavriel places the money before Gershon Wolff, refuses an invitation to take refreshment, takes possession of the book, and begins his journey home from the non-Jewish section of the town, where the wealthy manufacturer lives. Skirting a noisy crowd of gentile townspeople, Gavriel is suddenly pointed to with the cry "He's the one!" and set upon and severely beaten and then taken off to jail. The narrator supplies the back story to this astonishing turn of events. The wife of the church sexton has discovered thefts from the holy bread it is her duty to bake, and it is soon discovered that the thief is none other than the jealous and gluttonous mother of the sexton's deceased first wife. To deflect guilt from herself, the crone claims that a spell was cast upon her by a Jewish wizard, and she has the good fortune of seeing at that very moment R. Gavriel walk by, with a big tome in hand. The crowd attacks him, and he is imprisoned. His imprisonment lasts two and a half years, at the end of which he is tied to a horse and dragged through the streets of the town and then cut into pieces before the eyes of a respectable gentile audience assembled for the spectacle.

Every aspect of Gavriel's treatment is incredible. After the heat of the moment, the gentile townspeople come to realize that the case against the pious Jew is bogus. They know Gavriel to be a holy man and his wife to be an admirable shopkeeper who deals fairly with all her customers. They know the mother of the sexton's first wife to be a harridan. Moreover, even in a Polish legal system hostile toward Jews, since when can a few monetary favors not influence officials to do the right thing, especially when the charges are already so obviously flimsy? Yet no amount of bribes can lessen the torture or avert the death sentence. R. Eliezer Simḥah mortgages his home and impoverishes himself trying, but to no avail.

Gavriel's fate is altogether outrageous, but the story cannily diverts our attention from the aspect that is most provocative. Modern readers undoubtedly are appalled and indignant at the baseless victimization of an innocent Jew. Gavriel's contemporaries, more inured to such persecutions, are described in the story as being troubled by the problem of theodicy it poses. What can explain God allowing a man of such exemplary piety and righteousness to be subjected to unspeakable torments and even denied a Jewish burial? "All the sages of the generation struggled with this dilemma until they came to the conclusion that Satan had become jealous of him because his prayers had aroused stirrings of repentance in the hearts of the worshipers" (p. *111*, 137).[31] Is this the story of a holy man who falls prey to the sin of acquisitiveness? Modern readers, too, may struggle with a secularized version of theodicy that derives from an expectation of moral economy in literature. We bridle against the disproportion between Gavriel's minor transgression and the horrific consequences visited upon him.

Yet these are all distractions and false leads placed before us by the narrator at the conclusion of this long story. What is truly radical and radically disturbing is not the persecutions but Gavriel's response to them. His radiant happiness increases in proportion to the severity of the tortures meted out to him. When his wife Rivkah Devorah is finally allowed to visit him in prison, a privilege for which R. Eliezer Simḥah had to leverage vast amounts of political and monetary assets, she is aghast at what she sees. Bound by iron shackles, his battered and emaciated body peeps from among the tears in his soiled garment. But in response to her shriek, which shakes the walls and startles prisoners and guards alike, Gavriel comforts her by saying:

> Why are you weeping and why do you distress yourself? Is it not, after all, for my glory that I have been placed here, and is it not for the glory of He of whom it is said, "The earth is full of His glory"? You might truly protest that it is impossible to observe the *mitsvot* in such a filthy place. But the Rabbis, of blessed memory, already ruled that under conditions of coercion, the Torah absolves one of a requirement to observe the commandments. I trust in Him about whom it is said "His mercies extend to all His works," that He will view my presence here as equivalent to my sitting in the synagogue and the beit midrash. (p. *105*, 128)

Is Gavriel a holy fool such that he can remain wholly insensible to torture and take a growing delight in his ordeal? If his behavior is a wonder to his coreligionists, it becomes an object of veneration for the Christian prisoners who consider abandoning their faith and clinging to the God of Israel, who is the source of Gavriel's luminous strength. It is this fear that hastens the priests in charge of his torture to bring his ordeal to its end.

Gavriel's delight in suffering turns out to be the real scandal. As moderns we are less troubled by gratuitous suffering allowed by God than we are by the embrace and beatification of suffering, especially after the Holocaust. The key to Gavriel's mentality can be found in the admission that he makes to Rivkah Devorah when she visits him in prison. "All my life I placed before my eyes those tsaddikim who martyred themselves for the sake of Heaven by means of their death. The day that I went to purchase the book *Torat ha'olah* I could barely stand because of the intensity of my desire to offer myself as a burnt offering before God" (p. *106, 130*).

The articulation of this passionate desire for self-sacrifice activates two symbolic contexts that together help to explain why Gavriel's ordeal renders him ecstatic and others dumbfounded. The first symbolic context is the persecutions of 1096 in the Rhineland Valley community of Worms, Mainz, and Speyer during which Crusader soldiers presented Jews with the choice of conversion or death. Many pious and learned Jews chose to kill themselves after slaughtering their families rather than convert.

These ritual homicides and suicides went far beyond anything required in Talmudic sources regarding behavior under conditions of persecution. In the piyyutim written to extol their behavior, the standard rationales for collective suffering based on sin and punishment had to be put aside in light of the unimpeachable righteousness of the martyrs. Instead, an older rabbinic notion that had previously applied only to individual suffering was now extended to collective suffering. This is the concept of yisurin shel ahavah, affliction that is motivated by love. According to this doctrine, as amplified by the sacred poets of the time, the suffering of the martyrs of 1096 was not a punishment but an opportunity for spiritual distinction awarded them in recognition of their superior virtue.

The martyrs chose to kill their family members and themselves rather than *being* killed by the enemy because they sought to control the conditions under which they themselves became sacrifices to God, which not only resembled the wholly burnt sacrifices in the Temple, the *'olot*, but became those sacrifices *in fact*. The ecstatic transcendence that accompanied their deeds expressed the conviction of their offering being accepted. Living in the Exile, they felt acutely the distance and remoteness from God imposed by the Destruction and the abrogation of the concrete and embodied means by which direct service to God was offered and direct absolution obtained. Seizing the moment of their martyrdom enabled them to collapse the thousand-year gap that intervened between them and the Temple and, if only for a moment, to make the sacrificial milieu real again.

Gavriel's martyrdom is modeled on these precedents, but it is distinguished by his vocation as ḥazzan. This is the second symbolic context. As prayer leader, he is called upon to serve both the congregation and God. But the service he provides the congregation is not identical with the service he offers to God. His congregants rely on him to "facilitate" their religious experience by arousing them to repentance during the Days of Awe and providing them joy on the great pilgrimage festivals. Gavriel's own awe and joy come from a different direction: from the teivah he faces rather than from the worshipers seated behind him. The role of prayer leader affords him the chance not only for representation but for presence. His stance before the teivah is the privileged space granted to him to draw closer to God. But the closer he is the closer he wishes to be.

Although he leads a life of study and devotion that would seem exemplary on all accounts, he himself experiences the limitations imposed by an attenuated regime of worship, which is a replacement for the visceral and embodied service of the Temple in which God's presence dwelt. The service of the heart, *ha'avodah shebalev*, is not enough. Gavriel's passionate desire to acquire *Torat ha'olah* represents his longing to overcome this barrier through theosophical meditation. Attaining secret knowledge of the innermost dimensions of the Sanctuary and the high spiritual meanings of its sacrificial ritual is a great attainment; yet, in the last analysis, it remains only that, an illumination that takes places in the individual spiritual imagination. It is ironic, then, that Gavriel possesses the longed-for book only a few minutes before the attack, which opens the way for him to skip over the stage of reading and meditating and to proceed directly to the higher opportunity of making himself into a direct and embodied sacrifice to the Lord.[32]

The figure of R. Amnon of Mainz is the bridge between these two symbolic contexts. According to medieval legend, R. Amnon is the author of the famous prayer "Unetaneh Tokef" ["Let us now tell of the power of the day . . . "], which describes the awesomeness of the Day of Judgment and is one of the most solemn moments in the liturgy for Rosh Hashanah and Yom Kippur. The legend tells that in the eleventh century the Bishop of Mainz attempted to convert R. Amnon to Christianity and that R. Amnon asked for three days to consider his course of action. Immediately he regretted giving the appearance that he was wavering and failed to appear before the bishop. When the bishop had the rabbi brought before him, the rabbi pleaded that his tongue be cut out because it had expressed doubt in his Judaism. Instead, the bishop cut off his hands and feet. Rabbi Amnon begged to be brought to the synagogue on Rosh Hashanah together with his severed limbs, and just as the reader was beginning the Kedushah prayer, he intoned the hymn that was to become so famous. The figure of R. Amnon makes three appearances in "The Man Dressed in Linen." The first, which I already alluded to, occurs on Rosh Hashanah shortly after Gavriel contracts his desire to acquire *Torat ha'olah*, when R. Amnon appears to him and conveys the original melody in which the hymn was composed (p. *98*, 118). The second occurs as he walks across the town to purchase the book from Gershon Wolff; he remembers how, upon completing the intoning of his hymn, R. Amnon "disappeared from the world before all because the Lord had taken him" (p. *106*, 129). The third is related after his death by his wife, who, after describing how Gavriel had expressed the desire to be a sacrifice ('olah) before God, says "my heart tells me that on that day R. Amnon was revealed to him" (pp. *106*, 129–30).[33]

In addition to fusing the worlds of martyrdom and liturgy, the figure of R. Amnon makes it clear how profoundly and demonstrably Gavriel does not belong to his time. All the circumstances surrounding his imprisonment, torture, and death are not only incredible but anachronistic. The drama of Gavriel's consummation belongs to the eleventh century and not to the seventeenth or the beginning of the eighteenth, and it belongs to the ancient communities of Ashkenaz and not to the more recent communities of Galicia. Even during the Khmelnytskyi massacres of 1648, instances of sacrificial suicide and homicide were rare. Now several generations later, in a very different political climate, behavior based on this model is out of place. The rationale for self-sacrifice has been forgotten, and therefore Gavriel's ecstatic transcendence in his torture seems incomprehensible and theologically troubling, even scandalous. It is the reader-listeners of the story who remain uncomfortable, whether they belong to the narratorial audience contemporary to the time of the story or to the authorial audience of post-Holocaust Israeli literature. It is only for Gavriel himself that his passion makes rapturous sense.

Some of the same confusion attaches to the fate of the gifted narrator who recounts the first Gavriel's story. Shortly after the holiday season, a traveler from Buczacz passes by the village of the linen man and pauses in his journey to seek him out. It happens that on that very day the linen man, who is called by his fellow villagers "Yedid Hashem" [beloved of God], has decided to return his soul to God despite being in good health. He wraps himself in his tallit, recites the confessional, summons his brethren, and, with the words of the Song of Songs on his lips, departs the world. His motives remain a mystery, and those who were privileged to have heard him descend before the teivah speculate that he has been called to join the Heavenly Choir.

These final words of the story invite us to see an analogy between the final "consummations" of grandfather and grandson. The latter's self-willed death is a paler and belated version of the former's operatic martyrdom. The grandson returns his soul to God after accomplishing the great, long-deferred task of his life: telling the story of his grandfather. It will be recalled that when the grandson was being egged on by the curious Buczacz notables to tell that story he states that recounting the deeds of the righteous is a mitzvah only if the act of telling leads to deeds. *His* deed is that very act of telling, and, having accomplished it, he is now free to disentangle himself from dilemmas of serving before the teivah in this world and to join the choral singing of God's praises in the next.

"First as Tragedy, Then as Farce"

The third panel of the cantorial triptych abandons the rarified holiness of the linen man and his sainted grandfather to bring us into the world of ordinary ḥazzanim, which, despite its workaday immersion in money and status, remains a dangerous place. The third story is simply called "Haḥazzanim, hemshekh" ["The Ḥazzanim, Continued," pp. *113–21, 140–153*],[34] as if it is a continuation of the first story, "Haḥazzanim" about Miriam Devorah and R. Elya. There is no small irony in the fact that its protagonist is also named Gavriel despite the extreme difference between his nature and that of the two Gavriels who preceded him.

Already in the opening paragraph of the story we are plunged into an account of ḥazzanut that is very this-worldly; this is a picture of ḥazzanut as a profession rather than a spiritual calling. In his chronicler voice, the narrator informs us that by general custom ḥazzanim are released from the duties to their home congregations between Passover and Shavuot and allowed to make guest appearances in other communities to supplement their incomes. It is also an opportunity for ḥazzanim to advertise themselves and be looked at for new positions. Their employment, like that of rabbis, operates under conditions of an unregulated free market, and there is nothing that prevents a successful ḥazzan from being poached by a community that can offer him better terms.

We are further informed about the typical career path of a ḥazzan. He begins his training as a boy singer in the private choir of an established ḥazzan; with luck when he is older he becomes an associate ḥazzan in a community (*ḥazzan sheni*); and finally he becomes a ḥazzan on his own. This has been the path followed by Gavriel, the ḥazzan of Kamenets Podolskii, who arrives with his choir to spend a Shabbat performing in Buczacz.[35] His Buczacz appearance turns out to be a great success. He is held over for a second week, and Saturday evening after Shabbat the community leaders are enthralled when the troupe gives a heart-rending version of a hymn that tells the story of the fortunes of a pious but impoverished believer. On the spot Gavriel is offered the position of ḥazzan of Buczacz, a post that has lain vacant for many years.

Gavriel's triumph turns to dust when the terms offered him become clearer. He has badly misread the situation and assumed that because of its august reputation, Buczacz is a wealthy community that can easily sustain the expenses not only of a ḥazzan but also his choir. But as we the readers know from the beginning of the previous story, the community's resources have indeed been badly depleted by oppressive taxes and sums laid out to ransom captives, and paying the salary of a ḥazzan alone is already a significant challenge. Employing the choir with the ḥazzan is out of the question.

Yet what is evident as an unfortunate but necessary reality is experienced by Gavriel as fraud and chicanery of the worst kind. Promises had been made—at least in his mind—and then flagrantly violated. His feeling of betrayal is exacerbated by the defection of his bass singer Menasheh, who is recruited by a visiting leader of a neighboring community for the dual position of ḥazzan and husband to his widowed sister. Gavriel's response to these setbacks reveals much not only about him but also about ḥazzanut as a profession. He is consumed by rage. He threatens to bring the community to court until a sympathizer convinces him that this would be a futile effort. He and the members of his troupe parade through the streets of Buczacz barefoot to dramatize the unfairness done to them. He heaps abuse upon Buczacz and calls his troupe together to make a preemptory and contemptuous departure from the city only to find that no wagoner, Jew or gentile, will provide him with transportation, leaving him a humiliated prisoner in a city he reviles.

Gavriel's antics, it is implied, are part and parcel of the self-absorbed theatrics of the profession he practices. Like the maestros and prima donnas of the great age of opera, there are ḥazzanim who are by nature monsters of ego and grandiosity despite their ability to make angelic music. The first two Gavriels were exceptional creatures who occupied the highest rung of ḥazzanut as a sacred vocation; the belated, third Gavriel, alas, represents the norm. But rather than simply establishing that fact and leaving us with a caricature of the ḥazzan as a puffed up performer, "The Hazzanim Continued" tells the story of Gavriel's transformation into a complex figure worthy of our respect and pity.

One of the agents of Gavriel's change is none other than Buczacz itself. When Gavriel finally procures transport out of the city, he hears the wagoner singing in a pleasant voice one of the Sabbath melodies that he had performed during his stay in Buczacz. The wagoner suddenly stops his tune and when Gavriel asks why, he is told that the melody was so vivid in the wagoner's mind that he thought it was the Sabbath and was suddenly seized with fear that he was transgressing the law by driving his wagon. As the wagoner continues to sing more of Gavriel's melodies, the ḥazzan's anger begins to subside. He allows the wagoner to give him an account of the history of the ḥazzanut in Buczacz going back hundreds of years to the earliest of the Wernick family, to R. Elya's seventy-year tenure as ḥazzan, and to the story of the Gavriels, whose rejection of compensation for cantorial services this Gavriel finds incomprehensible. When the wagoner politely declines to sing some of the melodies of those ḥazzanim, Gavriel turns to the members of his troupe and says in a tone in which admiration overcomes sarcasm, "Have you ever in your life seen people as well-mannered as the people of Buczacz, who refuse to sing the melody of another ḥazzan in my presence?" (p. *116*, 144). His begrudging admiration reminds us of how the people of Buczacz reacted to his invectives and accusations. Rather than responding in kind, they refused to be provoked, they offered him some funds to help him place his charges in other cantorial choirs, and the good women of the town responded with empathy at the sight of the barefoot choristers.

It is in fact for the purpose of marrying one of these good women that Gavriel returns to Buczacz two years later. As a matter of principle, the narrator declines to track what befell him during that interval because it lies outside the subject of Buczacz and its ḥazzanim. What happens outside Buczacz apparently stays outside Buczacz. And what happened to him must have been substantial and extreme because when he reappears he is so utterly transformed that at first people don't believe it is the same person. "R. Gavriel was demanding, ill-tempered, and irascible, whereas this person speaks peaceably and amiably to everyone" (pp. *116–17*, 145).

The reasons for his transformation are mysterious; to be sure, we are informed that his wife has died, but it is implied that the real agent of change, or at least the catalyst for it, is Buczacz and its manners. Gavriel's unnamed second wife embodies what is best about the town. She is competent, well mannered, expert in the Bible, pious, and possessed of a good sense of humor (p. *117, 145–146*). Because she is disinclined to move to Kamenets Podolskii, Gavriel gives up his post there and, without position or standing, lives with her amicably in Buczacz. Soon, he is invited to pray before the teivah for the High Holidays, and eventually he is formally made ḥazzan of the community, this time with no histrionics on his part. There are some reminders of his old pride; he refuses to flatter the rich and odious at weddings and circumcisions ceremonies, a behavior to which the narrator gives a wink of approval. But all considered he acquits himself admirably.

Suddenly, after five years of service as ḥazzan, Gavriel recuses himself and resigns his position. "From that moment on he did not draw near to the teivah or pass before the teivah even on the anniversaries of the deaths of his father and mother" (p. *118, 147*). This abrupt and harsh self-imposed severance from his profession, the narrator informs us, is the result of a series of three bad dreams. The first two are neutralized by the comforting interpretations of his friends, but the third, which he reveals to no one until he is on his deathbed, proves his undoing. The first dream finds him leading public prayers on Yom Kippur when his *tsitsiyyot*, the fringes of his tallit, fly away from him eight times as he tries to gather them up during the Ahavah Rabbah prayer. His friends convince him that the dream cannot be probative because that prayer belongs to the morning service, which is not one conducted by the ḥazzan on Yom Kippur. The second dream also occurs on Yom Kippur. This time he is a boy serving in the choir of the ḥazzan of Lublin when he is struck on the forehead by the master and rebuked for not wearing his tefillin. Again, his friends argue that the dream has no real power because tefillin are not worn on Yom Kippur, and at the time he was a minor who as yet does not don tefillin. He is somewhat heartened until he is defeated by the third dream.

The third dream is the one that recurs eight nights in a row.

When he served as the associate ḥazzan in the Jewish community of Ostrog in the great synagogue and stood before the teivah during the morning service on the first day of Rosh Hashanah, a cannon that had been suspended in

the synagogue from the days of Khmelnytskyi fell on his maḥzor and on the
teivah, which sunk into the ground from the force of the impact. He heard a
kind of voice speaking, saying: "All this is the result of your actions." (p. *118*,
147–48)

This time he does not allow his friends to explain away the baleful implication of the dream—he does not even tell them—because he knows that
there is no comfort that can be given. He becomes a penitent, resigns his
position, and never again under any circumstances approaches the teivah.
He does, however, continue to be vigilant concerning the exacting standards governing the teivah. The slightest error in pronunciation or melody
made by a prayer leader is sure to provoke his visible disapprobation. This is
a mortifying dream under any circumstance but all the more so in an epistemic world in which dreams are not projections of the unconscious but
communications from heaven. The narrator offers no interpretation of the
dream, but none in truth is necessary because the structure of the story does
the job. The theatrical grandiosity and irascibility that Gavriel displayed on
his visit to Buczacz in the first part of the story is undoubtedly taken as a
symptom of his ongoing violation of the sanctity of the teivah by his antics.
To be sure, he is chastened when he returns to Buczacz two years later, and
after having been domesticated by the city's manners, he is allowed a period
of five years to serve as ḥazzan. But because of the severity of his offense,
payment eventually must be exacted.

The Impossible Profession

The fate of this third Gavriel brings to a close the third panel of Agnon's
cantorial triptych. The cantorate is presented in two aspects. It is an occupation; a salaried office; one of the kelei kodesh, the communal functionaries that include the shamash, the gabbai (unsalaried!), and, yes, the
rabbi, too. The relative wealth or poverty of a community often determines
the quality and character of the ḥazzan it can secure. At the same time, the
cantorate is a calling, a religious vocation in the classic sense, and this is the
dimension that interests Agnon. The calling is founded on an endowment
of spirituality, musical talent, and creativity that is inborn and distributed

unpredictably. An inordinately generous portion of this endowment descends upon the ill-fated Miriam Devorah, but because of the religious and social constraints of the world in which she lives, the gift becomes a curse. Not only is her life sacrificed but a hoary dynastic line of ḥazzanim is brought to an end.

Being a ḥazzan turns out to be a calling that is both necessary and nearly impossible to fulfill. The space next to the teivah before which the ḥazzan passes or into which he descends is a dangerous place for many reasons. The teivah does not suffer fools, and it demands exactitude, selflessness, and fear of heaven. But its most acute danger issues from the desire to close the distance between the self and the teivah. Sincere intimacy with the teivah, as we saw in the case of the first two Gavriels, breeds a desire for even more intimacy and for an unmediated path of worship and service and engenders impatience with the gap that the Exile has imposed. For such a soul, purveying the estimable commodities of Sabbath pleasure and holiday joy to a thankful congregation can never be enough.

The chronicles of the ḥazzanim of Buczacz cannot be brought to closure without a connection being made to Agnon's own self-myth. During the second half of the nineteenth century Buczacz was fortunate to enjoy the services of a ḥazzan from Russia. He crossed the border to Galicia, in flight from the authorities because he had rescued two Jewish boys from the hands of Jewish kidnappers and thereby prevented the boys from becoming cantonists, conscripts into the Tsar's army. He was accepted as ḥazzan in Buczacz because of his solid skills and good character despite his unfamiliar origins and despite the fact that his primary recommendation came from a Hasidic rebbe.

The narrator and the implied author merge as Agnon explicitly explains that this is the ḥazzan who played an important role in the autobiographical story "The Sign," which Emunah Yaron placed at the end of *A City in Its Fullness*, and which I placed at the beginning of the English edition. Like the earliest ḥazzanim of Buczacz, the narrator points out, the Russian ḥazzan served for many decades, and this longevity enabled a short overlap between his old age and the narrator's boyhood.[36] It is the "old ḥazzan," whose name curiously never is given in either story who first exposes the narrator to the pathos and power of Solomon Ibn Gabirol's piyyutim, and it is to this lofty tradition of sacred poetry that the narrator, despite his fallen métier of storytelling, later affiliates himself.

The last ḥazzan, also nameless, before the "First Destruction," Agnon's term for World War One, was a studious man who spent his days in the beit midrash when the narrator studied there as an adolescent. These were the years when the narrator first tried his hand at writing, and the first products of his pen were, of course, religious poems. Referring to the ḥazzan, the narrator tells us of his neighbor in the beit midrash: "I sometimes had the chance to speak with him and I even showed him some of my poems. Over the years he put them to music. Because I am not an expert in music and play no instrument, they did not remain in my mouth, and those poems and melodies were lost" (p. *122*, 152–53). Thus the narrator brings his chronicle of the ḥazzanim of Buczacz to a close, although we know, by virtue of the story we have read, that Buczacz would not remain forever without its sweet singer.

4

Rabbis and Scholars

The Crisis of the Rabbinate

"And these are the names of the early rabbis who reigned in Buczacz...."
(p. *301*). In this line, the opening words of book 2 of *A City in Its Fullness*, we may well pause over Agnon's choice to have his narrator use the
language of kingship to describe the role of Buczacz's community rabbis.
When referring to the Polish magnates who exerted total authority over
the city, the narrator uses the term *mashlu*, "they ruled"; but when it comes
to the rabbis and heads of the rabbinic court, it is always *malkhu*, "they
reigned." The lists of rabbis the narrator goes on to present, in the high
chronicle mode he has adopted, resemble nothing so much as the king lists
in the book of Genesis.

The notion of rabbi-kings reigning over Jewish city-states in an autono-
mous Polish Jewish commonwealth lies at the heart of Agnon's normative
vision of East European Jewish life in the early modern age. Normative, as
we have been using it in this study, connotes an ideal type, a structure of
value, a collective aspiration, and a choice of how to organize the memory
of the past. The fiction represents the constraints on these norms and the departures from them, but the norms themselves always remain palpable in the

ground beneath the fiction. There is undoubtedly a polemical charge to the assertion of this norm of autonomy.

Agnon is conducting an embroiled dialogue with Zionist historiography. On the one hand, as a religious Zionist, he is projecting the categories of nationalism backward onto to the history of the Jews in Eastern Europe and claiming their experiences for Zionism. Buczacz came into being as an accidental way-station for Rhineland Jews who had set out to ascend to Zion, according to the myth of origins that opens *A City in Its Fullness*. And after they were settled and able, the Jews of Buczacz and other settlements sought to create self-sufficient and self-governing Jewish polities. On the other hand, writing in the 1950s and 1960s, Agnon is doing battle with the nativist Zionism of Ben-Gurion and the young people from the youth movements who fought in the War of Independence. For them, the establishment of Israel represented victory over the Exile, which was conceived of as a gentile-ridden and shame-inducing aberration that made Jews dependent for survival upon the obfuscations of religion. Against this view, Agnon presents Buczacz as a highly evolved corporate organism that deployed a politics appropriate to the challenges that faced it and, in the best of times, maintained a balance between this-worldliness and religious culture.

Agnon widens the focus from Buczacz to the totality of Polish and Lithuanian Jewry at the conclusion to the introduction to the two great narratives about rabbis in book 2. In decrying the forced disbanding in 1764 of the Council of Four Lands, the quasi-legislative body that governed Polish and Lithuanian Jewry for almost two hundred years, Agnon's narrator makes this claim.

A nation worn down and vexed,[1] which lacking the force of a monarch and his ministers and possessing only the authority of the Torah, comes together to formulate and promulgate decrees and ordinances that are accepted by the entire people like the edicts of kings. When a king establishes a police force to subdue the people by rod and whip and impose his decrees, they flaunt those decrees, and many are the rebels who sin against the king's will. Yet the holy people Israel willingly accepted all that was placed upon them by the eminences of the Council of the Lands, which was like the Sanhendrin in the Chamber of Hewn Stone in the Temple. (p. *308*)

Now, our proud chronicler may be guilty of over-praising his coreligionists and denigrating the workings of the gentile regime, but his claim is profound and far-reaching. Despite the fact that the Jews had no state and were ruled by others, they contrived to constitute themselves as a self-governing commonwealth, and they were able to do so because of the universally accepted authority of the Torah, which purchased compliance out of respect rather than fear. Rather than religious belief being a surrogate for true national existence, as argued by the standard Zionist critique of the diaspora, it is in fact the opposite. It is the allegiance to the Torah that allowed Jews to maintain a coherent corporate existence under conditions of adversity.

The sway of Torah, according to the normative worldview of the narrator, depends upon the true rabbis who reign over the poleis that make up this vast invisible Jewish state. The true rabbi-king is both a scholar and a decisor (*posek*; *poskim*, plural). He studies and teaches Torah for its own sake and at the same time functions as a judge who interprets the law and applies it to concrete ritual and commercial problems. He is the *mara de'atra*, literally, the master of the locality, the religious authority of the community in which he serves; and, if his legal opinions are astute and published in book form, his authority is recognized beyond his locality and brings him, and his town, fame.

In truth, however, the chronicler's image of the rabbi-king reigning over the Jewish city-state is a norm that bears a tangled relationship to historical actuality. Far from being sovereign, all rabbis were employees of the kahal and served for limited terms at the pleasure of the community's lay leadership. (A précis of such a letter of rabbinic appointment, a contract delineating duties and compensation, appears at the beginning of the great saga about the quest for a rabbi for Buczacz [pp. *312–13, 257–59*], which I discuss below.) Although the rabbi had authority in legal and ritual matters, his employment ultimately depended upon his acceptability to the wealthy householders who controlled the kahal.

However, the constraints on rabbinic autonomy did not come solely from within the Jewish community. In many cases the office of rabbi was a leasehold that must be purchased from the Polish magnate who owned the town in which the Jewish community was located. For the magnate it was just another resource that could be monetized, another source of revenue. Just in the way that a Jew would buy the rights to operate a tavern or a flour mill or, in the case of the story we are about to discuss, to operate fish ponds or salt works, a rabbinic seat often had to be acquired by the rabbi himself or by his family on his behalf. This in turn forced the rabbi to exact payment for his services, especially from the Jews living in surrounding villages, to recoup the steep investment made in purchasing the office. The degree of interference by the local lord or the estate administrator in rabbinic appointments differed from place to place, but never was it wholly absent.[2]

By the eighteenth century, the communal rabbinate in Poland was an institution assailed from many directions. Community rabbis, it was often held, were "ignorant, venal, politicized, and dependent on outside power to maintain their authority."[3] Communal leaders, who sought to preserve the viability of their communities in the face of the magnates' demands for ever-increasing revenues, resented the rabbis' interference and competition in their negotiations with the gentile authorities.

The scholarly elite found many community rabbis ignorant of Bible and Mishnah and the works of the early Talmud commentators (the *rishonim*). They argued that likely in any given community, numbers of individual scholars resided who were more accomplished than the community's rabbi and better able to sort out thorny legal cases. The maskilim found the rabbis' ignorance of proper Hebrew and Polish and general history to be as disturbing as their unfamiliarity with Bible and Mishnah. They advocated rabbis being elected by the whole community rather than its commercial elite, and they wanted their influence restricted to kashrut and other narrow ritual matters.

The early leaders of Hasidism found rabbis guilty of aloofness from the needs of the people, both spiritual and social. In their drive to maintain their sinecures, it was argued, rabbis ended up oppressing the people rather than caring for them.[4] Although some of these generalizations do not always apply to Buczacz as presented by Agnon, this may be due in part to the exceptionalism of Buczacz encoded in *A City in Its Fullness*.

One might conclude from this broad-based critique that the continued existence of the rabbinate was endangered or deserved to be. But historians have cautioned us not to construct a false sense of crisis out of these criticisms. Similar criticisms long had been lodged against the rabbinate; yet the reality is that the position of communal rabbi continued to be a nearly universal feature of Jewish towns and cities. This coexistence of dissatisfaction with the rabbinate and its persistence helps us to understand the composite and complicated stance of Agnon's narrator in *A City in Its Fullness* toward the institution. He is deeply conservative and traditional in his desire for allegiance to a vision of a rabbi who combines the roles of erudite scholar and communal spiritual leader, and who retains his independence in the face of pressures from gentile authorities and from Jewish interests that are not aligned with Torah. The narrator identifies with the Holy Community of Buczacz in longing for the kind of rabbi that Buczacz feels it is entitled to according to its sense of itself and its spiritual aspirations.

At the same time, as an honest chronicler with an allegiance to historical actuality, the narrator has a duty to present the record of Buczacz's foiled, ineffectual efforts to secure the kind of rabbi it desires. The narrator is constrained to present and analyze the forces that conspire to frustrate Buczacz's quest: the city's inflated sense of its power and importance, the growing wealth of other cities that enabled them to poach the rabbis of Buczacz with impunity, and the baleful interference of the Polish magnates and their agents in internal Jewish communal appointments to maximize their own revenues. It is the interplay between longing and truth-telling that informs Agnon's engagements with the rabbinate in *A City in Its Fullness*.

Aside from the chronicle-like introduction to book 2, there are three major textual formations that deal with the rabbinate of Buczacz. Two of them are the long stories that comprise book 2: "In Search of a Rabbi" or "The Governor's Whim" ["Hamevakshim lahem rav" o "Beruaḥ hamoshel," pp. *309–93, 253–368*] and "The Parable and Its Lesson" ["Hamashal vehanimshal," pp. *394–440*]. The third is an assortment of stories in book 3 (pp. *441–46*, and *543–57*) that report on the tenure of three beloved rabbis who served roughly continuous terms from the end of the eighteenth century to the middle of the nineteenth. Their names together with the books by which they were known are: R. Zvi Hirsch Kra, *Net'a sha'ashu'im*; R. Avraham David Wahrman, *Da'at kedoshim*; and R. Avraham Teomim, *Ḥesed le'Avraham*. These three rabbis boast the further distinction—very important to our patriotic narrator—of faithfulness to Buczacz. Once they assumed their positions as rabbi of the town, rather than being lured away or bought off, they served until their deaths and were buried in the soil of Buczacz.

So, with such a run of good luck—however belated—where is the warrant for Buczacz's complaint about its ill-starred efforts to find a rabbi and where is the trenchant critique of the rabbinate? The answer hinges on the question of authority. These three later rabbis served the town after it passed from Polish rule and became incorporated into Galicia, a province of the Austrian monarchy. One of the hallmarks of this change, which is broadly described in the story "Disappeared" ["Hane'elam," pp. *448–91, 369–426*], is the diminution of rabbinic authority and the transfer of all but ritual matters from the town's beit din, of which the rabbi served as dean, to the civil courts.

The sway of Torah had been generally constricted. These rabbis may indeed have been exemplars of learning and piety, but because of the altered social and political conditions under which they served, it cannot be said that they "reigned" over Buczacz. The events of their rabbinates are conveyed through vignettes and reportage but not through the kind of sustained and organic fictions that were possible when rabbinic authority mattered more. It is not accidental that in the formidable stories in the last third of *A City in Its Fullness*, all of which take place during the terms of these rabbis and all of which deal with themes of social oppression, rabbis make virtually no appearance. They have no power to ameliorate the suffering and injustice corrupting the community over which their predecessors once exerted the prerogatives of Jewish law.

When it comes to adducing the paragon of a rabbi, then, it is little wonder that a true example can be found only in an earlier age. Such a figure is R. Moshe in the story "The Parable and Its Lesson," which, as mentioned

above, is one of the two major narratives of book 2.[5] The time of the action is the generation after the Khmelnytskyi massacres and the Tatar and
Turkish invasions, a century before Austrian rule and the tenure of the three
long-serving rabbis.

As seen through the admiring gaze of his assistant, the shamash,
R. Moshe is presented as the apotheosis of the rabbi-king. He is the opposite of the aloof scholar who cares only for impressing others with dazzling
legal dialectics. He is deeply engaged not only with the material rebuilding
of his community after the massacres but also with healing the theological
wounds inflicted by the trauma. His empathy is emblematized by his devotion to an orphaned girl who is the only one of his relations to survive. She
becomes a fifteen-year-old agunah (*agunot*, plural) when she is abandoned
by her husband, the rabbi's most beloved student, whose questioning of
God's justice has dispatched him on a path of self-destruction. It is to save
her that the rabbi risks a descent into Gehinnom.

As revealed at close quarters by the shamash, R. Moshe is shown to be
a holy man of great discipline and integrity. He guards his mouth from
speaking guile. He not only knows the Bible intimately, but his speech is
made up of verses that are quoted with exquisite precision. He is devoted
to the studying and reciting of Mishnah as well as the Talmud and its commentators. He uses his sermons not to show off his learning but to respond
to the community's need for consolation and healing.

Most of all R. Moshe reigns over Buczacz. His reign may be benevolent
and wise but his authority is manifest nonetheless. The shamash recalls an
incident in which a rich Jewish tax collector was summoned before the rabbinic court because he had slapped and humiliated a poor *melamed*. When
the powerful man refused to appear, the shamash was dispatched to brave
angry dogs and brazen servants to deliver his master's message. "That tax collector paid for his sin in this world on top of what awaits him in the world to
come," the shamash concludes and says, "No one defies our Master" (p. *401*).

This picture of the rabbi's sway over his community is surely, in part,
a projection of his assistant's adulation of his master and nostalgia for a
past that is now more than fifty years distant; and, moreover, absent from

the picture is any pressure from gentile authorities or any resistance from wealthy householders. But the possibility of the existence of this kind of authority, despite the iconographic heightening, is supported by the historical conditions. In the years after 1648, the Polish nobles were busy rebuilding their estates, which had been overrun in the Cossack Rebellion, and they needed the commercial acumen of the Jews to reestablish the urban market economy. Among the Jews as well, the process of rebuilding and recovery had not yet produced the extremes of wealth that would encourage commercial elites to challenge rabbinic mandates.[6]

Between the commanding authority of R. Moshe and the belated marginality of the three rabbis, we find the historical world of "In Search of a Rabbi, or The Governor's Whim" (pp. *309–93, 253–368*).[7] The events are set in the second half of the eighteenth century, both before and after the partition of Poland and the introduction of a centralized Austrian administration.

Note the two-part structure of the story's title carefully. In the first position is Buczacz's quest for a rabbi, with all it assumes about the very possibility of authoritative rabbinic leadership and the unremitting desire for it. In the second position stands the will or desire of the gentile rulers. Both parts of the title encourage a reading in a mildly mocking tone. "Look who is looking for a rabbi!" is one of the ways the first part can be understood, as if to call attention to Buczacz's inflated sense of itself. In the second part, the ruler's ruaḥ—one of the most plastic words in the Hebrew language— can move anywhere along a gradient from "spirit" to "temperament," as if to underscore utter dependence upon his whim or will.

Finally, there is the matter of the "or" that separates the two. The use of "or" after a primary title, as in Richardson's *Pamela, or Virtue Rewarded*, is a familiar, if now disused, convention. The question here is whether the "or" implies an equivalence or identity between the two, or whether it presents the second as an alternative to the first, and if so, whether this prospect sounds an ominous bell that indicates that the first (the Jews of Buczacz) will be appropriated or taken over by the second (the ruler). The reader embarks upon the story with these possibilities in mind and returns later to see which are confirmed. At the very least, the title suggests that the narrative, in its theme and structure, will likely be divided in two, and this turns out to be very much the case.

This narrative lies at the vital, epic center of *A City in Its Fullness* as a whole. It comes at the midpoint of the book, and, novella-like at nearly ninety pages, it is by far the longest story. It is also the most ambitious, both thematically and compositionally. The first half of the story addresses nothing less than the question of what is the true nature of Torah study and whether the vocation of the sage who engages in such study can still be combined with the role of the community rabbi. The second half explores the conflict between two wealthy Jewish arrendators who lease the rights to large-scale projects (fish ponds and salt works) from separate Polish noblemen. The competition between them is brought to a pitch of violent reprisals by the vagaries of nature and by the rival interests of the Gentile lords who back them. Because a conflict of this proportion threatens the Jewish commonweal, the parties are forced—not once but three times—to submit to the arbitration of a beit din; but the authority of the rabbinic court is flouted in all instances, the first two times because the businessmen withdraw from the proceedings and the last because a powerful lord over-turns a verdict inconvenient to him.[8]

Epic Designs

"In Search of a Rabbi" is an immensely ambitious work characterized by great shifts in time and space. When it comes to time, the novella has an envelope structure; it starts in the recent past but moves further and further back in time until it snaps back to the beginning. When it comes to space, the work begins and ends in Buczacz, yet all the significant action takes place elsewhere. The kinds of spaces in which the action unfolds are extreme in their differences; the cramped confines of a rabbi's study yield to an inn in an isolated village, which, in turns gives way to an immense landscape of fields, rivers, and pools and, most of all, the vast and unpredictable heavens above them. How—and whether—Agnon succeeds in holding together this vast composition is a question that I address below. First it is necessary to understand how the pieces of this complex work fit together. For that purpose the following I offer the following chart.

The Structure of Chapter Four

WHO IS TELLING THE STORY?	PRESENT	RECENT PAST	A GENERATION EARLIER	DISTANT PAST	NUMBER OF PAGES
The narrator	1. Embassy from Buczacz to Zabno				5
R. Avraham's monologue		2. R. Avraham and R. Mordekhai study together			17
Monologue continues			3. R. Mordekhai's education		14
Monologue continues			4. Conflict between Reuven and Shimon. The great flood		35
Monologue continues			5. R. Mordekhai and his teacher study together over Shabbat		3
The narrator resumes	6. The return to Buczacz and R. Mordekhai's rejection of the rabbinate				10

First, we observe that, although the story begins and ends in Buczacz, the great preponderance of the action takes place away from Buczacz. This structure represents the fact that fulfillment of Buczacz's desire to acquire rabbinic leadership is ultimately dependent on external factors over which it has little control. Second, the main action of the story is delivered through the late-night monologue of R. Avraham of Zabno. The narrator reports directly only the beginning and concluding sections (1 and 5). The felt "narratedness" of R. Avraham's monologue fades after section 2, but it nevertheless remains important to keep in mind that the story is told to us through the eyes of this scholarly community rabbi. Third, the movement of the plot is recursive. The action moves from the near present back in time through at least two generations and, as we see, this movement crosses—in reverse—the boundary represented by the partition of Poland in 1772.

The motive for reaching back into the past is the desire to explain how the Buczacz tinsmith R. Mordekhai came to become the prodigy he is. We read first of his remarkable education at the hands of a rabbi who had to flee persecution; then we learn the back story that explains the circumstances that compelled him to flee. Fourth, a glance at the number of pages devoted to each section indicates that section 4, which is the furthest removed in time from the present and ostensibly bears the least relevance to Buczacz's rabbinic search, in fact takes up half the novella. The disproportionate disposition of these narrative materials poses a challenge, especially because of the significant differences in the mode of writing between the story of the conflict between Reuven and Shimon and the earlier sections. I address this challenge below.

"In Search of a Rabbi" explores the relationship between two models of rabbinic leadership.[9] The first is the pure Torah scholar whose studies have no connection to the governance of a community and no connection to livelihood. His learning is disinterested. He views himself as a link in the great chain of tradition that began with the Sages of the Mishnah and Talmud, continued with great medieval authorities (early and late), and now passes through him. His responsibility to this tradition is to conserve it and purge it of error but also to advance it by novel interpretations and conceptual refinements. Even though he may not be engaged in tending to the pastoral needs of the community, the whole Jewish people depend upon the theoretical work he is undertaking to secure the enduring truth of the Torah. Needless to say, the only kind of rabbi who can fulfill this vocation is one graced with enormous mental brilliance and who possesses enormous mastery of the texts of the tradition.

The second model of rabbinic leadership is not different; it takes the first and adds to it. This is the community rabbi who manages his pastoral duties *in addition* to making signal contributions to Torah scholarship. His communal duties include delivering public sermons on special occasions, supervising the religious courts and serving as the final arbiter of halakhic questions, and offering advanced instruction in Torah studies. (I provide a fuller account of these duties as delineated in Buczacz's letter of rabbinic appointment below.) There seems to be no shortage of ordinary community rabbis during this period; but great rabbi-scholars are rare, and only wealthy communities can afford them.

Here's the rub. The kind of rabbi Buczacz is searching for is the great rabbi-scholar. The problem is that, in terms of its material wealth, Buczacz is a second- or third-tier Galician city, and it simply cannot compete. Yet, in terms of its spiritual wealth—the strength of its beit midrash and the large number of highly schooled members of the community—Buczacz views itself as fully deserving of a great rabbi-scholar. But over and over again it has been thwarted in its efforts to secure such a prize. Candidates are poached by other communities; unscrupulous lay leaders purloin letters of invitation meant for their rabbi; others are scared away because of what they have heard about the capriciousness of the family of Polish nobles who own the city. Buczacz has been without a rabbi for ten years because one such great man, R. Leibush Auerbach, who was born in Buczacz and educated in its beit midrash, was lured away by the up-and-coming community of Stanislaw.[10] Buczacz kept waiting for him to recognize the superiority of his spiritual home and return. It was only after his death that the good people of Buczacz come to terms with the finality of the rejection and acknowledge the necessity to fill the rabbinic seat.

This is the point of departure for the novella. After protracted divisiveness, Buczacz finally pulls itself together and coalesces around a single candidate for community rabbi. It sets its sights on R. Moshe Avraham Abush Margolis, the Rabbi of Zabno, known later after his work, as Tsiluta d'Avraham. (He is called simply R. Avraham throughout the story.) A delegation made up of three of the most venerable scholars in the city is appointed and dispatched to Zabno—a journey requiring a month's time—to present a formal letter of rabbinic appointment to R. Avraham, who as yet knows nothing of Buczacz's plans for him. What makes him such an attractive prospect? It goes without saying that his piety and family lineage are above reproach and are said to resemble in their depth those of Maharam Schiff, a renowned German rabbi from the previous century. (Little do the scholars realize that Maharam Schiff himself will descend from the heavens and make an appearance in the story that R. Avraham soon tells them.) After the worthies of Buczacz arrive in Zabno, they are invited to R. Avraham's home and they engage him in conversation. Because the embassy to R. Avraham is intended both to impress and probe, the early pages of the story (pp. *310–14, 254–60*) have the quality of an exquisitely refined dance; acting within the rarified etiquette and parlance of the scholarly class, the visitors use every opportunity to display their erudition to their host and observe how it registers on him.

But when it comes time for the rabbi to take charge of the conversation, he turns matters in a different direction. Although he seems entirely persuaded of the high level of Jewish learning in Buczacz, he is less sanguine about the city's political fortunes, about which he shows himself to be remarkably conversant. He knows that the city has a new ruler, and he inquires about his disposition toward the Jews and his susceptibility to bribery. He asks about a wagon, full of Jewish artisans from Buczacz who were kidnapped by a Polish lord and delivered to the ruler of Stanislaw as reparations for a Jew he had murdered. By making these inquiries, R. Avraham is not trying to better his advantage or to take Buczacz down a peg. Yet he is implying that it may be better to be a rabbi in a town like Zabno—smaller and less learned than Buczacz—than to officiate in a more substantial community that is constantly subject to the whims of gentile rulers (hence the subtitle of the novella). His skepticism on this score, bruited so early in the story—and in the very title of the novella itself—serves to adumbrate what becomes its major preoccupation.

When the representatives from Buczacz get down to the business that brought them to Zabno, they present the rabbi with a letter of rabbinical appointment that was carefully formulated by the communal leadership before their departure. This is a formal document, fully consistent with the practice of the times, which lists the duties of the position and its compensation. In giving us a précis of that document, the narrator omits the routine responsibilities and focuses on the issues that are of special importance for the community of Buczacz. Rather than being merely a checklist of responsibilities, the letter in fact reflects back upon its framers and opens a precious window onto the holy community of Buczacz and its aspirations.

The Rabbi of Buczacz, to begin with, should lead the community in peace and equanimity, avoiding intrigues and controversies, even those undertaken "for the sake of Heaven." If a case of an agunah presents itself to the rabbi, he should devote his attention to resolving it even if it comes from far away, and he should not be constrained by legal over-scrupulousness in pursuing a solution. When he delivers his major homilies several times a year, he should take care to include—in addition to the customary learned Talmudic arguments—stories and parables from the aggadah to attend to the spiritual nourishment of the common people. Coming from outside Buczacz, he should not use his rabbinic authority to supplant or replace the minhagim of the city, especially when it comes to the recitation of the piyyutim that are part of its ancient rite. He should refrain from writing amulets for the ill and restrict himself to praying on their behalf. Finally, when it comes to the fast of the 20th of Sivan, the day of remembrance for the victims of 1648, he should be steadfast in preventing erosion of its observance and insist that the fast be kept even by individuals visiting Buczacz from lands that were not affected by the massacres.

The letter of rabbinic appointment conveys the ideal of the rabbinate as a reflection of Buczacz's ideal image of itself. Buczacz sees itself as—or, more accurately, longs to become—a community that avoids divisiveness, defends the defenseless, cares for the spiritual needs of all its members, insists on the dignity of its traditions, and pays its debt of commemoration to its martyrs. All this is in addition to zeal in areas of worship and learning, which are taken for granted. Together these aspirations describe the true kehilah kedoshah, holy community, which is how Buczacz sees its best self. (If the city were larger and wealthier and unencumbered by capricious gentile rulers, it would be in a stronger position to secure a rabbi equal to its aspirations.) The image of the rabbi they seek is likewise aspirational. They seek a rabbi whose scholarship is impressive and publically acknowledged and who will also be actively engaged in supervising the spiritual life of the community, as well as being available, as in the case of agunot, to take on ethical challenges that go beyond the local level. They seek, in other words, the consummate scholar-rabbi.

R. Avraham declines to accept the great distinction offered him by the representatives of Buczacz. But, in the same breath that he gives his refusal, he presents his guests with an alternative candidate, one who he claims is not only far worthier than he but already dwells among them in Buczacz. This is the tinsmith R. Mordekhai. The worthies of Buczacz are dimly aware of his existence among the artisans of the city, but they are wholly ignorant of his scholarship. The very notion that the scholarly accomplishments of a common artisan could exceed those of a man like R. Avraham violates nearly all their assumptions about the way in which the world works and the way in which class, lineage, and scholarly achievement are woven together. That such a luminary of Torah should work in their backyard while they are unaware of his very presence is almost beyond belief, and it is only because the news comes from a man of R. Avraham's eminence that they take it seriously. Struggling with this stunning development, the Buczacz delegates press R. Avraham for information about this extraordinary tinsmith. Some ask for an account of his scholarship, and others ask for an account of his life.[11]

In deciding to supply an account of R. Mordekhai's life, R. Avraham makes the great, fateful decision that sets the whole of "In Search of a Rabbi" in motion. The decision is of course Agnon's. He has the general narrator of the story pass the baton to R. Avraham, who then proceeds to embark on a monologue that takes up almost the entire novella. To be sure, the monologue is a solution to a formal problem. The only way we can credibly be brought inside the intimate interaction between R. Mordekhai and R. Avraham is through the account of an eye witness. And, moreover, it is only to R. Avraham's ears that R. Mordekhai discloses the extraordinary story of his origins, and so hearing it from the former means hearing it first-hand.

However, the monologue is also an act fraught with ethical implications. R. Avraham's decision to relate the life of R. Mordekhai rather than his scholarship is made without its subject's consent. That the modest tinsmith from Buczacz is a scholar of phenomenal genius is a fact that has been hidden from public knowledge. That concealment has been the product of R. Mordekhai's own desire, and he had exacted an oath from R. Avraham to honor his wish. In acceding to the request of the Buczacz visitors, R. Avraham is supremely aware of the fatefulness of his choice. He announces to his guests: "I am about to reveal to you matters that I have concealed until now. This is what the rabbis meant when they said, 'There is no man who does not have his hour, and there is no man who does not have his place.' R. Mordekhai's hour has arrived, and I shall tell of it," (p. *314*, 261). With these words, R. Avraham launches into the great monologue that tells R. Mordekhai's story and in so doing violates the promise made to guard his secrets. The passage from Pirkei Avot (4:3) adduced to mitigate the willfulness of this unsanctioned choice is malleable and enigmatic. Even if the statement means that each person has his appointed hour to shine, how is it that R. Avraham arrogates to himself the decision about when the hour of another man has arrived?

The great irony of the monologue is that it is R. Avraham's secrets that are revealed rather than those of his erstwhile subject. True, R. Mordekhai's life is indeed exposed against his will, but in what is revealed there is nothing to cause anything but admiration. It is the story of a prodigy who came late to the study of Torah, mastered its monumental complexity, and then remained true to his teacher's counsel to avoid public office and live by his own handiwork. It is a principled and steady life whose only drama lies in its willed concealment. It is R. Avraham's soul that is unwittingly bared in the progress of the telling, and it turns out to be a soul far more vulnerable and unaware of itself than that of his younger colleague. His inadvertent confession is a great gift because it gives us the opportunity to look into the inner life of an eighteenth-century Torah scholar. Although R. Avraham was a historical character (c. 1720–c. 1800), the rich, subjectivity with which he has been endowed is entirely Agnon's invention. This is the kind of access that only Agnon's imaginative technique can grant us. R. Avraham's monologue becomes a confirmation of Agnon's foundational intuition that it is story rather than teaching that provides truth.[12]

Scholarship as Contest

R. Avraham is the perfect monologist because of his fidelity to the truth and his lack of self-awareness. Despite the fact that he is an astute and seasoned Talmudist, he is insensible to how he is perceived by others, and he is unresponsive to humiliation, because all he cares about is Torah. He is a well-regarded communal rabbi and a scholar of wide repute with a sense of his own worth; yet when his authority is assailed and his scholarship questioned, he has no difficulty stepping aside in favor of a deeper understanding of Torah presented by others, even if it is at his expense. When he becomes passionately dependent upon his late-night meetings with R. Mordekhai and their scholarly exchanges, he possesses scarcely any awareness of the obsessive nature of the relationship he has entered into. Taken together, these qualities make him an honest reporter of his experience, if a poor judge of it. He lacks the guile and self-interest to skew and manipulate, and this makes him that rare thing in modern fiction: a reliable narrator. His faithfulness to the study of Torah trumps his need for recognition. But his ability to put himself aside does not mean that he is without needs. When he becomes emotionally enmeshed in his relationship with R. Mordekhai, he is wonderfully capable of describing all the symptoms of his condition without the least consciousness of their meaning.

The opening scene of his monologue, in which he is publically humbled and first meets R. Mordekhai, is funny in the way that only Agnon can be. The scene takes place at a circumcision feast in a village outside of Zabno. In the learned discourse he gives to embellish the occasion, he presents what he considers a "great *hidush*" (an original, innovative insight; *hidushim*, plural) on the question of circumcision before the Giving of the Torah, and then to save the Ari (R. Isaac Luria) from suspicion of contradicting the Talmud, he goes on to present a "huge pilpul" that, in passing, resolves difficulties experienced by the scholarly world in parsing a passage in tractate Zevaḥim. As he is delivering what he considers a virtuoso performance, he notices seated at the table a man in his thirties with quick and acute eyes who is wearing strange garb and a ridiculous-looking hat. As the rabbi makes his points, the man makes dismissive gestures with his shoulders. This only provokes R. Avraham to pull out all the stops. "What did I do? I took up a matter that I had presented to great scholars who thought that it was as profound as the ḥidushim of Maharam Schiff," (p. *315*, *262*). But even to this pièce de résistance, the response of the man in the funny hat is a contemptuous hand gesture.

It was the comparison to Maharam Schiff, the reader may recall, that made R. Avraham so attractive to Buczacz in the first place. Maharam Schiff is a title of honor for Meir ben Jacob Hakohen Schiff, a German rabbi and Talmud scholar, who died in 1644 at the age of thirty-six. He composed comments and commentaries on all the tractates of the Talmud although only a small portion of them survived and were published. In a terse and often obscure style, Schiff engages his subjects directly without the digressive recourse to remote textual locations that characterized much Talmud scholarship at the time. His penetrating analyses display impatience with the positions of some of the greatest of the early authorities.

The connection between R. Avraham and Maharam Schiff turns out to be the farthest thing from a mere conceit. When the festive meal is over, R. Avraham approaches the stranger and asks what in his discourse caused him dissatisfaction. The stranger replies:

> "You are the one about whom the world says that his ḥidushim are as deep as those of Maharam Schiff. Neither you nor your ilk who make themselves out to understand Maharam Schiff know what they are talking about." I said to him, "Does the master have in mind a particular ḥidush?" He waved his hand and said, "What do I need one ḥidush when they are all the same? 'The dream of Pharaoh is one and the same.'" (p. *315*, 262)

A more summary and derisive dismissal is hard to imagine. In the meantime, the stranger proceeds to undertake a systematic critique not only of the arguments R. Avraham had made in his discourse but of "all the ḥidushim that are stated in my name in batei midrash and the yeshivot." The critique rolls on to lay waste to many of the insights of such towering figures as Yosef Karo, Moshe Isserles, and Shlomo Luria. Yet, again, rather than taking personal umbrage or expressing pain or injury, R. Avraham says of himself, "I stood like someone who is stunned and I shook my head at myself for having caused the words of our great sages, those from whose mouths we live, to become vulnerable to refutation" (p. *316*, 263).

It is at this moment that the figure who we discover to be R. Mordekhai intervenes to defend the honor of the Rabbi of Zabno. But rather than being relieved, R. Avraham is shaken by two disorienting revelations. The first is that a wagon driver dressed in workman's clothes is capable of engaging in the kind of learned discourse that is the preserve of the highest levels of the scholarly elite. The second revelation, which is told to him by the wagon driver, concerns the identity of the stranger with the ridiculous hat. He is none other than Maharam Schiff himself, who, according to R. Avraham's quick calculation, died 120 years earlier. The strange dress and hat are the costume German Jews were forced to wear, which is confirmed by the fact that a rabbi dressed in this fashion had once visited him in a dream to explain a perplexing passage.

Why does a great sage bestir himself from the Heavenly Academy to sully R. Avraham's reputation? Events happen so fast that the question remains unanswered. Still anonymous and incognito, R. Mordekhai takes leave to defend R. Avraham before Maharam Schiff. Displaying prodigious erudition and acuity, he undertakes a point-by-point refutation that attempts to buttress the ḥidushim of R. Avraham and restore the foundational authority of the great scholars whose views have been undermined. Maharam Schiff fires back with a rebuttal that disproves each of the counter arguments. And when R. Mordekhai is about to make a comeback, Maharam Schiff effectively tells him not to bother because he has already anticipated and negated all arguments he could possibly mount. Seeing no way out, R. Mordekhai shifts the focus to a different topic, and the two continue to contend, with the advantage moving back and forth between the two scholars.

The scene is intensely cinematic and resembles nothing so much as a duel between Samurai swordsmen. A lowly and nondescript commoner suddenly springs into action and takes on a grand master—a visitor from the Other World, no less—and, through a sustained series of dexterous moves, miraculously holds him at bay, all the while defending the honor of a well-meaning but limited bystander. The contest between Maharam Schiff and R. Mordekhai is a dramatic enactment of the concept of *milḥamtah shel torah*, the combat of Torah, the idea that the truth of the halakhah can be arrived at *only* through a contentious encounter between two antagonists who give no quarter and vigorously test each other's arguments. The more trenchant and searching the attack—and the counter-attack—the more likely it is to expose conceptual and logical flaws that must be rethought or shored up to secure the edifice of Torah. Although this contestation is fiercely adversarial, it remains impersonal because, ideally, it is entered into on behalf of the honor and integrity of the Torah and not on behalf of individual distinction or repute or ad hominem animosity. Scholars who hold one another in affection and respect assume the role of antagonists for the purpose of this necessary combat and revert to collaborative contact once the goal is achieved.

This is the exemplary model that describes the ongoing relationship between R. Avraham and R. Mordekhai after they encounter one another at the circumcision feast. Less exemplary, ironically, is the behavior of the magisterial scholar from the previous century. Maharam Schiff is moved to descend from heaven for more proprietary reasons. Having heard tell of a scholar whose ḥidushim are said to be as profound as his own, he undertakes a visitation upon earth to protect his reputation and safeguard his legacy. His affect is embittered and rancorous, and it is only after R. Mordekhai invites him to present teachings of his that were not preserved in writing that we come to understand the pathos of his life and the reasons for his defensive bitterness. Before his early death, he gave his unpublished writings to his daughter to keep in a locked strongbox for his descendants to release to the world. But the box was broken into, many of his ḥidushim were published unscrupulously by others under their names, and the box itself was destroyed in the great conflagration in the city of Frankfurt. The theft and the fire have been kept from him by Heaven so that he would not be anguished. Yet even without knowledge of these calamities, the fact remains that the majority of his life's work remains unknown, and the soul of this great scholar remains unquiet and unreconciled.

Where is R. Avraham while the duel rages? He has been pushed to the sidelines like a damsel whose honor is being fought over by others. Which emotions seize him? He is stunned, to be sure; but his emotional state is the opposite of that of the dour and bellicose Maharam Schiff. Oblivious to the fact that his own reputation in the academies and study houses is hanging in the balance, R. Avraham is so enthralled by the high-level scholarly thrust and parry unfolding before his eyes that he says, "my soul was about to depart from an abundance of bliss [*metikut*]" (p. *317*, 264). If it were not for the howling of the just-circumcised baby precisely at that moment, he claims he would have died of ecstasy and gone to the place from which Maharam Schiff had just descended. When the arrival of the time for the afternoon prayer brings an end to the battle of wits, the attention of the company is drawn to a new issue.[13]

R. Avraham's amalgam of insensibility and innocence stands him in good stead after Maharam Schiff departs. R. Mordekhai and Maharam Schiff were locked in combat during the great sage's visitation; but with his departure, the two mortals, men who had never met before, are thrown together and left to make sense of this extraordinary occurrence. And the occurrence *is* extraordinary. The world of this story, as that of all of the stories in *A City in Its Fullness*, is not a universe of magic realism in which violations of natural law are taken for granted. Both R. Avraham and R. Mordekhai are supremely aware that a miracle has transpired of which they are the stunned beneficiaries. What they do in the aftermath of this marvelous and uncanny experience is the test of their mettle. Their immediate reaction is to sit down and reconstruct for themselves the critiques the sage had lodged against the current scholarly consensus, of which R. Avraham's work is an integral part, as well as the unpublished ḥidushim the master had vouchsafed to them. Their response helps to explain the motives for Maharam Shiff's visitation. It is not thinkable that such an eminent master would cross the border between this world and the next to satisfy a personal grievance, like some Homeric god swooping down to meddle in human affairs.

His intervention, it is implied, is provoked by a crisis in the world of Torah learning that has disturbed both the upper and lower levels of the cosmos. The Torah has been put out of alignment and its study corrupted. Is this the result of an overly-ingenious, performance-oriented culture of learning that deflects from the true, plain meaning of the text? Readers familiar with Maharam Schiff's writings might infer this critique, although the substance of the crisis remains unelaborated. The all-too-easily admired teachings of R. Avraham, whose reputation has been enhanced by the association of his work with the genius of Maharam Schiff, are implicated in the crisis, but they are only a symptom of the problem. For the insensible R. Avraham, the cost to his reputation is nothing compared to the chance to participate in the process of putting the world of Torah back to rights.

What begins as an extraordinary one-time event becomes the foundation for an ongoing study partnership. R. Mordekhai has been contracted by the lord of Zabno to fabricate metal lanterns for the lavish wedding of his daughter, and his sojourn in the area affords him the chance to make late-night visits to R. Avraham. What takes places during these irregular study sessions constitutes a model for the norm of Torah study that Agnon makes into one of the pillars of his reimagining of Polish Jewry, and it is therefore important to attend to what these two scholars do when they meet. The first passage describes their response to Maharam Schiff's attack the next morning, and the second describes the nature of their intellectual work during the later nocturnal visits.

> We began to reconstruct some of the ḥidushim we heard from Maharam Schiff. We were astonished to find that each subject included multiple subjects and resolved many of the issues that the world finds difficult, and at the same time invalidated the explanations that the world has accommodated itself to. In the process, cruxes and contradictions were shown to exist in places where we had thought there were none. (p. *318, 265*)

> We sat as one in the midst of wondrous ḥidushim and magnificent pilpulim. He would offer a ḥidush and I would offer a ḥidush, and each ḥidush would be examined seven times over to determine if it could stand before the criterion of truth. For it often happens that people build one ḥidush upon another, sometimes up to eight or nine at a time; but once you realize that the first one is flawed, then all the others built upon it have nothing to support them. Worse than that is when people, because of their zeal for ḥidushim, sometimes become mired in error, God forbid, and end up inventing a new law that is refuted by an explicit gemara. (p. *320, 269*)

The activity upon which R. Avraham and R. Mordekhai embark upon, which on the surface of things may seem to be merely scholastic, in fact bears ultimate, even cosmic significance. But the gravity of their exchanges cannot be appreciated unless several assumptions are understood. To begin with, the world of Torah learning in which they are operating is dynamic and ahistorical. To be sure, they view themselves as coming at the end of a chain of tradition that began with Scripture, the Mishnah, and the Gemara and then proceeded through the Geonim to the early medieval commentators (the rishonim) to the later commentators (the *aharonim*), of which they form the latest link.

Yet the very belatedness of their position imposes a formidable burden: it is up to them to maintain the integrity of the entire edifice of the Tradition. That integrity is achieved by maintaining the logical coherence of the received body of Jewish law through a constant process of systematizing and rationalizing the vast profusion of opinions and dicta. The whole system is in constant organic movement as new rulings are added and revisionary conceptualizations of past opinions are proposed. Error enters the system when interpreters ignore the plain meaning of the text and build dazzling structures of casuistry to draw attention to themselves. The world of Torah has apparently been recently plunged into just such a downward spiral of inner corruption, and to pull it up short was the aim of Maharam Schiff's earthly intervention.

It is now left to our two lonely men of faith to continue the work of correction. Here is where the cosmic dimension enters the picture. They are not merely two study partners who, like chess masters, enjoy each other's acuity and take pleasure in testing each other's ideas. A better—but admittedly partial—analogy would be to theoretical physicists, whose contending notions of the fundamental building blocks of the universe have enormous real-world consequences. They apply themselves to reviewing the corpora of learned argument extant in their time and to submitting them to a rigorous standard of coherence and common sense. What is at stake is not just the theoretical integrity of the Tradition but the very norms of what is permitted and what is prohibited in the daily lives of all Jews. The fact they work in secrecy and anonymity is no bar to the cosmic efficacy of their work; the truth of Torah has in fact been diminished by the avidity of scholars who cannot help printing and disseminating their ḥidushim. A key to R. Mordekhai's capacity for incisive focus is his refusal to reveal himself as a *talmid ḥakham*. But at a metaphysical and mystical level, the work of R. Avraham and R. Mordekhai is helping to restore the world even if it is not published to the world.

Scholarship as Romance

A fundamental prerequisite for the success of the labor of R. Avraham and R. Mordekhai is that it be undertaken together. Without the complementary resources of the other, each scholar on his own is preordained to fall short and drift into error. The necessary model for working in tandem is, as we have seen, milḥamtah shel torah, the combat of Torah.[14] But the rules of engagement require neither the flashing swords nor the resentful antagonism displayed in the encounter between R. Mordekhai and Maharam Schiff. When R. Avraham and R. Mordekhai begin their working sessions, their exchanges are less fraught and more collaborative; yet the necessary competitiveness is not lacking. Their meetings usually begin with R. Mordekhai's presentation of a ḥidush that he has formulated since their last encounter. From this local insight he proceeds to clarify larger principles and correct the misinterpretations of earlier authorities. He would keep at this process of widening and deepening the import of his idea "until my eyes shone and I beheld the words of the Torah, both written down and transmitted orally, fitted together and rectified in their purity as on the day they were given by the Almighty and parsed by our ancient Sages" (p. 321, 270). Yet R. Mordekhai's brilliance cannot remain effectual if it is left only to be admired rather than scrutinized. This is where R. Avraham enters the picture.

> I also contested [pilpalti] with him, and if I won, he admitted without shame that the truth was on my side. But in the process of acknowledging this, he would begin to adduce proofs that contradicted my position and began to shore up his own. And if he was forced to leave the matter in the category of "needs further scrutiny," he would say to me, "I rely on the Rabbi of Zabno to discover in the course of his studies that my position is not foolish." (p. 321, 271)

R. Mordekhai's indefatigable assertiveness is a quality essential to his achievements as a scholar. Yet his brilliance and originality cannot reach their potential if they are not exposed to the astringent corrective of another strong mind, even if it is less brilliant and original. Competitiveness and amour proper guarantee the integrity of the search for religious truth.

The give-and-take of two students or scholars over the Talmudic text is of course familiar to us as the practice of *ḥevruta*, the Aramaic term for friendship or association. The intellectual potential unleashed by this kind of connection is embodied in the depiction of the study partnership between R. Avraham and R. Mordekhai. But it is in probing the affective dimension of the relationship that Agnon shows us something new. The hallmark of this new dimension is secrecy. As a condition for their studying together R. Mordekhai requires a solemn oath that his presence and identity be divulged to no one. (This, of course, is precisely the oath R. Avraham is flagrantly violating by narrating his monologue to the delegation from Buczacz.) His visits are timed to avoid the risk of exposure. He arrives after midnight when the rabbi has already slept several hours and arisen to the recite the midnight vigil (*tikkun ḥatsot*), and the streets of the town are deserted; and he stealthily disappears when the first footfalls are heard of the shamash who knocks on windows to wake worshipers for the first prayers. Even the members of the rabbi's household have no clue as to the identity of the mysterious visitor.

R. Avraham's experience of the relationship is deeply divided. On the occasions when R. Mordekhai materializes and the two launch their work of presenting and examining ḥidushim, R. Avraham enters a blissful state in which he is wholly absorbed in Torah study. With first light, R. Mordekhai transmogrifies from the radiance of a sage to the workaday demeanor of an artisan and departs. The Rabbi of Zabno is then cast into a state in which he is painfully aware of R. Mordekhai's absence and longs for his return. He is also thrown back upon the obsessive curiosity about R. Mordekhai's origins that assailed him when they first met at the circumcision feast. Who were his parents? Who was his teacher? These questions preoccupy R. Avraham until the moment of their next nocturnal meeting. But these questions are wholly forgotten the moment the door opens and R. Mordekhai begins to present his latest ḥidushim. They swarm back only at the moment the steps of the shamash are heard, and R. Mordekhai issues his ritual apology for not making good on his promise to tell his story, and he promptly disappears.

Because R. Mordekhai's visits are irregular and brief, R. Avraham finds himself at all other times in a state of forlorn anticipation.

> Because of my love of R. Mordekhai, my soul became attached to his soul. He was the object of my thoughts all day long until I could acquit myself of the regular lessons I offered and turn toward the *sugeyot* we had dealt with at night. Every night after tikkun ḥatsot I would listen intently for the sound of his footsteps. He had not yet told me where he came from or who were his forebears or who was his teacher. This was the case until things fell out such that he told me. And once he told me, he never came again. (p. *322*, 271–72)

We must account ourselves grateful to R. Avraham for his unselfconscious sincerity in naming his situation with the opening allusion to Jonathan's feelings for David in Second Samuel ("my soul was attached to his soul"). This is a relationship for which today we would use the term homosocial, a bond based on feelings of passionate friendship, here spiritual friendship between two men. As in the case of Jonathan and David, the feelings are not symmetrical. Although there is no confessional vehicle for R. Mordekhai to reveal his emotions the way R. Avraham has done, there is abundant evidence that for him the relationship is more instrumental than emotional. It is R. Avraham who is lovesick. He has lost interest in his regular duties; he comes fully alive only in R. Mordekhai's presence, and when he is not there, which is most of the time, he is suspended in distracted and anxious anticipation, made more acute by the irregularity of the visits and by his own inability to initiate contact. He must wait until R. Mordekhai comes to him. And the time spent waiting is consumed with his obsessive curiosity about the secrets of his life that have been withheld from him.

The imposed condition of secrecy becomes a source of anguish on another front. At the same time as he longs to know the true facts of R. Mordekhai's early life and scholarly formation, Zabno is abuzz with speculation about the identity of the mysterious stranger, whose visits cannot long be concealed in the small town. The members of the rabbi's own household, who have heard the visitor's movements but not seen his face, presume the secrecy prevails because the rabbi is giving spiritual guidance to a wealthy sinner or is counseling a Polish lord concerning conversion. The good Jews of Zabno, ever eager to aggrandize themselves through the magnification of their rabbi, make the automatic assumption that because of his greatness R. Avraham has merited private study sessions with no less than the prophet Elijah himself. (The facile recourse to the supernatural hits close to home because this is exactly the presumption that R. Avraham made at his first encounter with R. Mordekhai to explain his phenomenal erudition [p. *318, 266*].)

Having heard the rumor, R. Avraham is now obliged to gather the town elders and demonstrate to them, citing chapter and verse from holy books, exactly how the press of exhausting responsibilities (attending circumcisions, writing indulgences for faithful keepers of the Sabbath, and so on) could not possibly leave Elijah with even a moment of disposable time. Cowed by the rabbi's learning, the elders insist that if it is not Elijah who visits it must be the Holy Ari, the great kabbalist who lived in Safed in the Holy Land in the sixteenth century. Now R. Avraham has to explain to them that it is well established that tsaddikim from the Holy Land cannot survive in the air of the diaspora; but then his well wishers ask why such a great soul could not wrap himself in a cloak of holy air to travel abroad. The more the rabbi denies these absurdities, the more his followers are strengthened in their belief that it is only modesty that motivates his denials and the more they relish the confirmation that his humility is as great as his learning.

This adulation makes him miserable because the inflation of his reputation is the exact inverse of how he feels about himself. For despite the exhilaration of his study hours with R. Mordekhai, he has been humbled by a nimbler and more original mind. The disproportion between what he knows he is and the grandiose claims of the townspeople on his behalf is both painful and shameful—so much so that he begs R. Mordekhai to take his place as the community rabbi; he will vacate his position and become a *dayan* serving under the younger but greater scholar. R. Mordekhai declines the offer with the oft-repeated explanation that he already has a livelihood, thanks be to God; and R. Avraham is constrained to continue keeping his secret and, as a consequence, making his own life a living lie.

The rabbi's situation goes from bad to worse. He becomes embroiled in a tangled legal case concerning a derelict husband who has abandoned two women—one of them the young daughter of his own shamash. The man is being held by a rabbinic court in a distant city, where the older of the two women has confronted him, and the rabbi has to decide whether to request his removal to Zabno. He faces an impossible choice: if the man remains in the charge of the rabbinic court, he will probably slip off and never be heard from; and if he is consigned to the gentile authorities for transport, he probably will be beaten to death.

R. Avraham reassigns all his routine tasks to others and devotes himself to wrestling with these fraught legal issues. (By devoting himself to this case of these agunot, R. Avaraham fulfills the ideal explicitly enunciated in the letter of rabbinic appointment brought by the worthies of Buczacz.) Yet despite the full mobilization of his formidable powers, he gets nowhere; and at the end of each day's exhausting research, he hits the same unyielding wall. He is terrified by the prospect that the capacity to originate ḥidushim has been taken from him. He tries setting aside his investigations into the case of the two agunot and returning to his regular studies; he has found that an insight from a remote context often jogs loose the solution to an impacted problem. But this time the opposite happens. The passages that were clear to him when he originally studied them are now opaque. He enters a downward spiral in which " . . . the letters began to fly away and my eyes felt like they were sunk in sand" (pp. *326–27*, 278–79).[15]

The crisis comes to a head in a surprising betrayal. After a prolonged absence, R. Mordekhai materializes one midnight and announces that he is leaving the locality and moving his family to Buczacz. Because this will be their last meeting and time is in short supply, they are faced with the necessity of choosing between taking leave of each other by deliberating a matter of halakhah or paying the debt owed by R. Mordekhai to tell the story of his origins. While R. Mordekhai is undertaking a dexterous pilpul on the dilemma, his companion has a singular experience. Two halakhot appear before R. Avraham and ask pleadingly, "When you sat struggling to determine the law in our cases, you used to say that if only R. Mordekhai were here you would present us to him. Now that R. Mordekhai is standing before you, are you not going to mention us to him?" (p. *328*, 280).

One of the halakhot was the case of the agunot that he had taken on an emergency basis; the other was an issue about ritual slaughter discussed in the tractate he had been reading as part of his regular daily studies. There is an endearing touch of magic realism in the way in which the rabbi's guilty conscience animates these neglected claimants.

But the night is moving on, and the Rabbi of Zabno knows full well that the time will suffice for accomplishing only one task, and he makes his choice. He had intended to enlist R. Mordekhai's help in finding a way to liberate the agunot.

> But now my mind is addled and my spirit exhausted and I lack the strength to outline the issues, not to mention entering into a serious give-and-take about them. All I ask is some words to restore my soul. Let the master tell me where he came from and who were his ancestors and with whom he learned Torah. (p. *328*, 280)

R. Mordekhai accedes to his wish, and we get our story. R. Avraham's decision is not meant to be taken as his yielding to vulgar curiosity. Yet the fact remains that the rabbi does indeed sacrifice the interests of the abandoned women in order to hear R. Mordekhai's narrative. What is his true motivation? We are already accustomed to the fact that his innocence makes him a reliable reporter of his symptoms (the addled brain and exhausted spirit), but when it comes to their origins he remains clueless. His desperation is of course rooted in the feelings that have been churned up by the affective dimension of his study partnership with R. Mordekhai. The bragging of his congregants and the insoluble challenge of the agunah issues bore down on him, and he has undergone what would be called in another age a nervous breakdown. But these are only exacerbating factors.

The cause lies elsewhere. R. Avraham has come to realize how much it means to him to share the passionate life of learning with another scholar and how much he has missed in the past by walking this path alone. The overwhelming desire to be told R. Mordekhai's story comes from a thirst to know everything there is to know about a man who has become so central to his life. This desire, which was present from their first meeting, was repeatedly deferred so long as the two were vitally immersed face to face in their scholarly exchanges. But now at their final meeting the possibility for deferral has run out, and his need for connection to this holy man trumps an ethical commitment to the law and to the fate of the hapless victims of another, evil man.

What, in the end, does the relationship between R. Avraham and R. Mordekhai tell us about the grave questions concerning the nature of the rabbinate broached in the novella? Let us summarize the options represented by the narrative's main characters. R. Avraham comes close to being an exemplar of the scholar-rabbi. As the rabbi of a community, he is admirably engaged as a teacher and as a halakhicist. His commitment to utilize his scholarly acumen to alleviate human suffering is manifest in his extraordinary efforts on behalf of the two women deserted by the same man. His political awareness is similarly admirable; he is conscious of the pressures exerted on rabbis of larger cities ruled by capricious magnates, and he prefers to remain in a modest community with a more predictable relationship to its ruler. When it comes to scholarship, his achievements seem at first glance to be unassailable. His teachings are widely known in the study halls of the time, and his ḥidushim are said to rival those of Maharam Schiff in their brilliance. Yet the scholarly edifice he has built turns out to have shaky foundations, which are aggressively probed by Maharam Schiff himself in an extraordinary visit from Heaven. It takes R. Mordekhai's intervention to defend his reputation and help him rethink and rebuild what has been destroyed.

For his part, R. Mordekhai would seem to be the embodiment of the pure scholar. His life perfectly conforms to the exhortations of Sages of the Mishnah to practice a trade and thereby avoid dependence on the rabbinate for livelihood and to steer clear of entanglements with gentile authorities. He is the complete scholar because he combines intellectual brilliance (ḥarifut) with mastery of the tradition (beki'ut). (The special circumstances of his formation as a scholar are described in the next section of the novella.) But his achievement comes with a price: he is aloof of human connection and lacking in empathy. When R. Avraham undergoes a serious crisis, he is oblivious to the ordeal of his intimate study partner and does nothing to mitigate it.

Yet together they make beautiful music. The white nights they spend together proposing and rebutting each other's arguments describe an idyll of Torah study. At the center of this experience lies a passionate yet disinterested contestation—a dialectic of unrelenting critique—which is the only way in which the truth and the inner logic of Torah can continually be reestablished and protected from error. But the idyll, as crucial as it may be to the welfare of Torah learning, cannot last. There are three factors that bring it to an end.

To begin with, the partnership can work only in a dyadic relationship that is removed from the world. R. Mordekhai's condition of secrecy is merely an extension of the necessarily centripetal movement of the relationship. It cannot be integrated into the world, and for R. Avraham to participate in it he must be derelict in his duties to his community and, in the case of the two agunot, to ethical responsibilities beyond. Second, the emotions opened up by such intense partnership can lead in unpredictable directions. Although R. Mordekhai's temperament allows him to remain controlled and reserved, R. Avraham is a different story. He is so exalted by the bliss of study that he is as incapable of avoiding transference to the man who makes it possible as he is incapable of the least awareness of his situation. The great monologue itself, which recounts R. Mordekhai's origins, is a way of maintaining contact, if only through words, with the object that has been lost to him. In this sense, there is a parallel between the dangers inherent in pure worship, as discussed in the previous chapter about the ḥazzanim, and the dangers inherent in pure study.

Finally, gentile power, which becomes the grand theme of the novella's second half, makes a quiet appearance as a factor that contributes to the disbanding of the partnership between the two scholars. Their late-night sessions became possible because R. Mordekhai has been engaged as a tinsmith in the preparations for the wedding of the daughter of the local lord. When the job is done, he decides to move his family to Buczacz, a larger community in which he could earn his livelihood working for Jews and living among them.[16] The irony of the novella's ending, in which the tinsmith decamps from Buczacz because of the (positive) interference of the lord, will not be lost on the reader.

This first substantial segment of the great monologue at the heart of "In Search of a Rabbi" concludes with a superbly orchestrated intersection between the two narratives: R. Avraham's monologue and the frame story of the delegation to Zabno. Just as the rabbi of Zabno is about to embark on the story of R. Mordekhai's origins, the shamash knocks on the window to remind them that the night has passed, and morning prayers are in the offing. Within the story that R. Avraham has been telling, this is precisely what happens each time R. Mordekhai promises to reveal his background in their late-night meetings. There is a knock on the window, R. Mordekhai slips away, and the story is deferred.

And so the inverted Scheherazade motif crosses over into the main narrative. Already on the edge of their seats, the visitors from Buczacz must be patient and wait for the mysterious origins of this hidden genius to be disclosed.[17] And once that story is complete and the monologue brought to an end, they will have before them the return trip to Buczacz, the delivery of the surprising news to their fellow townspeople, and, ultimately, the rejection of their offer by R. Mordekhai. A great deal happens before that final disappointment, but it is all old news in the sense that it took place in the past. The recursive structure of the novella trains us, like the worthies of Buczacz, in the sweet discipline of deferral.

Origins of the Hero

We are rewarded for our patience by eventually discovering the reasons for unexplained behaviors. Why is R. Mordekhai so adamant about concealing his greatness? Why does he dismiss out of hand the possibility of accepting the office of community rabbi? Why must he move to a different city to have fewer gentile employers? We might write off his choices to temperament and perversity if we did not have the narrative that comes next. What we discover—all in good time, of course—is that the integrity of the rabbinate is highly vulnerable to calamitous interference on the part of the ruling gentile powers. Yet this political dimension is largely absent from the first story, which is enclosed within the hidden, intimate exchanges between the two Torah scholars.

It is exactly this dimension that is foregrounded in the opening lines of "R. Mordekhai and His Teacher" ["R. Mordekhai verabo"], the second narrative unit in the novella.

> R. Mordekhai's birth was due to the commandment of ransoming captives because his father redeemed a young woman from captivity and then married her properly according to the laws of Moses and Israel. The son she gave birth to was called Mordekhai, after the name of her father, who departed from this world in the midst of fleeing from the wrath of a lord.
>
> Let us now relate the details. (p. *331*, *285*)

Those details prove to be interesting and complicated, but it is obviously a matter of urgency for the narrator to begin by condensing their import into a banner headline. The job of this story is to present the origins of the hero, and those origins are inextricably embroiled in the experience of persecution. His mother's life has been decisively shaped by her victimization, and her son's name is a memorial to her father's death under conditions of cruel oppression. Added to their ranks will soon be the figure of the anonymous saintly rabbi, fleeing for his life from the malevolent reach of a great nobleman. Fortunately, this opening précis also cites an act that resists this cycle of suffering and foreshadows the role that R. Mordekhai one day plays in restoring the integrity of Torah learning. Even though ransoming captives (*pidyon shevuyim*) is an important ethical imperative, it is usually undertaken by communities in collective negotiation with an enemy captor. The private initiative undertaken by R. Mordekhai's father is an entirely spontaneous act of kindness.

The story displays a fine-grained attention to the historical moment and the shifting winds of power. Consider, for example, the plot's originating misfortune. The family of Sarah Rivkah, Mordekhai's mother, operated a tavern as a leasehold from the local Polish lord. The meager profits from the tavern could not satisfy the lord's cupidity, and he repeatedly threatened to take action against the tavern keeper. Knowing he cannot pay the mounting debts and knowing what the lord is capable of, the Jew flees with his daughter. He dies when they are apprehended by the lord's men. The daughter is taken from her father's corpse and imprisoned in a pit, where she, too, will surely die because her jailers steal the food allotted to her. This grim scenario is one that could—and was—played out at any point over the course of the seventeenth or eighteenth centuries when local Polish lords and estate administrators answered to no law but their own.

Now there is a second episode involving a tavern, and the circumstances under which it plays out indicate that an important historical corner has been turned. Once Sarah Rivkah has been ransomed and married to Yisrael Natan, they settle in the city, where he is an assistant to a successful merchant. But instead of flourishing Sarah Rivkah declines; she cannot abide the city and longs to return to village life. Her situation is so dire that Yisrael Natan is ready to abandon the career for which he had been training all his life and relocate to the countryside. The merchant is sad to lose his protégé, but he cares about his welfare enough to help him find a way to manage the change. It so happens that a Polish lord he knows has built an upscale country inn and is looking for a lessee to run it. In his shrewd negotiation with the lord, the merchant points out times have changed, and it is no longer possible to resort to brute force to intimidate and extract payment of the leasehold fees. If the lessor does not have the money to pay, then "there is nothing you can do to him, not even throwing him in a pit. Former times were very different from the situation now, under His Majesty the Kaiser" (p. 335, 290). Under these new conditions, the argument continues, what counts is a talent for management—which Yisrael Natan has in abundance—because if a Jew can't pay his fees, what does torture avail, or as the merchant puts it pungently to appeal to the lord, "you can't make sauce out of tears."

The mention in passing of the His Majesty the Kaiser provides us with a key locus of orientation for the succession of narratives in this novella. The partition of Poland, in which the Polish lands that would make up the province of Galicia passed to the sovereignty of Austria, took place in 1772 and 1775. From the merchant's remarks we understand that this momentous shift has taken place only recently, so much so that the lord has not yet absorbed the implications for the exercise of his own authority. This dividing line enables us to grasp in a general way the time line of the narratives within "In Search of a Rabbi." The birth and education of R. Mordekhai, as well as his later encounter with R. Avraham, take place after the partition; the grand narrative about Reuven and Shimon before. The effect of the imposition of an Austrian administration on the Polish nobility is a complex phenomenon that is explored elsewhere in this study. On the one hand, with the institution of an imperial legal system the nobles were no longer a law unto themselves; on the other, they maintained much of their wealth and influence. Agnon notes these differences with a keen eye, but the advent of the Austrians simply compounds and enlarges the concept of gentile interference. Both the old nobility and the new rulers constitute the "whim of the ruler" (ruah hamoshel), which remains toxic to the higher study of Torah and to the possibility of a pure and disinterested rabbinate.

The abandonment of the city for the village is the central moment in the first half of the story. It is ostensibly a regressive movement, because in these stories Jews generally aspire to move to town, where they can live among their brethren, pray in a quorum, and educate their children. The city, moreover, is the place where more advanced commerce flourishes, in contrast to the countryside, where the principle occupation is tavern keeping.

Yisrael Natan would seem to be the embodiment of this urban entrepreneurial spirit. Eager, ambitious, and loyal, he is apprenticed to a successful merchant, who treats him like a son—he has a sister and brother-in-law in town but no parents—and he sleeps in their attic among the merchandise for trade. The day he accidently comes upon the ruins of the tavern Sarah Rivkah's father operated happens to be the first time his mentor had given him the authority to act on his behalf in a commercial transaction, and the young man is very proud of his new status. The instinctive act of ransoming Sarah Rivkah changes everything and reverses the trajectory of his life. His efforts to incorporate her into his city life fail, and, in a second instance of love and kindness, he gives up his promising career to save her from a wasting melancholy. To be sure, the inn he operates is more like a boutique bed-and-breakfast than the old-style tavern catering to thirsty peasants; but it remains a reversion to an older Jewish occupation whose essence is serving the needs of gentile customers.

The retreat to the village is presented as a temporary seclusion that serves several purposes. It is necessary, to begin with, to restore Sarah Rivkah's mental health. The trauma of loss and victimization can be palliated only by contact with the rural life she is familiar with and its ongoing intimacy with nature. The seclusion is also providentially necessary for the purposes of hiding the rabbi in flight from persecution and providing him a venue in which to recover from *his* trauma. As an astute business move to preempt competition, Yisrael Natan had bought a disused inn on the other side of the village and planted foliage to conceal it from passers-by. This turns out to be the perfect "safe house" in which to place the rabbi, whose identity and whereabouts require extreme protection.

The Jewish marginality of the village further provides the sort of sterile laboratory conditions under which the young Mordekhai can grow up uncontaminated by erroneous notions about Jewish learning. His suitability as a tabula rasa is almost ruined by a boring and uncouth melamed brought to the village to instill in its ragged band of Jewish children some shreds of literacy. Before the arrival of the elderly rabbi, Mordekhai grows up in the lap of nature like the gentile children of the village devoting their time to climbing trees, imitating animal sounds, fishing, and swimming. The pious narrator—remember that it is R. Avraham who is telling the story—accords no romantic pantheism to this scene as Bialik surely would have. He, like Mordekhai's parents, is appalled that the boy is growing up ignorant of Torah. But it is not impossible that Agnon, who in his Nobel Prize acceptance speech stated that God's creation was one of his inspirations, accords to this "child-of-nature" phase a positive, propaedeutic function as a basis for the textual learning that will be placed upon it.

Finally, the isolation of the village, together with the hidden house secreted within it, create a multivalent parallel between the first and second stories in the novella. The secret tutorial R. Mordekhai receives from the rabbi in the second corresponds to the secret nocturnal meetings he conducts with R. Avraham in the first. Because the stories are reversed in time, we now discover that later relationship has a precursor in the concealed dyadic intimacy of the boy and the aged scholar.

The function of this story, it should be recalled, is to satisfy R. Avraham's unrelenting curiosity about how so formidable a scholar as R. Mordekhai could come from nowhere. The second half of the story therefore sets about answering this question by describing the formation of the young scholar-to-be. It is presented as a two-stage process. The first stage is devoted wholly to observation. The rabbi—whose name, like that of the village, is withheld to conform to the protocols of secrecy—is discovered in a nearly catatonic state wandering in a random field when Yisrael Natan goes in search of a lost cow. His feet are so swollen and blistered that Yisrael Natan has to wash them and apply salve. The reader is left to imagine how many days he has been in flight and what it means for a respected and elderly rabbi of an important community to leave his family and everything familiar to him and how terrified he must have been and how real he believed the threat to be in order to simply to walk out the door and into the woods. It takes a long and unspecified time for the rabbi to thaw, as it were, and return to himself. It is during this interval that Mordekhai observes him closely.[18] The boy has been assigned by his father to see to the rabbi's needs. He brings his daily meal and ferries over his father's tallit and tefillin—so exigent was his escape that even these were left behind!—after his father has donned them. Mordekhai has never seen a rabbi, and, at such close quarters, he has abundant opportunity to observe him.

For the quick-witted boy, the rabbi is a source of endless puzzlement. The enormous reverence his parents feel toward the rabbi is an attitude he has seen them express to no other person, even to Hasidim who occasionally pass through the inn. Alone in the hideaway, the rabbi spends his days seated with his eyes closed and his hands on his knees while he keeps up a barely audible conversation with himself. When he listens closely, Mordekhai picks up a series of strange names, which the reader recognizes as the great later commentators on the Talmud. The rabbi is conducting scholarly inquiries from memory and restaging the dialectics of Torah study in his mind. When the boy observes him in prayer, the words are uttered with such fervor that it is as if he is hearing and understanding them for the first time. The Ahavah Rabbah prayer, the second blessing before the Shema in the morning service, describes how God's love for Israel is expressed by the giving of the Torah and the commandments. As the rabbi inhabits each word of the prayer with intense mindfulness, Mordekhai experiences his first intimation about the nexus between love and revelation. He is further astounded when he witnesses the rabbi performing the tikkun ḥatsot ritual, the midnight vigil mourning the destruction of Jerusalem. He cannot comprehend how it is possible that such a saintly and distinguished a man as the rabbi should have to flee for his life from the Duke. He goes on to reason that the Exile must be responsible for this vulnerability to gentile will, and he further intuits that it is better to be an artisan than a rabbi to elude provoking the ire of the regime.

All this is absorbed simply through observation and despite the fact that the rabbi remains in his shell-shocked state. When he emerges from his trauma and returns to himself, the rabbi takes note of the boy who has been serving him and offers to teach him Torah. This is the beginning of the second stage of Mordekhai's formation. The rabbi sends to Yisrael Natan to have volumes of Talmud and Maimonides provided him only to discover that such things do not exist in the village. So the rabbi makes do with the only text available, the *ḥumash* with Rashi's commentary, the most basic primmer in the Jewish library. The obstacle is turned into an opportunity. The rabbi is delighted to discover that the entire edifice of post-biblical Jewish law (Mishnah, Talmud and all the early and later commentators) can be derived from the verses of Scripture and, far from being merely an expediency imposed by the scarcity of books, this is in fact the proper way to study Torah.

Implicit in this discovery is a sharp critique of what passes for sophisticated scholarship and pedagogy, and this is connected to the complaints discussed at the beginning of this chapter about the preparation of rabbis in Galicia and Poland. Young men are being trained to be able to make showy use of the arguments of the early-modern Talmud exegetes (aḥaronim) so that they can appear formidable in their learning and make a name for themselves in current scholarly debates. This educational regime perversely inverts the pyramid of learning, which properly should end with the later authorities rather than begin with them. The Bible is the foundation from which all follows—as Mordekhai's teacher is demonstrating—but the reality in yeshivot is that students rarely study Scripture and come across it only when it is quoted in the Talmud. This is the case as well with the Mishnah, which is not accorded its own study and which is encountered as decontextualized fragments, also in the Talmud. And the plain meaning of the Talmud itself often becomes merely grist for the mill of over-ingenious legal disputations. The study and elaboration of Jewish law, the halakhah, has been dangerously cut off from the fundaments that undergird it and supply its divine authority.

> There are, to be sure, great scholars who have mastery over the body of laws and know the opinions of the poskim. They may even know the source of a certain law in the Gemara. . . . But they are ignorant of the verse in the Divine Quarry from which the law was hewn. (p. *343*, 301)

By beginning with the "Divine Quarry," namely, Scripture, and building upward, the rabbi is working to purge the existing educational regime of its systemic upside-down error and shaping a disciple who will help to bring the world of Torah back into alignment.

Mordekhai's education, then, rather than suffering from the absence of texts, instead becomes a grand experiment, on the model of Rousseau, in writing the right words on the blank slate of the boy's eager mind. It helps in no small measure that Mordekhai possesses a perfect memory. It would be imprecise to say he has a photographic memory because except for the text of the Hebrew Bible itself, the vast reservoir of the texts of the Tradition are imparted to him by the rabbi orally. The printed text of a single tractate of the Talmud providentially falls into their hands, but this takes place after the basic regime of study has been established, and it serves mainly as a springboard for learning—again, orally—about discussions that take place elsewhere in the Talmudic corpus. The oral nature of the education imparted to Mordekhai turns out to be of signal importance in establishing the norm of rabbinic learning in *A City in Its Fullness*. It is through oral transmission, of course, that Moses received the Oral Torah at Sinai, and it was by the precise memorization of oral statements in the first and second centuries of the Common Era that the early rabbis, the Tannaim, compiled the Mishnah. Committing oral teachings to writing was viewed by the Rabbis as a concession to historical necessity rather than a sign of arrival.

For these reasons, the exchange between the rabbi and Mordekhai presents itself as something more than another instance of a teacher-student relationship. The relationship, we have observed, has two essential features. It roots itself in the fundaments of the Bible and arrives at later teachings through a step-by-step process of exegetical demonstration; and it takes place by word of mouth and relies on the exertions of individual memory. This pedagogical transaction provides, to be sure, a model for how the Torah should properly be taught. But it does something more: it restages and recapitulates the drama of the transmission of the Tradition by the early Sages in the time of the Mishnah. It is as if Mordekhai and his teacher are giving the world of learning a chance to start over again and rebuild itself based on the pure and true principles that have been lost sight of.

Even a phenomenal memory such as Mordekhai's could not contain the whole of the Oral Law without some trick or method. Throughout history there have been many schemes for organizing memory. Jonathan Spence presented a remarkable one in his study of the sixteenth-century Jesuit priest Matteo Ricci, who traveled to China and wrote, in Chinese, a book on the art of memory, which proposed constructing a "memory palace" in whose various chambers are placed the various items to be remembered.[19] In a manner not so dissimilar, Mordekhai's teacher proposes taking the myriad of rabbinic laws and legal discussions from the Talmud and attaching them to the relevant verses in the Bible. The rabbi trains Mordekhai's mind to see key verses as containing and leading to long threads of rabbinic learning, and, because the text of the Bible has been made into an inalienable possession of Mordekhai's mind, it can serve as an organizing gateway to the ocean of postbiblical knowledge, each verse clearly leading to a defined and retrievable portion. At the very end of the novella, when a new delegation of Buczacz notables approaches R. Mordekhai's house, finally, to offer him the rabbinate of the city, they hear him learning aloud and quoting word-for-word from arcane legal sources; but when they enter the house, they are astounded to find that there are no books at all, and the scholar has been working entirely from memory. Unbeknownst to them, they were already inside one of the chambers in R. Mordekhai's memory palace.

"R. Mordekhai and His Teacher," the second narrative unit within the novella, concludes on an idyllic note.

> There were no days of Torah for the rabbi and his student like those in which they were utterly cut off from the whole world and sat and reflected on the Torah. For the Torah expands the mind, strengthens the soul, and makes one forget the troubles of the world. (p. 345, 304)

The fact that the rabbi can forget the troubles of the world after what he has seen is indeed a great tribute to the healing power of Torah study. Because of the inverted time structure of the novella, we the readers do not yet know what it is he *has* seen, and that, in fact, is the title of the next story "What the Rabbi Saw That Made Him Flee." But in this interval between the fact of his flight and our looming discovery of the evil that caused it, there is a moment of perfection. A scholar and his student together study Torah for its own sake and do so in a way that recaptures the original purity of the act of study and transmission. This consummation joins the picture of the late-night exchanges between R. Avraham and R. Mordekhai—later in real time, earlier in the progress of the story—to render a model of Torah study and scholarship in their most ideal form, which in turn form a central, normative pillar in the spiritual and conceptual organization of the universe of classical Buczacz as presented by Agnon in *A City in Its Fullness*. But make no mistake: the purity of these moments is wholly conditional upon their isolation from society. What I translated in the passage above as "utterly cut off from the world" is a gloss on a set of Hebrew terms (*perushim umufrashim ubedeilim umuvdalim*) whose grammatical and rhetorical duplication further underscores the removal from society. But this is a condition that is so difficult to meet, as we soon see, as to render the norm an important ideal but one whose power is largely virtual and heuristic.

Fish and Salt

The second half of the novella is so vastly different from the first that the narrator is constrained to address the reader directly: "Be assured that in the end everything will connect back to the beginning, to the holy community of Buczacz that went in search of a rabbi and to R. Mordekhai, some of whose praises we have already heard" (p. *345*, 304). No small amount of assurance is indeed necessary because the narrative arc of the story sweeps us so far from Buczacz that we often wonder if return is even possible. But for the time being we defer questions of coherence and proximity in favor of appreciating just how far afield Agnon permits himself to go. The two narrative units that make up the second half ("What the Rabbi Saw That Made Him Flee" and "Water within Water") tell the story of the conflict between Reuven and Shimon, two wealthy Jews with contacts in the highest reaches of the Polish nobility in an unnamed region of the country. Reuven seeks and obtains the leasehold to rebuild and operate two large fish ponds, which are located adjacent to Shimon's already operating salt works.[20]

The unmistakable differences between the two halves of the novella can be summarized under several headings: (1) Whereas the action in the first part takes places in hidden, closeted spaces (R. Avraham's study, the secret inn) and in the context of intimate and discrete relationships, in the second part the action unfolds in vast, outdoor spaces and among figures whose movements are public and widely observed. (2) With one or two small exceptions, gentile authorities are nowhere to be seen in the first stories; the later stories, in contrast, dramatize direct transactions between wealthy Jewish merchants and high-ranking Polish nobles, upon whose wills and desires the fate of many depends. (3) Time and space in the first half are recognizably Jewish; the events take place in Buczacz, Zabno, and the hidden inn; and time is marked by the need to offer morning and afternoon prayers. In the second half, events largely take place in the drawing rooms of the nobility or in the limitless open spaces of fields and rivers, and time is marked by the seasons and the elements with no mention of Jewish holidays or the Jewish calendar. (4) In the first stories, the examples of human interaction with the physical world are limited to the objects Mordekhai and his uncle fabricate as master tinsmiths; in the later stories, the scope of the earthworks Reuven undertakes to put the fish ponds into operation and later to protect them from destruction, deploying thousands of serfs, is nothing less than promethean. (5) Whereas in the first half, knowledge of Torah and respect for Torah are the markers of worth and authority, in the second half, the correlation is inverse or negative. Although Shimon is acknowledged as a talmid hakham, he exploits his Torah knowledge to berate his workers and deride his competitor. Finally, (6) in the second half, the sway of Jewish jurisprudence, which earlier on is so central to the exchanges between R. Avraham and R. Mordekhai, is challenged, marginalized, and, finally, undercut.

If, for the sake of argument, we make a radical reduction of these factors, we can say that the first half of the novella takes place in a domesticated Jewish sphere, and the second half takes place in the natural world and the sphere of gentile relations. The binary accords well with the bipartite title for the novella: "In Search of a Rabbi, or The Governor's Whim." What is the relationship between these two? The narrator takes this divergence as a challenge of emplotment: How can he fashion a credible and coherent story line which, after traveling so far from the orbit of Buczacz and its rabbinic search, can be brought back home? The reader who accepts the narrator's encouragement to be patient and stays with the story to its end will indeed be witness to the two pieces being snapped together. This closure may be a virtuoso instance of storytelling construction, but, on a deeper deconstructive level, the gentile part of the plot is not folded back into the Jewish part. Jewish existence and gentile power remain stubbornly unsusceptible to connection.

The grandiose, outsize scope of Reuven's enterprises draw forth from Agnon a kind of writing that cannot be found in his other work, and perhaps not in the canon of modern Hebrew literature altogether. This new kind of writing is necessitated by Reuven's penetration and manipulation of the material, natural world. When we first meet Reuven, he is already a man of considerable means. He is an arrendator who has leased the fishing rights to a river from a very powerful unnamed noblewoman. Fresh fish are a highly sought-after commodity, but because of their skittish habits—appearing and disappearing unpredictably in different parts of the river—catching them is an inherently unreliable business. To overcome the quixotic nature of nature, Reuven comes up with a scheme to rebuild two huge and long-unused fish ponds on the noblewoman's lands. Reuven proposes to invest his considerable capital and provide the managerial supervision of artisans and engineers if the noblewoman will provide the army of serfs, whose labor she owns, necessary to clear the pond beds of generations' worth of rocks, earth, and refuse. The agreement is struck, and the noblewoman, who owns 999 villages, issues an order requiring two or three stout youths from each village to report for duty.[21] Reuven divides them into two camps, one for each pond, and they set to work hauling and clearing the accumulated detritus of decades so that springs that originally had fed the ponds can be unplugged. In the meantime, he hires specialists from abroad to design and construct a system of sluices and spillways capable of controlling the water level in the ponds and preventing the possibility of overflow.

Behind Reuven's colossal ambitions and his massive engineering project lies the myth of Prometheus in its romantic scientific version. The name is of course nowhere mentioned in the text, and such an association would be unthinkable in the mind of the pious narrator. But that does not stop us as worldly readers nor Agnon as a worldly author from identifying Reuven's ambitions as promethean, especially in these later sections of the novella that are so drained of Judaic reference. Reuven's practical ingenuity, mercantile zeal, and entrepreneurial fearlessness lead him to a particularly modern form of hubris. He believes that he can tame nature and harness it for human profit and benefit and that rationale planning can successfully anticipate the vagaries of the elements. Putting these schemes into practice requires the tangible fabrication and manipulation of the material world on a vast scale. Here Agnon faced a choice. He could have merely reported, suggested, summarized, or referred to the nature and scope of these activities *in their generality*; this would have been the expected course for a writer largely concerned with the ethical and spiritual consequences of human affairs.

But Agnon does the unexpected. He aggressively immerses himself in the realm of the radically material and concrete. Here, for example, is a description of the techniques used to drive great pillars that will support the sluices into the floor of the ponds.

How were the sluices constructed?

They cut down the trees and stuck them in the ground next to each other and rigged a rope and pulley at their top that functioned like a scale, such that when one was full the other was depressed. A barrel with a beam inside was attached to the ropes, and eight men on either side hoisted it up until it reached the top. When they let it go, it hurtled downward and struck with such force that the barrel with the beam burrowed deep into the earth. The impact was so fierce that sound was heard throughout the countryside. All who observed how the barrel and beam were planted in the ground declared that all the winds in the world could never budge the barrel from the ground or the beam from the barrel, and therefore all the worries raised by Shimon were without merit. (p. *349, 309*)

Every object and activity in this passage bespeaks superlativeness. The lumber is the hardest and most ancient, the barrels the stoutest imaginable, the trees the tallest in the vast forests, the fit of the beams in the barrels not subject to dislodgment, and so on. The hugeness of nature is matched and bested by the hugeness of human effort. Through ingenuity and invention, the giantism of nature is domesticated and converted into devices and emplacements that are equally gigantic but now serve human purposes. Even though Reuven and his engineers have devised these plans, their execution in this passage seems undertaken by an anonymous, collective human will arrayed to grapple with nature. In this encounter, religion and nationality are irrelevant, and all markings of Jewishness have been erased. This immersion in "gentile space" is underscored—not without irony—by the total focus on material objects and their fabrication and manipulation. Nowhere else in Agnon's vast corpus is there a description of the materials of the physical world that is so tactile and so attentive to the independent reality of things in the world.

One must look back to the Mishnah to find a similar language of materiality in postbiblical Jewish literature. Although the Mishnah often is invoked, correctly, as the model for the clarity and symmetry of Agnon's sentences, the content of his writing has had more to do with human agency than with the "thingness" of the created world. In such passages as the one above in this section of the novella, we are witness to a fascinating substitution. To represent the gentile space of vast construction projects, armies of serfs battling ice flows, and flooding and extreme weather—the realia of the real world, as it were—Agnon gives up his measured and regular mishnaic style in favor of a novelistic, naturalistic flow of descriptive language that is adapted to cycles of human activity and natural forces.

In addition to the description of the construction of the earthworks for the ponds, Agnon displays this kind of writing in two more extended sequences of epic proportions. After a sudden thaw following a frigid winter, the ice on the ponds breaks up into ice flows that threaten to wash over the containing walls (pp. 353–56, 313–18). Again the army of serfs is summoned and armed with ancient feudal weapons from the castle armory, and they man the perimeter of the ponds to deflect the ice flows. The great catastrophe—the collapse of the system of sluices and spillways—comes later in the season when the rapidly melting ice and snow is joined both by unrelenting rain and a great upsurge from underground wells on the floor of the ponds (pp. 357–68, 320–32).

Yet before the implacability of nature reasserts itself and wipes away Reuven's projects, there is a palpable if illusory period of grace. During a stretch of years—the number is not given—in which nature behaves predictably, there is a reign of harmony in the feudal relations among the Poles, the Jews, and the Ruthenian/Ukrainian peasantry. The gentry take pleasure in skating parties on the frozen surface of the ponds. Wealthy Jews prosper from the profits on their leaseholds and contribute generously to charity while their brethren enjoy a period of lessened persecution. The peasants plant, harvest, and subsist. This is an entente based, in large measure, on fish. Reuven's success in regularizing and increasing the supply of fresh fish and suppressing its price is a blessing bestowed upon all. Evident in the depiction of this idyll are the echoes of the creation story in Genesis. Man as the crown of creation has asserted his rule over the creatures of the water and ushered the world into an Edenic state.

It is little wonder then that when the sluices collapse and the countryside is flooded and Shimon's salt works are washed away that the calamity should also be cast in the terms of the primeval creation story. The title of the final narrative unit is "Water within Water" ["Mayim bemayim"]; the unrelenting rains falling upon the melting snow and ice are the "upper waters," and the suddenly unplugged underground springs below the ponds are the "lower waters." In Gen. 1:7–8, heaven and earth are created by separating the waters above the firmament from those below. In the story of the

Flood that follows, the dry land of human habitation is swallowed up by the rejoining of the upper and lower waters.[22]

It is precisely this return to primordial chaos that Reuven surveys when he sits astride his horse, whose feet are so deeply mired in the mud that it is stuck in place. The individual contours of hills, valleys, fields, ponds, and rivers have been erased and submerged in the unforgiving flood waters. The great hierarchical world, momentarily propped up by human cleverness and sustained by an abundance of good things, has fallen into chaos. The fish ponds and the salt works are both destroyed and the fields of the peasants rendered useless. The visual intensity and epic sweep of these chapters are extraordinary, and they deserve the sort of close attention that cannot be given to them here. They give us an intriguing glimpse into a kind of realistic-naturalistic prose Agnon was supremely capable of writing but chose largely to keep in reserve, perhaps viewing the material world it described as gentile space.

The scene of watery chaos comes into focus through Reuven's consciousness. However much we the readers may be shaken and disheartened by the devastation, Reuven remains stoic and attentive to his economic interests. The young serfs who drowned while trying to stave off the ice flows; the ruin of the peasants' fields and, thereby, their livelihood; and the obliteration of Shimon's salt works and the actuality of his dire predictions of catastrophe—none of these are present to his mind. His sole concern is the wagon loads of fish he had contracted to supply for an army banquet and the valuable jewel he had given as a surety. With his own supply wiped out, he makes arrangements to purchase fish from another source only to have his shipment forcibly intercepted by agents of Shimon, who is enraged over the losses he has suffered.

The Faltering Reach of the Law

This is the pivot point of the novella. The vast vistas, the titanic ambitions to harness the natural world, and the chaotic force of the elements all disappear. In their place our attention is redirected—whether we like it or not—to the political intrigues among wealthy Jews and powerful Polish magnates and to

the compromised efforts of the Jewish polity in Poland to submit the conflict between Reuven and Shimon to arbitration in Jewish courts. We feel
the story being reeled back into the thematic orbit the narrator established
at the beginning of the novella; the theme is Jewish learning and Jewish law
as they are studied and applied by rabbis in the face of the gentile regime.
Step by step the narrator is making good on his promise to return his narrative to Buczacz's problematic rabbinic search. However dazzled we are by
Reuven's huge projects, by the eruptions of nature, and by the tactical moves
of one grandee against another, we are now called upon to turn our attention to the impact of these adventures on the authority of Jewish law.

The entire novella, it is important to recall, is poised in its various parts
around the shift from Polish autonomy to Austrian rule. The feud between
Reuven and Shimon is the novella's last unit—excepting the final return to
Buczacz—and, set in the period when great Polish magnates held sway, it
is the earliest chronologically. It is also the very end of the period in which
the Lithuanian-Polish Jewish polity could function as a meaningful body of
corporate will and as a kind of sovereign juridical system. (The Council
of Four Lands was abolished already in 1764, a decade before the Partition.)

Agnon stages the conflict between Reuven and Shimon as a test case
positioned along this unstable fault line. The question is thus posed: Is the
institution of Jewish law, both in its applied practice and its larger authority, capable of handling this crisis? The practical consequences could not
be direr. The narrator adduces the case of a rivalry between wealthy and
powerful Jews in Bohemia that was brought before the princes of the realm
for adjudication and ended very badly for the simple Jews as well as for the
great. "Because of disputes among the rich," the narrator rues, "householders
become impoverished and uprooted from their communities and must wander from exile to exile. The rich themselves did not escape without being
displaced and banished with the rest of their Jewish brethren," (p. *371, 337*).

If Reuven and Shimon are allowed to pursue their feud by leverag-
ing their clout with various noble lords and maneuvering outside of the
protocols of Jewish law, then the result could be a similar cascading of calamitous consequences at all levels of Jewish society. Therefore the elders

of the Jewish metropolis Lviv take note and bestir themselves to persuade the parties to the conflict to place their dispute before a beit din. If in the past it was in their power to insist, now they can only persuade. Their efforts take place against the background of two failed court procedures that took place before the great flooding. In both cases, Reuven and Shimon withdrew from the proceedings before a verdict was rendered because of impatience, on both their parts, with the perceived ineptitude of the judges and their limited capacity for comprehending complex mercantile transactions. Now, in this third iteration, when terrible losses and damages are a fact rather than a speculation, the very capacity of the Jewish polity to contain this rupture is at stake.

While Reuven agrees right away, Shimon resists. The narrative devotes not a little space to the visit of the elders of Lviv to Shimon and the arguments they place before him. (This embassy is the second of the three embassies in the novella. It is framed by the journey of the delegation from Buczacz to Zabno at the very beginning and by the delegation, composed of a different set of notables, whose members offer the rabbinate of Buczacz to R. Mordekhai at the very end.)

Shimon presents himself as the righteous, aggrieved party and as the victim who had foreseen the disaster when no one would pay attention. It would therefore seem that he would have the most to gain from a *din torah*, a rabbinic adjudication. Yet because the world had for so long been the happy beneficiary of the seemingly endless supply of fresh fish provided by Reuven, Shimon questions whether he can get a fair trial. He is well versed in Torah knowledge—Reuven is not—and he uses his erudition to spar with the learned emissaries and evade their arguments. His animus against Reuven is fueled not only by the financial ruin visited upon him but also by the accommodations to gentile mores he claims Reuven makes in his dress and physical appearance and in the education of his daughters. In the last analysis, Shimon seeks to avoid the Jewish courts because he believes he can put his trust in the influence of the Duke to protect him. His wife's deceased first husband had rendered a valuable service to the Duke, and Shimon thinks he can count on this indebtedness to advance his interests.[23]

But the visitors from Lviv prove themselves to be even more up-to-date on the rivalries among the nobility, and they observe that whatever putative favors owed Shimon will count for nothing in the light of the active hatred the Duke has recently displayed to the lord from whom Shimon had leased the commission for the salt works. To this argument Shimon must yield, and he finally agrees to hand the dispute over to a beit din. His recalcitrance has been overcome not by an appeal to the authority of Jewish law but by the calculation that his chances had dimmed in world of gentile power relations.

But even after the agreement of both men has been obtained, the first attempt to submit the case to a beit din is a humiliating public failure. The grandiosity of the arrangements is evident in the hyperbolic language. The notables of each man's city turn to the "statesmen and princes" [alufim verozenim] of the land, who, in turn, approach two extraordinary merchants [soharim muflagim], who are renowned for their wealth and their integrity, who then proceed to approach a rabbi with an international reputation. It is the rabbi who turns out to be the true man of integrity. The merchants make time available from their busy schedules and travel to the home of the rabbi, who lives in conditions of poverty that shock them. Rather than becoming the beginning of a legal proceeding, the visit is over almost before it has begun. With exquisite courtesy, the rabbi explains to his visitors that the commentators on the Shulḥan 'Arukh hold a court composed, even in part, of laypeople rather than Torah scholars to be invalid. The merchants turn around and go home.

"There are, thank God," the narrator assures us, "rabbis in Poland who are expert in the affairs of the world" (p. 377, 345). This second attempt succeeds, or so we think. Each side nominates a distinguished rabbi as his advocate, and the two rabbis choose a third, and thus the beit din is complete. The third, elderly rabbi is "famous throughout the land for his greatness in Torah, piety, and honesty," and he is, of course, none other than the rabbi who will become Mordekhai's teacher. For five long days the arguments are presented in all their closely reasoned moral and legal complexity. Like all trials, there is a mixture of tedium and suspense. The younger rabbis fear at

times that the attention and acuity of their older colleague may not be up
to the task. Yet when they have rested their cases and there is nothing more
to say, they are astonished by the elderly rabbi's total recall of every particular that has been uttered and his mastery of the relevant case law.

A verdict is rendered that acquits one party and finds the other culpable.
Yet the verdict is an anti-climax twice over. As if he is boxing our ears for
unseemly over-eagerness, the narrator withholds from us the identity of the
winner. After we have followed the escapades of these two men for so long,
the matter is simply dropped with no explanation. This provocation seems
intended to burst the bubble of the melodramatic interest we have taken
in the exploits of these high-flying Jewish grandees and in the intrigues
they conduct among the nobility. (Is there not a degree of bad faith in this
reproach? Is it not, after all, the narrator himself who has put these compelling affairs before us?) Yet our own disappointment pales in comparison to
the blow dealt the verdict of the beit din by the Duke himself. The Duke
rules over the city in which the elderly judge is the rabbi. Because the
Duke's interests align him with the losing party, he orders his men to take
the rabbi into custody for the purpose of forcing him to reverse the judgment; knowing what is in store for him, the rabbi flees. Thus, in one stroke,
are swept aside the vast and concerted efforts of the leadership of Polish
Jewry to maintain the sway of the Jewish legal system.

Back to Buczacz

Failure at this elevated level of Jewish-gentile politics is echoed in a minor
chord by the novella's conclusion: the final failure of Buczacz to make a rabbinic appointment. The delegates from Buczacz return home from Zabno
ebullient with the news that a magnificent scholar has been living modestly
in their own backyard. The community absorbs the news and consolidates
its will to make the offer to R. Mordekhai. When he is approached, he is
astonished that R. Avraham has recommended him for the rabbinic post,
an act that has in effect "outed" him. But rather than reject the offer outright, he agrees to give the matter three days of consideration in light of
the honor due to the opinion of the Rabbi of Zabno. Buczacz misreads

his hesitation as an expression of humility that precedes acceptance. In the meantime, word of the appointment reaches the gentile master of the city [*sar ha'ir*], who gives it his enthusiastic endorsement.[24] This agreement further strengthens the confidence and self-satisfaction of Buczacz; a distinguished delegation is put together to make the official presentation and finalize the appointment. With much ceremony and solemnity, they make their way to the tinsmith's house and make the offer, mentioning the approbation of the gentile official in order to cap the occasion. R. Mordekhai is confounded and stupefied by this news, which renders his rejection of the offer absolute.[25] By the next day, he has taken his family and disappeared from Buczacz.

The conclusion to "In Search of a Rabbi" is rife with compositional problems, signified by the numerous instances of broken horizontal lines, which indicate breaks in the manuscript.[26] The novella is sprawling and heterogeneous; Agnon's failing health did not permit him to return to the manuscript and linger over the problems of closure. Yet the trajectory is clear enough. It is an arc of failure, and that failure is the consequence of the unholy intermingling of power and rabbinic learning. Power is primarily gentile power, which inevitably exploits Jews for its own interests. But it is also power itself, the very desire for position and distinction—even within the internal Jewish community—that must inevitably lead to the corruption of Torah.

So we are returned to the bifurcated nature of the novella. The second half of the novella turns on the tragic inevitability of grandiosity and power in the widest possible public sphere, whereas the first half, set later in time and in secret enclosures, offers two relationships: (1) R. Avraham and R. Mordekhai and (2) R. Mordekhai and his teacher that exemplify disinterested Torah learning. If the events had been presented in their natural chronological order, we might have been tempted to take these exemplary instances as redemptive antidotes to the "bad old days" of the scheming grandees and their fickle gentile protectors. By reversing the temporal order, Agnon first exposes us to a set of ideals and then plunges us into a world in which spiritual nobility cannot survive. We are left with the feeling that power always and everywhere devours the norm of Torah no matter whether it is early or late, before or after.

R. Mordekhai, the putative hero of the novella, is the complete talmid ḥakham in his disinterested pursuit of Torah and his devotion to the active clarifications of its teachings. But at the same time he has foresworn all forms of leadership and declines to take responsibility for the application of his studies to the life of the community; he has gone so far as to conceal his gifts until the moment of his unwilling exposure. Aside from his testy independence, moreover, he is a man "without qualities" in the sense that we are shown nothing of his inner struggles, if they exist, in the way we are given access to R. Avraham's self-doubts and his need for connection.

The novella's conclusion, then, is unequivocal. At this period of time in the life of Polish-Galician Jewry, the political conditions bearing down on the communal rabbinate make it impossible for that office to be occupied by true exemplars of Torah learning. And, conversely, true exemplars of Torah learning can exist—survive might be the better term—only in secret, invisible and, for all practical purposes, not of use to the community.

The bleakness of this conclusion admits one mitigation. From all this communal conflict and frustration there is at least negative knowledge to be derived. To know the truth is a kind of consolation because it clarifies the norms of value around which the world is organized, despite the disappointments of reality. The monitory insight around which the message of the story is crystallized is made explicit in a scene that Agnon inserts into the penultimate position in the novella. After finishing the chronicle of Reuven and Shimon and before the story returns to the authority of its general narrator, R. Avraham brings his great monologue to a close by returning to the story of R. Mordekhai and his teacher (pp. *380–83, 350–53*). (This is section 5 in the chart above.) Representatives of the rabbi's town have come to the village to return him in glory, the Duke's carriage waiting at the ready. But he declines to leave with them, insisting that they come back for him after Shabbat. He uses the interval to take leave from his pupil by sitting and studying with him one last time. The text is Pirkei Avot, which is customarily studied on Shabbat afternoons during the summer months. But there is nothing customary or accidental about the individual mishnah (1:10) chosen for scrutiny.

> Ehov et hamelakhah usen'a et harabbanut ve'al titvad‘a larashut.
>   Love work, loath mastery over others, and avoid intimacy with the government.

It is no small stroke of genius on Agnon's part to adduce this laconic, tripartite statement, which brings together the work's key themes, and make it the cognitive climax of the novella. The effectiveness of the text for this purpose turns on a willed misprision of the term *rabbanut*. No commentator, traditional or modern, would mistakenly parse the word as an equivalent for "the rabbinate." Rabbanut does not take on that meaning until the Middle Ages. In rabbinic Hebrew—the author of the statement, Shemaya, belongs to the famous "pairs" who lived while the Temple still stood—the term means love of high office, domination, and mastery over others. But at the conclusion of this long narrative that hinges on the question of whether or not to be co-opted into the rabbinate, the opportunity is too good to pass up.

The venerable rabbi, Mordekhai's teacher, is an admirable figure on many counts, but there is one, according to his own lights, on which he falls short. Looking up from his parsing of the mishnah, he plaintively delivers his last words to his pupil.

> When I was a lad I longed to become a rabbi. Once I entered the rabbinate, I neither loved nor hated it. Now, with everything that has happened to me, I am in a position to fulfill the commandment "Loath the rabbinate." But I have not merited fulfilling the commandment "Love work" because I have no other trade to offer. I wish I shall have no need for "intimacy with the government," even when it seemingly works to my benefit. (p. *383*, 353)

Even if it was too late for him, his pupil learned well.

5

Jews and Poles

After being cut off from his hunting party, the great Count Potocki, lost
and enfeebled, is discovered by a charcoal maker named Naḥum Ze'ev, who
then carries the nobleman to his one-room hovel in the forest where the
count can regain his strength. Soon the count has sufficiently recovered to
be taken back to his palace in Buczacz, but before they can set out Naḥum
Ze'ev has to say his morning prayers; for he had been on his way into town
to pray with the community when he came across the exhausted magnate.
The sight of the Jew praying is utterly astonishing to Count Potocki, and
the narrator makes this ironic observation:

> Approximately eighteen hundred Jews lived on Count Potocki's estates.
> Among them were leaseholders of farm land and taverns, grain merchants,
> and businessmen who handled financial transactions, not to mention shop-
> keepers and artisans. But when it came to the customs of the Jews, he had
> not the least notion, and their prayers he had never heard, except for parodies
> of them by the banquet jesters who were a constant presence at his table.
> Now that fate had placed him in the home of a Jew who was preparing him-
> self for prayer, he lay there with eyes open waiting to see what the prayer of
> a Jew looked like. But fatigue and the brandy he had drunk overcame him,
> and he fell asleep. (p. *243*, 207)[1]

This episode, from the story "The Partners" ["Hashutafim"], is remarkable for what it reveals both about Jewish-Polish relations in eighteenth-century Buczacz and about the imaginative intervention in those relations undertaken by Agnon's fiction.

Buczacz was one of the many "private towns" wholly owned by an aristocratic family. In 1602 it passed into the possession of the Potocki family, headed at the time the story takes place by Mikołaj Potocki, who ruled over the town for much of the eighteenth century.[2] He was a man renowned both for his irascible temper and his great generosity to civic and religious institutions. Buczacz, the many villages that surrounded it and the serfs who inhabited them, as well as vast tracks of forest and rivers in the region, were but part of the family's hereditary holdings.

Yet all this land and its natural resources could be converted into wealth only with the help of the Jews. It was through their entrepreneurial, commercial, and managerial acumen that forests could be turned into timber, rivers harnessed to power flour mills, animal hides processed into leather, grain converted into highly profitable alcohol, and the agricultural bounty of the peasantry efficiently marketed in return for manufactured necessities imported from abroad; and this is not to mention the tradesmen and artisans necessary to sustain the civilized life of a city. The Jews and the great Polish landowners were far from equal, but it is no exaggeration to say they were interdependent. This was especially the case in the borderlands of southern Poland in what is today western Ukraine, where Buczacz is located, because it was the Jews who mediated between the Polish Roman Catholic nobles and the Orthodox Ruthenian peasants.

Yet despite the multiple, dense layers of interconnectedness between Poles and Jews, the knowledge of each other's culture remained paltry. Although the Great Synagogue was the most visible Jewish structure in Buczacz and synagogue prayer the most visible ritual of the Jews, the only familiarity Count Potocki has with these matters comes from the derisive mimicry of his court entertainers, who likely found in the Jews' penchant for gesticulation and movement during prayer rich fodder for their ridicule. The feeling was mutual, it is fair to say. For their part, the Jews evinced little interest in the theology or practice of Catholicism in its eastern or western forms and were repelled by the images and statuary that played such a prominent role on saints' days as well as in personal piety. So despite the fact that they lived in the same city—albeit in different quarters—and did business with one another day in and day out, Jews and Poles led parallel but separate lives. Parallel, but hardly symmetrical when it came to status and political vulnerability. Priests could whip up incitement against Jews; the students of the Basilian monastery school in Buczacz could vandalize Jewish property whenever it suited their high spirits; and the lord of the town, Count Potocki himself, could shoot a Jew to death with impunity after finding nothing else to shoot at during a long and frustrating day hunting.[3]

It is precisely at this point that Agnon's fiction makes its intervention. The Buczacz stories conjure up the embroiled relations between Poles and Jews with fidelity to the historical record. But instead of stopping there, the stories introduce an alternative plane of reality in which the asymmetry inherent in these relations is equalized or reversed. In the passage quoted above from "The Partners," Count Potocki is not only rescued from death's door by a poor Jew but exposed to the intimate gestures of his devotional life in a way that engenders respect rather than disdain. (Note well, however, that he falls asleep just at the moment Naḥum Ze'ev begins his prayers!) Did such an event ever take place? Was there even a legend to this effect that was passed down in local lore? Was the story retrofitted as an etiological myth to explain why a Jewish family possessed an inalienable writ to occupy the basement of the great town hall, as described in the remainder of the story?

Although the historical framework of the story is unassailable, the historicity of its central event, the rescue of a Polish count by a Jewish charcoal maker, is suspect and ultimately beside the point. This is not to say that simply by placing the text in the category of fiction it gets a free ride. Whether Agnon built his story around the armature of a legend that circulated in Buczacz or whether he created it out of whole cloth, the more interesting question is how his story envisions Polish-Jewish relations.

At the core of the other major story that deals with this issue, "R. Moshe Aharon the Mead Merchant" ["R. Moshe Aharon mokher mei devash"], is a similar instance in which a high-ranking Polish nobleman is saved from death by a Jew and which results in a temporary benefit for the community as a whole. In both cases Agnon is doing something new. He is "adding" to the historical record by imagining what could have or *should* have transpired between Jews and Poles. The wisdom evinced by Naḥum Ze'ev and R. Moshe Aharon, each in his own way, is not so much an individual distinction as an expression of the achievement of Buczaczan—read Polish—Jewish society as a whole. Agnon's contribution is to take this achievement, which is real, and create an imaginative experiment in which a great Polish lord in extremis is exposed to it and is compelled to acknowledge its truth.

Thus for Agnon to devote himself to the project of reimagining Buczacz in its golden age means not simply to accept the limits of the historical record but to enlarge them. He exploits the imaginative freedom accorded him as a storyteller to conjure up or reveal or bring into being developments that, if the right opportunities had presented themselves, could have taken place. This is not an indulging in denial or wish fulfillment but it is the creation of a more useable past. For despite the innumerable and variegated interactions we know to have taken place between Poles and Jews in Buczacz by virtue of their commercial interdependence, the paucity of documentary sources allows us to experience precious few of them. Agnon's intervention exfoliates that fraught potentiality. It performs imaginative experiments and interventions while remaining true to the thick texture of the historical record.

The stories that depict the encounter between Jews and gentiles in *A City in Its Fullness* are divided by the partitions of Poland at the end of the eighteenth century. This chapter deals with the interaction of Jews with the sovereign Polish lords who brought them to Ukraine to serve as their agents. The next chapter discusses the eclipse of the feudal paradigm and the effects of the subsequent Austrian rule on internal Jewish relations.

The Golden Prerogatives of the Nobility

Before Poland was dismembered and divided among Russia, Prussia, and Austria, it had been unique among European states in its governance. The office of king was elective rather than hereditary. As a protection against tyranny, the Polish nobility insisted on choosing a monarch from among its ranks without the possibility of dynastic succession. This "golden liberty" was first among a number of privileges that vested enormous power in the hands of the nobility rather than the monarchy. The nobility, which was called the *szlachta*, was an estate or a caste that included 6 percent of the population, a proportion greater than in other European states. The szlachta was a vast group whose members ranged from the landless and impoverished gentry to minor gentry and then to fabulously wealthy land owners. Over 60 percent of the land, towns, villages, and peasantry of Poland were privately owned by the nobility; and a few families, such as the Radziwills and the Potockis, owned networks of non-contiguous holdings numbering dozens of towns and hundreds of villages. These so-called magnates (members of the *magnateria*) exercised absolute authority within their estates (called *latifundia*; *latifundium*, singular), and their judgments on civil and criminal matters could not be appealed to any royal or centralized judiciary.[4]

It was the goal of the magnate to extract from his latifundium as much profit as possible to sustain a style of life based on expensive imported goods. The magnate could rely on the brute labor owed to him by his serfs to plant or harvest his crops. But when it came to exploiting the natural resources of his property—extracting minerals, felling and marketing timber, milling grains, and fishing and fish farming—he called upon the services of leaseholders called arrendators, who received a concession to operate in a specific economic sector in return for a fee or a share of the profits. The most abundant resource was agriculture, and the magnate faced a special challenge in realizing profit from surplus grain, which, even if he could export by virtue of proximity to river transportation, could not be sold at a premium. The solution was to distill the grain and convert it to alcohol and sell it back to the peasants at a significant markup to be consumed locally at rural taverns that were permitted to dispense only the landowner's liquor.

It is as leaseholders, agents, and bankers that the Jews enter the picture. It was beneath the status of the magnate to engage in business, although he might employ lesser members of the szlachta in the administration of the estate. Jews provided the commercial and managerial acumen and discipline necessary to maximize the yield of the latifundium. When it came to the retailing of alcohol, their sobriety was particularly advantageous. Whereas the peasants lived in villages, Jews made up the largest group inhabiting the market towns, where they provided goods and services for the hinterland. Although there were existing guilds of Polish artisans, Jews were often the most prominent tailors, haberdashers, butchers, furriers, and tanners. They maintained shops that stocked textiles and other goods not produced locally. Living in close proximity to the synagogue and the beit midrash, the Jews constituted a separate corporate entity, and the lord of the city would relate to them as such. He would deal directly with representatives of the kahal, the community's lay leadership, when it came to exacting taxes and granting privileges.

This pattern, which repeated itself throughout the Polish-Lithuanian Commonwealth, was intensified in what is today western Ukraine, where Buczacz was located. The Polish landowners had entered this region in more recent centuries as colonizers and had subjected the Ruthenian peasantry to their rule. The Eastern Orthodox Christianity of the local populace, along with its language, was treated with contempt, and their churches and religious orders received few of the resources lavished upon the Roman Catholics churches and institutions. (This was the case even after the creation of the Uniate or Greek-Catholic Church, which combined Eastern Orthodox ritual with obedience to the authority of Rome.)

Ukraine was the scene of the only serious peasant uprising in the history of the Commonwealth. This was the rebellion led by Bohdan Khmelnytskyi in 1648–49, which was responsible for the destruction of hundreds of Jewish communities and many tens of thousands of Jews, as well as a smaller number of their Polish patrons.[5] The uprising became possible only because of the location of Ukraine on the southern flank of the Commonwealth, which enabled the Cossacks to cross over from east of the Dnieper and join with the Tartars. The Buczacz fortress withstood the Cossack siege during the uprising, but the town was sacked several times in the ensuing decades by Tartar bands and by the Ottoman army, which had reached the gates of Vienna only to be turned back by the Polish King Sobieski. Subsequent border changes and the ceding of East Ukraine to Moscovy eventually removed Buczacz from its exposed position on the frontier. Yet the general region of western Ukraine known as Galicia remained one of the wildest and least developed in the Commonwealth. Its vast forests and marshlands provided refuge for outlaws and brigands as well as for Cossack adventurers who would cross the Dnieper to stir up trouble.

By the beginning of the eighteenth century, the external threats to the region had receded, and with them the prospects for mass violence against Jews. Buczacz was rebuilt under the patronage of the Potockis, and a charter was granted to the Jews reconfirming their right to take up residence in the town and do business there. They were as necessary to the project of reconstruction and civic prosperity now as they had been almost two centuries earlier when the Polish nobles had sought to develop the town's fortunes. But the usefulness of the Jews did not ameliorate their general situation. They were loathed by the peasants as the visible agents of the Polish oppressors. They were resented by the Christian townspeople for what was perceived to be their unfair commercial advantage and their domination of certain trades. And they were despised by the shlachta for not being Christians, for not being Poles, and for not being shlachta but living in town.

In *A City in Its Fullness* this misery is faithfully represented, but it is not left alone. Agnon writes two major stories in which the ratio of power is reversed: "R. Moshe Aharon the Mead Merchant" and "The Partners." Although the stories are very different in their conception and atmosphere, at the center of each is a Polish nobleman of immense stature who is rescued from death by a Jew. How and why Agnon constructs this alternative reality, which constitutes the imaginative supplement he adds to the record of Jewish-Polish relations, is the question that preoccupies this chapter.

Before exploring these two stories, it is important to survey briefly the more general canvas to appreciate the exceptionality of these stories. Many of the stories referred to below are discussed in the previous chapters and may be familiar to the reader. I do so under five headings.[6]

First is the Cossack uprising of 1648–49 led by Bohdan Khmelnytskyi. Even though the perpetrators of the massacres were not Poles, the Jews bore the brunt of the violence because of their service to their Polish lords, who generally saved themselves when possible rather than protect "their" Jews. In the collective Jewish memory, the particular identity of the enemy was absorbed into the figure of the *goy*, the gentile persecutor. The impact of this trauma is given its fullest representation in the story "The Parable and Its Lesson" (pp. *394–440*), which depicts Buczacz in the generation after the massacres as a community in which all of its members struggle with the murder of most of their family members. The collective experience of loss is marked by the fast day of the 20th of Sivan, whose solemn liturgy is lavishly and extensively described in the story.

Second is the incitement by Catholic priests and religious persecution. To deflect attention from her own misdeeds, the wife of a church beadle accuses a Jewish bystander, the community's ḥazzan, of witchcraft and desecrating the Host in "The Man Dressed in Linen" (pp. *84–113*, 98–139). The civil rulers yield to the appeals of the church authorities and the saintly Gavriel is convicted and condemned to death by being drawn and quartered. In "The Parable and Its Lesson," Aharon, the senior disciple of R. Moshe, who is afflicted by doubts about divine justice in the wake of the 1648 massacres, is lured into conversion and eventual death by the wiles of a local priest. Under this religious persecution category should be added the periodic waves of vandalism committed by the students of the Basilian monastery students in Buczacz.

Third is murder, authorized by aristocratic indulgence or by a personal whim. There is the famous story of Count Potocki, who, frustrated by a long day of hunting with nothing to show for his efforts, forces a Jewish woman to climb a tree so that he can shoot her dead with his bow and arrow ("The Little Town Hall," pp. *256–57*). The count, the narrator observes, was not an anti-Semite but a nobleman who was law unto himself and whose impulses and caprices had no regulation. Boredom on a Friday afternoon accounted for another incident in which the great count importuned a Jew on his way to Sabbath prayers and, using his whip, forced him to dance before him (p. *75*). Sometimes it was a great lord who strove to protect his Jews from the depredations of the lesser nobility. It was a failure to do so that resulted in the murder of Naphtali, the wine merchant, the father of Zlahte, in "The Parable and Its Lesson" (p. *409*). While Naphtali sleeps by his wagon one night on a trip through the lord's lands, the petty retainers open the wine casks and get drunk. When they come to their senses, they realize they have violated the lord's prohibition and hasten to murder Naphtali and bury his body to erase traces of their crime. A similar occurrence is recounted in "In Search of a Rabbi," in which the murder of a Jew from Stanislaw by a lesser nobleman evokes the anger of the ruling magnate. The murderer then kidnaps a wagonload of Jewish artisans from Buczacz and delivers them to the magnate as a replacement for the Jew he murdered (p. *311*, *256*).

Fourth is sexual victimization. "The Story of the Betrothed Maiden" (pp. *272–74*) tells the story of a young woman from Buczacz who is renowned for her fancy desserts and is hired to bake for the wedding reception of the local lord's son. While she is busy in the castle's kitchens, the bridegroom becomes so smitten with her that he lures her to an isolated place and rapes her, and she dies. In a parallel tale ("Sons Who Were Born to Them" [p. *154*]), the erotic obsession is homosexual. A Polish lord becomes entranced by the stunning beauty of a young Torah scholar, the only son of older parents, who is already engaged to be married. He too is lured to an isolated place and raped. But rather than dying on the spot, he becomes mentally deranged by feelings of pollution, and after his parents' repeated failures to cure him he throws himself off a mountain and falls to his death.

The fifth is economic persecution and intervention in internal Jewish communal affairs. An important source of income for Polish nobles was the manufacture and sale of alcohol made from excess grain production. The retailing of this commodity was largely placed in the hands of Jewish tavern operators, who leased the rights to sell alcohol to the peasantry on the lord's estate. When the lord's expectations of profit were not met, he could turn a family out of its home even if it had operated the tavern for generations—this is the case with Naḥum Ze'ev in "The Partners"—or the noble could throw the family in the stockade. It was from this latter fate that Yisrael Natan rescued Sarah Rivkah and made her his wife in "In Search of a Rabbi, or The Governor's Whim" (pp. *332–33*, *286–87*). That story makes its central theme the constraints imposed by Polish nobles on the most proprietary of Jewish communal choices: the appointment of a rabbi. In their audience with the Rabbi of Zabno, the representatives from Buczacz discuss the systemic bribery necessary to regulate relations with Polish rulers (p. *311*, *256*). But sometimes bribery is of no avail. When a Jewish law court decides a case in a way displeasing to a great nobleman, the latter simply sets aside the verdict and dispatches his men to put the presiding rabbi in prison. The rabbi flees for his life and, in hiding, conveys to his disciple, who is destined to become a formidable scholar, the utter importance of avoiding the office of rabbi.

A Jewish Statesman

The Polish nobles own cities, villages, lands, and forests and rule with a high hand. But to the significant degree that the Jews are allowed corporate autonomy, how do they rule themselves? Throughout *A City in Its Fullness* Agnon makes a strong argument for considering the large Jewish towns in Poland as self-governing city-states that manage their own affairs and negotiate as communities with the powers that rule them. The narrator takes pride in the Council of Four Lands and in its role in representing the interests of the Jews to the Polish-Lithuanian Commonwealth, and he expresses resentment at the abrogation of the Council shortly before the breakup of the Commonwealth, the latter event taken as punishment for the former.[7]

Who governs these proud Jewish polities? Because Agnon chooses to make learning and worship the normative pillars of his imaginative reconstruction, it would be natural to present rabbis and scholars as the rightful rulers. At the same time, he well knows that the notion of the rabbi as ruler is not the historical truth but a construct driven by desire, a longing for the way it *should* have been. And the stories themselves endlessly document the political constraints that weigh on the rabbinate and lead to the eventual diminution of its authority. So the question remains: If Jewish communal autonomy is real, who is it that rules? Now, we do not need Agnon's literary fictions to know that the kahal of each community was controlled by a group of well-to-do householders who took turns administering the

institutions of the community and representing it before the gentile authorities. The position is variously called the parnas or the gabbai. Yet in
the several instances in which the stories of *A City in Its Fullness* turn their
attention to the workings of temporal rather than spiritual authority, they
do something more than reconfirm the facts we know from the historical
record. Agnon exploits the freedom he has arrogated to himself to conjure
the mental world of Jews who rule other Jews and to explore how their
temperament is fitted to the task. He opens up an imagined and imaginative three-dimensional space behind and beyond the historical record and
populates it with flesh-and-blood figures whose experience is more real
than their historical cyphers.

Such is R. Moshe Aharon, the eponymous hero of "R. Moshe Aharon
the Mead Merchant." The story is one of three about gabbaim, and it joins
the larger taxonomy of kelei kodesh in book 1 of occupations, lay and professional, that serve the religious needs of the community. First come the
ḥazzanim and the shamashim, then the gabbaim, later the lomdim (men
who devote all their time to study in the beit midrash), and, finally, in
book 2, the rabbis. Passing from one gabbai to another, the narrator is conspicuously operating in his role as chronicler, fixing details of succession and
recording unusual events that took place during the term of each gabbai.
But, as happens so often in the flow of *A City in Its Fullness*, the chronicle
mode is suddenly disrupted and overtaken by a great narrative profusion
that soon reveals itself not as a digression, but as the story itself.

Rather than contenting himself with a quick sketch and some piquant
anecdotes, as he has in the case of the other gabbaim, the narrator undertakes an ample portrait of R. Moshe Aharon, detailing his lineage, his education and intellectual formation, his costume, and the autocratic manner in
which he governs Buczacz. Then there is a further surprise. When the portrait is on the brink of being completed, the narrator turns on a dime and
from out of nowhere introduces a long and lurid narrative about a great
Polish prince whose desperate search for atonement for a terrible crime
he committed leads him on a pilgrim's journey to Egypt and back. The
ostensible justification for the tale comes at its very end. Providence brings

the desperate prince to the doorstep of R. Moshe Aharon, who cures him and leverages the prince's gratitude on behalf of the welfare of the Jews of Buczacz. The connection to the main story, long deferred and often apologized for by the narrative, is finally made; but the nexus is flimsy, and the reader remains disorientated by the presence of a tale about a gentile nobleman that is so sensational that it threatens to take over the story proper.

Agnon's purpose in this strangely constructed story, I would argue, is to imagine what a successful Jewish prince might look like. The story-within-a-story of the penitent Polish prince has a function far more important than explaining why one Jewish mead merchant has garnered the favor of an illustrious magnate. Its real function is to establish a comparison—and by implication, a moral equivalence—between two unlikely parties: the lay head of a moderately-sized Jewish community and a great peer of the realm. The prince, whose name is never given and who is not identifiable as a historical figure, is referred to by that title—*rozen* in Hebrew—not only because he owns a fifth of Poland and is therefore no ordinary member of the nobility but also because the title "prince" carries the generic connotation of "ruler." In European culture the term automatically evokes Machiavelli's *The Prince*, and this is an association that Agnon might welcome. He wants his nameless Polish prince to function as a type for the gentile ruler, whose governance and behavior can be compared to the conduct of a Jewish ruler in his own sphere. As the ruler of a Jewish city-state, R. Moshe Aharon is every inch a prince, despite the constraints under which Jewish sovereignty operates. In analyzing how he governs, Agnon means his story to partake in the genre of "mirrors for princes" in which Machiavelli wrote. His portrait of R. Moshe Aharon is not a historical recollection of a unique individual but an exploration of what a Jewish ruler might be.

The Buczacz of Agnon's construction, to begin with, is a world that privileges learning and worship, and it is far from self-evident that civil leadership can be seen as anything more than a duty that falls to the lot of successful businessmen. "R. Moshe Aharon the Mead Merchant" makes the case that such leadership can—again, potentially—be a high calling. The narrator implies that nowadays Torah scholarship and communal leadership cannot be combined in the same person and the choice to follow one path or the other constitutes a kind of "either/or." It was not always so. R. Moshe Aharon's grandfather, R. Shaul was not only recognized as a great talmid ḥakham, but he took up arms to defend Buczacz at the time of the Turkish incursions and was wounded in battle.[8] The position of gabbai fell to R. Moshe Aharon through a kind of dynastic default. The office was held by his father R. Neḥemia, whose success in the mead trade had made communal leadership an expected duty. But the older he got the more his heart was not in his duties as gabbai, and he spent his time studying Torah in the beit midrash. Although the father bore the title, it was really the son who oversaw the affairs of the community. With his father's death, R. Moshe Aharon acceded to the title proper as he did to his father's business and the valuable contents of his cellar. In another story in *A City in Its Fullness*, the father's preference for Torah study might have been held up as evidence for the sterling attributes of the denizens of the city; but in this context it comes across as dereliction. Governance is a calling unto itself with its own discipline and skills.

"R. Moshe Aharon was not considered one of the scholars (lomdim), but he was well educated (*hayah ben torah*)" (p. *129*, 154).[9] The narrator makes a precise distinction, and an important one. As a boy he was given the kind of elite training that would have qualified him to devote himself to Torah studies, and his family certainly did not lack the resources to underwrite the pursuit of such a venerated vocation. But he chose another path, and the choice was made on the basis of an implicit recognition in himself of the kind of strengths and qualities necessary to protect the community and govern it. The stamp of his character was given important confirmation by the Rabbi of Yaslovitz, his kinsman and teacher, in the form of two gifts.[10] One is a jet black sheepskin hat given to express gratitude to Moshe Aharon for saving the rabbi's life when he was attacked by a bandit. He jumped the bandit from behind, threw him to the ground, trounced him, and drove the rabbi away to safety. This was a formative lesson in the vulnerability of the Jews among the nations and in the will necessary to resist victimization; and it is by no means insignificant that it was to a convocation of the Council of Four Lands, the parliament-like

Jewish deliberative body, that the rabbi and his young companion were travel-ing when the attack occurred. That the rabbi's gift is an expensive headdress, a symbol of office, and not a tome of Talmud commentaries—Moshe Aharon buys that for himself—is also telling. The rabbi is aware of what his pupil is just learning: his gifts lie in statesmanship and not scholarship.

The rabbi's second gift, given on the occasion of Moshe Aharon's wedding, is two works by R. David Gans (1541–1613): *Tsemaḥ David*, which chronicles Jewish and world history from the creation of Adam to the discovery of America, and *Sefer neḥmad vena'im*, which relates the discoveries of astronomy, "the shape of the four basic elements, the nine celestial bodies, the height of the sun and every star beyond the horizon and many other wondrous phe-nomena" (p. *129*, 155). The Rabbi of Yaslovitz was placing in the hands of his student the sum total of what could be known at the time by a Polish Jew reading in Hebrew about the human and natural history of the world.

Close study of these works has a transformative impact on the young man's worldview. The world of Buczacz and the communities of Galicia are revealed to be a miniscule locus within the vastness of the cosmos. His study of world history leads to the formation of a determined political consciousness as well as a sense of personal destiny. "As much as he learned about kings and emperors, he felt saddened that the glory of the Jews had been taken from them and given to the nations of the world. How could this have happened? All of the nations of the world have emperors and kings, princes, officials and rulers, whereas we, the holy people Israel, are mired in Exile without a king or a ruler or a sovereign" (p. *129*, 155). Unlike similar questions asked in the wake of the 1648 massacres by another Aha-ron, the tortured denizen of Gehinnom in "The Parable and Its Lesson," Moshe Aharon does not draw a damning conclusion about God's justice but rather takes Israel's fallen state as a personal charge to forge the kind of leadership that has not been given by grace.

These discoveries, especially pertaining to developments far away, would seem to open up a shared space of worldliness between Jews and Poles, a space of refinement and learning. In his enthusiasm, R. Moshe Aharon tells the noble who is the owner of Buczacz about the discovery of America only to be told in return that "this was just another of the fabrications the Jews fill their books with." Undeterred, he loans the noble his copy of *Sefer nehmad vena'im*, which contains a Latin précis as an appendix, to document the news. But the acknowledgement never comes, and the volume, the precious gift from his teacher, is never returned. From this painful early experience, R. Moshe Aharon draws two lessons: "A Jew should never engage a gentile in conversation about matters the gentile is not familiar with, and a Jew should not bring a book written in the language of the gentiles into his home."

R. Moshe Aharon's conduct in this episode suggests something about the man himself beyond these practical wisdoms. He converses with the lord of Buczacz as if he were his equal, as he indeed regards himself, no matter how contemptuously he is regarded by the Polish magnate. And he converses with him in Polish, a language he speaks with fluency and authority, as we are told near the end of the story (p. *141*, 172). Finally, we see him as a leader who learns by acting in the world and by turning rebuffs into sagacity about future statecraft.

R. Moshe Aharon has a further distinction. Of all the men and women who parade through the pages of Agnon's Buczacz stories, he is the only one to merit what amounts to a catalogue raisonné of his wardrobe.

> He wore an old felt coat lined with cotton and a grey turban, wide at the bottom and narrowed in a circle to the top. Although it appeared to be woven, it was actually not, because he never wore anything woven after once discovering that the threads in a garment he had purchased were woven in the shape of the cross.
>
> Wearing these garments he would go about his business and welcome the princes and lords who come to his home to taste his mead[. . . .] Whenever he recited the blessings after meals—and, there is no need to add, when he walked to the synagogue or went to circumcise an infant—he wore a coat over his garments with a lambskin turban in place of his regular one. On Sabbaths and holidays he wore a satin coat and a silk cap. On winter Sabbaths he wore a marten coat and a goatskin cap of such deep and shiny blackness that it seemed to give off sparks of blue light.[11] (p. *130*, 156)

What prompts the narrator toward this upsurge in sartorial specificity is a desire to suggest—through the indirection of metonymy—the different aspects in which R. Moshe Aharon presents himself to the world. We learn, for example, of his studied indifference to Christian mores. Although he would take great pains to alter his costume and put on finery for Sabbath and ritual functions, he makes a point of not doing so when he is receiving high-born visitors shopping for spirits. The avoidance of any woven garment because of cross-like stitching is surely a hyper-stringency, and it would seem to reflect a need to reinforce the conviction of an inner boundary on the part of a Jew who has frequent contacts with Christians. Most striking in R. Moshe Aharon's wardrobe is the variety of his headdress. There are four altogether: one for business, one for the observance of weekday ritual acts, one for summer Sabbaths, and one for winter Sabbaths. (This last one is the gift from his teacher for saving him from the hands of bandits.) The Hebrew term for this head gear *mitsnefet* is not the usual word for hat. It comes from the biblical name for the head covering of the high priest in the Jerusalem temple although it was also used later to connote a turban, that is, fabric wrapped around the head.[12] Whatever its precise meaning, the term projects an archaic, hieratic, and vaguely oriental tone and suggests, in addition to his exquisite awareness of his self-presentation, that R. Moshe Aharon sees himself as the re-embodiment of an ancient Jewish ruler, the very prince absent from the annals of postbiblical Israel.

The aggressive and autocratic manner in which R. Moshe Aharon discharges his duties as gabbai, the narrator informs us, has never before been witnessed in Buczacz. When a man with connections to the rulers seeks to avoid paying a tax levied on the community, the gabbai tells him coolly that he may be exempted, but when he dies he will not be buried until his heirs pay several times the sum to the community. When another complains that he has not been treated with the respect he deserves by a representative of the community, he is told by R. Moshe Aharon, "Wait until Yom Kippur, when he will want your forgiveness, and if it is difficult to wait, forgive him now" (p. *132, 159*). When still another criticizes the gabbai's brusque style by comparing it to his father's agreeable courtliness, he receives this riposte: "Why do you compare me with my father? My father dealt with men of understanding like your father, but I have to deal with troublemakers and malcontents like you." He makes enactments that are necessary for the community's welfare and only after the fact convenes the council of elders to inform them. If his measures fail to elicit approbation, "he would close his eyes as if he was asleep and no one could know whether or not he had heard."

R. Moshe Aharon's behavior is a subject of astonishment rather than judgment. In his role as the representative of communal opinion, the narrator reports: "Many people struggled with the question of where Moshe Aharon found the strength to act in this way" (p. *132, 159*). The elderly denizens of the beit midrash do not remember as well behaved a boy as he, and his contemporaries say that he was an agreeable youth who showed no signs of aggressiveness, except, that is, for the time when he grabbed a switch out of the hands of a melamed who was about to thrash him. The narrator can come up with no explanation, and he is forced to admit that this remains a question with no answer.

There *is* an answer, of course, but the narrator is looking for it in the wrong place. He assumes that Moshe Aharon's behavior as an adult must necessarily be an outgrowth of a core personality that was shaped in boyhood and youth; and he is confounded when he can adduce no early signs of the later man. We have in fact already been informed of the source: after reading about the kings and princes of the nations and the abjection of Israel, the young man decides, within the terms available to him, to become a ruler and statesman. That it could be will rather than temperament that is driving the gabbai's conduct is a notion beyond the narrator's mental repertoire, which has provision for neither the concept of a Jewish ruler or prince nor for the act of self-fashioning Moshe Aharon has undertaken. So even though it is the narrator himself who describes Moshe Aharon's revelatory experience reading history, he cannot put the two things together. Agnon invites us, the readers, to take that step.

"R. Moshe Aharon the Mead Merchant" is a portrait sketch of a singular communal leader until it suddenly becomes something else. The story goes about its business laying out the gabbai's lineage, education, and conduct in a manner that, despite an admixture of illustrative anecdotes, is essentially discursive. But then, with the flimsy excuse of explaining how Moshe

Aharon achieved prominence in the mead trade, the story launches into a lengthy and lurid narrative about a Polish prince who traverses most of the known world in search for atonement for a terrible crime. The narrator is well aware of the fact that he is taking the reader on a wild ride far away from Buczacz and deep into world of Polish Catholicism; and the longer the story goes on, the more frequent are the apologies and the requests that the reader stay with him, and the promises to be brief and cut to the chase. The narrator eventually makes good on his promise to bring his tale back home and demonstrate its relevance to R. Moshe Aharon and his milieu. Yet the ostensible connection between the two remains slight and unpersuasive, located somewhere between the vagaries of divine providence and the coincidences of melodrama. Again, Agnon as implied author urges us to discover a deeper nexus, one that lies beyond the ken of his narrator.

The Haunted Prince

The hero of this tale-within-a-story is no ordinary Polish noble, and the transgression for which he seeks remission is no ordinary sin. The noble is an unnamed prince who owns a fifth of Poland and whose vast wealth is beyond imagining. (He is not, it is important to point out, a scion of the Potocki family, and his estates do not include Buczacz.) His sin is hiring an assassin to murder his sister and her husband, whose independence after their marriage aroused a jealousy he could not abide. Although his exalted status places him above the law of the land, the prince cannot be defended from the afflictions of his conscience and from accusatory apparitions of the murdered couple. Feasting and drinking provide only fleeting relief, and when he tries to lose himself in hunting, the animal he is about to dispatch opens its mouth and says, "Are you going to kill me too the way you did your sister and her husband?" (p. *132*, *160*). He seeks refuge in a rural church, but the huge sums he contributes do not avail him. In the smoke of the candles his donations have purchased the shades of his murdered victims appear and lay hold of him, haunting him without respite. Next he consults with distinguished priests who are used to serving as father confessors to the nobility, and he is counseled to make pilgrimage to the grave of a saintly wonder worker.

That errand is a failure, but the prince hears from other penitents about a cave in Egypt that assures atonement to sinners who spend the night in it. Humbled, he foreswears his finery and joins a group of pilgrims traveling by foot to the holy site. By this time he is so hobbled by the consequences of his transgression that he can barely walk; he can proceed only with the support of the other sinners, who endlessly rehearse the tales of their own sins. The cave is the cell of a penitent who carved out a space only large enough for him to kneel in, and there he installed himself until worms devoured his flesh. The worms were overheard promising absolution to any sinner who spends three nights in the cave; a monastery was established on the site, and pilgrims came from far and wide. The claims prove true; arriving in a state of mental collapse, the prince spends just one night in the cave and suddenly feels free of the censorious apparitions that have haunted him so long. But that same night, alas, he contracts a wasting fever and lies languishing in the paupers' ward of a hospital. Having been immersed in the torments of the soul, he is now plunged into the torments of the body.

His luck changes when his aristocratic identity is discovered by a European nobleman visiting the indigent ill. He is brought to a proper hotel, loaned money, and given a carriage so that he can consult doctors and return home. He visits many doctors in many countries, taking the medicines they give him for the payment of enormous fees, but he does not improve. Finally, he comes under the care of a great court physician, who declares that the essence of his suffering derives from the toxic drugs he has been given by meretricious doctors. Under this new regimen, the prince's condition improves somewhat, and when the physician becomes too busy with his obligations at court to treat him, he decides to return to his estates in Poland and to turn his attention to his subjects, whose welfare he had ignored even before his troubles began. On the road home there is a terrible flare up of the fever, and his driver pulls his carriage into the nearest town.

The town is none other than Buczacz, and the house in front of which the carriage comes to a stop is none other than R. Moshe Aharon's. The prince is taken in and put to bed. R. Moshe Aharon descends into his cellar and retrieves a cask that was already 250 years old when his father laid it down fifty years earlier. The prince is given two beakers of this elixir to drink and falls into a deep slumber. Over the course of two days he sweats out his fever and arises restored to health and full of boundless gratitude to his host. When R. Moshe Aharon declines the purses of gold he is offered as thanks, the prince is astonished at the comparison between him and the many doctors who drained his pockets yet brought him no relief. The prince promulgates an edict placing the mead merchant under his protection; R. Moshe Aharon becomes the mead supplier of choice to the great estates, whose lords visit his home to taste the mead and converse with the worldly merchant. The prince himself sets aside a day or two each year for a visit. The two men sit together and discuss—in Polish, of course— "the affairs of the world, the prince basing himself on what he had seen with his own eyes and R. Moshe Aharon on what he had read in the volumes *Tsemaḥ David* and *Neḥmad venaʿim*" (p. *142*, *172*). The favor R. Moshe Aharon enjoys in the eyes of the Polish elite is converted to political capital in difficult times, and the fortune he accrues is left to the community upon his death.[13]

The prince's tale is finally concluded and folded back into the frame story. Yet the tale remains so sensational and exotic and lengthy that it threatens to consume the frame that is supposed to contain it. It is also a journey deep into a gentile Christian imaginary thick with mortal sins and mortifications. Why, then, is this tale here? What justifies the hefty narrative weight it displaces?

The prince's tale, I would argue, serves two purposes, one explicit and one implicit, one urged on us openly by the narrator and one implied structurally by the author. To begin with, the narrator justifies the prince's tale by virtue of its etiological value. It provides an explanation for the extraordinary fact that a Jew from Buczacz has frequent contact with the Polish nobility and counts one of its greatest magnates as his special friend. The coincidence that makes all this possible—the prince's carriage "happens" to stop beside R. Moshe Aharon's home and mead shop—is presented as a clear instance of providential orchestration. The narrator goes so far as to claim that the reason the prince does not lose a grip on his sanity, which would have been his likely fate in view of his extreme suffering, is because God wanted the prince to hold himself together just long enough to collapse on R. Moshe Aharon's doorstep and thus provide the mead merchant with the chance to cure him and put him in his debt (p. *135, 164*).

Yet despite its expository justification, this chronicle of obsessive sin and the quest for absolution drags the reader over a terrain of gentile Christianity that, though fascinating in a voyeuristic sense, is alien and polluting. The narrator feels called upon several times to address the reader directly, and he offers reassurance that we, as Jews, know that these beliefs and practices are nonsense. For example, regarding the belief that a night spent in the cave of the Egyptian penitent delivers absolution, the narrator says, "To you, my friend, it is not necessary to say that their sins were not remitted; would that at least thenceforth they desisted from sinning." The directness and intimacy of the narrator's address to the reader as "my friend" (*yedidi*) are unusual in Agnon's Buczacz stories. The phenomenon may signal a desire to reinforce the bond between narrator and reader and underscore the boundary between them and the Christian behaviors in the great gentile world being described. The need for differentiation may be all the more urgent in light of the fact that the prince refers to R. Moshe Aharon as yedidi when he has been purged of his fever and awakes in the mead merchant's bed (p. *140, 170*).

Agnon is up to something more ambitious. By placing the prince's tale alongside the portrait of the gabbai R. Moshe Aharon, he is inviting us to compare the two men in their aspect as rulers. On the surface of things, such a comparison would appear ludicrous. The gabbai of Buczacz is the volunteer head of a downtrodden confessional community that is not only subservient to the Polish magnates but owned by them outright. How is it possible to speak of him in the same breath as a prince of vast wealth, the owner of a fifth of Poland? It *is* possible, the author argues, because communities like (Jewish) Buczacz were invested with a real if conditional sovereignty, and they were, at times, ruled by men of great authority and power. Not only are the terms of the comparison valid but the results of the comparison turn things upside down; for it is the Jewish mead merchant who comes off as the ruler of true wisdom and aristocratic bearing.

The prince serves as a foil. Despite his control of vast estates, his life has been devoted to the pursuit of pleasure, and it is not until he has been chastened by spiritual and physical pain that he accepts responsibility for the governance of his lands. The act of murder, both in its commission and exemption from punishment, is the result of an indulgence unchecked by law. His self-centeredness persists despite his afflictions. In his search for atonement, it is striking that he never repents of his deeds or attempts to reform himself; the goal of his quest remains solely to palliate his suffering and banish his demons. R. Moshe Aharon's worthiness shines by contrast. Armed with neither great wealth nor the coercive power of the state nor the trappings of noble office, the gabbai of Buczacz governs with wisdom, dignity, self-assurance, and justice, qualities that should be the envy of princes and dukes.

R. Moshe Aharon's achievement, however, remains singular, and it is not presented without qualification and irony. The vocation of governance is realized at the expense of devotion to the study of Torah. R. Moshe Aharon and his wife, moreover, are childless, and that fate would seem to be a tragic payment for a consuming devotion to communal leadership. His brusque and autocratic manner does not make him much loved, at least during his lifetime, by his fellow townspeople and by the village Jews, whom he has forced to travel into the city for Rosh Hashanah and Yom Kippur. It is only after his death that the latter acknowledge his wisdom in this ruling and bring their heartfelt rustic tributes during the mourning period. Most striking is the fact that the boundary that separates him from the prince turns out to be more permeable than it appears. The man who will not wear woven garments because of the taint of cruciform stitching is the same man who discovers the will to rule not from the chronicles of ancient Israel but from the histories of the kings and princes of the nations of the world.

It is telling that the spectacle of world history is discovered by reading a book in Hebrew. The prince has traveled the known world, but R. Moshe Aharon may never have traveled farther from Buczacz than Yaslovitz, the neighboring town, yet he gets all he needs from reading the Hebrew books of David Gans. The worldliness the gabbai attains by reading in Hebrew draws attention to the prevalence of the theme of languages in the story. The gabbai reads texts in Hebrew, talks with his fellow Jews in Yiddish, and converses in Polish with the Polish lords, who, in turn, can read texts in Latin and converse in French, the international language of European aristocracy.

These attainments are, perhaps, only to be expected among members of the ruling elite. But the narrator adduces two instances, one more bizarre than the other, in which the knowledge of a "foreign" language becomes a marker of secret and effectual wisdom. One concerns the cave of the Egyptian ascetic. After his death, the worms, who formerly feasted on his flesh, are overheard conversing by the monks, who, not knowing languages, cannot make out their meaning. It is only when the sagacious abbot translates for them that the good news about the cave's powers can be recognized and broadcast (p. *134*, 163).

The other incident occurs earlier when the prince is searching for diversions that would blot out the afflictions of his conscience.

> He went out hunting. He sighted an animal and was about to take aim, when suddenly the animal spoke up! "Do you intend to kill me as you killed your sister and her husband?!" That the prince understood what the animal was saying should not surprise you, because wild animals and birds are able to speak Hebrew, as we know from the incident of Balaam's talking ass. Now the prince did not know Hebrew. However, animals, beasts, and birds do not waste a word, and they were not party to the sin of the generation of the Tower of Babel and remained unaffected by its punishment. They therefore retained their unitary language from the time when the entire world had one tongue. So when the animal opened its mouth to speak, the prince understood what it was saying. He threw away all his weapons and began to run. (p. *132*, 160)

In his desire both to promote the primacy of Hebrew and to favor us with a reproachful talking bird, the narrator gets lost in the thicket of a casuistical argument. We know from Balaam's ass that animals speak Hebrew; we know that the unitary language spoken before Babel was Hebrew; and we know that animals were not implicated in the sin of Babel. Ergo, the bird spoke Hebrew. But Hebrew is a language the prince does not understand; so how he understands its accusatory message remains tangled in the overly-knowing syllogism.

Despite this confusion, a kind of principle emerges that is embodied in the careful balance of R. Moshe Aharon's conduct. So long as Israel lives in exile among the nations of the world with their many different tongues, Israel's leaders must of necessity be worldly men who can converse with their rulers and understand their intentions. But this worldliness is only a functional necessity, an appurtenance of statecraft. When it comes to true wisdom about the world as opposed to mere worldliness, Hebrew remains the font of truth, whether it is the Hebrew of Scripture and the ancient sages or the Hebrew of an astronomer, cosmographer, and historian like David Gans, who lived only in the previous century.

A final thought about R. Moshe Aharon. Although he is elevated above his brethren by virtue of his demeanor and authority, he shares a great deal with them when it comes to his occupation, because, like them, he is an alcohol retailer. The wide prevalence of rural taverns run by Jews, as was discussed at the beginning of this chapter, was the result of an economic logic. The surplus grain produced on the magnate's estates would lose much of its value if it had to be transported to distant markets. But distilled into alcohol locally, it could be sold under monopolistic terms to the Ukrainian-Ruthenian peasants and who better than the Jews, with their reputation for sobriety, to do the selling? The coarse intoxicants dispensed in the taverns were not of much interest to the nobility, who preferred wines imported from Hungary or mead, a beverage that is made from fermenting honey and is capable of aging and great refinement. R. Moshe Aharon inherits a cellar of old casks from his father, and, thanks to its role in healing the prince, his mead becomes a sensation.

Being blessed with a superior product and a superior clientele gives him the wealth and connections necessary to lead and protect his community. But the tony and upscale nature of his business should not obscure the fact that R. Moshe Aharon is plying a trade that is not essentially different from the rural Jewish tavern keepers. The point is made ironically in the particular way in which the excellence of his cellar is praised by his highborn clients. At their banquets, "[t]he priests would sing that all the Jews' houses should burn like stubble except for the cellar of the Jew who makes mead" (p. *131*, 157).

The Jew who makes mead knows that his exemption is highly contingent and that his fate is shared with that of his people. With sober purpose and statesmanlike resolve, he leverages his advantage on behalf of his community.

Town and Village and the Longing for the Sacred

Rarely does a title deliver so much meaning with so much concision. "Hashutafim," which means the partners or the sharers, describes the circumstances under which the descendants of a humble Jewish charcoal maker named Naḥum Ze'ev came to acquire permanent tenancy of the basement of the great town hall of Buczacz, thus becoming "partners" with the descendants of Count Potocki, who erected the building.[14] The word *shutaf* (singular) is a rabbinic, postbiblical term that connotes a variety of commercial and legal arrangements in which two or more persons share responsibility.[15] Persons become partners when they join in a business or in the ownership of a property; persons can also become partners even in the absence of a commercial relationship, when, for example, their houses abut a common courtyard. The verb stem, *sh.t.f.,* means to join or associate as in the many midrashim in which, as an act of grace, God associates his name with Israel. The verb also has a connotation of empathic sharing, as in participating in the joy or sorrow of another.

With this lexical instrument in hand, Agnon probes the ironies of the Jewish-Polish relationship. What seems, especially viewed from the hauteur of the Polish nobility, as a relationship based on ownership or domination, or at the very least, feudal obeisance, turns out, viewed from other angles, to be less stratified and differentiated. There are nodes of entanglement between Jews and Poles in business, in the conduct of everyday life and in the management of the great estates. Although they would be loath to acknowledge it, the Poles were dependent upon the Jews for their success in colonizing Ukraine; and the Jews, no more eager to admit as much, were grateful to the Poles for conditions of commercial stability and communal autonomy that did not exist elsewhere in Eastern Europe. Although this was a relationship hardly based on equality, it was, for all intents and purposes, a functional partnership.

Like most partnerships of necessity there was little intimacy. The Jews did not know, and were not interested in knowing, much about the domestic and religious life of the Poles; and the Poles were interested in the inner sphere of Jewish life only as fodder for drinking songs and the doggerel of court jesters. The relationship can be summed up as one of pragmatic enmeshment together with mutual disgust and willed ignorance. For this very reason, the intimate encounter Agnon stages between a Jewish charcoal maker and a Polish magnate in "The Partners" is truly remarkable. As described in the passage quoted at the beginning of this chapter, the count observes the Jew in the homely act of praying from his position prostrate on his rescuer's rustic pallet. Later the same day, Naḥum Ze'ev penetrates the palace precincts, traverses the great dining hall, and installs the count on a couch. Throughout much of the day, the count's enfeebled body has been carried in the arms of the charcoal maker or supported by him, the physical distance between these unlikely partners closed entirely.

The tale of the charcoal maker and the count, so fraught with coincidence and drama, is told by the narrator for an ulterior motive. It explains the origins of a singular and surprising situation whereby a Jewish family enjoys the inalienable right to live in the basement of Buczacz's magnificent town hall. The tale discharges an etiological function similar to that of the tale of the mead merchant and the prince in the account of the gabbai R. Moshe Aharon, whose wealth and worldliness are anomalous and require explanation. Both stories have a similar envelope structure. An anomalous feature of Jewish-Polish relations is described in a discursive opening section; in the middle comes the sensational tale that accounts for the phenomenon; and, finally, a report on its fate given in the narrator's longitudinal, chronicle mode.

In "The Partners," Agnon fashions a spatial metonymy with extraordinary resonance. The permanent and irrevocable installation of a Jewish family in the basement of the grandest edifice in Buczacz stands for the place of Jews in Polish society in general. True, the Jews are in the basement, but their right to be there has been secured, and there they persist and thrive, maximizing the real but constrained opportunity given them for religious expression and mutual assistance. They are permanently wired into the subconscious of the host culture. The power of this spatial metonymy depends on the special importance of the town hall, whose magnificent but dark history is recounted in the story that immediately precedes "The Partners."[16] "The Great Town Hall," discussed in Chapter 1, recounts the tale of Theodore, the Italian architect who was forcibly baptized as a child and whom Count Potocki imprisoned in the tower of the finished edifice.

The account that the story describes is Mikołaj Potocki's desire to build in Buczacz the grandest civil structure in Poland and his recruiting of an Italian architect and sculptor named Theodore to design the project and oversee its realization. The project is a success. The magnificent, many-storied town hall festooned with lifelike sculptures, towers over Buczacz and gives this modest town bragging rights throughout the country. The dark dimension of its history concerns Theodore's fate. A Jewish child by birth, he was seized by priests, forcefully baptized, and apprenticed to a master sculptor. In this Jewish version of the Icarus tale, Theodore fashions a set of wings and escapes the tower. His strength lasts only long enough for him to reach the other side of the River Strypa, where he crashes to his death. The Ruthenian peasants working in the fields observe his fall and, pronouncing his name in their dialect, call the place Fedor Hill. The name endures, and it is on this hillside, the narrator informs us, that the Nazis made five hundred Buczacz Jews dig their own graves.

There is another shadow cast by the splendor of the town hall, and this is the first thing the narrator tells us at the outset of "The Partners." Despite the building's conspicuous display of wealth and power, it is built upon a cavern-ous basement designed as a place of refuge in case of Tatar or Turkish attack. The basement connects to a series of underground passageways that would enable the Polish rulers to flee the city rather than being picked off for de-portation and ransom. This was not, needless to say, an emergency evacuation scheme that included the Jews, who would be left together with non-noble Poles to defend the city with their lives. But as the bloody seventeenth cen-tury receded into the past and with it the terrors of Ottoman incursions, the basement of the town hall fell into disuse and became a cobwebbed place re-markable only for the cries of demons heard from it on occasion by local ears.

When Naḥum Ze'ev is given the basement as a reward for his rescue of the count, he fills this vacuum with purposeful life. He cleans it, sanctifies it as a Jewish dwelling place by affixing *mezuzot* to its doorways, and, because he needs only a fraction of the space for his living quarters and his business, he makes the basement available at no charge to the poor stall operators in the adjacent market square. These are the poorest vendors who cannot afford shops of their own and who can now store their merchandise overnight rather than carting it back and forth each day to the distant quarters where they live.

Thus, without the need for explicit statement, Agnon allows his spatial metonymy to suggest, in the largest possible terms, the place of the Jews in the edifice of Polish society. The Jews took the inferior and disused sectors of society allotted to them and made them productive, and they leveraged the good fortune of the few on behalf of the many. Now, this global, affirmative reading of Polish Jewry is not, to be sure, the only account rendered in *A City in Its Fullness*; as we see in the next chapter, in the stories set after the Partition and under the Austrian regime, Agnon adopts a far more acerbic stance toward the behavior of Jews toward each other under conditions of oppression. But in this earlier period, when Jewish communal and rabbinic authority have not yet been significantly undermined, his eye remains more benevolent and seeks out instances of piety, ingenuity, and steadfastness.

This is why at the beginning of the story Agnon has his narrator single out the figure of Naḥum Ber standing at the doorway to the basement of the town hall. As we come to understand by the end of the story, Naḥum Ber, who lived at the end of the nineteenth century and was a friend of the narrator's parents, is a direct descendant of Naḥum Ze'ev, who was granted the tenancy of the basement sometime in the middle of the eighteenth century. All these years the family has held fast to its subterranean home and rejected the escalating offers from the Potockis to buy it back.

Although it would be in his financial interest to sell, Naḥum Ber responds to the latest offer thus: "If I have merited to have been made a partner of the majestic counts from the House of Potocki in the town hall that is the glorious splendor of the city and an object of envy throughout

Poland, could I possibly dissolve the partnership? I would not dissolve it for all the money in the world," (p. *239*, 202). Naḥum Ber's response, tweaks the noses of his "partners" with its inflated, sycophantic diction and makes the point that, come what may, the Jews will not relinquish their rightfully-acquired ownership of their portion of the Polish polity. And this is a time, it must be remembered, when the sway of magnates like Potocki has been diminished by Austrian rule, and the magnificent edifice of their authority has already been heavily mortgaged.

The issue of Polish oppression does not disappear as the narrator now proceeds to tell the tale of the charcoal maker and the count that explains how all this came to be. Before he became a charcoal maker, Naḥum Ze'ev was the leaseholder of a rural tavern that had been operated by his family for generations. When the tavern's profits disappoint the Polish lord who owns it, he turns out Nahum Ze'ev and his family and installs another Jew who promises a better return. Dispossessed and wandering in the country-side in search of work, Naḥum Ze'ev comes across an elderly Ruthenian peasant who remembers kindnesses shown to him by the Jewish tavern keeper in former times. He is a charcoal maker by occupation; and he offers to teach the trade to Naḥum Ze'ev, who gratefully accepts his offer. The old man has no heirs to take over the business—one son joined the army, one hired himself into domestic service, and one was arrested for brigandage—and when he dies, Naḥum Ze'ev, who is already not young himself, takes over the hard work involved in producing charcoal: cutting down trees, chopping them up, burning them down under controlled conditions, and transporting the sought-after finished product to town for sale.[17]

Once the problem of livelihood has been resolved, there remains a large hole in his heart.

> He got up early that day, as was his wont, and set off. What was in his heart at that moment? Although one cannot know what is in the heart of another, one can conjecture that he desired what most village Jews desire: to live in town with other Jews, to pray daily with the community, especially the morning prayers. For at dawn one senses palpably the Lord's work as he re-turns our souls to our lifeless bodies, and one wants to praise God in a house of prayer where there is an ark, religious books, and Jews. (pp. *240–41*, 204)

Naḥum Ze'ev's typicality is at odds with R. Moshe Aharon's edicts regarding village Jews. The gabbai views their Judaic literacy as woefully substandard and fears the erasure of their Jewishness altogether if they are not compelled to spend Rosh Hashanah and Yom Kippur with their brethren in town. Naḥum Ze'ev is a strong witness for the defense. In our story, the maintenance of his piety in isolated circumstances is presented as characteristic of his class of Jews rather than as exceptional.[18] He is not a zealot or a holy man but a representative figure, and on that basis the narrator justifies the license he takes to imagine his unspoken thoughts as he makes the long predawn journey on foot from his home in the forest to pray with the community in town. This is a trek he undertakes twice a week, on the days when the Torah is read in the morning service, as well as on Sabbaths and holidays. Even long after he has accommodated himself to the rigors of his occupation as a charcoal maker—the story is vague on time but informs us that his children are now grown up—the feeling of being deprived of daily communal prayer has not grown less acute.

Note well the nature of Naḥum Ze'ev's religiosity. The spring of his desire to pray with the community is not rooted in issues of moral duty or halakhic requirements or communal solidarity. The narrator presents it as the instinctual response of a religious person to the created world. This is the instinct to praise God for the wonders of life, which are experienced with special urgency upon arising from the demi-death of sleep and encountering the mystery of creation.

Note also the importance to Naḥum Ze'ev of the presence of the ark, the *aron kodesh*; it takes the close proximity of the ark, together with other Jews and the tomes of sacred writings and commentaries, to fulfill the potential force of communal prayer. The term for the ark used here is aron, but, recalling the discussion of the stories about ḥazzanim in Chapter 3, the alternate term is teivah. In those tales, which concern religious professionals whose very business it is to draw close to the teivah, proximity verges on danger. The oft-personified teivah does not suffer all who approach it, and, for those with the requisite superior spiritual resources to do so, dwelling in its presence requires either self-sacrifice or self-disqualification. The problem is the opposite for the hero of "The Partners." Naḥum Ze'ev is too far away from the source of holiness. As an unlearned layman he will never draw too close for safety, but as a Jew of steady faith he needs something more than the strength of his own devotion. He seeks to be warmed by proximate distance to the holy, and this can be achieved only by joining the congregation in the synagogue.

The thematic significance of this desire cannot be stressed enough. Naḥum Ze'ev's longing to take part in daily communal prayer is not presented as an endearing idiosyncrasy or the product of a special spiritual endowment. Rather, it is an instantiation of what is most essential about Buczacz in Agnon's reimagining of the town. As I argue at the beginning of this volume, Agnon decided to anchor his reconstruction of Buczacz to two normative pillars: Torah study and communal worship. The path of study, even with its many compartments and levels, is open to those who have had the good fortune to have been educated in their youth. The path of worship is open to all, and the case can be made that there is no better embodiment of this than the figure of a charcoal maker whose circumstances have hitherto kept him at a distance and who, now that a fortuitous opportunity has, literally, crossed his path, is determined at all costs to seize this prize, which is taken for granted by town dwellers but has eluded him all his life.

Strange Bedfellows

To be sure, coming across Count Potocki prostrate on the forest floor eventually turns out to be Naḥum Ze'ev's great chance. But it is crucial to keep in mind that initially, and for a long narrative duration, the encounter with the stricken magnate is fraught with danger rather than opportunity. It is still night time when the charcoal maker comes across the body of a man propped up against a tree. He identifies the great man by his clothing and is relieved to discover that his lifelessness is sleep rather than death. But he sees that the count has been out all night exposed to the cold air, and he reasons that there is a serious danger of what we would today call hyperthermia. Lest you think the course of action is self-evident—taking the count to safety indoors—it is well to remember that this is the same Count

Potocki who was well known for having shot dead two Jews in the marketplace simply because he was frustrated after a day of hunting produced nothing else to shoot. Moving the ill magnate and then having him get worse or even die as a result of the intervention would have deterred many from touching his body. Yet Naḥum Ze'ev does not hesitate. Because the count is too weak to walk, he puts him over his shoulder and carries him, in addition to the bundle of charcoal he was taking into town for sale and the satchel of his tallit and tefillin, to his home.

The picture of Naḥum Ze'ev that emerges from the set of deliberate actions he takes is startling. He is a Jew who is at home in the physical world. No longer a young man, he displays enormous strength in hoisting up the count on his shoulders and carrying him through the woods. It is in those woods that he displays a preternatural intimacy with nature. On his predawn trek to the synagogue in town he strides from wood to wood, from thicket to thicket, along a path that only a veteran woodsman can discern. "And if summer rains or winter snows have erased the path, the smells of the trees show him the way. Passing through trees, each with its own smell, he suddenly gets whiff of a human being. Following the smell takes him to a broad oak tree and a man propped up underneath it," (p. 241, 204). From his days in the forest Naḥum Ze'ev has developed the autochthonous wisdom of a Ruthenian peasant, but, in his case, it is a knowledge deployed for purpose of navigating his way to the divine service in the synagogue.

There can be no greater contrast than that between Naḥum Ze'ev's dexterity, sturdiness, and decisiveness and the count's enfeeblement. True, he has been suffering from exposure and dehydration, but he exhibits a near total collapse of faculties far beyond his physical situation. His disorientation stems from his sudden isolation and from his removal from the network of helpers and servants that customarily surround him and answer to his every whim. As one of the great magnates, he resides at the pinnacle of shlachta culture; beneath him are serried ranks of lesser nobles who eat at his table, serve in his army, and administer his estates. That he is allowed to go missing from this legion of minions, retainers, and servants may or may not be a plausible plot development; nevertheless, this is where he finds himself, depleted and debilitated and alone and in the hands of an uncouth and decidedly non-noble stranger.

Intimacy, both physical, domestic, and spiritual, is the keynote of the time the two men spend together, which, although it is only one day, is spread over many pages. First, there is the contact of their bodies. Naḥum Ze'ev places the count over his shoulder and carries him to his home in the village, and after the count has sufficiently recovered to travel, he has to hold on to him with his arms and support him as they proceed on foot through the forest because the way is impassable to wagons and the count is unsteady on horseback. Although he was only semi-conscious when he was carried to the village, he is fully aware that it is a Jew who is holding him up as they trek through the forest to the palace. The count is then installed in the Jewish couple's one-room cottage and placed on the pallet of stones and straw that is Naḥum Ze'ev's bed.

It is there that Naḥum Ze'ev takes his life in his hands by disobeying the count's peremptory order to return him to the palace immediately. He had not yet said his morning prayers because he had discovered the count on his way to the synagogue in town and was subsequently occupied taking care of him. Now that it is clear that the count's life is not in danger, he takes leave—respectfully but unilaterally—to pray before they depart. It is precisely at this point, as Naḥum Ze'ev puts on his tallit and tefillin and begins the swaying motions of Jewish prayer, that the narrator makes the observation, cited at the opening of this chapter, that although thousands of Jews live on his estates, the count had never seen Jews at prayer. He looks on as this Jew prays and is not reviled.

The whole long day is one of boundaries crossed and identities inverted. The social distance that collapsed between the two men is so enormous that it is unthinkable, or thinkable only in the imaginative space of the story. The mighty have been humbled, and the meek have been raised up. This is a reversal that has taken place without any violent reckoning. The puissant aristocrat's collapse stems from an internal insufficiency; cut off from his retinue, his executive self shrivels. The Jewish charcoal maker, on the other hand, is elevated only by virtue of the accidental situation he has stumbled upon; for he remains unchanged and continues to apply to this radically unanticipated event the same God-fearing values he applies to all aspects of his life.

This awkward, intimate connection between the two men can exist only so long as they remain in the liminal, interstitial zone of the forest. Their troubles begin at sunset when they emerge from the woods in sight of Buczacz. Angered and confused by the sight of the city lit up as on a festival, the count instructs Naḥum Ze'ev to ask a drunken and rowdy tough what is going on. In reply he gets only vulgarity and curses hurled at him, and he is told "Shut your mouth, Jew, and don't get in the way of superior lords" (p. 245, 210). This odd couple soldiers on and arrives within sight of the palace. When one of the torch bearers sees a Jew in these precincts—and apparently missing the shrunken figure next to him—he lands a blow on Naḥum Ze'ev's legs that brings him to the ground together with his noble charge. There they lay, one exhausted and in pain and the other dazed and disoriented.

Eventually they get back on their legs and hobble into the palace, which at that moment is completely illuminated and completed deserted. It is at that point that the count utters the most risible line in the story. The poor charcoal maker, who has never before been anywhere near the magnate's residence, is given the command, "Set me down on my bed!" (p. 246, 212). Earlier in the day, the count had lain on Naḥum Ze'ev's rough-hewn pallet, but now any notion of a mutual or reversible intimacy is absurd. Just then a couch is found in the corner of the dining hall upon which to deposit the count, and the room begins to fill up with hungry and impatient retainers returning from combing the countryside for the missing magnate. Naḥum Ze'ev is filled with dread by the prospect of being caught in this company, and he slips away just before the count's presence is discovered and the jubilation over his return begins.

To the count's credit, he does not forget what happened to him in the woods once he regains his strength and is again surrounded by those who do his bidding. His gratitude to the poor Jewish charcoal maker is genuine, but his efforts to fasten on a reward that would be acceptable to his rescuer prove challenging. Money in itself is of no interest. The one thing Naḥum Ze'ev wants is the same thing the narrator assumed was on his mind when he happened upon the count's body in the woods. He wants to live in town so he can pray with the community. And fulfilling this desire turns out to be one of the few things the great magnate cannot do with the mere issuance of an order to his minions.

In a series of exchanges with his well-informed major domo, the count learns that, because of a recent fire, housing in the Jewish quarters of Buczacz is not just at a premium but impossible to obtain. But the count perseveres and comes up with the idea of granting him the right of tenancy in the basement of the town hall. A solution is also found to the problem of how the charcoal maker will find livelihood in the city. He will be assigned the town's yeast-selling concession, a trade traditionally given to a rabbi's wife to supplement the limited salary paid her husband by the community. Because of illness, the wife of the current rabbi of Buczacz cannot avail herself of this opportunity. The count purchases the concession from the community and assigns it to Naḥum Ze'ev and his descendants in perpetuity, that is, on the same basis on which they are given the basement.[19]

In the final sections of "The Partners," the typicality accorded Naḥum Ze'ev at the beginning of the story is rubbed away to reveal a man of singular faith. Living among the gentiles in the villages and forests, as we know from the reasoning behind R. Moshe Aharon's edicts, is a test of Jewishness that many cannot withstand. But the charcoal maker's convictions, embodied in the unremitting desire for public prayer, remain unsusceptible to environmental conditions. The narrator begins to refer to him as *hatamim*, "the innocent" or "the perfect," and he is presented as an ideal type of unlettered piety. This is not a piety to which any mystical appurtenances attach; rather it is a distinctly urban piety that can be fulfilled within the worldly and mercantile space of the city. The narrator hastens to inform us that Naḥum Ze'ev did not treat the yeast commission as a sinecure or just as a source of income. In possession of a monopoly, he could have sold an indifferent product; but he made it his business to produce yeast of a quality rarely found in other cities. As a result, the weekday breads and Sabbath loaves of the housewives of Buczacz rose gloriously, making a modest but real contribution to the gross domestic happiness of the community (p. *251*, *219*). Naḥum Ze'ev's boldest gesture, as described above, is to alleviate the daily travails of the poorest of the city's commercial class: the market sellers who have no shop but only their merchandise and a stall.

With the account of Naḥum Ze'ev's generosity, the narrator announces that he is bringing to a close the amazing tale of how a poor Jewish family came to share the great town hall with the noble Potockis. By way of a coda to the story, he jumps ahead by over a century to the 1890s to focus on the figure of Naḥum Ber, the last descendent of his family to occupy the town hall basement and the author of the proud rebuff to the Potockis quoted earlier. This latter-day Naḥum is an avatar of his namesake: a busy man who works for a living but never fails to join his brethren in the synagogue for daily prayer. Although he is not learned, he is, literally, warmed by the light of Torah, as evidenced by his habit of popping into the well-heated beit midrash on a cold winter afternoon and enjoying the sound of Torah being studied aloud.

There is something noticeably different in the way the brief account of Naḥum Ber is rendered. Jumping to the end of the nineteenth century places events within the lifetime of the narrator and enables him to use childhood memories as an epistemological source. (This is one of those sporadic moments in *A City in Its Fullness*, discussed in Chapter 2, when the chronicler-narrator fashioned by Agnon bleeds into the voice of the autobiographical implied author.) There is a family connection as well. The narrator's mother served as a kind of adoptive parent for Naḥum Ber's younger daughter Neḥe after the death of her mother. The reasons given for the death of Naḥum Ber's wife are fraught with historical moment: "It was because nature and the temper of the generations had changed that her mother died. They said it was because of the air in the basement that she died" (p. *254*, *221*). The widower abandoned the basement and took an apartment in a location that would make it easy for his daughter to make frequent visits to the narrator's mother. Even if he had persevered in the basement of the town hall, the narrator informs us, the special arrangement that had guaranteed his family's tenancy—and together with all it represented about Jewish-Polish relations—was shortly to be dismantled and cast aside by the cataclysm of World War One.

Surprisingly, here at the end of the story, as he deals with vast historical changes in gestures that are necessarily telegraphic, the narrator seems to have plenty of time to tell us about Naḥum Ber's two daughters. We might account for this late-in-the-game digression as a familiar expression of the narrator's fondness for telling us more than we need to know about the families of his beloved city, especially when there is a link to his own family history. But Agnon is doing something much more astute. He is using the fates of the two girls to represent the forces responsible for the collapse of the two phenomena dramatized in the story: the embroiled "partnership" between Jews and Poles and the steadfast though unlettered piety expressed in the desire to pray with the community.

The older girl, whose name the narrator cannot recall, was married to a hard man who ran through her dowry and divorced her but not before teaching her bad habits. Now back home in Buczacz, she has not only rejected religious observance but she flaunts her apostasy by installing herself on a bench on the Sabbath where she can be seen knitting by the worshipers exiting the synagogue (p. 253, 221–22). The narrator and the good people of the town profess to be stupefied by her provocations in light of her estimable family background. Yet the reader can infer that her "bad luck" can be put down to acculturation, pauperization, modernization, urbanization, and a host of other forces that transformed East European Jewish life at that time.

The younger orphan, Neḥe, is nurtured by the maternal mentoring of the narrator's mother and married to Feivush Ringelblum, an upright grain merchant who is a kinsman of the narrator's family. Their son, born in Buczacz in 1900, was none other than Emanuel Ringelblum, the historian and social scientist whose name will live forever because of the extraordinary archive he assembled in the Warsaw Ghetto, near which he was murdered on March 7, 1944. Ringelblum is the last transformation, in secular form, of the spirit of Naḥum Ze'ev, which, after the decimation of the First

Destruction (World War One), has now been extinguished by the "accursed and polluted minions of the defiled abomination" (p. 255, 223).

Rather than ending the story with a reference to the final destruction wrought by the Holocaust, which is his practice in a number of the stories in *A City in Its Fullness*, Agnon closes on a distinctly elegiac and liturgical note. He returns to Naḥum Ber's midday visits to the beit midrash when he used to stand surveying the men and boys learning Torah and sing a song.

> There are many melodies I have heard and forgotten, but this melody has stayed in my heart. When I recall the days gone by when our city was full of Jews and the old beit midrash full of learners, the melody that R. Naḥum Ber used to sing when he came into the beit midrash sings itself in my heart. Although the melody itself I am incapable of conveying, I can set down the words. These are the words in Aramaic:
>
> Exalted is the Lord from the first to the last,
>
> He wanted us and was pleased with us and gave us the Torah. (pp. 254–56, 223)

The forgotten melody resonates strongly with the ending of "The Sign," the story that describes Agnon's consecration to the task of memorializing Buczacz, which was discussed in the introduction to this book. There, Shlomo Ibn Gabirol, the dean of medieval Hebrew poets, mystically appears to the Agnon-like narrator and composes a poem that will perpetuate the name and memory of the city. Concerning that poem, the narrator says, "[i]f I don't remember the words of the poem, for my soul left me because of its greatness, the poem sings itself in the heavens above, among the poems of the holy poets, the beloved of God."[20] To be sure, there is no comparing Ibn Gabirol's awesome elegy to the ditty sung by Naḥum Ber. Yet both are melodies that sing themselves (*mitnagen*) in the narrator's heart in their respective realms, one august and one homely. Both gesture toward the music of memory beyond the reach of story.

Etiological Fictions

In summary, "R. Moshe Aharon the Mead Merchant" and "The Partners" are stories that run against the grain of the general picture of the relations between Jews and Poles in the Buczacz tales as being rooted in political vulnerability and persecution. Here the ratios of power are reversed. In both stories, it is a noble of superior rank who becomes vulnerable and exposed to danger, and it is the Jew who rescues him and restores him to his former potency. In both cases there is a fortuitous circumstance—the carriage of the sick prince stopping in Buczacz or the lost count lying on a forest route to the synagogue in town—that affords a Jew an opportunity to display his inner qualities. The stories dramatize a contrast between the personal attributes of the characters and, again, reverse the external perception of the Jew especially as seen through Polish eyes. The Jewish mead merchant and the charcoal maker are consistently disciplined, steadfast, strong willed, resourceful, generous, and loyal to their faith and their community. The prince and the count are variously arrogant, impatient, self-indulgent, coddled, and fragile. The act of rescue has positive consequences for both sides. The rewards received by the two Jews are converted into enduring benefits for the whole community. And the Polish magnates are saved from themselves and given the chance to become better and more enlightened rulers. In the process, a barely-imaginable common space is briefly opened up, a space of shared worldliness in one case and a space of shared physical and domestic intimacy in the other. Although these commonalities are hedged in and demarcated by many forces, they nonetheless establish a basis for softening if not undoing the polarization of Jewish-Polish identities.

Where does this softening take place? Is it in the historical world, of which the story presumes to give us a truthful account? Or does it exist only within the imagined world of storytelling? I am intentionally simplifying a complex situation in order to recall the issue I raised at the beginning of this chapter concerning Agnon's "intervention" in the historical record. It is reasonable to assume that the stimulus for these stories comes from established facts about Buczacz in the eighteenth century. There were wealthy Jews in the mead trade, heads of community among them, who had contact with prominent members of the nobility. Presumably, there was a family of Jewish yeast dealers who occupied the basement of the town hall.

Yet when it comes to the sensational tale of the penitent prince or to the intimate account of the rescued count, we feel we are in the domain of invention. Whether there were kernels of legends that Agnon had in hand when fashioning these tales is something that is difficult to know but also essentially beside the point. The tales of the prince and the count can be considered etiological fictions, inventions intended to explain the origins of anomalous phenomena.

Of course, in the eyes of Agnon's traditionalist narrator, it is taken for granted that these tales are not only truthful but also the handiwork of the Creator. It is evident to him that the prince's sanity is preserved for the purpose of being cured by R. Moshe Aharon, just as Count Potocki was separated from his hunting party so that he would be discovered by a poor Jew whose family would be installed in the town hall. Yet, as we have seen in many other instances, the audience the narrator addresses is not identical to the modern readers addressed by the implied author. For this audience, in which we are belated participants, providential rationales are of limited utility. We are brought back to a blunt question about the status of these fictions of rescue and reversal. When all is said and done, are they compensatory and counterfactual fantasies that deny the larger framework of Jewish–Polish relations?

They are something much more, I would argue. The stories presume to present the deeper, unseen truth about Jews and Poles as experienced from the point of view of the Jews. This can be called an aspectual difference. In the historical record, Jews in Poland were subservient to the ruling Polish nobility, very much the "lord's Jews," as Moshe Rosman has put it. But viewed from a different aspect, one that is rooted in Jewish experience, the role played by the Jews in the region looms much larger. Despite the vast wealth and power of their rulers and owners, it was the Jews in their constancy, sobriety, initiative, and good sense who were the secret spring behind the maintenance and progress of this society.

Agnon's imaginative resourcefulness takes this further, into the realm of alternative history.[21] The tales of R. Moshe Aharon's curing of the prince and Naḥum Ze'ev's rescuing the count are events that *should* have taken place, and, given their power to explain features of Polish-Jewish relations, *might* well have taken place if the fullness of the historical record could be disclosed. For Agnon, what we call fiction and what he calls storytelling are mechanisms for correcting a skewed perception of the Jews as a community oppressed and constrained in spirit. Agnon knew the truth was deeper and richer, and his writing was committed to making that known.

We might then usefully think of these stories as acts of tikkun—correction or restoration. Agnon thought of his fiction as the last great chance for the reimagining of Polish Jewry. As fixed in the medium of his writing, *this* was the way that this civilization was destined to be remembered, and he was determined it should be the right way.

6

Austrian Mandates

The half million Jews that Austria received upon the first partition of Poland in 1772 was an equivocal gift. The number of Jews in the empire doubled and presented Vienna with the sudden challenge of governing the populous new province of Galicia. Without the benefit of accurate or substantial demographic and economic data about the region, Maria Theresa and Joseph II did not hesitate to issue a raft of legislation aimed at bringing the Jews within the orbit of enlightened absolutism. What ensued in the following decades was a jittery dance between an incessant imperial desire to reshape Galician Jewry and a resourceful determination to resist that control. Agnon sets several of the major stories in *A City in Its Fullness* within the turmoil caused by the Theresian-Josephine reforms, and these stories contain a surprise. Rather than allowing his Hebrew reader to settle comfortably into an opposition between gentile malevolence and Jewish resistance, Agnon subverts this binary and presents the new regime as merely an external pressure that reveals deep moral fissures within the Jewish community. Yes, the news is grim, these stories imply, but the source of the evil is closer to home.

The disorientation occasioned by the accession of Galicia was even greater for the Jews than it was for the Austrians. The Jews had lived for centuries within the Polish-Lithuanian Commonwealth as a kind of fifth estate with a degree of judicial and communal authority. Some Jews lived on Crown lands, and others, like the Jews of Buczacz, lived in towns wholly owned and governed by wealthy nobles. Jews might be despised by their Polish overlords, but as a corporate entity they were often granted privileges on par with the Christian town dwellers. A willful seigneur could intervene in internal communal affairs and rabbinic appointments, as we have seen in several stories; yet commercial conflicts and acts of deviance and criminality were generally adjudicated in rabbinic courts. Persecutions occurred, of course, and Jews enjoyed few legal protections because the lord of the manor *was* the law; the lessee of a tavern or a mill who failed to produce enough income could be thrown into a stockade at the will of the master. But these eruptions of cruelty—*gezeirot* (*gezeirah*, singular) in Jewish parlance—were not the everyday norm, and they could usually be mitigated by bribes or ransoms. Compared with what was to come, moreover, these troubles had the advantage of being neither ideological nor bureaucratic. For better or worse, they represented a true picture of the irrational feelings of two groups living in close contact.

The lives of Galician Jews changed dramatically as an immediate consequence of a geopolitical development in which they had no role. (The Polish nobility and the Ruthenian peasantry were also profoundly affected.) Upon the Jews of Galicia, writes Stanislav Gordziski,

> fell an avalanche of rules that changed their legal status, limited their autonomy, raised their taxes dramatically, imposed military service, and interfered deeply even in the sphere of private life. In contrast to the much rarer legal changes during the period of the 'noble republic,' a powerful administrative apparatus bolstered these legal amendments. It was difficult to evade the laws, dangerous to disobey them.[1]

Avalanche is an apt term because of the volume and suddenness with which laws and regulations were issued from the Austrian capital. Because the regime in Vienna was both enlightened *and* absolutist, it had a prolific enthusiasm for framing reforms as well as the unilateral power to legislate them. Many measures met significant opposition and evasion and went through several iterations; other measures, such as taxation and military conscription, were tightened over time.

This extremely complex story can be summarized for our purposes by listing seven areas in which Austria sought to impose changes on the Jews of Galicia. First, the regime sought to implement a process of Germanization by conducting all government business in German, requiring Jews to take German surnames, and requiring German to be taught in schools. Although elementary Jewish schooling managed to resist the penetration of German and remain traditionalist, German names were widely adopted, and the knowledge of the German language paved the path of many Galician Jews to the universities of Vienna. Second, as a strongly Catholic country, Austria tried to induce Jews to convert to Christianity; these efforts failed on a popular level, but legislation enabled forced child baptisms and made it impossible for someone once baptized to return to Judaism. Third, the Austrians resented the inordinate size of the Jewish population of Galicia and sought to reduce its numbers by requiring couples who wished to marry to be above a certain age, to obtain permission from the gubernatorial authorities, and to prove their tax worthiness. The Jews generally evaded this regulation by entering into ritually sanctified unions, and the measure was eventually dropped.

Fourth, the tax burden of Galician Jews was made much more onerous under the Austrians, and the Jews were made the target of a special candle tax (explained below), which was levied on no other group. Fifth, out of a desire to push Jews into agriculture, the Austrians forbad Jews from leasing taverns and mills, which represented a significant sector of the Jewish economy. This displaced a vast number of Jews and turned them into itinerant paupers, without increasing the number of Jews in the agricultural sector. Sixth, although Austria exploited the kahal (the council of elders) to enforce many of its decrees within the Jewish community, it severely limited the role of rabbinic authority and the jurisdiction of Jewish courts, which were now largely limited to ritual matters. Last, in a move that was unprecedented in the historical experience of Polish Jewry, Jews were conscripted into the imperial army for long terms of service. In response to passionate outcries concerning kosher food and Sabbath observance, some accommodations were eventually made. But the insistence on military service was never abrogated, and it was rigorously enforced.

All of these changes are referenced in *A City in Its Fullness*. How could they not be in a work that seeks to convey the vicissitudes of Buczacz over the course of two hundred years? Yet, as became evident in the previous chapter, although Agnon takes history very seriously, his vocation as story-teller gives him license to make interventions in the historical record for what he regards as higher purposes. The Jews of Buczacz may in fact have been subservient to the will and whim of the lord of the city, but that cir-cumstance does not prevent Agnon from imagining a set of events in which puissant Polish nobles are brought to acknowledge the wisdom and worthi-ness of their Jewish subjects.

In a similar way, the Austrian accession is submitted to the Agnon imagi-nation. But this time the outcome takes a different direction. Instead of re-pairing the humiliation the Jews were forced to undergo, Agnon undertakes an unsparing critique of Jewish communal hypocrisy and indifference to suffering. The viewpoint becomes internal: the issue is not how the Jews deserve to be viewed in the eyes of the gentiles but how the Jews should view themselves. In "Disappeared," the greatest of these stories, Agnon takes the indictment beyond social criticism into the realm of the metaphysical. In a world from which the holy has been eliminated, he wonders, can the evil potential in human nature, Jew as well as gentile, be constrained? The march of history in Galicia at the turn of the nineteenth century does not offer much cause for optimism.

A City in Its Fullness evinces a clear plan for apportioning fictional treat-ment of the major Austrian decrees. "Feivush Gazlan"[2] deals with the cruelties that attended the collection of the candle tax by Jewish tax farmers and their enforcers. "Yekele One" and "Yekele Two"—two versions of the same story, whose relationship I discuss later—deal with the dictatorial conduct of the kahal and the marginalization of religious courts. These stories are the subject of this chapter. Chapter 7 places at its center the extraordinary story "Disap-peared," which deals with the social iniquity perpetrated by the community in satisfying the demand for Jewish young men to serve in the military.[3]

In each of these cases, the reader who comes across these stories in the final sections of *A City in Its Fullness* is likely to experience something of a double-take. Suddenly torn down is the partition between the Jews—toiling peaceably to make a living and serving their Creator—and the gentiles, exploiting the Jews for their gain while despising and occasionally beating them. All of a sudden, gentile malevolence is moved to the background and made into a real but remote condition of communal existence. The focus shifts to the violence visited by Jew upon fellow Jew, the powerful upon the weak, by the leaders of the community upon the marginal and voiceless.

Feivush Gazlan

All the peoples of Galicia were taxed heavily by the new masters, but the Jews were forced to pay additional taxes that applied only to them. Among these was the *Lichtergefälle*, the candle tax, which was instituted in 1797. Because Jews are ritually obligated to light a minimum of two candles on Sabbaths and holidays, placing a tax on candles proved an effective way to exact a stream of revenue from this group alone. Candles lit at weddings and other family celebrations were also taxable. The tax was geared to produce more income from the wealthy, who could afford more illumination in their homes. Although the tax was onerous and predatory, it did reflect some "enlightened" elements. Certain categories of Jews—unmarried women, widows, farmers, soldiers, and apprentices—were exempted from the tax, and the collectors of the tax were enjoined from making their rounds of Jewish homes after noon on Friday. The collectors themselves were Jews employed by wealthy Jewish tax farmers, who subcontracted from one Shlomo Kobler in Lviv, a Jew who had proposed the tax to the chancellery in Vienna and administered it on its behalf. The tax was in force until the revolution of 1848.[4]

Of the burdens thrust upon Galician Jews by the new regime, the candle tax was especially loathed. The tax penetrated into Jewish domestic space and encroached upon the one time during the week when Jews turned inward and felt protected from the world. The legislation from Vienna ostensibly protected against overly aggressive collection practices. But as depicted in "Feivush Gazlan," the reality defied regulation from above. Feivush is the thug who is employed by the tax sub-contractor for Buczacz to enforce the payment of the tax. On Friday evenings Feivush takes two gentile helpers with him and makes the rounds of Jewish households. He stomps into homes unbidden, and when he finds lit candles for which the tax has not been paid, he orders his helpers to extinguish not just the unpaid for candles but all the candles in the home. Aggrieved and affronted, the family must sit in the darkness, especially in the long winter evenings. Taken away is the pleasure of reviewing the weekly reading from the Torah; and even the eating of fish, so beloved of Jews on the Sabbath, must be suspended for fear of choking on unseen bones. The insult is all the greater because the institution of the tax and its collection are the work of Jews.

This particular evil decree provides Agnon with the opportunity for a fictional exploration of how the community of Buczacz responds to the very existence of evil. In the eyes of Buczacz, Feivush is the embodiment of all that is base and villainous, and the population views its victimization at his hands as another of the ordeals that Jews are called upon to endure. Their accommodation to their fate is understood as an expression of the strength of their faith before God. It is this mixture of theological consensus and collective self-perception that is submitted to scrutiny and found wanting in the course of the story.

Part of this deconstruction comes from what we are shown of Feivush's life. He turns out to be motivated by a banal industriousness and loyalty rather than venality, and his greatest desire is to enjoy the domestic respectability of a Jewish householder. When he and his wife are injured and crippled and then abandoned by his employer, Feivush is defanged and becomes an object of sympathy; and in contrast to the Jews of Buczacz, who have wholly domesticated the problem of theodicy, he refuses to be reconciled with the fate God has visited upon him.

The other part of the deconstruction comes from the behavior of the good people of Buczacz, especially the denizens of the beit midrash. In their rush to vilify Feivush and arrogate moral superiority to themselves, they end up exposing the depths of their own violence, their indifference to suffering, and their denial of responsibility for their actions. In the final analysis, these deconstructions and reversals yield no Purim-like restoration of the moral balance. The story concludes with a dark vision of evil and cruelty as inscribed in the human condition rather than as an accident of historical victimization.

Here, as in all the stories in *A City in Its Fullness*, the narrator takes us in hand and guides us through the moral and theological quandaries of the tale. Here, as well, this guidance is highly unreliable. As a chronicler of Buczacz, on the one hand, the narrator is obliged to lay out the facts of Feivush's life as they happened. But as a standard bearer of the values of Buczacz, on the other hand, the narrator "spins" those events in accord with his worldview, as well as not restraining himself from overtly editorializing in an effort to shape the reader's attitudes.

In "Feivush Gazlan," the narrator is aligned with the moral consensus of the town, which views Feivush as nothing more than a brute and his behavior execrable. His downfall is well deserved in this view, and it confirms the wisdom of Buczacz's stoic endurance of persecution. But in his role as implied author, Agnon works adroitly and subtlety to stoke our suspicions of the narrator's guidance and his apology for his townspeople. Agnon does this in a number of ways. He has the narrator mention competing perspectives in order to refute them, and, once they are mentioned, there is nothing to stop the reader from finding them more persuasive. His most effective tactic is allowing the narrator to represent Feivush's domestic sphere and inner life, thus providing us with a more empathic grasp of the man, one the town either cannot see or is not interested in seeing. Finally, by further empowering the narrator at the end of the story to penetrate the sordid inner sanctum of the tax farmer who employed Feivush, we are afforded a glimpse of venality that wholly subverts the narrator's conformist piety.

A House on Stilts

"Feivush Gazlan" has a three-part structure. The first part (the prologue and chapter 1) introduces us to Feivush and the secluded area of Buczacz where he has built his home and paints a general picture of the town's tribulations under the burden of the candle tax. The second part (chapters 2–6) describes the events surrounding the injuries sustained by Feivush and his wife on one summer Sabbath afternoon. The third part (chapter 7, longer than all the rest) concerns Feivush's unsuccessful efforts to reinstate himself with his employer and to find theological reasons for his suffering; and it further describes the kindness extended by Buczacz to its handicaped former oppressor.

In presenting Feivush at the outset of the story, the narrator curiously has nothing to say about his ancestry or childhood and is wholly preoccupied instead with the location of his jerry-built house. The house stands in a secluded little valley on an island formed by a bend in the Strypa and a canal dug to power a flour mill. Despite its proximity to the town proper, the valley is free from the stale urban air and graced by stands of willow trees and chirping birds. Yet no one except for Feivush lives there because of a series of inauspicious historical associations. It faces the ruins of a castle that the Tatar invaders forced the Polish nobles to tear down, and it is the location of a synagogue destroyed by Khmelnytskyi. Most ominous of all is the fact that the valley contains the ruins of the house in which Jacob Frank was born. Jacob Frank (1726–91) was the founder and leader of a sect that sought to perpetuate and develop the antinomian and anti-rabbinic teachings and practices of the messianic pretender Shabetai Tsevi (1626–76). (It is important to note that the historical evidence points to Frank having been born in Karolivka, and Agnon is alone in asserting his birthplace in Buczacz.) It is from the detritus of Frank's house that Feivush has built his own home. He has built it on stilts, so he can pull up the ladder at night and feel entirely protected against intruders. In this beautiful but haunted spot, Feivush and his wife live "free as a bird with no worries about rent" (p. *280*, 229).

On the face of things, it would seem that the narrator is merely doing due diligence in supplying us with information about the story's main character. Yet, perhaps unwittingly, all the information supplied carries with it a floating sense of primordial unease. Unspoiled and verdant, the Valley of the Willows, as it is called, is truly an Edenic site; but it is only at the expense of others that Feivush can live there freely and without rent. It is, furthermore, a liminal space in which he lives apart from the rest of Buczacz, intentionally disengaged from the bonds of mutual obligation that would make him part of the community. Most disturbing of all are the ruins and remainders of carnage and heresy that scar this idyllic site. The deep duality that attaches to this place foreshadows—and provides a spatial correlative to—the duality that will be exposed in the figure of Feivush. On the one hand, his brutishness and malice are revealed to be merely the banal result of a desire to please his employer. But on the other, his ruthless work as an enforcer ineluctably connects him to a genealogy of radical evil whose historical echoes still resonate in this rustic bower.

Further information about Feivush's name and his appearance raises similar questions about whether he himself is a source of malignity or whether he is principally an instrument for the malignity of others. When it comes to Feivush's name, the narrator offers a tortuous and withholding explanation.[5]

> For reasons that I will keep to myself I will not call him by his real name but rather will call him Feivush. Why Feivush and not another name? Because he served Feivush the tax collector and gave his life for Feivush the tax collector's money and was ready to jump into Gehinnom for the sake of Feivush the tax collector. Therefore do I call him Feivush in the name of that other Feivush. (p. *280*, 227–28)

We are surprised to discover that the infamous name of Feivush, which figures in the lore of Buczacz and gives the story its title, is a fraud. The narrator's coyness in withholding his true name only underscores the motives for the substitution. Because Feivush has made himself into the self-sacrificing tool of the tax contractor, the narrator implies, he deserves to have his own name effaced. But does this act of renaming, which the narrator arrogates to himself, exculpate Feivush from responsibility for the suffering he visits on others, or does it ineluctably fuse him with this source of evil?

Part of the answer is given when the narrator, in his role as ethnographer as well as chronicler, provides us with the text of a folk dirge that laments Feivush's cruelty. The fact that it is in Yiddish is meant to attest to its popular origins, although the concluding couplet is in Hebrew and consists of a pastiche of biblical verses. The song depicts Feivush as a bogey monster capable of blotting out the light of the Sabbath created by God, and God in turn is admonished for tolerating Feivush's impudence. The song concludes with a curse: "Let him be burned together with his beard and his ear locks!" These signs of Jewishness are precisely the point; it is the fact that Feivush is one of us that rankles most deeply. In the end, it is the existence of the song as an artifact that connects it to the general line of Buczacz's response to persecution. Making a myth of Feivush, mildly complaining to God and cursing the evil, and wrapping these altogether into a song—all this affords Buczacz a mechanism for coping and denying at the same time. The greatness of Buczacz, the narrator informs us more than once, lies in its capacity to accommodate itself to the sorrows placed upon it.

With chapter 2, the story shifts to the fateful events of one summer Sabbath. It happens that year that Tisha be'Av (the ninth of the summer month of Av), the solemn fast day that commemorates the destruction of the Jerusalem temples and other calamities, falls on the Sabbath. Because fasting on the Sabbath is not allowed—except for Yom Kippur—the fast and its attendant rituals, such as reciting the Book of Lamentations, are shifted to Saturday night and Sunday.[6] Because of this juxtaposition, the young men who sit in the beit midrash on that Sabbath afternoon turn their attention to the legends about the destruction of the temples in the Talmud and the Midrash.

It is not long before they make a connection between the great calamities of Jewish history and the present-day persecution of the candle tax. The idea of the tax, they point out, was originated by someone just like them, one Shlomo Kobler, a brilliant Talmud student from a nearby Galician town. Kobler had hoped to marry the daughter of the Neta Sha'ashu'im, the previous rabbi of Buczacz. When he was rebuffed, he went off to Vienna, and there, as a way of getting rich, he conceived of the idea of a candle tax and successfully proposed it to the court. Wealthy Jews increased the value of the contracts to enrich themselves, and this in turn sharply increased the tax burden on the Jews. Thus was initiated the reign of domestic terror that snuffed out the joy of Sabbaths, holidays, and weddings.

"There was no trouble that Israel suffered in which a Jew did not bear some responsibility" (p. *284*, 234). This is the moral that sums up the discussion in the beit midrash. In one sense it is a worldly wise position, because, rather than railing at the gentiles alone, it admits the complicity of Jews in their calamities. But in another important sense the admission is circumscribed because it clearly draws a line between rich and assimilating Jews on one side and the good folk of Buczacz and certainly the denizens of the beit midrash on the other. The latter remain safely ensconced in the conviction of their righteous victimhood. True, the category of persecutors has been enlarged to include unscrupulous Jews, but the "genealogy of morals" has not been altered fundamentally. The source of the persecution remains the implacable, millennial hatred of the nations for the Jews. As they sit in the beit midrash reading the legends of the Destruction, they perceive a direct line from Nebuchadnezzar, Titus, and Vespasian to their home-grown oppressor Feivush the enforcer.

Genealogies of Evil

An alternative genealogy of evil is presented in the next section of this story. It is offered by an old man in the beit midrash who is one of a small number of elders who stand apart from the rest of Buczacz because of the independent and critical stands they take toward the policies of the official community. They are distinguished by their devotion to studying the books of the Bible, especially the Prophets, from which they derive their habit of speaking their minds on moral issues and even on occasion undertaking covert actions to right egregious wrongs. When it came to Austria's insistence on conscripting Jews into the military, these men were particularly exercised by the community's practice of paying and detaining itinerant poor young man to substitute for the sons of the city's householders. And they took action rather than just talking. One morning Buczacz awoke to find that "the room where the detainees were kept with its door open and the guard drunk, and all the young men who were to be sent to the army had vanished" (p. *285*, 234). The narrator evinces an ambivalent attitude toward these elders. While he admires their cleverness and attention to Scripture,

he thinks they "overdid their study of the biblical books," and he views
them as a destabilizing element because they speak what is in their heart
without regard for the powers that be. Yet despite this suspicion, the narrator—or rather the author behind the narrator—allows the old man to tell a
story that offers a very different construal of Feivush's motive.

The story concerns an impoverished and abashed young man who turns
into an autocratic monster once he is given a little power. It is customarily the job of the shamash of the beit midrash to unlock a cabinet and
distribute candles to students studying in the evening. When he had to be
absent one day, the shamash asked the lad to perform this task in his place.
Granted this moment of authority, the lad is transformed from being a
"formless entity" into a frightening new creature. His body goes through
physical changes, and he gazes on the other young men studying in the beit
midrash, before whom he had formerly groveled, "the way a parnas would
look at the dolts he would deliver up to the army" (p. *286*, *235*). He plays
one recipient off against the other, switching "one candle with another
even though they all were identical." The next time the shamash puts him
in charge, a message is tacitly conveyed to the lad when a burning candle
is "accidentally" tipped over and burns his clothing and singes him as well.

Within the narrative syntax of the story, there is obvious relevance in
the mention of candles, and the significance of a fire of suspicious origin
soon becomes evident. But it is the lesson the old man derives from the
vignette that amply justifies the digression. He admits to his young listeners
in the beit midrash that the oppression of Jews by Jews represented in the
candle tax is shameful. "If you want to use your money to make a living,"
he opines, "go and make it in a proper business and don't make money off
Jewish blood." Nevertheless, he sees the case of Feivush the enforcer as embodying a different truth.

> When a hungry person hires himself out in order to put bread on the table,
> it is not he who determines his actions but the work that he engages in.
> The task he is assigned to perform, whatever it is, will undo him. The very
> fact that he is assigned to do something will unhinge him. Even if his heart
> tells him to do this and not that, his unsettled state will disconcert him and
> subvert his actions. We see this in the cheerless way most of those charged

with administering communal affairs walk around. Why are they cheerless? Because they are not at peace with themselves. What they do is not in line with what they believe. (p. *285, 235*)

Human beings, in this view, are subservient to their needs and appetites, whether it is for food or respect. And their nature is malleable. Given a job that puts food on the table and provides a legitimate license to exercise authority over others, an ordinary person, especially a person of low status or self-esteem, cannot help being undone and remade into a different creature. What follows are acts of cruelty and evil. The evil may not be inherent in human nature, but a susceptibility to it most certainly is. Because this negative potentiality is universal, it makes little difference whether the heart in which it actualizes itself is Jewish or gentile. The source of the evil is therefore not the millennial hatred of the nations for the Jews or even the predisposition of Jews to become collaborators in their own persecution. Furthermore, the evil is potentially resident in all hearts, like those of the young denizens of the beit midrash, who are quick to establish a cordon sanitaire between themselves and perpetrators of evil like Feivush.

Feivush is a villain who, though he commits cruel acts, is following the orders of his employer, and at home he turns out to be a rather ordinary Jewish husband. It is difficult to assess his behavior without thinking about the issues of evil and ordinariness that were raised by the Eichmann trial a century and half after the time in which the story is set. Let there be no ambiguity about the timing: "Feivush Gazlan" was published in *Haaretz* in 1956, five years before the Eichmann trial and the polemics around Hannah Arendt's banality thesis that followed. Nonetheless, these embroiled issues were in the air for the entire post-war period, and it is hard to imagine a Hebrew reader not detecting echoes of them, whether or not Agnon intended them to be picked up.[7]

Arendt's argument about the banality of evil is complex, and the fierce debates that followed make it difficult to make use of the concept productively. Moreover, there is, of course, no commensurability between the Nazi regime and Austrian rule; nor between Nazi perpetrators and those who collaborated with them and Jewish tax collectors and their agents.

Yet, with all of these caveats in place, the notion of banality helps us to shed some light on the alternative construal of Feivush that is advocated by the old man in the beit midrash and advanced by the way the story is told despite the opinions of the narrator. In the chapter that follows, Feivush is described in his domestic lair and shown to be just another Jewish husband seeking respectability from other Jewish townspeople and respect from his wife. The acts he commits are certainly reprehensible, and, like the boy with the candles in the beit midrash, he is transformed into a thug when he carries out his duties, and he is fully responsible for his cruelties. But it is the evil framework that has triggered the potential for evil that resides in all hearts.

At Home on a Sabbath Afternoon with Feivush and Mamtchi

Our comprehension of Feivush is deepened by the ingress we are granted to his domestic space in chapter 4.[8] While he is being discussed in the beit midrash, Feivush is just waking up from his Sabbath afternoon nap, putting on his spectacles, and getting ready to read to his wife Mamtchi from the *Tsenerena*, a work written in Yiddish in the early seventeenth century that includes traditional commentary and folklore on the weekly Torah readings. "Even though those Yiddish books were written expressly for women," the narrator informs us, "Mamtchi did not know how to read them" (p. 286, 236). Orphaned in childhood, Mamtchi hired herself out as a maid and never had the time or means to learn how to read. So Feivush reads to her and takes much pleasure in being thought of by her as a wise Jewish husband. It is his favorite time of the week. What is remarkable in this domestic scene is the fact that Feivush and his wife are no different from other Buczaczers. They may be less literate, but they view Jewish learning as an essential obligation and engage in it as their capacity allows; and the same goes for their careful observance of the laws relating to cooking and heating food on the Sabbath. In their humble way, in short, Feivush and Mamtchi aspire to be thought of as respectable Jewish householders.

The scene is affecting and surprising given what has been previously said about this man. But lest we fall for an image of the enforcer with a heart of gold, the story provides several means to correct and complicate our view. The first has to do with the subject about which Feivush reads to his wife from the *Tsenerena*. Because it is the Sabbath before the Ninth of Av (Shabbat Ḥazon), the text is full of legends about monstrous oppressors of Israel throughout the ages who were eventually themselves brought low and who met grotesque ends. The chief example, and the one most relevant to the imminent fast day, concerns the Roman general responsible for the destruction of the Temple. A gnat "got into the evil Titus's nose and burrowed into his brain for seven years, and when he died they split open his skull and found there something like a bird weighing two *selas*, with a beak of brass and claws of iron" (p. *287*, *237*). So that if you see wicked oppressors eating and drinking and having a good time, know that God has raised them up on in "order to destroy them in the end, so that they should feel their sufferings to the fullest extent." "God does not countenance the wicked who bring distress to Israel," and to bring them down He gives them enough rope to hang themselves.

Now, there is nothing strange in Feivush taking pleasure and solace from these tales, as do other Jews who read the *Tsenerena* on Sabbath afternoons. The problem is that he has absolutely no inkling that he himself belongs to the category of oppressors of Israel who one day will be toppled from their positions of power and that, in essence, he is reading about himself. To be sure, he cannot be expected to know that his reckoning will come later that same afternoon when the house built on stilts will come crashing down. There is nevertheless a total disconnect between the reality of the cruel acts he performs and his naïf desire, at once homely and deluded, for Jewish respectability and self-regard. The ironies abound and move back and forth in different directions. To the best of his meager ability, Feivush studies Torah of a Sabbath afternoon, and Mamtchi pays particular attention to staying within the bounds of Jewish law as she keeps warm the special pre-fast meal she has lovingly prepared for her husband. "If anyone had desecrated the Sabbath," as we shall soon see, "it was the Torah students cloistered in the beit midrash," those selfsame students who are so self-righteously assured that Feivush is an evil doer.

The tone in which their domestic coziness is described is further disturbed by the language used to describe Mamtchi. It is because she was orphaned and impoverished that she is illiterate. Yet attend to the language used to describe this disability.

> If Feivush did not read books to her on the Sabbath, she would be inferior to a cow. Except with a cow you can write a Torah scroll on its hide or make tefillin straps from it, whereas Mamtchi in this life was a mere mass of flesh, and in death would be dust and food for the worms. (p. 286–87, 236–37)

Who is responsible for this vulgarity? We might suppose that it is the narrator's hostility to Feivush and his wife that has unwittingly broken through and interfered with the job of telling the story. But a few minutes later when Feivush interrupts his reading for a moment, we are told:

> Feivush looked at his wife to see if she had noticed his cleverness. Her excesses in food and drink had fattened her heart and shrunk her brain and she did not grasp the holy matters that he was relating to her. Feivush's expressive voice spiced up the telling but it meant nothing to her.

Here it is not clear whether the observation occurs in Feivush's mind as he looks to his wife for comprehension and finds none, or whether it is the narrator intervening to explain the reason for that failure. While the confusion may not be easy to sort out, the rhetorical effect is clear. If Feivush is fooling himself, Mamtchi is too. The astuteness she appreciates in her husband comes not from his ability to read Torah legends to her but from the money he earns—the 1 percent of the fines on the candle tax he is allowed by his employer to keep for himself. As for the stories about the destruction of the Temple, the only meaning she discerns lies in the encouraging fact that the pent-up demand for weddings after the three-week period of mourning preceding Tisha be'Av will provide a great multitude of candles to be snuffed out and fined.

The same kind of disconnect is on display at that very moment in the beit midrash. (The action in chapter 5 is parallel in time to the previous chapter, Sabbath afternoon chez Feivush and Mamtchi.) The young men have listened to the old man's story about the lad and the candles, but they have absorbed nothing of his meaning, and they revert to telling tales of

Feivush's brutalities before returning to their readings in the Midrash on Lamentations. Of the innumerable passages from this body of literature, Agnon has them read the exegesis of the Sages on verses from Proverbs and Psalms. Although their relevance to Feivush is unmistakable to the reader, it remains totally opaque to the students in the beit midrash: "When a wise man contends with a fool, there is anger and laughter but no rest" (Prov. 29:9) and "One who rebukes a buffoon will bring shame upon himself" (Prov. 9:17).[9] The verses are a direct rebuke to the denunciations they are indulging in and a warning about the dire consequences of contending with a fool or rebuking a buffoon. But they read on in the sing-song of Torah study, clueless to the connection.

It is precisely at that juncture that the news is delivered that Feivush's house has caught fire. The report is false, but neither the denizens of the beit midrash nor the reader yet know this to be the case. At first the news is discounted as merely the expression of an unspoken wish that "the one who fed us with suffering taste a little bit of it himself" (p. *288*, 239). (Ironically, this presumption turns out to be true.) But with a second report of the fire, the news is deemed reliable, and a discussion ensues concerning the meaning of the event and whether it demands immediate action.[10] The discussion becomes a festival of *Schadenfreude*. The high point is the proffering of a three-fold exegesis that justifies the sure but sometimes tortuous ways of God's justice. Feivush extinguished the flames of the candles that provided light for Torah, and now his life was being ruined by fire. He invaded the homes of others and now his own home is being consumed. He ruined the Sabbath pleasures of Buczaczers, and it is therefore on the Sabbath that his own life is being ruined.

But this earful of righteous homiletics is nothing next to the legal casuistry that follows. It is evident to a Hebrew reader with even a passing knowledge of Jewish practice that, when saving a life is at stake (*pikuah nefesh*), it is not only permissible but obligatory to break the Sabbath restrictions. If Feivush and his wife may perish in the fire, the law leaves no room for ambiguity. Yet rather than bestir themselves to deal with the emergency, Buczacz's finest young minds settle into submitting the issue to the kind of academic scrutiny they routinely use to deal with purely theoretical matters. Most provocatively, they consider the case *as if* the house were unoccupied. For indeed, if it is not a matter of life and death, a burning house can be left to burn down if the fire does not endanger neighboring inhabited structures. And since Feivush's house was isolated and built on marshy ground, they reason, it presents no danger. Eventually, they conclude that the question must await further investigation; they shelve their books and go outside to see what is happening.

Their behavior does not receive a pass from the narrator, either in his editorializing or dramatizing functions. As the denizens of the beit midrash join the throng moving toward Feivush's house, the narrator comments directly on the various commandments they are transgressing. They believe themselves "motivated by a desire to fulfill the mitzvah of witnessing the downfall of the wicked." But, in fact, "there was no end to the commandments they were transgressing in the name of a mitzvah they had fabricated," (p. *289*, 240). Their hypocrisy is further documented when the crowd reaches the Courtyard Valley, where Feivush's house stands, and it is discovered that there is no fire and hence no emergency. (The origin of the false rumor is never explained, and we are left to infer, as was hinted, that it was a product of wish fulfillment.) The captivating natural beauty of the place, which was described in the opening paragraphs of the story, overwhelms the Buczaczers, who do not regularly visit it because of the negative associations with Jacob Frank and other disasters. The time is the end of the nine days preceding Tisha be'Av during which traditional Jews do not bathe or launder their clothes, and they are in a state of physical discomfort. The water and the fresh breezes and the lush vegetation are almost too much for them.

> [T]hey quite forgot about the destruction of Jerusalem and rejoiced at having come to such a pleasant and airy place. I am quite sure that there were some among them who were quite ready to conduct the afternoon service in the valley without a Torah scroll to read from, and to wait there until dark and enter into the chanting of the Tisha be'Av dirges with a joyful heart. (p. *290*, 241)

In addition to the prospect that such a scene would be very funny to contemplate, there is a darker point. The righteous citizens of Buczacz, the victims of Feivush's cruelties, turn out to be made of the same malleable and imperfect human materials as their victimizer. During this, the most somber day in the Jewish calendar, when Jews are called upon to identify with the victims of the great catastrophes of Jewish history, it takes very little to move them to thoughts of gamboling in the stream among the willows. This is less a sign of their religious shallowness than of their human frailty, a commonality with Feivush that they are hard pressed to acknowledge.

Chapter 6 is the climax of the story not only because it depicts the dramatic fall of the house of Feivush but also because it utterly tears down the boundary between the pious souls of Buczacz and their so-called oppressor. The scene is both bathetic and deeply disturbing. When Feivush sees a throng of townspeople gathering beneath his house—a place that Buczaczers make a point of steering clear of—he is at first surprised and pleased. Based on the day's readings in the *Tsenerena*, he has learned that Tisha be'Av is not only the day on which the Temples were destroyed but also the day on which the Redemption will take place. He therefore considers the possibility that the crowd is a sign that the Messiah has come. (The narrator snootily observes that Feivush is apparently unaware of the fact this cannot take place in a year when the fast falls on the Sabbath.) Feivush is the picture of geniality as he greets them, welcomes them to his home, and inquires why they have come, regretting only that he does have not enough cold drinks to offer all of them. Earlier in the story we saw Feivush as he sees himself within the domestic sphere, a proper Jewish husband studying with his wife of a Sabbath afternoon. Now he warmly projects the same self-perception of respectability to the community as a whole. Totally absent from his awareness is the fact that these are the same people who view him as an evil oppressor and who have gathered below his house in the hopes of seeing it burn down.

That no flames are shooting from the house, which stands undisturbed rent-free in its verdant valley, proves to be an unspoken disappointment that cannot be abided. Individuals in the crowd turn on each other with abusive accusations about who started the false rumor of the fire. The shouting turns to shoving and jostling, and soon enough the old, termite-eaten stilts that hold up the house begin quivering. Enraged and fearing the collapse of his house, Feivush begins cursing them furiously. "There was not one profanity he did not utter about them, their homes, their belongings, even their ancestors" (p. *291*, 243). And the good people of Buczacz "in turn cursed and blasphemed" Feivush, giving as good as they got.

It is Mamtchi who moves the conflict from cursing to action. She opens the oven in which she has been lovingly keeping warm her husband's prefast meal and systematically begins throwing the scalding food and the pots upon the heads of the assembled throng. Evoking the defense of Buczacz that took place in the Courtyard Valley more than a century earlier, "Mamtchi did with the groats exactly what they had once done with pails of boiling millet when they poured them out over the invading Tatars." Inevitably, the house crashes down and together with it the lit oven, which set fire to the whole structure. The fire that never was now finally becomes a reality.

Feivush and Mamtchi both sustain broken bones in their hands and feet in the collapse. And it is now, when they have been, literally, toppled from their perch and made into homeless cripples that the town of Buczacz mobilizes to take care of them. The moral drawn from this event is articulated in an exchange between one of the bystanders and Elisha, the town's medical expert, who has been called to the scene. It happened that it was the daughter of this same Elisha who lost her grip on her baby one Friday night as a result of one of Feivush's home invasions. Referring to that incident, the bystander remarks: "This shows us that the Holy One, blessed be He, does not let the wicked go unpunished but pays them back in kind," (p. *292*, 245).

Elisha's response is both impassioned and instructive: "Your punishment is worse than Feivush's. Feivush was stricken in body, while you have been stricken in soul because you watched someone writhing in pain while rehearsing to him the sins he had committed" (p. *292*, 245). Elisha, the narrator informs us, is a member of a small voluntary society, influenced by the writings of Menaḥem Mendel Lefin, whose members are devoted to moral self-improvement especially regarding intemperate speech.[11] Having rebuked the bystander for his moral sanctimony, Elisha immediately rebukes himself "for putting his mouth before his mind and not overcoming his bovine nature that allowed his tongue to gore other people the way an ox gores with its horns" (p. *292, 245*).

Although the episode with Elisha is a very brief interruption in the rush of events, it is important for establishing a frame of reference for evaluating the behavior of the Buczacz community, and for that of Feivush as well. Elisha alone possesses the will and honesty to understand the motives for his actions and to assess them critically. He is allied with the old man in the beit midrash who tells the story of the boy who distributes the candles, as well as with other "elders who were wont to search after the root causes of events" (p. *297, 251*). As a dutiful chronicler, the narrator notes the existence of this perspective, but he also lets us know that it is not his own.

The Heart of Darkness

"Feivush Gazlan" is a story with two climaxes. The first, the crash of Feivush's house, is related in an antic tone befitting the collapsing of moral boundaries between the townspeople and their supposed oppressor. The second, Feivush's meeting with his employer after his injuries, is far darker and pushes the story into a vertiginous moral freefall. Soon after the calamity, Feivush picks himself up off his pallet in the almshouse that serves as Buczacz's rude hospital and, limping in pain from his broken bones, drags himself to the house of his employer Reb Feivush. It will be recalled that, even though the narrator has referred to him throughout as Feivush and we have come to know him by that name, it is in fact not his given name, and he has become known as Feivush because of the rich tax collector whom he serves as an agent and into whose identity he has submerged his own. It is that groveling loyalty to his employer that moves the afflicted, ailing Feivush to present himself. In the course of the scene we discover another bond between the two: Feivush's mother was the wet nurse for the tax collector in his infancy at the same time as Feivush was being nursed. Most of her milk went to the baby of the rich family, and when her own child cried out in hunger, she would "dip a rag in licorice water and stuff it" in his mouth (pp. *294–95, 248*).

Feivush's meek respectfulness edges into servility. He stands in pain and hunger propped up on his crutches while Reb Feivush, sitting, finishes off a sumptuous meal and then stretches out on his bed for a nap. Wickedly entering the role of a rabbinic sophist for the moment, the narrator adopts Reb Feivush's smug perspective and appropriates Maimonides, "the towering giant of Torah," to justify his self-indulgence.[12] Finally, Feivush's abused and starved body "mutinies against him," and he falls over. "Yet even in his collapse," the narrator notes, "Feivush was polite, not crying out in pain lest he interrupt his employer's slumber" (p. 293, 246).

The thud of his fall, however, bestirs the members of Reb Feivush's household to rush to the scene and gather around the prostrate enforcer, who, with no help from them, finally succeeds in getting back on his feet. While Reb Feivush continues sleeping, these anonymous voices gaze upon Feivush in his wounded, enfeebled state, "wondering whether this was the same Feivush whom the whole town feared" (294, 247). Their attitude is detached and bemused as they observe Feivush and debate with each other about the relative qualities of his injuries and deformities. Into this surreal scene now saunters the nameless muscle-bound thug who was given Feivush's job the moment he was incapacitated. Looking at the pathetic cripple before him, the thug

> crossed his arms over his chest, swayed back and forth, laughed, and said, "You jokers, you're making fun of me," and then he spat in Feivush's face and said, "Too bad for you Buczacz that you had to make do with this undernourished mouse." He then pursed his lips like a cat and let out a long "Meow!" (p. 294, 247)

The spirit of raillery continues when Reb Feivush finally gets up. He burps and yawns and observes jokingly, "The hour of the Resurrection of the Dead must have come if Feivush has gotten up from the beating he took." Finally, it is made clear to Feivush that there is no more work for him, despite his thirteen years of devoted service and his loyalty in reporting for duty so soon after his injuries, and the point is reinforced by a violent kick delivered by the thug. The thick wadding of denial is pierced, and, acknowledging the finality of the betrayal and the rejection at last, Feivush withdraws and drags his aching body back to the almshouse.

This is a journey into the heart of evil: heartlessness, cruelty, abandonment, ridicule, humiliation, sadism. Yet the reader surely remembers that although Reb Feivush's household may be the worst setting in Buczacz in which Feivush the enforcer has been maligned and treated badly, it is not the only one. The whole town has heaped imprecations on Feivush, made him into the villain of a folksong, destroyed his home, and caused him grievous bodily injury. We might instinctively feel that the two are not comparable. It was not, after all, the overt intention of the townspeople to destroy Feivush's home and injure him and his wife, and, once the damage was done, Buczacz mobilized to see to their needs for food and shelter. Yet the comparison holds on many levels. The people of Buczacz longed for Feivush's downfall even if their longings were unacknowledged to themselves or over-layered with moralizations. In contrast to the townspeople, to be sure, the tax collector and his household show no remorse or pity once the downfall has been brought about. But it is difficult not to admit that the two cases exist along a continuum of evil rather than being separated by an essential distinction.

Yet this is precisely the truth the narrator sets out to refute in the closing pages of the story. By virtue of his diligence as a reporter, the rancorous heart of Buczacz has been exposed, and now the narrator launches himself into a campaign to contain the effects of what he has exposed. His goal is to install a partition between the radical evil manifest in Reb Feivush's household, which he abjures, and the contingent evil manifest in the behavior of the people of his town, whom he esteems.

The first step in this project is to describe how Buczacz spread a social welfare safety net under Feivush and Mamtchi to soften their fall. People contribute old clothes and shoes and dishes of food, and invite the couple for Sabbath and holiday meals. And do not think that this was easy to do, the narrator tells us, because Mamtchi sorely tried the good will of her hosts "because she continually complained and lamented the loss of her goat and her hens" (p. 296, 249). The narrator does not stint in giving us an ample portion of her chatter about the goat's milk that "would make even Count Potocki lick his lips" (p. 296, 250) and the hens who knew how to show respect, and it takes little to imagine how truly vexing her inanity must have been to her hosts. The extended mimicry of Mamtchi turns out to be an example of just the sort of bad faith the narrator condemns in others. Abject and abashed, Feivush is himself an easy target for moralistic reproach, and the narrator pats himself on the back for showing admirable restraint.

> Here I could easily make fun of this hapless man as he sat anxiously in fear of the thug bastard who had taken over his job suddenly coming in and doing with the candles in this house what he himself in his heyday had done in others. He was particularly nervous when they brought fish to the table. Fish was his favorite food. Fish were his neighbors in the days when he lived in his house on the Strypa and he had established a relationship with them. But I do not make fun of the poor and the unfortunate. (p. 295, 249)

But that is exactly what he has just done in the guise of describing the opportunity he has supposedly passed up to take pleasure in saying, "I told you so," and savoring the nice ironies of the tables being turned in Feivush's present situation.

The narrator's condescension to Feivush is further extended by presenting him as a kind of Job manqué. In light of the brutal thug who succeeds him in his office, Feivush's own former acts of brutishness recede into the background. He remains stubbornly unreconciled to God's justice. (As was the case before his fall, he is of course conscious only of his unwavering and unrequited faithfulness to his former master and not of the harsh acts he committed on his behalf.) But for now he knows only that he has been crippled and made homeless while Reb Feivush prospers. The theological justifications offered to him as consolations leave him unsatisfied. He is told that his suffering in this world will offset his account in the next world. He is told that his suffering is justified as a punishment for the sin of building his dwelling from the detritus of Jacob Frank's house. But Feivush is having none of it.

His defiance is both obtuse and heroic. The narrator persists in viewing his refusal to accept God's ways as pathetic and simple minded. Yet the reader is led to a different standpoint in reaction to the narrator's campaign to endorse and even extol Buczacz's readiness to submit to God's will. "As it always did, Buczacz accepted its vicissitudes and did not rise up against them.

In fact, it lovingly embraced each and every calamity that befell it and repudiated none of them," (p. *297*, *251*). Long gone are those dissenting points of view once bravely voiced by the "elders who were wont to search after the root causes of events as they unfolded," those same elders, like the old man in the beit midrash, who took the admonitions of the biblical prophets seriously. Feivush's protest against God's justice may seem ridiculous coming from a man who himself did bad things, but it looks quite otherwise when put alongside Buczacz's meek submission to its persecutions.

The narrator uses the last moments of the story to shore up a traditionalist/preservationist interpretation of the events related in the tale and to tamp down their subversive potential. To pull off a general exoneration and affirmation of the community of Buczacz, he anticipates the reader's discomfort with the behavior of the townspeople and concedes the sinfulness of the subset of citizens who participated in the disturbing events on that fateful Sabbath. "Darkened by the distress of that desecration," the narrator tells us in a rueful voice, "they walked around mournfully, not a smile on their faces. They gave much to charity and took upon themselves many fasts, some as prescribed by the Shulḥan 'Arukh and some according to the numerical reckoning of the word *Shabbat* until their strength gave out and they died" (p. *297*, *251*). (The numerical value is 702!) Note well, however, that the sins for which they are so extravagantly atoning have little to do with Feivush and Mamtchi's injuries and much to do with the ritual laws of the Sabbath. In conveying their extreme devotion to their penances, the narrator is in essence praising them rather than taking them to task. Their misdeeds constituted a regrettable but isolated eruption, a one-time offense which was amply paid for and, moreover, proves the rule of the town's rectitude.

The narrator's valedictory defense of Buczacz's quiet submission to its tribulations represents a shrewd case of hedging one's bets. On the one hand, the town is piously bending itself to God's will and submitting to divine justice without complaint. On the other, the rationale for its submission is based on a calculation of self-interest, a dour realpolitik. The narrator imagines Buczacz explaining itself thus: "We accept our fate not because we are so upright but because we live in fear that the new tormentors and oppressors will be worse than the old ones." The replacement of Feivush by the heartless new thug is the point at hand. But whether it is this way or that, the narrator has succeeded in inserting a buffer between the good people of Buczacz and the source of the evil, whether it comes from the gentile persecutors or from unscrupulous coreligionists. The scandal of that summer Sabbath remains an embarrassing anomaly that says nothing essential about the community and the darker recesses of the human condition.

Considering the concluding lines of "Feivush Gazlan," it is well to keep in mind that the story first appeared in the pages of *Haaretz* in 1956.

> [E]vildoers grow progressively worse as the generations proceed. Each one is more fiendish than his predecessor. For evil feeds off those who do it; the wickeder they are, the more wickedness grows. I hope I am not proved wrong when I say that it will continue to grow and grow until that day comes when wickedness will vanish like smoke. When will that be? On the day when the Messiah will appear, may it happen speedily in our time, Amen. (p. *297, 252*)

For the narrator's traditionally minded contemporary audience—contemporary, that is, to the turn of the nineteenth century—this pious peroration likely goes down very well. There is certainly support in classical sources for the idea that the Messiah will come when things cannot get worse. The expression of this hope, furthermore, conforms to the homiletical convention of ending a discourse on a redemptive note. But for the author's audience at the time it was published, a dozen years after the Holocaust, these sentiments would seem tasteless and perverse. This audience had lived through a time when wickedness had indeed grown and grown, but what came at the end of that downward spiral was Hitler rather than the Messiah. This duality is cannily caught in the phrase "wickedness will vanish like smoke" (*veharish'ah ke'ashan tikhleh*), which is a very specific allusion to the text of the Amidah prayer for Rosh Hashanah and Yom Kippur.[13] In its liturgical context, the prayer expresses an eschatological yearning for a time when Israel will be released from the grip of the nations. Uttered in the context of the murder of European Jewry, however, the notion of vanishing like smoke takes on quite another meaning.

There are many stories in *A City in Its Fullness* that conclude abruptly with a reference to the slaughter perpetrated by Hitler's depraved minions. The reference is abrupt because it is wholly extraneous to the story and unanticipated by anything that came before. And this shock and disconnection is exactly the effect Agnon seeks to achieve. Its absence here, at the end of "Feivush Gazlan," is palpable, and effective in its own way. Instead of that tonic coup of reality, we are given the narrator's pious denials and his saccharine messianic uplift. And if that weren't enough, how are readers who have witnessed the Zionist revolution and the creation of a Jewish state to react when the narrator says in praise of the people of Buczacz that they "bowed their heads and did not rise up against their tormentors"? Agnon has allowed his narrator to dig his own grave, and it is up to us as readers not to fall in.

Yekele, Juvenile Delinquent

Every human community has its misfits, and Buczacz is no different. Throughout *A City in Its Fullness*, generally Buczacz is presented as a place in which the norms of worship and study are broadly respected. The norms may be realized only by a few, but most citizens participate in their practice to the degree their education allows. Even someone like Feivush makes an effort, as we have seen, doing his best to approach the holy texts through a Yiddish digest meant for women. Yet when deviance occurs, and it must occur, how is it handled? Terms such as deviance and delinquency, products of mid-twentieth-century sociology and criminology, actually make a good fit for understanding Buczacz, whose rules of conformity may not have been much different from those of small towns in America. There will always be some young people who, because of the temperament they have inherited or the deprivations they have experienced in childhood, cannot or will not accept and live by the values of the society into which they have been born. If the existence of "wayward youth" then is a given, the question becomes what to do about them.

The eponymous hero of "Yekele" is just such a home-grown variety of juvenile delinquent, Buczacz style. The existence of a lad like Yekele is no cause for sensation. Rather, the story's focus is trained upon the ways in which the new Austrian regime has affected how Buczacz deals with delinquency such as his. As discussed at the beginning of this chapter, one of the major changes after the partitions was the constriction of Jewish legal authority. Under the Polish–Lithuanian Commonwealth, to be sure, the magnate was the law of the land in the towns he owned; but when it did not affect his interests, he generally allowed the Jewish community to police itself and adjudicate its internal conflicts. This adjudication took place through the local rabbinic court (beit din) or through policies enacted by consensus among the elders who constituted the kahal, the community's official body. When the Austrians created the province of Galicia and brought its population within the civil practices of the Empire, the administration of justice was transferred to state courts. Aside from ritual matters, civil litigation and criminal offenses were now adjudicated through the state apparatus. By mutual agreement, two Jewish businessmen could choose to submit a business conflict to a rabbinic court, but if one refused the matter would be taken to a civil court. In the stories from the Austrian period in *A City in Its Fullness*, rabbis are seen very little, or, as in the case of "Feivush Gazlan," not at all. When they do appear, they have to be forced to take action by emergent circumstances. And this is a period, moreover, when Buczacz was lucky in its rabbis and had a succession of figures, much beloved and respected and, perhaps more importantly, who stayed in Buczacz.[14]

Unlike the rabbinate, the kahal did not decline in importance, but its role shifted. Even after the establishment of a civil administration, the Austrian provincial government continued to relate to the Jews as a kind of separate estate for certain purposes, and it used the kahal to do its will, or at least to communicate its will to its Jewish subjects. "Disappeared," the great story on this subject, which I discuss in Chapter 7, shows the kahal charged with the task of providing a fixed quota of young men for army conscription. Who it provides and how it obtains the conscripts are left entirely to the kahal.

The kahal, it should be remembered, was not an elected body but a self-perpetuating council of elders. At its head stood a man who held the position of parnas; the office could be variously held for a sustained time or rotated for short periods. The kahal was by nature an oligarchic form of communal leadership, and the qualifications for membership included commercial acumen, wealth, Torah learning, charitable generosity, knowledge of gentile languages, and strength of character. The particular mix of these characteristics varied, of course, according to time and place. In the stories that take up Chapters 7 and 8 of this book, the profile of the Buczacz kahal is far from generous. Its members are represented as being vain, corrupt, and dictatorial; and in addition to being used by the Austrian rulers to do their will, the members of the kahal become adept at getting the Austrians to do *theirs* as well.

Before discussing the case of the defiant and ill-used Yekele, I must point out that Agnon left us two recensions of his story. *A City in Its Fullness* contains side by side two stories with the identical title "Yekele," distinguished only by subtitles—supplied by Emunah Yaron—indicating "One Version" and "Another Version." Neither version appeared in Agnon's lifetime. His daughter found both texts among the stories intended for the project and, rather than making a determination that one was the final version and the other a preparatory draft, she chose to include both. Upon reading the stories, it is easy to see that she acted very responsibly.

The major plot events are the same, as is Yekele's sad fate, yet the events are shaped differently in each; there are different emphases and different details. Moreover, "Yekele Two," which is what I call the second version, is about a third longer. But yet again, it is not simply a matter of added material but of different or varied material. Each is a self-contained and finished story with its own pleasures. Why did Agnon write both? It is likely, simply, that he wanted or needed to tell the story in two different ways because one would not do. For the purposes of this chapter, I have chosen to discuss the second version because it makes a more coherent station in the examination of the Austrian theme and because it would be distracting to jump back and forth between the two. Some of the elements of comparison are noted along the way.

The keynote difference between the two is Agnon's decision to make R. Yisrael Shlomo, the parnas (leader) of the kahal, the focus and point of departure in the second version, whereas Yekele plays that role in the first.

True, the story is named for Yekele and the reader is naturally drawn to the misadventures of the colorful and insubordinate scamp. Yet the crushing reality the story exposes derives directly from the authority wielded by the parnas, an authority abetted by Austrian rule and unregulated by rabbinic morality. Thus Agnon seeks to prevent us from mistakenly thinking that it is Yekele's incorrigibility that is at fault; instead, he makes it clear that the genealogy of evil is rooted in the way in which power is concentrated and abused, whether it is in gentile or Jewish hands. In the unblinking presentation of this truth, the narrator, as we have found so often in these stories, is more hindrance than help. As chronicler, he must convey the events that took place. But his own subject position is identified with the generality of the community, and the generality of Buczacz is beholden to R. Yisrael Shlomo for his largesse and inclined to be compliant with his will. The conventionality of the narrator's sentiments is at odds with the horrific act of injustice at the center of the story, and the gap between the two embroils the reader in a spreading web of tragic fatalism.

In the narrator's sympathetic introduction of R. Yisrael Shlomo, the parnas's power is presented as both unprecedented and justified. There has never been in recent memory, whether in Buczacz or the province as a whole, a leader who has attained his prominence. His achievement is explained by his being "wealthy, philanthropic, well bred, elegant, resolute, and unyielding" (p. *508*, 438). In a more conceptual mode, the narrator ascribes his success to three factors: a distinguished lineage, his personal forcefulness, and Buczacz's readiness to yield to authority. This third necessary condition, which makes a strong connection with the image of the community in "Feivush Gazlan," is presented without criticism as merely an enabling factor. But there is a telling difference. In "Feivush Gazlan," the community consensus, portrayed as a kind of collective actor, is the main force moving events. In the Yekele stories, by contrast, the broad will of the community possesses no independent force because it is entirely subsumed in the will of its strong leader.

The narrator, perhaps despite himself, provides an excellent account of how R. Yisrael Shlomo goes about purchasing the good will of the good people of Buczacz. His blandishments are everywhere at once: gifts at circumcision ceremonies and weddings, dowries for poor brides, and meals to comfort the bereaved during their week of mourning. His beneficences find grateful recipients, who in turn are further disposed to defer to him. His influence becomes such that the narrator "can say with some certainty that there was no one in the town who did not accept R. Yisrael's authority unconditionally" (p. *408*, 238).

With one exception, that is. Yekele is an orphaned youth who occupies a rung on the social ladder of Buczacz that is as low as R. Yisrael's is high. He has the distinction of being the only person in the town who scoffed at the parnas, "spoke ill of him, and did not even deign to address him as 'Reb,' a title of respect the whole town gave him even when he was not present" (p. *409*, 439). At first report, the powerful man is amused that there should be anyone who does not respect him; but when reports of Yekele's insolence are repeated, his equanimity is disturbed, and he utters the wish that the boy come to an early end. This intemperance reaches Yekele's ears, and the exchanges between them escalate in vituperation until their mutual antipathy is common knowledge.

The narrator makes a show of investigating the origins of their antagonism, but his efforts miss the point entirely. There can be no "real" reason why a man of R. Yisrael Shmolo's immense prestige and power should be affected by *anything* said by a social nullity such as Yekele. That is, unless his grandiosity rests on so precarious a basis that anything other than complete acclamation can topple it. In the face of such danger, there is no telling what a man would do to preserve his position.

There are undoubtedly comic possibilities inherent in this picture of inflated self-importance vulnerable to the wiles of an irreverent mischief maker. But Agnon decides instead to take the story in the direction of tragedy, and he builds a plot about the inexorable crushing of a minor delinquent by an insecure oligarch, full of rage, while the community looks on impassively and the traditional organs of conscience are neutralized by the new gentile regime. Now, one might think that this plot-line would be advanced by filling out Yekele's character and thereby strengthening our bond with him. Yet, although we are surely sympathetic to Yekele and abhor his victimization, Agnon declines to tell us much about his life or to develop him as a character. (There is more of this is in the first version of the story.)

Instead, a disproportionate amount of narrative investment is devoted to his pre-natal origins and the peculiar figure of his father, R. Moshe, and it is from these that we are asked to make inferences and understand something essential about how Yekele came to be the way he is. And if this were not enough of a digression from the ostensible main business of the story, this excursus is followed by another long passage, which lists, in exhaustive and often absurd detail, the voluntary benevolent associations that operated in Buczacz.

Who is this R. Moshe whose life gets more attention than the eponymous hero of the story? He is introduced to the reader as being "the youngest of the early Hasidim in Buczacz" (p. 409, 439), and this identification does a great deal to explain who he is, while still leaving unexplained contradictions. The timing helps to date the story because the Baal Shem Tov, the founder of Hasidism, died in 1760, and Dov Ber of Mezerich, the disciple who helped to spread the new doctrine in the region, died in 1770. If R. Moshe died around this time, just on the eve of the partitions of Poland, then Yekele would have come of age during the second decade of Austrian rule, a time of the legislative activism in the Viennese chancellery regarding the Jews of the new province. The timing also helps to explain why R. Moshe's behavior is so peculiar in the eyes of Buczacz.

The city's scholarly culture and its proud loyalty to the liturgical practices of medieval Ashkenaz made it more resistant to the explosive spread of Hasidism than other communities in the region. The laxity in the fixed time for prayers and the shift to the rite associated with the kabbalist Isaac Luria (*nusah ha'ari*) were disturbing and subversive changes, which almost amounted to a seccession from the community. The seccession was literal when it came to the separate prayer houses established by the Hasidim. Contempt for the new movement was not limited to the elite. In "Feivush Gazlan" when the new thug accompanies the brutal kick he gives Feivush with the taunt: "If you want to lie around, get yourself over to the bath-house or to the place where the jokers pray." By jokers (*letsanim*) he means the Hasidim.[15]

Of the joy and earthiness that later characterizes Hasidism, there is little in R. Moshe. In his disregard for the body and the world, he embodies more of the asceticism of the Hasidism of medieval Ashkenaz. He is a holy man not in the sense of being a wonder worker but in his desire to immerse himself wholly in contemplative worship and the study of mystical texts. He takes no responsibility for the practicalities of life and leaves the burden of earning a livelihood to his wife. While others don the tallit and tefillin only for early morning prayers, R. Moshe wears them all day long as a sign of his withdrawal from the world and his desire block out all but the sacred. He devotes himself to studying and teaching the esoteric lore of the Zohar and the writings of Isaac Luria, and the mystical treatise *Ḥemdat Yamim* never leaves his hands.[16] He spends half the week running to the town's synagogues checking to the make sure the Torah scrolls contain no scribal errors.

Similarly, married life for R. Moshe is an institution that exists only for a higher purpose. He divorces his nameless wife after ten years when their union produces no issue, in accordance with Talmudic guidelines.[17] But in accordance with another Talmudic principle he takes her back so she will not be alone for the Passover holiday at the end of a brutal and impoverishing winter. Wondrously, after so many years of childlessness, she conceives a son on the Friday night before Passover. Sadly, R. Moshe dies soon afterward, and his wife dies giving birth to the son, who is Yekele. The miraculous circumstances surrounding his birth come to light as the narrator explains the origins of the boy's name. That Passover R. Moshe and his wife were facing the holiday with no provisions when a man from the village drove up with a wagon full of meat, fish, and vegetables, as well as a large purse full of coins, which he proceeded to bring into their house. It was later reported that this Elijah-like figure, whose name was Ya'akov, drowned with his wagon in the river. "And when the boy was born as she was dying," the narrator informs us, the mother "instructed that he be named Ya'akov. But because everyone loved him, they called him Yekele. He is the Yekele of our story," (p. *511*, 442).

But of course he is anything but beloved and blessed. From the tragic ordeal of Yekele's life we realize retrospectively, if we have not already worked it out from the precious stylization of the episode, that the story of his origins is a parody of a Hasidic wonder tale. The only wonder is that he survived—until he didn't. Our narrator is not a maskil, who would openly and wickedly ridicule the miraculous pretentions of the Hasidim, because he cannot discount the pillars of religious faith he shares with them. But he is not above showing us that R. Moshe took the quest for holiness so far as to push it over the top and empty it of meaning. His obsession with holiness is impotent and barren, and he and his wife can create a child only by supernatural intervention. A child created in this way must of necessity be a blasted vessel into which evil can enter more easily than good.

Now the miraculous wagonload of good things is necessary to create an essential premise of the plot. R. Moshe donated the excess wine he received to the Ḥevra Kadisha, the town's burial society, in exchange for a promise that if his wife gave birth to a boy he would be registered as a member of the society. The promise was kept, and it was this membership that eventually entangled Yekele in the concatenation of events that led to his execution. (In "Yekele One" much more space is devoted to Yekele's early life, his resistance to attending ḥeder, and the fearlessness that makes him a good gravedigger.) The very idea of a truant, delinquent, and penniless boy belonging to the Ḥevra Kadisha is patently absurd, and the narrator knows it. The burial society was the wealthiest and most prestigious and exclusive club in Buczacz or in any Polish Jewish town, and there was a long waiting list of the successful and pious waiting to gain admission. The narrator issues one of his famous understatements: ketsat kasheh, it is a little difficult to understand. "Nothing happens without a reason, of course," he admits, "but why this was we do not know, and so we will have to be content only with the facts" (p. 511, 443).

Involuntary Societies

As if to divert attention from this quandary, the narrator launches directly into the second long digression in this short story. This is a catalogue of some twenty voluntary associations that existed in Buczacz, some devoted to the study of sacred texts and others to social welfare. The catalogue is a fascinating document unto itself, but its value as an ethnographic source is equivocal because it mixes important and weighty endeavors, such as the study of Mishnah and the providing of poor brides with dowries, together with activities of a far more peculiar valence, such as the society "founded by craftsmen in town in order to provide hens for the *kapparot* ritual to those who could not afford to buy them" or the society whose members "made lanterns which they brought to illuminate the ceremony of sanctifying the new moon" (p. *513*, 447). The whole lengthy catalogue sticks out like a sore thumb and works to impede the forward movement of the story. And that seems to be exactly the effect that the narrator seeks to achieve, consciously or not. Not only does he wish to camouflage the preposterousness of Yekele's membership in the Ḥevra Kadisha, but he wants to anticipate and neutralize the calumny and moral diminishment that will likely be Buczacz's lot in the reader's eyes for standing by while a terrible injustice is carried out. Buczacz is more and better than that, the narrator urges us to see. Just look at the many ways in which the community takes care of the poor and the needy.

When the narrator finally returns to the story, events take place at a rapid pace. R. Yisrael Avraham, one of the richest men in town, has been waiting for years to become a member of the Ḥevra Kadisha, and to celebrate his admission, he has contributed funds to turn the society's annual banquet into a sumptuous, once-in-a-lifetime affair. While R. Yisrael Avraham and the other men are celebrating all night, his wife is at home asleep. Deep in the night, his home is broken into, and all the silver and gold and promissory notes from Polish nobles are stolen from his strongbox. The greedy thieves even take the golden earrings from the sleeping wife, who awakes and shouts. Then "one of the robbers gagged her with a handkerchief, and in a gentile language told her, '*Cicho bestia!*' meaning, 'Shut up, you animal,' or I'll strangle you" (p. *514*, 448). The matron identified the voice as belonging to Yekele.

The journey from this accusation to Yekele's being condemned to the gallows takes place with startling rapidity. Because of the prominence of R. Yisrael's wife, inquiries are made, and it is soon discovered that Yekele was not present at the banquet and he is nowhere to be found. Two days later he returns to town of his own accord. He is wounded and roughed up, and, under pressure from his relatives, he reveals that he absented himself from the feast because he thought he would be forced to serve the leaders of the society. He went to a neighboring town to buy a cask of aged mead so he could show up his fellow members by producing a beverage superior to theirs. He ended up drinking the mead himself, and in his drunken state he was an easy mark for a gang of peasants who attacked him. Unaware of the break-in at the home of R. Yisrael Avraham, he assumes that R. Yisrael Shlomo is seeking to punish him for failing to report for duty at the banquet. He is insolent with the magistrates and calls them shills of the powerful parnas.

Once he is informed of the severity of the accusations against him and taken to prison in iron shackles, he utters, "God help Reb Yisrael Shlomo. I swear he will not leave my hands alive" (p. 515, 449). The parnas is shaken by his threat, and he "moved quickly to bring the matter to the attention of the regional judges, and he was not satisfied until they condemned Yekele to the gallows." Before anyone knows it, an official hangman arrives from Czernovitz, sent for by R. Yisrael Shlomo, and a gallows is erected on the river hillside, a location that will create a natural amphitheater for the members of the Polish nobility who will come from wide and far for the public spectacle.

Yekele's fate is dispatched so quickly that we are barely aware that the entire drama is staged exclusively by R. Yisrael Shlomo. If even a modicum of due process and civil procedure exists, he controls it and rides roughshod over it. Savor the irony here: the Austrian regime has taken over many areas once dealt with by rabbinic courts, but now a single powerful and wealthy Jew uses the Austrian regional courts for his own purposes, for a vendetta against one impudent and offensive youth. Where is the rest of the Jewish community? The unhappy answer is that this man has *become* the community. Still, several leading figures come, together with the rabbi of Buczacz, before the parnas to protest. They assume, mistakenly, that the hangman has been brought merely to frighten Yekele, and they protest that even "tormenting him is still a grave sin." The dismissive answer they receive is instructive.

> Reb Yisrael Shlomo sighed and replied, "What can I do? The matter is now out of my hands and there is nothing more to be done. I'm not the judge or the one in charge or the one giving orders, and besides, the law of the land is the law." (p. *516, 450*)

The imperious parnas is not only deceitfully camouflaging his own initiatives, he is also invoking—and traducing—the well-known halakhic principle *dina dimalkhuta dina*, the law of the land is the law. This principle, enunciated first in the Babylonian Talmud (*Nedarim* 28a and *Bava Kamma* 113a) and developed by innumerable medieval authorities, states that in certain circumstances regulations imposed by the royal authority or the state, such as paying taxes, are binding in the same way as the statutes of Jewish law.[18] The application of this principle is complex and fraught, especially at a time when rabbinic authority is being curtailed. But here it is evident that R. Yisrael Shlomo is adducing it as a piece of sophistry to conceal his own machinations.[19] The picture becomes clearer when the rabbi and the notables, unsatisfied with the parnas's response, attempt to register their concerns with the Austrian officials directly. They are rebuffed and told that any matter pertaining to the Jewish community or to a Jewish person goes through the esteemed Israel Salomon Behrmann (a.k.a. R. Yisrael Shlomo), and any further protest will be punishable as an attempt to unduly influence the judiciary.[20]

This is the story, in short, of a lopsided duel between a powerful oligarch and a boy who refuses to acknowledge his authority. Cowed and enfeebled, the community fails to play a mediating role in the confrontation, and their entrance into the drama is sadly belated. They withdraw and cede the stage to the police officials, the hangman, and the gawking Polish nobles. The narrator allows the Jews of the holy community of Buczacz to put in a cameo appearance at the story's conclusion.

> On the day that Yekele was taken out to be executed, all the God-fearing people of Buczacz went out into the fields and forests outside of town. They walked about the whole day weeping and crying. From time to time they

spread out their hands in the direction of the town saying "Our hands did not shed this blood." (p. 517, 451)

The verse they utter comes from Deuteronomy 27, which describes a ceremony to be performed by the elders of a town near where a corpse has been found and the murderer cannot be identified. The town has incurred guilt and impurity because it has failed to provide the hospitality and protection that might have prevented the man's death. To expiate the guilt, the elders sacrifice a calf by a stream outside the town and recite the formula quoted above stating that their hands did not shed the blood of this man.[21] The picture of the God-fearing of Buczacz weeping as they wander the fields is an affecting and surreal image of regret and ineffectuality. They are guilty, to be sure, of many sins, foremost among them accepting R. Yisrael Shlomo's blandishments in return for acknowledging his rule over them. Yet their heartbreak and contrition also are real. But tragically they come too late.

At the same time as the righteous are forlornly wringing their hands, Yekele is having the last laugh. Availing himself of a final wish granted the condemned, he is allowed to ride a horse around the gallows area. Seeing lords and ladies arriving late for the spectacle, he shouts to them jokingly, "You need not hurry as long as I am here. It won't happen without me!" It is not clear whether Yekele has come to terms with what is in store for him or whether he persists in believing that it is all a show to frighten him. In either case, he embodies a defiant, anarchic principle of revolt against authority. He *is* deviant and he does confess to many crimes, but not to the one of which he stands condemned. And sure enough, after he has been hanged, a rider arrives from the capital to confirm his innocence.

7

Disappeared

Of all the measures imposed on the Jews of Galicia by the Austrian Empire, the one most feared and loathed was conscription into military service. That a Jewish young man should be plucked from his home and community, sent far away for many years—the term of service varied from ten to fourteen years—made to live among gentiles, eat non-kosher food, and desecrate the Sabbath—this prospect struck dread in the hearts of Jewish families. The conscription was not universal, to be sure; Jewish communities were given yearly quotas to fill, and, as we see below, ways were readily found to exempt the well-to-do and the scholarly among the young male population.[1] Yet army service for Jews was very real, and by 1821, it is estimated that thirty-five thousand Jews had served as soldiers in the imperial army.

The Jews of Galicia experienced this measure very differently from the imperial government's intent in imposing it. For the Jews, it bore the markings of a classic gezeirah, an edict issued by gentile rulers aimed at their persecution. For the Austrian monarchy, however, it was a sign of the equal status of the Jews in relation to the many peoples and provinces of the multi-ethnic empire. Even though all religious and ethnic groups in the empire were required to provide quotas of young men for army service, there had indeed been a serious debate within the government about whether Jews should be included or exempted. The military itself was dubious whether Jews could make competent soldiers and, if they were inducted, whether it would be possible to make the arrangements necessary to accommodate their religious practice. It would be more trouble than it would be worth, in their eyes. The civil branch of government, and the monarch himself, on the other hand, put forward the argument that military service is the defining obligation of all subjects of the empire, and without the fulfillment of that duty no ethnic or religious group could hope to be granted rights to participate in other aspects of civil society. This argument prevailed. Despite the military's concerns about the practicability of making Jews into soldiers, the enlightened ideology of inclusion won out.[2]

The question of the religious needs of Jewish soldiers was taken very seriously. Austria was a deeply Catholic country, whose rulers believed that religion plays an essential role in the preservation of morality. While exerting its dominion over many regions and peoples in central Europe, the empire followed a liberal policy in respecting the rights of non-Catholic groups and supporting their institutions. In Galicia, in particular, Vienna strengthened the position of the Greek-Catholic or Uniate church as a counterweight to the Roman Catholicism of the Polish nobility. The Greek-Catholic church, which observed the Eastern rite but was loyal to the authority of Rome, was the religion of most Ruthenians.

When it came to the fierce conflicts between the Hasidim and the maskilim among the Jews of Galicia, the Austrian government declined to persecute the Hasidim; and this was despite the urgings of the enlighteners conveyed in the many German-language memoranda they submitted to the government. In designing the legislation regulating the conscription of Jews into the Austrian army, much thought was given to anticipating the religious needs of the recruits. Although there would be no separate Jewish units, Jews would be concentrated with their co-religionists in the transport and artillery branches of the army. Efforts would be made to locate units with Jews in parts of the empire with Jewish communities so that Jewish soldiers would have some access to kosher food and holiday observances when possible. When it came to Jews and the Sabbath, the policy was to be similar to the guidelines for Christians on Sunday, which allowed for observance according to ad hoc conditions. Jews were not required to attend Christian worship. Uniforms free of *sha'atnez* would be provided for them to avoid the prohibition against mixing certain kinds of fibers.[3] Although it is difficult to know how these mandated accommodations were put in practice in the field, the liberal intent of the legislation is clear.

Agnon does two things with this historical information in "Disappeared" ["Hane'elam"], the major story in *A City in Its Fullness* that deals with the Austrian period.[4] First, he disregards much of it and makes his protagonist Dan Hoffmann undergo many of the deprivations the legislation was designed to alleviate. Dan appears to be the lone Jew in his unit, which has been deployed very far away to Upper Austria, where Jewish settlement has long been erased by persecution and expulsion. Outfitted in his sha'atnez uniform and compelled by circumstance to violate the Sabbath and eat non-kosher food, he struggles bravely to maintain his Jewishness. Second, Agnon declines to frame the Austrian rulers as persecutors. To the contrary: in comparing their behavior toward Dan with that of the representatives of the kahal, the official Jewish community of Buczacz, it is the Jews who come away looking villainous. The Austrians may have no love for the Jews, but their bureaucratic rationality requires fair treatment of the empire's subjects. The only kindness shown to Dan by anyone is extended by an Austrian sergeant, who shows him how to address his letters so they will reach his mother. When Dan fails to return home after he has been demobilized, the whole of provincial officialdom is roused to try to locate him. And when disturbing reports surface concerning the behavior of a Polish noblewoman toward a Jewish young man, the local authorities cannot desist from investigating and uncovering the crime.

The Austrians, in short, are not demonized. As in the case of "Feivush Gazlan" and the Yekele stories, the gentile regime in the far-away capital is responsible for onerous impositions, but it is the morally compromised response of the Jewish community that moves to the center. "Disappeared" is a larger and more ambitious story, and part of its power derives from the fact that the main Jewish drama is flanked by scenes from the Austrian world and the Polish world between which, and within which, contemporary Jewish life unfolds. The Austrian bureaucracy and military, at several levels of operation, are present in the ways mentioned above. The milieu of Polish nobility is represented by a cameo appearance by none other than Count Potocki himself and by an extraordinary document, the diary of the unnamed noblewoman who keeps Dan chained to a wall for six years. By bringing both the old and new gentile regimes into the story, Agnon gives "Disappeared" an impressive historical breadth at the same time as he inverts the historical sequence. The story begins with the Austrians, the present rulers of Buczacz, and ends with the imprisonment of a Jew by a member of the Polish nobility of the sort who once owned and ruled towns like Buczacz. The story thus enacts a movement backward in time, a disengagement from the rationality of enlightened absolutism and the German language as a vehicle for modernity and a regression back to feudal autocracy and the Polish language of its former rulers.

It was not just the Jews who seemed strange and ungovernable when Austria suddenly found itself in charge of a portion of the former Polish lands. In the eyes of Vienna, the province that came to be called Galicia was a kind of Wild West filled with unpoliced outlaws, oppressed serfs, medieval and mystical Jews, and swashbuckling Polish noblemen who, despite their kindred Catholicism, exploited their freedom from authority to indulge their perverse individual wills.

As enlightened monarchs, Maria Theresa and Joseph II set a task of bringing order to Galicia by ridding the roads and forests of bandits, alleviating the plight of the Ruthenian peasantry, making the Jews into citizens, and curbing the unbridled appetites of the Polish nobles. The success of this civilizing mission was at best equivocal, as can be judged from the stubborn traditionalism of the mass of Galician Jewry. The Polish nobility, in its own way, proved just as recalcitrant. The ending of "Disappeared," which discloses a web of hidden violence and erotic cruelty, relates the history of a noblewoman's mute servant, who becomes an emblem for all of primitive nonrationality the Austrians failed to extirpate from the benighted region. He is a survivor of the bands of robbers and murderers that were largely wiped out when Austria took over the region. His tongue was cut out by his comrades so he would not talk under torture. Rescued by the noblewoman's father, who had often used him to exact vengeance on his enemies, he now loyally serves the daughter in the execution of her own perversions.

Between the enlightened absolutism of the Austrians and the residuum of Polish feudalism lay the Jews and their corporate structures. "Disappeared" deals with the choices made by the organized Jewish community of Buczacz in filling the conscription quotas and with the consequences of those choices for the lives of the individuals involved. Here, more than in any other story in *A City in It Fullness*, political history is laid out in detail and presented as knowledge the reader must acquire before the meaning of the events about to be related can be understood. In discharging that responsibility, the narrator plays a role different from the other Austrian stories. He is more worldly, reliable, and omniscient. He knows what is in the heart of a poor widow as well as the words exchanged between two Austrian officials; he follows Dan and his unit bivouacked in the far reaches of the empire just as he keeps track of life in Buczacz. He must, in short, become something of a novelist, and in this he shares more with Agnon in this story than in others.

The story begins in an expository mode by explaining the hard practical choices faced by Galician Jewish communities in filling the conscription quotas. These deliberations are a world away from the discourse about empire and civic duty that took place in the capital surrounding the decision not to exempt Jews from military service. Each year the parnasim of the community would gather and compose a list according to clear criteria: "If [a young man] was from a prominent family or a Torah scholar they would pass him over and in his place take some clod or numskull who would be no loss to the town. If they did not have enough men to fill the government quota, they would recruit from itinerants in the region who sold themselves for military service" (p. *448*, 369).

Described here are the workings of the kahal, and it is well to recall the status of Jewish communal leadership under the Austrians. Although the name of the institution was changed from the kahal to the *Kultusgemeinde* and it lost its titular privileges, the institution retained considerable power, and it constituted the means whereby the regime procured what it wanted from the Jews.[5] Although it remained a self-perpetuating council of wealthy elders, the kahal is presented here as reflecting the consensus of the larger community.

This is the scale of value: a boy from a wealthy family or a boy who is himself learned in Torah is given a pass, and the opportunity is exploited to weed out and ship off "undesirable elements" within the community. (The term in Hebrew is *poḥez* from Judg. 9:4, connoting someone who is a mischief-maker or a dunce.) On the next rung down on the scale are the itinerant poor. The narrator takes great care in explaining the severity of this new phenomenon. The fact that a great many Jews earned their livelihood by operating taverns was disturbing to the new Austrian rulers because peasant drunkenness, morally offensive in itself, led to the under-utilization of agricultural production. Expelled from this employment, Jews were forced to leave their villages in search of work. In the absence of other prospects, some were willing to be conscripted into army service in return for payment, and with these hired bodies a community could fill its quota.

But what is a community to do when it not only has run through all of its undesirables but has no money to secure the services of the wandering poor? "If the quota set by the regime was still not met," the narrator explains, "they took from the ranks of the unlettered" (p. *449*, 371). The unlettered (*'amei ha'arets*) are not the rebellious or uneducable but simply those young men, usually workers or apprentices, whose poverty has not allowed them to learn Torah. This is exactly what happens one year. There happen to be no good-for-nothings or adulterers in Buczacz at the time—a reason for the community to pat itself on the back. And the reason why there is no money to hire outsiders is very peculiar. Because of a recent plague, the community needed to expand the cemetery and arranged to purchase an adjoining field from a gentile. They delayed paying him because of the need to deal with unusually heavy taxes and bribes. To display his displeasure, the gentile let his pigs loose to graze in the cemetery. Because of the "danger that the repose of the dead would be disturbed," the community paid up and drained its coffers, and thus there is nothing left to "purchase" itinerant strangers.[6] Thus the community chooses to sacrifice a blameless youth rather disturb the repose of the dead.[7]

A Perfect Storm

Having set out the historical background concerning Galician Jews in general and Buczacz in particular, Agnon now devotes himself to launching the story of Dan Hoffmann, the unfortunate young man who has been selected for involuntary recruitment. But the story we get is not the story we expect. Instead of following the adventures and tribulations of the young Jewish recruit in any direct way, "Disappeared" is taken over by a variety of digressions and preoccupations for most of its long span until the story returns at the end to Dan's victimization at the hands of the Polish noblewoman. Yet, as we have seen throughout these stories, digressions are precisely the place to search for what Agnon is up to. With that in mind, I focus the following discussion on those features of "Disappeared" that seem anomalous or excessive and pose an interpretive challenge. The following is a list of the unexpected formations in the texts, which I consider in the course of this chapter. (1) The story is thickly emplotted—multiple strands of causation are knotted together—only in its opening scene. (2) The emotional experience of the women on the home front (Dan's mother and his unofficial fiancée Bilhah) receives the preponderance of narrative attention rather than Dan's fate in the army. (3) Nearly a quarter of the story is devoted to the subject of letter writing and to the portrait of a professional scrivener named Dovidl. (4) In the second half of the story, considerable space is given to the fraught relations between the Polish nobility and the new Austrian rulers. (5) At the end of the story proper—before the revelation of the noblewoman's diary—the narrator shifts focus away from the elders of the kahal as representative of Buczacz as a community and instead gives us an epic rendering of the people of Buczacz as a kind of body politic. (6) The "Diary of a Lady," the Polish-language document that mysteriously comes into the hands of the narrator and is placed after the conclusion of the story proper, begs many questions about the narrator's motives. I list these issues in the order of their appearance in the story, and it is in that order that I consider them in this chapter.

First is the knotted opening scene that becomes the generating premise of the plot. In weaving together the multiple factors that result in Dan's being pressed into the army, Agnon is attempting to account for the concatenation of events and forces that leads to this fate. The forces are all grounded in the historically conditioned reality of the story's time and place, yet *how* the threads are entangled is determined by the creative discretion of the writer. Any single one of these threads by itself is troubling but not dangerous; knotted together, they produce tragedy. Agnon executes this fateful entanglement in one long passage.

> That month Reb Leibush was serving as parnas. The young man's mother had come to him to receive her share of wheat money to buy Passover matzah.[8] He gave it to her, but she demanded more. Reb Leibush said to her, "Look, this is what you are entitled to receive, this is what I gave you, now be gone and on your way." Whereupon she started screeching and hollering and recounting to him all her troubles. Her husband had died and left her with an only son and no visible means of support. Over the winter they sustained themselves with whatever she could earn in her impoverished state. She would buy a chicken from a Gentile woman and sell it at a small profit, she would salt the slaughtered chickens to remove the blood and render the meat kosher for the local women. She would prepare goose fat for them for Passover, or pluck feathers; she would prepare the chickens for the wedding feasts the wealthy families made for their daughters. Now that Passover was approaching she wanted to buy provisions for the festival so that she and her orphaned son would not go hungry as they had all winter, when there was nothing in their mouth but saliva. Reb Leibush replied that there were many poor widows in town and many orphans too.
>
> "What makes you better than they?" he asked. She grew angry at the way he compared her to the other poor widows and retorted fiercely, "Whoever envies us, may his children be orphans and his wife a widow!" Just at that moment Godil the tailor came in. He wanted to measure Reb Leibush for a garment. I am not sure if the garment was for him to wear on the approaching Passover holiday or to impress the officials of the provincial capital when he brought the recruits there to present them. When the widow saw Godil she exclaimed, "Well now, here's Godil! He can say whether I deserve to be

treated well or not. And if not on my own account, then on account of my son, who works with him."

Godil was silent. Said the widow, "Godil, why are you silent? Why do you swallow your tongue? Say something. Let Reb Leibush hear my son's praise." Said Godil, "What can I say about your son? He works for me." The widow shrieked in anger, "That's all? Nothing more?" Godil continued, "What more do you want me to say? That he is worthy of being a *Landesrabbiner*?[9] He does his work, and I have nothing against him." The widow raised her voice at him and screamed, "That's how you treat an orphan, the son of a widow? That's all you have to say about him?"

Godil grew angry at the woman for addressing him that way in the presence of Reb Leibush. It might make him think that she was his, Godil's, equal. "Sha! Sha!" said Godil to her, "If you insist, I will praise your son to the skies." The widow replied, "So open your mouth and say something." Godil turned to Reb Leibush and said, "He may be young but he's as strong as a grown man. He's as powerful as a mighty oak and taller than everyone his age. Twenty year-olds, twenty-two year-olds, men who sell themselves for the imperial army don't even come up to his shoulders."

Her love for her son prevented her from catching the import of what Godil had just said. Indeed, his earlier silence was better than the words he had now spoken. Triumphantly she said to Reb Leibush "So has Reb Leibush heard what Godil has said about my son? I will add to his words. One Sabbath last summer I took a walk with him. We came to a village and sat down in a park belonging to a Polish noblewoman from whom I buy chickens and fruit. The lady passed by and asked me who this young Jewish man was. I said to myself, "May the eyes that this shiksa can't take off my son wither away!" She then said, "A fellow like this, a fellow like this by us would be made a commissioned officer." And within two or three days the widow's son was taken for the imperial army. (pp. *450–51, 372–74*)

Let us begin with Godil in untangling the plot complications. Godil is a tailor with social aspirations. In the paragraph directly preceding this one, we are told that he owns a house and serves as a gabbai in the tailors' synagogue and that several generations back his forbears were related to R. Leibush, the member of the kahal who is taking his turn as monthly parnas. Godil plans to use the prospect of his daughter's marriage to a prominent family as a major avenue in his ascent. But his daughter Bilhah has fallen in love with Dan, one of his apprentices. Although it is Bilhah who has "cast her eyes" on the young man, her father's anger is trained on "this father-less son of a widow with nothing more than a shirt on his back [who has] worked his charms on the girl and stolen her heart" (p. *450, 372*).

R. Leibush too has his aspirations. The reason for Godil's appearance is to measure him for a new suit of clothes. The purpose of the suit is to make an impression on the officials in the provincial capital when he travels there to hand over the recruits. So, the ceremony that marks Dan's being torn from his family and condemned to many years of lonely military service is the same ceremony that the parnas from Buczacz hopes to use to inflate his importance in the eyes of the regime. But the new suit will be for naught unless he can deliver the quota of inductees. Even though Dan's name may have been discussed in the kahal, the slot was not yet filled at the time this scene takes place. Ironically and tragically, it is only after Dan's mother sings his praises that the deal is done, and R. Leibush can walk away knowing that the complement of recruits is now complete.

Dan's mother is bereft but not powerless. The fact that of all the characters she alone has no name of her own lends a primal, archetypal force to her being. Her encounter with R. Leibush occurs within the context of an official occasion, in which charity funds are distributed to the poor in advance of Passover to enable the purchase of holiday necessities. Rather than accepting her allotment demurely, she launches into a harangue denouncing the tightfistedness of the community and dramatizing the demeaning and exhausting jobs she undertakes to make ends meet. Her accusatory invectives and her expressions of raw emotionality are the features that are most identified with her throughout the narrative. Stripped of other resources, she possesses only "screeching and hollering" and rehearsing her travails as sources of power. These means are not wholly ineffectual in her encounter with R. Leibush, but, tragically, not for the purpose she intended. Rather than being moved to greater charity, he becomes defensive and provokes her to greater shrillness by asking what makes her more deserving than the other poor widows of the town.

The tipping point in the situation takes place with the arrival of Godil, who has come to measure the parnas for his new suit. To bolster her claims for increased charity funds, she demands that the tailor give a testimonial to her son's worthiness. The reader knows what she does not: Godil is already predisposed against Dan for interfering with his plans to make an advantageous match for Bilhah. So when she screams at him and abuses him for his tepid response, Godil is provoked from a resentful withholding into a destructive rage. It may not be clear whether the mother is aware that her son is a candidate for forced induction, but Godil certainly knows. With his extravagant praise for the apprentice as being mighty as an oak and taller than the "men who sell themselves for the imperial army," he has effectively sealed the boy's fate. For the one reservation that has been holding back Dan's selection is the fact that he is below the minimum mandated age of eighteen. The obstacle falls away now that R. Leibush sees that he will be universally perceived as at least that age.

As if this weren't enough, the mother makes the situation even worse by proudly recounting the anecdote about the Polish noblewoman who could not take her eyes off of Dan and who declared that he is strapping enough to be made a commissioned officer. This additional nail in the coffin, as it were, is not necessary to bring the sad business to a conclusion, but it serves several functions. It sharpens the terrible irony of the mother's triumph unwittingly condemning her son. It foreshadows the grotesque consequences of another Polish noblewoman's attraction to Dan at end of the story. (Agnon differentiates between the two noblewomen by calling the local one a *peritsah* and the other an *adonit*.) And, most crucially, it introduces the fact of Dan's beauty.

Considering the scene as a whole, one is struck by the complexity of the emplotment. Each strand brings with it a set of circumstances that have to interlock with the others for the tragic outcome to be set in motion and the knot cinched tight. The scene, moreover, is not just a piling up of circumstances but a dynamic field of potentialities, and to actualize them requires the mother's mounting hysteria. It is the devastating irony of the scene that the more unrelentingly she ratchets up her appeals on behalf of her son's welfare the more she undermines the very outcome she seeks. The stark finality of it all, the brute fact of the fait accompli, lands like a blow:

"And within two or three days the widow's son was taken for the imperial army" (p. *451, 374*).

It is evident that this complexity makes it impossible to obtain a simple answer to the question of who is responsible for Dan's fate. Yet it is possible to make distinctions between contingent circumstances and more essential causes. So, for example, R. Leibush happens to be the parnas on duty when the Passover charity is being distributed. Dan happens to be an apprentice in the workshop of an ambitious tailor with an attractive daughter. It happens to be a year in which a cemetery expansion has emptied the communal coffers. Chief among the essential causes are the Austrian government's decision to conscript Jews and the Jewish community's policy of sacrificing the poor and unlettered. But there is another, less evident essential cause that has nothing to do directly with historical or political events. This is Dan's physical beauty. This fact is never told to us by the narrator; and, indeed, Dan is not even aware of it himself. We see it only through the reactions of others to him: Bilhah casting her eyes on him, Godil testifying to his size and height, the local noblewoman's compliment as reported by his mother, and, most of all and most deferred, the erotic obsession of the Polish noblewoman at the story's conclusion. If it weren't for his strapping handsomeness, he may never have been inducted into the army in the first place, and the noblewoman would never have overcome her loathing for Jews and made him into an object of desire.[10]

Dan's beauty represents a different kind of causality. It is a natural endowment; he is born with it. Does it come from God, from the randomness of nature? The answer depends, of course, on one's fundamental view of life. Yet to the degree that the story is not life but artifice, the answer must be that it comes from Agnon, the author of the story, who is responsible for making Dan so attractive and thus supplying the premise that moves the plot. If Agnon's goal was to write a story about the consequences for the Jewish community of the Austrian decision to force Jews to serve in the military, there are many ways he could have built his plot. He chose this one. The "accident" of Dan's beauty is different from all the other circumstances in the story, which are givens of social, historical existence: imperial regimes seek to exploit and integrate new territorial possessions; tradesmen seek to better their social standing; a young woman falls in love with a handsome man who works in her father's shop; and communal leaders are zealous of their authority. But whether to make a boy be plain or handsome is a choice.

Making Dan be born handsome underscores two important truths about the story. First, "Disappeared" is more novelistic than many of the other stories in *A City in Its Fullness*. The voice of the garrulous narrator-chronicler has withdrawn deep into the background and emerges to make observations only occasionally. Gone is the self-assured, know-it-all voice of a narrator who informs you about how busy he has been managing the telling of the story. And managing is *all* he does, because it is God who has created human destiny and orchestrated human affairs. But in "Disappeared," the world-shaping work of that God has also receded, and in its place there is a sense of reality being shaped by historical and social mechanisms. This is the domain of the modern novelist, who mixes a mimetic responsibility to the world as we know it with the prerogative of fixing the points of departure for the plot. If the story is an equation, Dan's physical appearance is the unknown, the radical that has been inserted by Agnon.[11]

Second, the particular variable Agnon has chosen to insert is far from arbitrary. The erotic attention and the erotic desires elicited by Dan's appearance raise a theme that is not a comfortable presence in the traditional Jewish world of Buczacz. Throughout the epic world of *A City in Its Fullness*, there are virtually no instances of romantic love preceding marriage or leading to marriage.[12] This does not mean that such attractions did not exist or that their suppression did not cause pain to those who had to abandon them. But these instances do not have a place in the Buczacz Agnon has reimagined. So when Bilhah falls in love with Dan and gives her heart to him as he is taken off for induction, it is a very significant moment not only in the story but in the cycle of the Buczacz stories altogether. She suffers terribly because of her attachment not just because Dan is removed from her for so many years but also because she has no standing as an official fiancée and must therefore hide her love and grieve in secret. Her persistence in considering herself betrothed to Dan, despite the lack of her parents' approval and his protracted absence, indicates not only a strong will but a sense of herself as fulfilling some positive ideal rather than merely transgressing the norms of the community. By the time of the action of the story, sometime after 1815, the Austrians have been ruling Galicia in the German language for over forty years, and it is difficult to imagine that no adumbrations of European sentiments, with their idealizations of true love, have infiltrated the consciousness of young Jews.

If the tragedy of "Disappeared" came only from the separation of the two lovers, it would be sad enough. But Dan's horrible and grotesque plight at the hands of the Polish noblewoman occupies a very different rung of tragedy, and it opens up the chilling dimension of the erotic. Erotic longings and the attraction to physical beauty remain controlled and even chaste within the context of the Jewish community during the early stages of modernization, at least as refracted in these stories. Those same energies are more combustible when they are located, not in the more advanced European society, but rather in the persistence of the pre-modern Polish feudal order. It is in this older regime that the noblewoman is rooted, a regime formed by a configuration of local autocracies in which the desires of the lord are absolute. When it comes to the character of the noblewoman, one of Agnon's achievements is *not* to make her a cutout of her class but to give her a psychological history that supplies some motive for her behavior. What she does to Dan, however, is driven not just by her own deprivations but by the position in which she has been placed by the Austrian accession. Having rejected the proposals of Austrian officials earlier in her life, she lives alone on her vastly reduced estate, accompanied only by her Catholic piety and her mute ex-murderer servant. Her inability to control her desires, as I discuss below, is directly connected to her isolation and to the radical diminution of her prerogatives.

Finally, there is the question of Dan's own possession of his erotic appeal. When the noblewoman opens her door to find Dan on her doorstep, she is struck by his handsomeness, and when she teasingly tries to engage him in conversation during the many unnecessary dress fittings, she asks him whether a strapping youth like himself has worked his charm on other ladies. Dan is dumb in response. He does not perceive himself in that way and is wholly unaware of his effect on women. Without making that assumption, his blindness to the noblewoman's intentions is either inexplicable or fatuous.

Dan's innocence and lack of consciousness in this area should be understood not as an individual trait but as a reflection of the society that has formed him. Although European sentimental norms have just begun to make their presence felt, Jewish Buczacz remains a traditional world in which men's handsomeness is not talked about. A girl's beauty or lack of it may figure in the calculation of her marriageability, but a boy's appearance, not to mention his erotic appeal, generally remains an unacknowledged quantity. The story does not consider whether this is a good or bad thing in itself, but it does explore what happens when this complex of innocence and denial is exposed to a world in which the controls of Jewish traditional society are not operative. The consequences are unsettling.

Women Alone

One of the biggest surprises for the reader of "Disappeared" is discovering that the dire consequences concerning military service announced in the story's opening turn out not to be so dire. The real suffering is borne not by the recruit on the front but by his mother and beloved at home. For some Jews, Buczacz turns out to be a much more dangerous place to be than the Austrian army.

Dan manages to hold on to his identity and his soul despite enormous challenges. Agnon was likely aware of the accommodations for Jews in the military that were part of official policy, as discussed above. Yet he chose to make the circumstances of Dan's service more trying by virtue of the absence of any of these measures. He is the only Jew in his unit, and he cannot understand the gruff German they speak. The unit is deployed to Upper Austria, a region of the empire at the greatest possible distance from Galicia. Rather than offering a description of Jewish communities in the vicinity that could offer support for this lone Jewish soldier, the narrator makes a point of telling us the grim history of the Jewish settlements that flourished in the Middle Ages in that region. Envy of the success of the Jews led to the promulgation of blood libels, persecution, imprisonment, and banishment until "the only trace of Jews was their cemeteries from which the despoilers took the gravestones to use as foundations for the houses they built" (p. 455, 379). Agnon seems to have made the Jewish conditions of Dan's service more severe in order to make his perseverance more remarkable and meritorious.

Dan is acutely aware of the transgressions of Jewish observance that his situation imposes on him. To be forced to work on the Sabbath, to eat non-kosher food, to wear a uniform made from mixed fibers, to live in a dwelling without mezuzot, to arise in the morning without putting on tefillin—all these constraints and deprivations sadden him deeply. Yet rather than being unnerved and crushed by his plight, Dan resists by holding on to the few expressions of Jewishness he has internalized. "At such times as he found himself alone with no one around, he would put his hand on his forehead, close his eyes, and stand and recite the one or two prayers he knew by heart" (p. 456, 380).

There is a telling cleavage between how the narrator reports Dan's predicament and how he judges it. Dan's discouragement comes less from the strictures he is forced to transgress than from an emotional connection to Jewish experiences from which he is cut off. This is especially the case with the Sabbath and its warm embrace of both home rituals and synagogue liturgy. Yet, although the narrator reports Dan's experience, his own attitude toward it is tinged with anxiety bordering on dread. "Woe to the person who performs purposeful labor on the Sabbath, all the more so when the biblical punishment for that grave sin is stoning." The narrator must surely know that, according to Jewish law, constraint (*'ones*) is a mitigating factor and that Dan has little choice in these matters; yet he makes no effort to imagine any remission of the punishment. This failure stems less from a desire to censure Dan than from a horror of a world denuded of commandments into which he has fallen. This is the apotheosis of gentile space, the antithesis of Buczacz; and the very idea that a Jew should be forced to find his way in this world is profoundly unsettling to the narrator.

To sum up Dan's army experience, Agnon uses a poignant and finely calibrated metonymy. The only Jewish possession that Dan has is a prayer book that he took from home. It is from this prayer book that he learned to recite the Mourner's Kaddish after his father's death. He guarded it carefully and kept it near his pillow at night.

> But then it was taken from him. Forty soldiers, all gentiles, lived with him in one room. They all smoked and were always in need of kindling paper to light their pipes. At one point they came upon a bundle of tattered pages. They took hold of it and divided it up among them without knowing that it was the prayer book of their fellow soldier Hoffmann. They had not taken it and torn it up and used its pages for kindling out of any malevolence but for their smoking needs. In any case, Dan's prayer book was gone. (p. 456, 381)

Like the circumstances around the loss of the prayer book, Dan is not the object of malice. To the contrary, his comrades and commanders respect his industriousness and humility. But they have their lives to live and their pipes to smoke, and they possess no knowledge of what is dear and tender to their Jewish colleague. The mundane conduct of their lives and their harmless everyday pleasures necessarily and unwittingly entail using up the spiritual resources of his life. The process is collective and matter of fact. And before they know it, all the pages are gone.

The great truth of the story's structure is expressed in its title. One of the chief senses in which Dan has or is "disappeared" is lodged in the fact that he is largely absent from the plot. After the narrator gives a summary of the Jewish privations he endures and how he copes with them, the narrative returns to him only two or three times, and briefly in each case, before his embroilment with the noblewoman at the end. "What more can I say about Dan?" the narrator opines, "That he was a soldier in the imperial army" (p. 457, 382). That seems to say it all; the narrator is simply not interested in further exploring this gentile, martial space. Dan is the occasion for the story but not, until the very end, its true subject. He is an absent presence. When we first approach the story after reading the historical background at the beginning, we naturally assume the title refers to an action or a fate visited upon Dan by the kahal under the constraints of the Austrian regime. Yet once we are more deeply inside the story, we realize that Dan's disappearance is also a choice made by the author and his narrator. And this is because the real action is elsewhere.

That elsewhere is at home in Buczacz with Dan's mother and Bilhah. Dan himself manages to stay afloat in the army thanks to his sturdy constitution, his native modesty, and a nature not overburdened by self-awareness. It is the moral genius of the story to shift our attention to the family members and loved ones, women all, who are paying the heaviest price. If the emotional costs were equally or randomly distributed, the burden would be heavy enough. But because of the community's tainted values, the burden falls on the shoulders of those who can least bear it—women, poor and alone who lack networks of support to sustain them.

Agnon does a brave thing in "Disappeared" by giving Dan's nameless mother more sustained attention than her son, the eponymous hero of the story. All the more so because the mother, for all her desperate advocacy for her son, undergoes no beatification; to the contrary, she is an abject figure whose hysterical harangues importune us, the readers, as much as they do the random passersby in the marketplace. Being in her presence is not comfortable, but Agnon makes us stand there, and in so doing he opens up a new space within *A City in Its Fullness*, which is defined by both gender and class.

Bilhah joins the mother in bearing the burden of Dan's absence, and the narrative explores their experiences separately and together. As for the mother, before her son's conscription, she was the embodiment of the working poor, and in her tirade at the handing out of the Passover charity, she was not shy in telling R. Leibush the lengths she goes to make ends meet. She goes out to the villages to buy chickens and vegetables so she can sell them at a profit in town; she makes the rounds of the wealthy families to perform the chores of plucking and salting that the housewives avoid doing themselves. Through this dawn-to-dusk industry she manages to subsist and provide for her son; and by dint of this effort she literally holds things together. But the trauma of Dan's removal proves too much for her, and her fragile mental organization collapses.

> The widow's thoughts were all confused. Her distress and her agony muddled her mind. As in a nightmare, fantasies raged within her; she was totally discomfited. Her fantasies, though vague and shadowy, appeared before her as frighteningly real. Their actuality terrified her relentlessly and endlessly. (p. *453*, 376)

Her mind is pictured as a vacant chamber lacking the separate compart-ments that would aid her in making sense of what is happening to her. In the absence of structures and defenses, her mind is invaded and terrified by terrible imaginings, which she experiences as true and actual. She laments her son "as if the Angel of Death had snatched him away" (p. 453, 377).

The only "possession" she has left is her expressivity. She stops making the rounds of the villages and the wealthy homes. She shuts herself alone in her ramshackle hut and talks to the four walls. When she realizes no one is listening, she wanders the streets reciting her laments to anyone who would listen. "Sometimes she mistook a shadow for a real person and talked to it as if it were" (p. 453, 377). Her capacity for bewailing and keening is her signature and one that is deeply gendered. She howls because she lacks the language possessed by better educated men and women for explaining and appealing. But the howling can be used as an instrument, as well as being a sign of breakdown and dissociation. In her encounter with R. Leibush, alas, her screed was perversely effective, and there are important instances later in the story in which she projects her abjectness through her wailing and forces a response from people who either cannot bear to hear her go on or who are moved to examine their conscience.[13]

Bilhah deals with her own trauma differently. Not only is it not in her nature to bemoan and expostulate, but she is enjoined from any public expression of her grief because she is an unmarried woman with no recog-nized tie to Dan. In contrast to the mother's wild ideation, Bilhah "frames her thoughts quite clearly." She takes stock of her situation and looks at the future. "I am eighteen and half now. If I add the twelve years that Dan will serve in the army, I will be thirty and half, a half year older than Mother is now. Will I be too old for Dan to still have feelings for me?" (p. 453, 376). The narrator sympathetically points out that her imagining of the future is one-sided and misses the obvious fact that Dan, too, will have aged in equal measure. (Little does she realize alas that aging will be the least of Dan's problems.)

Even if Bilhah can make only imperfect use of her capacity for reason when it comes to herself, she uses it to good effect in helping the mother.

She realizes that one of the greatest threats to the older woman's sanity is the feeling of not being heard and she knows she is the one person in the world who does not mind hearing about Dan "ten times or twenty times, or even fifty times" (p. 454, 377); so she sits with the mother and listens, and the narrator pays her the compliment of acknowledging, "No greater kindness can be done to those who suffer than listening to their sighs and sighing in sympathy with them" (p. 454, 377).

Bilhah further understands how important it is for the mother to return to work and be occupied by something other than her grief. She sagely comes up with arguments for why Dan would want her to support herself, and she persuades her to throw herself back into her round of buying and selling and haggling, and she thereby succeeds in keeping the darkness at bay. But only temporarily. Five months go by, and the two women do not receive a line from Dan. When they seek to send a letter to him they come up against the fact that no one knows the address of his unit; neither the worldly Jewish merchants who have contact with many lands nor the officials of the imperial court. Having taken her son away from her, now these clever people will not let her communicate with him.

The mother lapses back into the distraught, disorganized state she inhabited before Bilhah helped her to return to her buying and selling. She stands in the marketplace and accosts passersby, even gentiles, with her troubles. She storms into the old beit midrash and thrusts her head into the ark. Beating her breast, she turns to the Master of the universe, "You are the only One who sees my suffering. Help me! Help me! How many more tears can this broken vessel hold? It is already overflowing. If you don't help me, God, Your children, the Jews You love so much, certainly won't" (p. 458, 383). Her appeal reminds us how much the hand of God is absent from this story, and it raises the question about whether its title, "Disappeared," refers exclusively to the hapless Jewish soldier.

By diverting the focus of the story to the two women, Agnon is locating the only place left in Buczacz where moral sensitivity survives and endowing it with narrative attention. Rabbinic leadership has been silenced, ordinary Jews have been cowed, and the oligarchic lay heads of the community decide what is expedient. The heart of Dan's mother and that of Bilhah, each in its own way, may not be conventionally fertile fictional soil, but Agnon works hard to make us care.

La Lettre avant la Lettre

One of the challenging features of the structure of "Disappeared" is Agnon's decision to devote the substantial central section—a quarter of this long story—to the subject of letters and letter writing. The decision is very much a part of Agnon's insistence that the difficult experience of Dan's mother and Bilhah at home in Buczacz be considered the "true" plot of the story, or at least one that should compete with the more melodramatic tale of Dan's fate. It is evident that letters would be the only form of communication between the soldier and his loved ones. But why so much attention should be devoted to the medium itself is not so obvious. A whole new character, Dovidl the scrivener, is introduced and described at length; he has little to do with the plot beyond having taught Dan the rudiments of writing. Described in detail, as well, is the physical and mechanical process of learning how to write, from the preparation of ink and quills to the formation of the letters. We are given scenes of Bilhah reading Dan's letters to his mother over and over again, even though the letters themselves, when the standard salutary rhetoric is subtracted, contain precious little real news. The investment in this theme, in short, is substantial. In the same way as letters make connections among separated correspondents, Agnon uses them to draw together and entangle the separate components of his story. But he goes further: he points to letter writing as a key sign of the modernization that has been accelerated by the German-speaking regime that now controls the lives of Galician Jews.

For an epistolary transaction to succeed, it goes without saying, each party must know the address of other. This is precisely where Dan's mother founders, because no one can supply her son's military address. For his part, far away on the other side of the empire, Dan knows where his mother lives, but he lacks the language tools to address a letter to her. Eventually, a kindly sergeant takes Dan in hand and shows him how to address a letter to Buczacz, and their arrival gives Agnon the opportunity for a send-up of communal hypocrisy worthy of Abramovitch or Sholem Aleichem.

The background to the scene lies in the fact that before Dan was shipped off to the army he was given a German last name by one of the members of the kahal. The taking on of German last names—largely for taxing and administrative purposes—was an Austrian edict that was widely enforced. Jews had traditionally referred to each other by patronymics (X the son of Y) and occupations (e.g., Godil, the tailor), and they continued to do so among themselves. When Dan was handed over to the state apparatus, he was given the family name of Hoffmann and known henceforth as Private Dan Hoffmann in the army.[14] But not in Buczacz.

The mother is known only by the name of her deceased husband, a name that has not come down to the narrator. So there is widespread bafflement when a bundle of letters arrives at the post office from a senior army officer in Lviv addressed in large, clear script: "TO THE HONORABLE WOMAN, THE WIDOW MRS. HOFFMANN IN BUCZACZ" (p. *461*, *387*). Agnon has all sorts of fun in explaining through his narrator why this address constitutes such a difficult nut to crack. Hoffmann could be either a gentile or a Jewish name, and the existence of such a distinguished personage would have to be known either to the important Jewish merchants in town or to local Austrian officials. Then there is the very formulation of the name. "If she was Jewish, it was unheard of for a Jewish woman in Buczacz to be called by her family name," the narrator reasons, "because if she were important and well known she would be called by her given name, and if she were important but not so well known she would be called by her husband's name." Eventually, the members of the kahal are forced to assemble to dispel the embarrassment this has caused them in the eyes of the local Austrian government, and it is R. Leibush himself who remembers that they stuck the name Hoffmann on Dan before he was shipped off.

The ongoing perplexity exposes the tensions in Austrian-Jewish relations and the vulnerable subservience of the Jewish communal leadership. Because there is no solution to the problem of the honorable widow's identity, the head of the post office is forced to cut open the letters, and, upon discovering them written in Jewish script, he summons two leading members of the community and tells them in no uncertain terms that the wishes of a senior army officer cannot go ignored and that they are instructed to take matters into hand forthwith.

Although today we may not be inclined to see post office officials as especially formidable, the postmaster of Buczacz, in uniform and insignia, likely embodied the full weight of the empire. As the parnasim assemble in the meeting chamber of the kahal, we see them in a different light: not as wealthy, autocratic eminences but as subalterns reprimanded by the ruling power to keep their house in order. The meeting is a desultory affair, beginning with a pious homily—through which R. Leibush dozes—on a verse from Genesis (49:17) that contains the name Dan.

The name is all they have to go on, but no one can make a connection between that name and the honorable widow Hoffmann. Slowly, R. Leibush begins to remember something about an orphaned tailor's apprentice on whom they may have stuck the name Hoffmann. The others find the idea ridiculous. "If the officer really had the mother of that poor orphan in mind, then who should we laugh at first, the officer or you, R. Leibush, for thinking he would do something like that?" (p. *463, 389*). But as the others begin to recollect the actions taken by the kahal, what was formerly unthinkable now presents itself as fact, and soon the shamash is delivering the packet to Dan's mother. The pompous and self-satisfied members of the kahal likely persist in regarding her as a person of no account; yet, the fact that she has been addressed as the Honorable Widow Hoffmann must make a difference. The appellation is not a mistake. Although they threw him away, Dan has in fact become a faithful servant of the Kaiser in ways they themselves cannot approach, and as a mother of such a soldier she has to be seen differently.

There is great joy and the shedding of tears of relief and gratitude. Bilhah rushes over and they weep and rejoice together. Yet, "in the euphoria of receiving letters from her son she forgot to ask what he had written in them," and they soon gather themselves and go to Dovidl the scrivener, who reads to the two women. But this forgetfulness is not beside the point.

The content of the letters is far less important than the existence of the letters. Throughout the years of the correspondence, the letters come to serve as a stand-in for her son. She comes to cherish the physical letters—the very paper they are written on and the ink used to form words—as totemic objects, and she gives much thought to the wonder of how letters are created and how they bridge vast distances.

As for what they contain, they are poor things indeed.

> How were the letters written? The first line had the name of God in big letters in the center. On the second line was written: "To my revered, humble, and beloved Mother, *most blessed of women in the tent*" (Judg. 5:24). The third line said: "I wish to inform her that her son, whom she reared and nurtured and brought him to this day, is well." The fourth line said: "May the beneficent God grant life and goodness and let us hear only good tidings." The fifth line said: "These are the words of your son who every day hopes for your well-being and happiness." Following all that was his name, printed, because he was not a practiced writer and could not write in cursive script. Even so his mother remarked that though she was completely uneducated, if she saw a letter from her son in a dream she would recognize the letters of his name. (p. *465*, 391–92)

Today, when we are accustomed to thinking of letters as little parcels of spontaneous subjectivity, it is well to recall that among the working poor in places like Buczacz at the beginning of the nineteenth century, it was quite otherwise. Composing a letter was a challenging and arduous process, and when Dan was younger he was sent to Dovidl to take lessons to learn how to do it. After first learning how to make ink and prepare quills and form letters, Dan proceeded to the more advanced task of composing model letters for different purposes. The templates—a sample of a letter from a young man to his betrothed, for example, or from a son to his mother—were taken from *brivnshtelers*, Yiddish letter-writing manuals.[15] In this method, letters are put together out of modular units. Each unit has a function, such as the salutation (the opening greeting) and the valediction (the closing greeting). Each is formulated in exalted, florid, and pious diction and embellished by biblical verses. The aspiring correspondent learns these topoi by heart and reproduces them when he sits down to write a letter; he then adds the news or message that is particular to the communication.

Dan's letters are almost entirely stock sentiment with next to no message. This missing essence is of a piece with the overall nullity with which he is presented as a character. Make no mistake: his inner strength is demonstrated by the respect he wins from his comrades and commanders, by his retention of his Jewish identity, and by the very fact of his surviving the long military service unbroken. But he possesses little interiority, and he lacks sufficient literacy to represent his experiences in writing. Agnon has chosen to invest his narrative resources back home and there, as his mother and Bilhah devour his letters, the conventionality and lack of substance are considered no detriment. Dan's mother presumably cannot read, and she relies on Bilhah to read the letters to her. Their similarity enables her to get to know them by heart over time, and she delights in discerning the nearly negligible differences among them. She treats the physical letters as she would a *teḥinah* book, a small, pocket-sized book of Yiddish prayers written for, and often by, women, and she cries over them like a woman reciting those prayers. In a naively revealing observation, the mother comes close to preferring his written words over his spoken voice. "Were I not so anxious to hear his voice I would say that writing is better than speaking. A letter that he writes I can listen to ten times, even a hundred times. As many times as I want" (p. *465–66, 392*).

She can listen to the letters so often because Bilhah reads them to her. Bilhah herself, as the narrative points out more than once, cannot be an addressee for Dan's letters. Their bond is secret, and the impropriety of letters being addressed by a soldier, or any unmarried man, to an unmarried woman would be discovered immediately. Besides, the letter-writing manuals offer examples only of correspondence between formerly betrothed couples. Dan's letters thus do double duty and deepen the bond between the two women. "Dan's mother strokes the cat lying in her lap, fixes her eyes on Bilhah and listens attentively to every word coming out of Bilhah's mouth" (p. *467, 394*). For both of them, the ritual of reading and rereading the letters in each other's company becomes a great solace. Dan, or more precisely his absence, is the reason why their connection is formed, but the relationship takes on a life of its own. They establish a quasi–family unit in which men play only a virtual role. It is a community of mutual support, a community of empathy, of *ḥesed* (kindness), and it stands in sharp contrast to the Jewish community of Buczacz as a whole and the kahal in particular.

These scenes of tranquil letter reading come almost exactly at the middle of the story considered by length, and they form a charmed still point in the narrative. Here a remarkable thing happens. This woman, who was barely recognizable as a human being as she ranted hysterically in the marketplace, is now utilized by the narrator as a vessel for meditations about the wondrousness of letters and the unacknowledged wisdom of Dovidl the scrivener. This kind of combined discourse the narrator is embarking upon is preceded by a rationale that manages to be both telling and opaque at the same time.

> Here I connect these thoughts of Dan's mother to things she did not say but which amplify her thoughts about this matter of writing. They contain some of the mother's thoughts that did not reach a final formulation.[16] (p. *467, 392*)

The mother's thoughts, as we shall see directly, are observant and even wise, but inchoate. Not only can she not articulate them in speech, but she lacks the mental language to express them to herself. The narrator, who has access to the thoughts of the characters, declares that he is going to extend to her some of the powers of his craft and enter into a sort of joint partnership. He will take these unarticulated intuitions and bring them into language so they can be understood by the reader. It is a singularly generous gesture, and it results in fine passages of *style indirect libre*, which are gifts to us in their insights and the reclamation of the mother as a character.

The mother's meditations focus on the wonders of writing and the figure of Dovidl the scrivener, and we can appreciate the fruits of the narrator's "partnership" with her by comparing how Dovidl is presented first by the narrator alone and later through their combined discourse. We hear of Dovidl for the first time when the mother and Bilhah are desperately trying to send Dan letters. The scrivener is sympathetic but unable to help them in the absence of a useable address. They next visit him under happier circumstances when the bundle of letters is first delivered; he helps them read the letters. It is he, after all, who taught Dan to write them. On this second visit, the narrator gives us a profile of the man. He is a small man living in very modest circumstances, and he observes the commandments like other Jews in Buczacz.

To learn his craft Dovidl poured over epistolary collections. But once he became adept at letter writing, he began to read "more uplifting things, books that served to remind him that good people could do good things and writings from which he could derive moral instruction that would bring joy to his heart and peace to his soul" (p. 464, 390). The source of this edifying literature is Josef Perl and the circles around him. Perl (1773–1839) was a well-to-do merchant from Tarnopol who fiercely opposed the spread of Hasidism by submitting critical memoranda to the Austrian government and by writing a series of scathingly brilliant parodies of Hasidic writing.[17]

To the Jews of Galicia, Perl—referred to familiarly by Dovidl as Reb Yossl—was largely known as an educator who established and maintained a school in Tarnopol in which German and general subjects were taught alongside the traditional curriculum of Torah studies. As an aid to the students, between 1813 and 1815 Perl produced a series of almanacs (*Luah halev* and *Tsir ne'eman*), which interweave words of moral instruction and useful information with the Jewish and secular calendars.[18] These are the texts that Dovidl reaches for when he returns from prayers each night.

This combining of traditional observance with an interest in moral self-improvement and general culture places Dovidl within the wider orbit of the moderate Galician Haskalah, which set out on a path very different from the radical Berlin Haskalah at the end of the eighteenth century. Influenced by Austrian rather than German cultural models, the Galician Haskalah emphasized a widening of the Jew's worldview, but it remained loyal to the Hebrew language and did not advocate departing from or reforming Jewish practice. It criticized the hypocrisies and inequities of communal leadership and encouraged the ethical improvement of common Jews. This is a trend that gains force as the century progresses and interacts in complex ways with other forces of modernization. Within the social world of Buczacz, Dovidl may be a figure of no account, but the ideals he embodies play an increasingly important role. This is true as well of the writing skills he teaches, which become essential for participation in an expanding world.

The picture we receive through the eyes of the mother is not contradictory but different. Because she knows nothing about Josef Perl and the intellectual ferment in Galicia, she is the perfect medium through which to appreciate the wonder of the new developments. The basic acts of reading and writing, which have long undergone a process of reification, are defamiliarized in her eyes and made into objects of radical amazement.

> Consider the power of the letters of the alphabet as they appear on a page. They are tiny as peas and in Dan's case, as beans. Only a trained reader can tell one character from another. They all sit on the page immobile and mute. But when a girl like Bilhah looks at them, the letters immediately start talking and reveal to us what is happening in far off places. (p. 466, 392–93)

Dan had not received enough instruction in writing so that he could reduced the size of the letters that he had laboriously learned to write to the smaller size of an adult hand. In the mother's homely metaphor, he writes in peas rather than beans. To someone who cannot read, the letters indeed resemble random, undifferentiated dried legumes. They remain dry, immobile, and mute until they are brought to life by the gaze of someone like Bilhah, who has learned to decipher them, having secretly been taught by Dan. Only then do they fulfill the potential so dear to Dan's mother: "to reveal to us what is happening in far-off places" (p. 466, 392). The art of writing is even more wondrous to her. She now recalls that under Dovidl's tutelage, Dan spent three months learning how to make ink and sharpen quills before proceeding to the rudiments of penmanship. He learned how "to hold the quill and dip it in the ink, and how much ink to draw, because if too much is drawn the paper will get spattered, and if too little, the quill will scratch." And Dovidl "continued teaching him until he knew how to write the letters of the alphabet and became adept at joining them together" (p. 467, 394).

But not much more. Now that the letters serve as her lifeline to her son—"His letters keep me alive!"—she regrets that she prevented Dan from taking lessons with Dovidl after he reached this rudimentary level, but instead had pulled him out. Back then, she could not fathom the real benefit of further mastery; the lessons cost money, and the choice presented itself as a stark either/or. "For the good money you waste on tuition every month," she told her son at the time, "I could buy you every day a cup of milk with licorice and a bun with sesame seeds, and you would eat and drink and put on some weight and start looking like somebody successful" (p. 466, 393). Dan stopped his training just at the point when he was able to assemble and copy the conventional sentiments he was taught to write; but he did not continue long enough to achieve the capacity to convey his own experience. The mother realizes now that her shortsightedness has deprived her of a deeper connection to her distant son. What she does not realize is the ill-fated irony that the narrator has put us in the position of knowing: by opting for helping him grow and put on weight, she was turning him into a lad who looked old enough to be taken by the army even if he was not.

Being herself among the downtrodden and dismissed of Buczacz, the mother can view Dovidl through the sympathetic lens of social class. The skills he has mastered and teaches to others are established by the narrative as being a powerful tool for self-representation as well as for more pragmatic communication. They are furthermore linked to emerging trends in the opening up of Galician society to European culture. Yet in the eyes of traditional Buczacz and its contemptuous leadership, Dovidl will never be thought of as anything more than a scrivener, a tradesman (ba'al melakhah) whose quill is not better than a cobbler's awl or a tailor's needle. "In the synagogue he stands by the door with all the undesirables in town. And if once or twice a year he gets called up to the Torah, why do they call him? For the pittance he will pledge to contribute" (p. 466, 393). Yet, despite the slights and insults he has to put up with, Dovidl knows his own worth, and he knows that his standing depends on his ability to dress decently, which he cannot afford to do. So he cleverly talks Godil into making a new suit for him for free in exchange for teaching Bilhah how to write. He persuades the tailor that this is a necessary skill for an unmarried young woman so that she can correspond with her fiancé once she becomes engaged.

As in the story's opening scene in which so many factors conspire to condemn Dan, this scene replicates that dense, ironic emplotment in miniature and to less tragic effect. Dovidl gets his new suit, Bilhah learns how to write and need not rely on Dovidl's services to write to Dan, and ironically Godil subsidizes her lessons without any hope of there being a fiancé other than Dan.

The Missing Correspondent

Does Dan serve ten or twelve years in the Kaiser's army? It is twelve at the beginning of the story and ten toward the end.[19] "Disappeared" is one of only a few of the major stories in *A City in Its Fullness* that did not appear in serial form during Agnon's lifetime. Having not prepared it for press, he probably did not catch the discrepancy. And it matters little. After describing the mother's connection to her son's letters, the narrative skips the intervening years and jumps to the end of his service. This leaves us to assume that in this long interval, life has continued on course; Dan perseveres in the army, and the mother and Bilhah cling to their epistolary lifeline. The only new information we learn about Dan is that toward the end of his service he finds a way to make use of his tailoring skills as a sometimes dressmaker to the wives of the officers. The time of his demobilization finds him untrammeled and optimistic. He plans to return to Buczacz, marry Bilhah, and set himself up as a master ladies' tailor. Because he has no money in his pocket, he sets out to return home on foot while making occasional stops to sew dresses for the nobility, so he will not come back empty handed. On the road, he falls out of the habit of letter writing because he lacks the proper equipment and the focused attention necessary to a task that for him remains laborious.

At first, the cessation of letters is a puzzle and an annoyance. But soon it turns into an enigma tinged with dread and eventually a trauma leading to demoralization and madness. It is six years until Dan's fate is discovered, and the intervals of time are clearly marked: first two months, then one year, three years and then six. Agnon makes us experience this long duration as more acutely measured out than in the first half of the story, which covers the ten to twelve years of his service. The vacancy in the story's title takes on a more frightening resonance. Dan's having "been disappeared" by an act of communal cruelty in the first half is balanced by his stolid perseverance and the fact that we know where he is.

There is nothing metaphorical about his disappearance in the second half. The vacuum of his absence is filled both by the futile grindings of bureaucratic wheels and by the imagining of gruesome disasters, which turn out to pale before the true horror of the boy's fate. Here, again, even more so than in the first half, the focus is on the home front and the consequences of Dan's disappearance up until the disturbing, melodramatic ending. But the focus is widened this time. Although it begins with the escalating desperation of the mother and Bilhah, it expands to include Buczacz's rabbi and several great merchants, contemptuous Polish nobles, and local and regional Austrian officials. The ending of the story proper—before the noblewoman's diary—balloons into a theatrical, even operatic, spectacle, whose epic sweep nearly overwhelms the tortured fates of mother, son, and beloved.

Uneasy, the two women endure the first two months of silence. Bilhah's parents force her to limit her visits to Dan's mother and at the same time to receive a series of suitors for her hand. Penelope-like, she acquiesces to her parents' wishes, but she manages to elude their intentions and remain true to Dan. In the meantime, the mother goes from neighbor to neighbor asking what the possible meaning can be of the delays in hearing from her son. She begins having nightmares and ends up seeing terrible visions by day. What she sees in these dark imaginings begins a process of foreshadowing that unfolds inexorably. She realizes that now, after the French wars, the country is at peace, and the Austrian rulers have cleared the roads and forests of robbers and murderers. So to find a credible source of horror, her imagination goes back to before the partitions and dips into the primordial imaginary of Polish barbarity. In her dreams, she sees her son fallen "into the hands of a she-demon in the guise of a noblewoman." When she goes around town talking about her terrible vision, she is roundly rebuked. For "in Buczacz belief in demons was thoroughly repudiated, and so there was no pity at all for the unfortunate woman." Even if the reader is inclined to share this rational outlook, the hint has been registered and filed away. The all-seeing narrator also does nothing to call attention to this prophetic intuition. Instead, he wanly opines, "Let us rely on God who guides the steps of man to guide Dan's steps and bring him back to where he belongs" (p. 472, 400), a sentiment that serves only to redouble our awareness of how deeply hidden is God's hand in this drama.

The rebuke pushes her out of the shadows and into a one-woman public campaign to get the regime to inquire into her son's disappearance. First, she knocks on the doors of the homes of the parnasim, requesting that they write to the Emperor on her behalf; they think she is joking. She importunes a wealthy merchant with political influence who is visiting the city. She then places herself in the face of R. Avraham David Wahrman, the rabbi of Buczacz, and demands that he do something. Although once confronted he does takes steps, the marginalization of the rabbinate is again illustrated by his removal from this key moral drama that is being played out within his congregation. The machinery of Austrian officialdom is finally moved to launch an inquiry, and before long the parnasim are summoned to hear a court official read them an orotund epistle from the capital certifying that the soldier Dan Hoffmann had been honorably discharged from the Kaiser's army after fulfilling his term of service and that "it is attested in his file that he is on route to his hometown Buczacz" (p. 474, 404). When the parnasim relay the import of the message to Dan's mother, all she can do is shriek, "If he has come back, why isn't he here? And if he's not here, then where is he?"

For a time after the matter is officially recognized, the missing soldier becomes an item of public concern and conversation. Searches are made and inquiries conducted in all the towns around Buczacz, and even the imperial officials are placed on the alert. When a year goes by and then another the urgency of the matter fades from general consciousness. "But in the mother's mind and in Bilhah's mind it was as sharply felt as ever, asserting itself anew every passing day" (p. 475, 405). The story catches the way in which the trauma and isolation of victims persist and deepen after the sensation of their case recedes from public view. The mother's deterioration is precipitous. She stops taking care of herself, cooking food, and mending and laundering her clothes. Soon she becomes a disheveled madwoman. "Had Bilhah not protected her, children would have thrown stones and dirt at her and called her crazy, the way people treat those who are despondent and have descended into melancholia" (p. 476, 406). During the summer, Bilhah takes her to bathe in the Strypa and makes sure she puts on a fresh dress and stockings. For her kindness to the poor woman, Bilhah is upbraided by her parents who see her ministrations as proclaiming a kinship that does not exist.

This is the last we see of the two women until the end of the story. The narrative has sustained a focus on their ordeal for a considerable time as if to serve as a model against which the behavior of Buczacz is judged. After the initial sensation of Dan's disappearance has worn off, the narrator has stayed with the true victims of the community's actions. But even for the narrator there is not much more that can be said about their forlorn situation, and the focus now pivots toward the higher reaches of Austrian-Polish relations and the tangled skein of plot lines that lead up to the grotesque finale.

Austrian Officials and Polish Nobles

At this moment, which is the midpoint between Dan's discharge and his discovery, the narrator pauses to make a jaundiced observation about the progress that has been made so far.

> Three years went by and nothing came of all the searches and inquiries other than reams of paper, the voluminous correspondence sent from Buczacz to the head of the district and from the head of the district to various officials in several localities. All that paper became in time the pages we find in the bindings of the Talmud and other books. When the government offices became cluttered with old documents and space was needed for the new ones, the old ones were sold to storekeepers who re-sold them to bookbinders. The bookbinders would insert a sheet before the first and after the last pages of a book and then paste those sheets inside the front and back covers that bound the whole book together. There are elders in Buczacz whose excellent German was learned from those pages inside the binding. And there are elders in Buczacz whose proficiency at composing letters to the law courts was acquired from those pages. (p. 476, 406–7)

Administrative rationality is the great civilizing gift the Austrians have conferred upon Galicia, in addition to banishing brigands and murderers. Yet in the face of a real evil, all that can be mustered is a busy and officious production of paper, more and more ineffectual memoranda. The narrator extends his interest in the materials and mechanics of letter writing by following the fate of the mounds of documents used up in the failed inquiries after the soldier's whereabouts. Jobbers buy the paper in bulk and sell it to bookbinders, who use it as endpapers in the binding of Talmud volumes. If the story ended here, we would have a moralistic anecdote about the enduring superiority of Torah study. But there is one more loop to the recycling: the German learned by the elders comes from these random endpapers. For these denizens of the beit midrash, German is not a cultural medium, the language of Herder and Goethe, to be studied in and for itself, but rather a pragmatic tool for dealing with the gentile world. And this tool has ironically been acquired through the mediation of discarded memoranda bound into the ur-text of Jewish learning.

The story now jumps to the sixth year of Dan's disappearance, and it is only then that a concatenation of circumstances takes place that leads to the discovery of his whereabouts. The discovery is played out against the background of the fraught relations between the Austrian rulers of Galicia and the Polish nobility, whose power has been altered by the new political order. This is a pronounced shift in the historical framing of the story. Until now, "Disappeared" has focused on the consequences of the Austrian annexation for the Jewish community, and it has traced the machinations that led to a Jewish lad being handed over to the Kaiser's army. After he goes missing, the story increasingly focuses on how the new Austrian administrators of Galicia reckon with Polish nobles, who still own estates and forests, and with the legacy of "barbarity" they associate with centuries of Polish rule.

It is in this new arena that the plot begins to unspool. It so happens that a new district official is dispatched to Buczacz by Vienna, and he and his wife are dissatisfied with the house they have been assigned to live in. The house is being rented from the Potocki family, and the Count himself comes to inspect the problems when he is next in town. After deigning to look around, the Count observes, "I am surprised that the district head is unhappy with his living quarters. My horses would be happy to live in a place like this" (p. 477, 408). The official is stung by the insult, with its equal measures of condescension and resentment, and he refuses to stay in the house. He finds himself a new residence, but it is still being completed when he moves in, and one day he approvingly observes the work of a Jewish tradesman who is installing a stove. He sees an opportunity. As a colonial official newly arrived in unfamiliar territory, he is in search of trustworthy native informants. "Most Jews find ways to go around the government's laws, and we would never catch them," he reasons, "if it weren't for the few honest ones among them who turn in the cheaters" (p. *478*, 408). He engages the tradesman in conversation, but the sensational information he extracts from him ironically has nothing to do with the scofflaw behavior of the Jews. The tradesman recounts what he saw by accident when he was called to repair an oven in the house of a noblewoman in a certain village.

> A human-like creature that was neither male nor female. I couldn't tell if it was a Jew or a gentile. It looked like a woman because it had long hair like a woman's, with braids and bows, and it had on a blue satin dress. It looked like a man because there was hair on the cheeks like a beard, or maybe it wasn't a beard but long hair hanging down. It looked like a Jew because of the pain I could see in the eyes. And the person was tied to the wall with an iron chain. (pp. *478–79*, 409–10)

It is this grotesque sight that triggers a cascade of inevitable consequences. The noblewoman whips the Jew across the face and cautions him to remain silent about what he saw on pain of death. The Austrian official is so enraged by what he has heard that he smashes an expensive flower pot and accuses the Jew of being a liar.

The matter will not go away, no matter how loathsome it is. His superior, the regional governor, happens to be visiting Buczacz at that moment, and the two officials sit together and curse their luck that this incident has landed on their watch. Their concern lies not with the hapless Jew but with the restiveness of the Polish nobility. Although their political autonomy has been curtailed, they remain a powerful and potentially violent factor in the affairs of a region upon which the Austrians are seeking to impose civil tranquility. The destabilizing factor in the recent revelation is shame. The noblewoman in question was once an attractive woman and a prominent landowner, whose hand was sought by the great nobles of the day. She rejected them and remained unmarried. But now? "I can already see how much anger and jealousy and hatred there will be," says one official, shaking his head, "when the noblemen that woman rejected find out that she has taken a Jew for herself" (p. *480*, 411). "Yes," responds the other official, "when I look at these Jews with their beards and side curls, I am amazed that a woman of her class would even get near one of them." They both well understand the rageful humiliation of the Polish nobles, because, even though they pride themselves on their superior culture and comportment, they feel the same disgust and insult. Their reactions, it is important to point out, are based on the assumption that the enchained Jew is being used as a sexual slave by the noblewoman, and this is the same assumption that will be made by the Jews of Buczacz when they witness Dan being wheeled into the town in the police wagon.

The same tensions are manifest when the chief of police is ordered to put a party of men together to ride out to the noblewoman's estate and investigate the disturbing report. The first exchange between the chief and the lady is all courtesy and deference on both sides. But once the policeman insists on searching the residence, the meeting breaks down into outrage and insult as the Polish noblewoman vainly resists the dominant position of the Austrian occupiers. When the policeman insists on the authority behind his inquiries, she screams, "No! You are not officers of the Emperor! You're a bunch of robbers, and you are so-and-so, the head of them. How dare you surround the house of a noblewoman living alone?" (pp. *480–81*, 412). It does not take long for the police to discover in the stable a "young man with shaggy hair wearing a woman's dress tied to an iron chain, and the old servant holding the chain and straining to fasten it to a large stone resting on the stable floor." The woman and the servant are arrested, and soon a convoy is formed: the police chief and the noblewoman in the first coach and the servant and Dan in the second, with a detachment of mounted officers at the head and in the rear.

Buczacz in Full

Agnon could have ended the story at this point or wrapped it up expeditiously in any one of a number of ways. But instead he insists on slowing down and attenuating the pace by adding two narrative blocs. The first is the spectacle of Dan's being returned to Buczacz while the entire town looks on, and the second is the account of what happened to Dan as related by the lady in her own words. What is the rationale for these additions?

Consider first how the spectacle of Dan's return is constructed with its manipulations of time and space. Long before the clatter of the wagon wheels and the hoof beats of horses announce the approach of the police procession, the Jews of Buczacz have been gathering en masse, alert to the fact that something important is transpiring. The arrival of a runner dispatched by the police chief heightens the mystery and hastens the production of theories that are baseless. Times dilates, and the "minutes passed as slowly as the sluggish waters of the Strypa in mid-summer" (p. *482, 414*). The throng grasps at wisps of speculation like a vast organism starving for nourishment. Finally, a spark of rumor ignites the crowd. The news circulates that a Jewish man has been kept prisoner by a Polish noblewoman. No one knows his name or her name or the name of her village, but there is certainty—false, of course—that the room in which he was chained was her bedroom. In the meantime, the crowd has packed the area between Fedor Hill and the cemetery. A rumor that the lady is being brought in from the north provokes a mass rush in that direction, which is followed shortly by a rumor of the arrival from the opposite entrance to the city, which causes a concomitant shoving toward the south.

Among the crowd are Bilhah and her mother. The narrative exploits the apprehensive tedium of waiting to bring us up to date on her life. Her father Godil, we learn, died after a long illness, his death hastened by his heartbreak over his daughter's refusal to marry and by his pangs of conscience for his role in Dan's recruitment. Dan's mother, who had long been closer to death than to life, finally passed away, and now Bilhah is taking care of her own widowed mother. Exhausted, jostled by the roiling crowd, and drained of desire to participate in the spectacle, Bilhah is about to return home just as the convoy enters the town and the faces of the passengers become distinguishable. Agnon has carefully prepared for the anagnorisis, the recognition scene of a classic tragedy. In contrast to the initiated reader, Bilhah and the assembled townspeople of Buczacz have no idea of the identity of the Jew imprisoned by the lady and no reason to associate him with Dan Hoffmann, whose disappearance has faded from public awareness. Yet even if there is no surprise for the reader, the recognition scene still unfolds with horrifying, tragic inevitability.

> Bilhah beheld the boy and emitted an ear-piercing scream. Another scream came from Dan as he looked at her. Dan is the boy dressed in woman's clothing, and from the way his eyes smiled at her everyone knew that this was the soldier who disappeared. (p. *482*, 416)

Although this electrifying exchange takes place between Bilhah and Dan, the narrator turns his attention to the "everyone," the entirety of Buczacz that has assembled for the spectacle. The passage that follows is a small masterpiece of collective portraiture. For a moment, "everyone" remembers Dan's mother and her incessant weeping for her son, and they further remember how they treated this suffering woman. But rather than being consumed by regret, especially now that they see with their own eyes that the reality is worse than her histrionic suspicions, they focus on rationalizing their behavior. They say sagely that, "ironically, the greater a person's troubles, the less sympathy he gets," a worldly-wise observation that shifts the blame onto the mother (p. *484*, 417). If she had been quieter about her troubles and less abject in her misery, then she would have fared better in gaining support from others. But soon enough the people of Buczacz come to terms with how they had acted, and they move their attention away from themselves and begin to make pronouncements about the mother's fate, some lamenting that she had not lived to see her son be returned and others arguing that she was better off dead than to have seen the horror that has just been paraded before them. They all join together "in wishing death upon the wanton woman whose depravity in taking a Jewish boy and using him for sinful purposes few could surpass" (p. *484*, 417). Vilifying the alien woman allows them leave off interrogating their own behavior.

This self-serving communal introspection is brought to a halt by the policemen's shouts and the demand that the Jews disperse and go home. The breakup of the crowd makes us realize how extraordinary these scenes have been. Within the corpus of *A City in Its Fullness*, there are only a few times when Agnon assembles the entire community of Buczacz. One instance takes place in "The Parable and Its Lesson," a generation after the 1648 massacres on the occasion of the 20th of Sivan, the fast day for the martyrs, when every man, woman, and child in the small community of survivors gathers in the synagogue to recite laments and listen to Rabbi Moshe's homily. Another takes place almost two hundred years later at the conclusion of "In a Single Moment," when the community dissolves into joyous dancing upon hearing the news that a young Talmud scholar is going to wed a young woman who has been insulted and rejected by an avaricious bridegroom. Here at the end of "Disappeared," "[e]very man and woman, old and young, came out that day to hear and to watch in what became one huge throng, the biggest gathering of people Buczacz had ever seen" (p. 483, 415).

These are scenes in which Buczacz undergoes a process of totalization. Individual desires, temperaments, and social standing are momentarily unified and submerged into an entity called Buczacz, which is then treated as if it were itself a character in the narrative. If in the other stories the motives for totalization are exalted, here they are fallen. Compelled by sensation and rumor, Buczacz has gathered to gawk, and when the identity of the central character in the spectacle is revealed, the reflex is to evade responsibility and to demonize the gentile victimizer and to cluck about the sadness of it all.

From the first pages of the story, the responsibility for Dan's ordeal is placed upon the shoulders of the parnasim, the oligarchical elders of the community, and the dynamic of entreaty and rejection takes place among them and the dyad of Dan's mother and Bilhah. With the spectacular recognition scene with the entire community of Buczacz assembled en plein air, Agnon takes a forceful step to widen the radius of accountability. It may have been the elders who shipped Dan off, but they did not do so without the tacit support of the good folks of the town who thanked God that it was not *their* son who was taken and who did their best to avoid having to deal with the supplications and ravings of the mother.

The conclusion to the story proper is quickly wrapped up, and it contains no glimmer of uplift or learned wisdom. At first Dan is enveloped

by Buczacz in a great spasm of solicitude. The outward signs of his forced
feminization are erased by Jewish barbering, and he is given proper Jewish clothing and fed kosher food. Afterward, the community doesn't know
what to do with him because his mother is dead and he was never married
to Bilhah and the municipal Jewish almshouse is full. Ever thrifty, the elders
find a way to kill two birds with one stone. There is a melamed who has become paralyzed, and as a way of providing for him, a group of householders
each agree to pay a weekly sum to his wife for taking care of Dan in their
home. Even then the melamed's wife has to spend all of Thursday trying to
collect the payments for Sabbath necessities, ending up with only half the
promised amount. We are not surprised to learn that "Bilhah, to her credit,
would bring Dan food and drink two or three times a week, and on Fridays
a clean shirt" (p. 485, 418). There is a glimmer of recognition in Dan's eyes
when she is with him, but he remains semi-catatonic and does not hold on
for more than a year. "The sorrow pent up within him brought on the illness from which he died." Of Bilhah we are told nothing more. But of the
noblewoman we are told that she voluntarily entered the Mother of God
convent, to which she consecrated all her possessions, including her mute
servant. Devout in her faith, she lived on for many years.

The Lady and the Bear

It is difficult to count the many ways in which "The Lady's Diary" is a remarkable artifact.[20] The narrator's explanation conceals more than it explains.

> Thus ends the story of Dan Hoffmann. But the diary of the lady has come
> into my possession, and so I would add here that it is clear and apparent from
> what she writes that Dan was steadfast in his righteousness and his integrity
> and never submitted to transgression. He suffered much at the hands of that
> impure woman and never gave in to her seductions, served well by the merits
> of Joseph, the paragon of a virtuous man who did not succumb to the seduc-
> tions of an alien woman. (p. 486, 419)

How the intimate diary, written in Polish by a Roman Catholic noblewoman who finished her days in a convent, should simply "come into the
possession" of our traditionalist Jewish narrator is a rather large question, and

it is one that Agnon has not the slightest intention of answering. The same applies to the justification for violating the privacy of the diary. It is, simply, just so. All that is important to the narrator is the vindication of Dan's reputation. The sensational, scandalous, and publicly played-out nature of Dan's discovery has made his fate one upon which both Austrian officials and the Jews of Buczacz make shocked pronouncements with utter certainty.

The narrator knows they are mistaken, and he adduces the diary as conclusive evidence of the truth. Their error has been to assume not only that Dan has been used to satisfy the lady's sexual lusts but also that he must have yielded to her seductions. The diary will demonstrate, in her own words, that sexual violation and sexual relations never took place, despite the perversity of her desires. Through the traditional lens of the narrator's consciousness, the great strength necessary to withstand the lady's seductions must have been augmented by a source beyond Dan's own determination, and he names this source as the merit (zekhut) stored up by the biblical Joseph when he fled from Potiphar's wife. Thus, Dan is not only cleared of complicity but he becomes a latter-day fulfillment of a biblical type.

It should not be surprising to find Agnon, the master ironist, traducing his own narrator's purpose. The demonization of the lady is undone by the access we are given to her inner life, which has been stamped by the trauma of her mother's murder and by her own struggles with sin and temptation. Dan himself, moreover, is in no sense a simple embodiment of Joseph the Righteous. He is surely innocent, but his innocence is so extreme that it renders him insensible of threats to his safety. The narrator, furthermore, is naïve about the contradictory powers latent within the diary as a form. He sees the diary simply as a source of documentary evidence for establishing Dan's purity; and he himself remains unaware of the potential for sympathy—or at least the neutralizing of judgment—that is realized when we are made privy to the lady's inner thoughts and motivations.

What the diary reveals, which the story proper does not, is the power of Dan's beauty. This quality was noted only in passing early in "Disappeared" when Dan's mother unknowingly reports that another Polish lady had remarked on her son's strapping appearance. It was always there, of course, but the conventions of Jewish social discourse do not mark male physical beauty and attractiveness as a noticeable or special characteristic. This may remain inconsequential within an internal, shared community of value. Yet when the community is exposed to the outside and Jews move into gentile space, unacknowledged male physicality can trigger unforeseen and untoward behaviors. There can be no greater dramatization of this exposure and reaction than the opening lines of the diary.

> This is how it all began. A soldier newly released from the army came and knocked on the door of my palace. I asked him what he wanted. He said he was a tailor who knew how to make dresses for ladies and noblewomen. I looked him over and saw that he was good-looking and well built and charming. (p. 486, 419)

The attraction is instantaneous. "When the boy started to unroll the blue velvet, my eyes were attracted to his. I couldn't tell which was bluer—the velvet or his eyes." From that moment on, the lady finds herself in a web of erotic obsession. She rushes off to bathe and perfume herself and assumes all sorts of postures that show off her figure as he takes her measurements, and then, upon her insistence, takes them again and then again. She is aware he is a Jew and that it "does not befit the daughter of a nobleman to be so interested in a Jewish boy" (p. 487, 420). She addresses Mary, Mother of God, and protests that she did "not sin and did nothing that could be construed as foolish." Nevertheless, her attraction takes over. She instructs her servant to tell anyone who comes to the door that she is not at home; she neglects the affairs of her estate; and she stops writing in her diary, in which she nightly records the events of the day. Instead, she sits transfixed and bewitched watching him sew her dress. "I have never ever seen such delicate fingers," she confesses, "and I don't know anyone whose movements are so lovely." But she looks forward to the spell being broken once he finishes the dress and leaves to return home to his sweetheart.

But rather than resisting she gives in. And he does, too, in his own way. The dress turns out to be a success, and as she is about to take her leave from the ex-soldier, she jokingly asks him if he would be willing to delay his departure to make a second dress for her. Knowing what is on his mind, she increases the payment for this job so that he will have more money to take home to his "dearly beloved." He agrees to the offer. But this time, the job is not completed expeditiously. She delays several days in giving the fabric he needs to make the dress, and then she changes her mind several times about the style she wants. She then settles into a routine of sitting near him while he works and observing his nimble movements. She remains fixed in her erotic reverie. Of the tales he tells her about ladies for whom he has made dresses, "what amazed me most" she reports, "was that in all his stories he never once mentioned that he had gotten near a woman, and here was a good-looking boy with all his juices" (p. 488, 422). This is the situation in a nutshell: Dan speaks freely about his proximity to women's bodies without the slightest awareness of the attraction he may be exuding while at the very same moment, that is *all* that the woman sitting across from him is experiencing. In Hebrew, "with all his juices" is *bimlo' ḥumo 'amad*, literally, he stood in full heat. For the lady, he radiates sexuality; for himself, he is merely plying his needle.

Soon she makes him her prisoner, but it doesn't start out that way. In thrall to her obsession, she stumbles from step to step with no premeditation. When the ex-soldier announces that he must take his leave because the great holiday of Passover is approaching, she spends a sleepless night in the throes of chaotic emotions. When praying on her knees to the Holy Mother to stand by her in her hour of need brings no answer, she believes she has been abandoned for "giving her heart to a Jewish man" (p. 489, 422). She instructs her servant to take away the boy's clothes and lock him in his room while she escapes to ride in the countryside on her horse. She rides out again the next day, and this time she comes back with a small she-bear she has bought from a gypsy. The bear becomes a complex stand-in for the boy. She is delighted by its antics, but after only three days the bear stops frolicking and starts to decline. "A kind of sadness could be seen its eyes," (p. 489, 423), and this is the characteristically Jewish quality that the oven maker saw in the eyes of the strange, chained creature he discovered. The mute servant puts the animal down with a shot from a rifle and buries its carcass. For a brief interval, the bear had provided a diversion, and she can reflect that "the sinful thoughts

I had now faded and were not as wicked or as troubling as they had been before." Does this mean that her sexual urges have become muted, or does it mean that her conscience has become inured to her wicked thoughts?

The denouement of this dilemma, which is to last for six years, makes an argument for an uneasy stalemate. The boy/ex-soldier is dressed in the blue dress, his beard is shaved, and his hair allowed to grow long and be done up like a woman's. He is chained to the same peg used for the bear. His needs are seen to by the mute servant, and whenever he has been bathed, the lady visits him and caresses his face and murmurs, "If I didn't know you were a man I would say you're a girl, your skin is so soft and smooth, like a virgin's, or maybe you really are a virgin. Sometimes I am not even sure you're a man" (p. *490*, *424*). If we rely on the truthfulness of her account, the attentions she forces on him are limited to fondling his face and feasting on him as a spectacle. Why does she not molest him genitally? Is it because such contact with a Jew would be degrading to her? Is it because his resemblance to a virgin woman arouses feelings that are too disturbing?

The only clue we are given concerns the "winter palace," the deeply hidden building on her grounds into which she moves during the cold weather. It was built by her father to house a mistress he brought back from Dresden. In one of the rooms there was a bear chained to the wall, and when her mother stepped into the room to observe the bear, the mistress locked the door behind her and let her die of fright and starvation. The identification with the mother and the trauma of her gruesome death provide an explanation for why she avoided marriage and turned down the offers of the Polish nobles who sought her hand. Why, after all, would she consider ever placing herself under the thumb of a man like her father? Yet rejecting subjugation to a man does not mean that she possesses no sexual feelings, and those feelings suddenly assert themselves in the presence of a beautiful object of desire who not only poses no threat to her but whom *she* can subjugate.

What, then, has the narrator wrought by providing us with the lady's diary? In a narrow sense, he has indeed succeeded in his professed purpose: defending Dan from the taint of submitting to seduction. But the victory is pyrrhic. In the process of achieving it, he has exposed the poor boy's un-defended innocence, the haziness of his moral agency, and the humiliation of his abasement. And in providing the lady with a credible psychology, he has made it difficult for us to hold on to the perception of her as a monster.

If there is a monster in the story, it is the lady's father and his mute re-tainer. The closing passage of the story presents us with a final quandary. She grows tired of the boy and wants to send him packing, but she is afraid that he will reveal her shame. The mute servant knows that more final mea-sures are in her self-interest. But when he slides "his hand across his neck like one about to slaughter a chicken or a cow," she backs down and tells him that no harm should come to the Jew. Precisely at this moment, the lady declares: "This is the place for me to tell why the slave was mute and why he was so loyal and attached to me" (pp. *490–91, 425–26*). Why indeed is this, the final lines of the story, the place for her to give us his history? His origins evoke the violent period one or two generations earlier when the new Austrian rulers set themselves to routing out bands of murderers and robbers lurking in the mountains and the forests. On the strength of his power as a nobleman, the lady's father intervened to save this man, whose tongue had been cut out by his comrades so he would not talk under tor-ture. The intervention was not undertaken on humane grounds. The man had presumably served as an assassin secretly dispatching the father's en-emies, and saving his life made him into a servant unconditionally loyal to the family's interests.

Now, we might think that this gruesome tale serves to illustrate and en-dorse the binary between Austrian notions of civil society and the gothic feudalism of the Polish nobles. But its placement as the lady's final thought pushes in a different, deeper direction. She returns to the acts of cruelty and violence she observed as a girl because she herself remains arrested and incapable of releasing herself from the consequences of those traumas. The ancient tongue-less servant, with his amoral blood loyalty, embodies what is carried over from her father to her. The darkness in her heart, despite her piety and desire for expiation, connects her to the darkness we have seen elsewhere in the Austrian stories in the hearts of Jews as well. The cruelty of

Reb Feivush as he looks on as his namesake and longtime retainer is being beaten up, the vindictive malice of R. Yisrael Shlomo in assuring Yekele's hanging, the aloof heartlessness of R. Leibush and the other parnasim as they pluck Dan from his mother—all these point to a depth of evil in human affairs that is the possession of no one people.

Yet, in the final analysis, it is the soul of Buczacz that Agnon cares about. That soul is deeply compromised and mired in turpitude in "Feivush," the Yekele stories, and "Disappeared." In all of these stories the policies promulgated by the new Austrian rulers, in themselves onerous and pernicious, serve to expose the degradation of the Jewish community of Buczacz. In earlier historical periods, reflected in earlier sections of *A City in Its Fullness*, Buczacz had been held up for admiration as a kehilah kedoshah, a holy community. That distinction has now become deeply tarnished. This picture of the city reveals a painful cleavage within Agnon and his narrator. The moral realism of the Austrian stories bespeaks an allegiance, however disturbing, to truth-telling and to the relevance of historical forces. On the other hand, identification with Buczacz and anguish over its decline leads to an urgent quest to purify the image of the beloved city and to find some path toward redemption, even if it is fleeting.

8

Moments of Redemption

Buczacz Lost?

Is there any good news to relieve the utter bleakness of "Disappeared"? Can any image dispel the grotesque horror of the catatonic tailor's apprentice turned-soldier being returned by the police to Buczacz in his blue dress? As described in this important story, the world of Buczacz is bereft of human feeling and communal responsibility. The benign oppression exerted by the distant Austrian regime engenders a base and unworthy response, which in turn reveals a Jewish community that has become wholly unmoored from its connection to Torah. The community has relegated its rabbi—an admirable man and estimable scholar—to the margins of communal life; and callous and smug men, whose only recommendation is their wealth, dominate the kahal. The victimization of the innocent unfolds with tragic inevitability.

This picture of a fallen Buczacz poses a threat to the integrity of *A City in Its Fullness* as an undertaking. From the outset, to be sure, Agnon rejected nostalgic idealization as a premise for his grand project, and he took the notion of "fullness" in his title to be understood not as fulfillment or consummation but as epic inclusiveness. The shortcomings of individuals and the collective are indeed presented in full, but they are always located in their

337

relationship to the norms of learning and worship, whose privileged status is never far from our awareness. The fullness to which Agnon is committed, we have seen, takes on a different coloration in the stories set before and after the Partitions.

During Polish rule, that fullness, though variegated, is richer with admirable if flawed men. The rabbis, ḥazzanim, lay scholars (lomdim), and community heads (gabbaim), as well as humble shamashim and tradesmen, who populate these pages are complex figures whose holiness does not obscure their humanity. As a collective entity, Buczacz itself is a character playing a recurring role. At times the holy community of Buczacz is prideful about the preeminence that its learning should—and fails—to entitle it to, and at other times the community is portrayed as a slothful enclave given to recirculating rumor and truckling to the well-healed. But Buczacz is also a town that is capable of pulling itself together and returning to its professed values.

A key text in this regard is "The Parable and Its Lesson." The aged shamash, who is brought before a court on charges of humiliating the son-in-law of the town's wealthiest man, tells the story of his journey to Gehinnom fifty-four years earlier in the company of the saintly R. Moshe. The picture that emerges of this earlier period, a time when Buczacz was a fragile band of survivors in the throes of recovering from the 1648 massacres, is of a community united in reverence for its magisterial spiritual leader and obeisant to his will. In the present time in which the story is narrated, however, a recovered Buczacz has become complacent, and the force of God's word, as read aloud in the synagogue on Sabbath mornings, has been blunted and obscured beneath a mesh of protocols based on social status. At the same time, Buczacz is a community capable of *teshuvah*, return to the right path. The shamash's story, with its gruesome images of the consequences of competing with God's word, shocks the community into reexamining its ways and recommitting itself to valuing Torah over wealth.

In the stories that take place after the Partitions of Poland, that capacity for inner reform seems exhausted. Earlier in *A City in Its Fullness*, Agnon's narrator never ceases pointing out that the Jews always have a hand in their own troubles; and at the same time, he does not let us forget the capricious cruelty of the Polish nobles and their contempt for their Jewish subjects. But when the Austrians become the rulers of Buczacz that balance is disturbed. In "Feivush Gazlan," the Yekele stories, and "Disappeared," it is the Jewish community itself that hands over to the authorities its weakest and least protected members.

The Austrian overlords are represented as being more preoccupied with their procedures and policies than with harassing the Jews, although those protocols certainly have the effect of applying harsh fiscal pressures on the community. Those pressures in turn create the conditions for an inner moral corruption upon which the restraints imposed by the Torah have been neutralized. The evisceration of rabbinic authority is further accelerated by the gathering momentum of modernization ushered in by the access to German-language culture.

The very status of Buczacz as a kehilah kedoshah, a holy community, is imperiled by these dark late stories. The ideal of fullness, with its balance of norm and deviation, which has structured the entire project of *A City in Its Fullness*, is in danger of being polluted beyond repair. To gauge the distance fallen from the idealized image of Buczacz, it is worth recalling the dedication that appears in large font following the volume's title page:

> This is the history of Buczacz that I have written in my aguish and sorrow so that the children who come after us should know that our city is a city full of Torah and wisdom, love and piety, life and grace, kindness and charity from the time of its founding until the abominable enemy and his polluted and deranged accomplices utterly destroyed it. May God avenge the blood of His servants and visit vengeance upon His enemies, and may He redeem Israel from all its foes.

Even if we make a considerable adjustment for the liturgical and martyrological function of this cri de coeur, there is no getting around the gap that opens up between the city full of Torah and kindness and the city that sacrifices its most vulnerable as depicted in "Disappeared."

In response to this threat Agnon takes a path of addition rather than denial. The moral debasement of Buczacz represented in the stories from the Austrian period cannot be controverted. The honest storyteller, no matter how devoted he is to the cradle of his soul, must tell the truth. He may, however, place beside these truth-telling stories *another* story that presents a truth that acts not as a refutation but as a supplement. This is the case with the extraordinary story "In a Single Moment" ("Besha'ah aḥat," pp. *558–89*, 445–97), which together with the equally extraordinary story "Pisces" ("Mazal dagim," pp. *602–32*, 518–59), anchors the conclusion of *A City in Its Fullness*.

"In a Single Moment" describes a wholly abrupt and precipitous individual act of kindness that sends ripples of joy throughout Buczacz. Although this sudden act lacks the power to brake or disrupt the forces responsible for the degeneration of community, it represents an eruption in the present moment of what was best about Buczacz in former times. It is, in every sense, a breakthrough, despite its evanescence. In exploring the theme of redemption, this chapter takes the story "Until Elijah Comes" as an example of the spirit of the earlier sections of *A City in Its Fullness*, which survey the period "when Buczacz was Buczacz." The story "In a Single Moment," located at the end of the book's historical arc, deals with the time when Buczacz had become something else.[1]

Moments of Redemption

The special status of a privileged moment has a long provenance in Jewish literature. The title "In a Single Moment" quotes the words uttered in the Talmud by Rabbi Judah the Prince upon observing the martyrdom of Rabbi Hanina at the hand of the Romans (*Avodah Zarah* 10b). Below I discuss the connection to the story. In later legend, Elijah the Prophet, who did not die according to the biblical account but was transported to heaven in a fiery chariot, appears in the guise of a beggar or a poor man. He is the precursor to the Messiah, but his disguise presents a challenge that exists for the duration of a moment. If true kindness is shown to him despite his loathsome appearance, then the world will be redeemed. But the opportunity is always lost, and, although some uplift is gained from the encounter, the unredeemed state persists.

This is a key motif within Agnon's writings as a whole. In the important earlier autobiographical story "The Kerchief" ("Hamitpaḥat," 1932), the protagonist comes across a particularly repellent beggar on his return from the synagogue on the morning he has become a bar mitzvah.[2] Rather than avert his eyes, he hands the beggar the silk kerchief his mother had tied around his neck for this special occasion. The story evokes the traditions of Elijah as the harbinger of the Messiah as they are played out in the boy's fantasies only to demythologize and humanize them. In ironic contrast to the hapless characters in the legends, the boy does not miss his chance and seizes the moment. But what is triggered by the act is not a fairy-tale deliverance but the beginnings of a moral conscience, which may become the first steps taken in a process of redemption. It is the boy's arrival at a sense of responsibility for the suffering in the world that Agnon makes the reinterpreted significance of becoming a bar mitzvah.

The moment is either seized or lost. If the world we live in is, by definition, unredeemed, then the Buczacz of the late stories, represented as a city withdrawn into a hardened carapace of indifference and self-satisfaction, is doubly lost. This fallen Buczacz describes a world perilously close to the one inhabited by modern man. In conceiving of the larger parameters of *A City in Its Fullness* as a project, it will be recalled, Agnon sought to halt his epic story before the march of modernity, embodied by emancipation, succeeded in finally enfeebling the capacity of the Torah to serve as a normative anchor for Jewish society. In looking ahead to that inevitability, "In a Single Moment" describes the only kind of redemption that will be possible in that desacrilized space: isolated moments of grace.

Thought of in theological terms, a moment can be more than a moment. A moment of *redemption* can be defined as a moment in which the divine axis, the axis of eternity, intersects with the human axis, the axis of temporality. Even if the moment itself is of the briefest duration, the significance of what is revealed or unlocked overflows the limitations of the experience. In the case of "In a Single Moment," the act at the story's climax reveals the depths of Torah learning that were once intrinsic to Buczacz and have now been repressed; and at the same time it looks toward the future by participating in the process of repair upon which the Redemption depends.

Agnon's considerable achievement in "In a Single Moment" is to give this theological moment narrative extension. The single moment in question is the decision made by Avraham David, and acceded to by his son Menaḥem, that his son wed a poor bride who was supposed to be married that very day only to have the bridegroom withdraw from the marriage agreement. With the ḥuppah erected and the bride in her wedding dress, though deeply traumatized and humiliated, one bridegroom is substituted for another on the spot. This is a momentous decision made in a moment; it is an instantaneous, headlong leap with lifelong consequences. Yet "In a Single Moment" is a lengthy story because a carefully constructed set of background circumstances and cultural explanations must be put in place so that, when it finally comes, the great, astonishing act bursts with significance. To this end—or rather fruitfully to delay a too-soon arrival at this end—Agnon makes maximum use of his narrator's characteristic penchant for digressive asides; for with each dilatory excursus on Buczacz affairs past and present, the plot truly thickens so that when the explosive moment finally comes we can adequately register how much is disrupted and how much is invoked.

"In a Single Moment" stands at the center of this concluding chapter. It is preceded by a discussion of "Until Elijah Comes," a story from an early section of A City in Its Fullness, which uses the Elijah legends to explore the relationship between redemption as a human process and redemption as an eschatological concept. The story is also an argument for Buczacz's suitability as a community that possesses a special link to the footsteps of the Redeemer.

The significance of the figure Elijah in Jewish legend lies precisely in its constituting a point of intersection between this world and the next.[3] The fact that he did not die in the biblical account made Elijah available to be considered the author of a long list of beneficent interventions that continued to grow in the early modern period. Agnon uses this expanding inventory to comic effect in "In Search of a Rabbi," when R. Avraham tries to dissuade his congregants from presuming that his frequent midnight visitor—in reality R. Mordekhai—is Elijah himself, who has come to study with the rabbi in acknowledgement of his exalted spiritual status. The rabbi provides his followers with a huge list of exhausting miraculous acts of charity that keep Elijah so occupied that it is inconceivable that he would have the time to spend long nights of study with a provincial rabbi.

The popularity of Elijah is attested to by the wide variety of legends about him, both oral and written, that circulated in Eastern Europe. Common to most all these variants is the fact that Elijah appears in the form of a pauper or a beggar, and his disguise poses a test that reveals the presence or absence of true righteousness in those who come upon him in his decrepit guise. The poor, childless couple that shares with the beggar the little it has, for example, is rewarded with the birth of a child, while the bumptious merchant realizes that his condescension to the beggar has caused the redemption to tarry. In both cases the recognition of Elijah's true identity comes belatedly, in the aftermath of his disappearance. It is a moment, and one that has been either seized or lost.

Because Elijah was such an indelible part of the folk imagination of East European Jewry, it would be difficult to think of Agnon presuming to conjure up Buczacz as an archetypal community *without* including him. The real question is how Elijah is connected to Buczacz specifically and how Agnon puts a distinct stamp upon a topos that has already been so widely elaborated and disseminated. In answer to the first question, it is worth recalling the guided tour of Buczacz described in Chapter 1.

The narrator's commitment to introducing the reader to the details of the town's geography and its key institutions leads him to focus especially on the peculiarities of Buczacz. One such peculiarity is a trunk that has rested undisturbed for generations in the passageway between the old beit midrash and the new one, and it is this unexplained object, in addition to Elijah's chair used in circumcision ceremonies, that becomes the stimulus for the story at hand. The fact that the story's protagonist is a shamash binds it in an additional way to the business of book one of *A City in Its Fullness*: presenting and explaining the kelei kodesh of Buczacz, the various occupations and roles in the religious life of the town (rabbi, ḥazzan, gabbai, shamash).

What steps does Agnon take to make the Elijah topos his own is paradigmatic of the movement of his imagination in *A City in Its Fullness* as whole.

In the corpus of legends about Elijah, characters are generally described in terms of their occupation and social status and the clear-cut emotions that move them, such as piety, hunger, joy, and regret. The poor are most often pious and the rich overweening. It is a world inhabited by stock figures who are types rather than differentiated characters. Agnon takes the conventions of traditional literature and, without disturbing their familiar lineaments, infuses them with the psychological realism of modern writing.

In a traditional rendering, the kind of shamash who is the centerpiece of "Until Elijah Comes" might be only hardheaded, unctuous, irascible, and susceptible to temptation. He inhabits those qualities in Agnon's telling as well, but he is provided with interiority and subjectivity, and this makes all the difference. The fixed humors that seem a function of his difficult occupation become unfixed when the psychological mechanism behind them is explored by a narrator who, though not without judgments, makes his chief duty to explain and understand. The unexpected development in "Until Elijah Comes" is the opening of the shamash's heart to feelings of longing and attachment. Within the logic of the story these changes come about because of his encounter with Elijah in the guise of a destitute vagrant. But at an antecedent level of the telling, what enables this shift is the narrator's capacity to confer subjectivity upon his character by the empathic opening of an interior space.

The Curses

The premise of "Until Elijah Comes" is simple and effective. Two sections of the Torah (Lev. 26:14–43 and Deut. 28:15–68) contain lists of horrendous punishments that will befall Israel if the covenant with God is disobeyed. These passages are called the Tokheiḥah or the Curses. The second of these is read on Sabbath morning in the synagogue in the late summer as part of the weekly portion Ki Tavo. Even though the Curses belong to the past of ancient Israel, the ferocity of the language engenders a sense of fearfulness within popular piety, and the person who is called up to the Torah for that section is held to be exposed to this negative potentiality. When hiring a shamash, the narrator explains at the outset of the story, it was customary to make it an explicit condition that the shamash be that person and take this exposure upon himself unless he can find someone to replace him. Because the shamash is as disinclined as other members of the congregation to put himself in harm's way, he looks for a poor man who, for payment, will stand in his place. This has worked for the shamash in the past, but when we meet him at the opening of the story, it is already Thursday in the week in which the portion will be read on the upcoming Sabbath and no candidate has materialized. What's worse is that the shamash has recently been guilty of acts of dereliction and misappropriation, and although his actions have not been discovered by the community, he feels acutely vulnerable to divine judgment, and this redoubles his motivation to avoid exposure to the Curses.

In describing the orbit of the shamash's duties, the story opens up territory not previously explored in *A City in Its Fullness*. It is the religious and communal leadership of Buczacz that the narrator has hitherto foregrounded. The shamash, however, holds sway over a kind of subterranean religious world which, despite taking place in the same synagogues and study houses, is far removed from the circles of scholars, ḥazzanim, and pious merchants. The gap is most evident when it comes to caring for the souls of the departed. Early death was a fact of life in this society, and it was believed by rich and poor alike that the souls of the dead underwent a postmortem journey. The outcome of the journey depended in part on the deceased's righteousness while alive and in part on the efforts made on his or her behalf by surviving relatives after their passing. Those efforts include reciting the mourner's Kaddish, studying chapters of Mishnah, and giving charity; without these interventions, the soul of the departed was certain to be condemned to the torments of the grave (ḥibutei hakever).

Successfully carrying out these measures, however, depends upon two things the poor lack: textual literacy and money. Gender is an added aggravating circumstance; women must rely on men to recite Kaddish and learn Mishnah. The Mishnah looms large and takes on a new role in the pious practices surrounding the dead. Rather than being an integral element in the complex of Talmud study—the Talmud, after all, is a commentary on the earlier code—the Mishnah is broken off from this complex and made into a kind of totemic object in itself, whose very recitation (rather than study) confers benefit on the dead. The effectual power of Mishnah recitation is established by the fact that the letters in the word "mishnah" are the very same letters in the word *neshamah* (soul).

Here is where the shamash enters the picture. To supplement his meager salary, the shamash in our story, like shamashim everywhere, is available for hire by those, principally women, who themselves cannot recite Kaddish or learn Mishnah. He is paid to recite Kaddish on behalf of a beloved deceased parent or child where there is no male available or capable of doing so. Whereas the Kaddish cannot be customized for an individual, the Mishnah lends itself to that practice. The shamash has put together a list of twenty-two chapters, each beginning with one of the twenty-two letters of the Hebrew alphabet, and he recites them in combinations that correspond to the names of the deceased. He is not a learned Jew, but his literacy suffices for this purpose. His standing as one of the functionaries of the synagogue, as modest as it is, should be sufficient to reassure the women who contract his services that the duties paid for will be performed, even though there would ordinarily be no way to make sure.

But the shamash become derelict in his duties, and one day he is caught. The way this happens tells us a great deal about the epistemological world of the story.

> There was a certain poor woman in our city. Her husband died, bequeathing her nothing but a young son. The widow took comfort in her son. But the father pined for his son and took him. One night, the young boy appeared to his mother in a dream, sadness on his face. She said to him: What ails you, my son? Does being with father not suit you? He said to her, Things would be fine for me if only someone in the world below would say a Jewish word for the ascent of my soul. (p. 57, 59)[4]

The poor woman is horrified and anguished, for she had sold the kerchief her late husband had given her as a gift to pay for the shamash to perform just those services that would ensure the boy's comfort in the afterlife.[5] When she pays a surprise visit to the beit midrash and finds the shamash dozing over the volume of Mishnah, the widow's "heart filled with fury, and she cursed him with all the maledictions in the Curses" (p. 57, 59). When the narrator tells us that "the curses of a widow are never ineffectual," he is corroborating the shamash's dread; if he finds no substitute and is himself forced to ascend to the Torah for the reading of the Curses, the danger to him will be very real. It is essential for the reader to attend carefully to the narrator's promptings to comprehend the theological underpinning of the story's world. It is easy to label the shamash's dread superstitious, but in the eyes of the mostly reliable narrator this is not the case. The world of the story is one in which a dead father can "take" his young son to mitigate his loneliness beyond the grave, from which the son can communicate with his mother through a dream. These occurrences are, in this context, entirely plausible. Now, to be sure, the turning point of the story comes when the Elijah figure demonstrates that the shamash's dread is groundless. But this is not so much the debunking of a primitive belief as its substitution by a superior and more constructive, but no less supernatural, belief.

The widow's curses are not his only problem. During the unrelenting cold of the previous winter, the shamash had taken home some firewood that belonged to the synagogue so that his young children could have some warmth. Over Hanukkah he did the same with oil that belonged to the community because there was none left at home to light the menorah for the holiday.[6] His actions have not been discovered, and may never be; but the shamash lives in a world in which sins are visible to God and in which a reckoning is certain. This is sure to be the case even if his punishment is not triggered by the reading of the Curses. He has become mired in melancholic resignation; in his mind he tries various calculations to minimize his culpability by shifting his sins into categories of lesser gravity, but he knows the game is up: "regrets broke his heart." He knows his punishment will be set in motion by his exposure to the Curses if no substitute is found. It is Thursday and the clock is ticking.

At just this moment the door to the beit midrash opens and a vagrant enters.[7] Of the many comic ironies in the story, this one is especially rich. The shamash seizes on the poor man as a candidate to be his substitute. Yet while a redemptive moment is indeed in store for the shamash, little does he know that his breakthrough from dejection to joy will come precisely because he will *not* be replaced and will have to face the Torah on his own. Another irony that subtends the story as a whole derives from the fact that the shamash is ignorant of the vagrant's true identity, while the reader knows the truth from the outset. Not only the title of the story but a common familiarity with folk tales about Elijah make that knowledge taken for granted.

The shamash's ignorance not only makes him a figure of comic ridicule, but it also serves to underscore the differences between the two men. Taking the Elijah figure for a common itinerant pauper, the shamash projects onto him a set of assumptions he supposes to be true about the poor generally: they are moved first and foremost by their bellies, they are ignorant of Jewish learning, they faun upon the well-to-do town Jews and look down upon uncouth village Jews. He knows these things to be true because they are true of him as well. Admittedly, he is not homeless or destitute or entirely ignorant, but he most assuredly inhabits the world of poverty. He too lives on the edge, and his misappropriation of synagogue property is motivated by want. He is not far removed from the poor widows who hire him and whose trust he abuses. He is, ordinarily, an effective manager of the vagrants who collect at the synagogue precisely because he knows them all too well. The shamash, in short, is a creature who has been shaped by the conditions of deprivation within which he lives and works.

When the door swings open and the vagrant enters the beit midrash, the shamash is confronted with a radically new order of value. The dialogue between the two men stages a brilliant and, again, very funny encounter between two ways of seeing the world. Throughout the uncanny duel that unfolds, the petty privation in which the shamash is immured doesn't permit him to question his superiority to the vagrant. And all the while, the reader shares in the knowledge that this small-minded functionary, unwittingly, is crossing swords with Elijah the Prophet.

Yet despite his heavenly pedigree, the Elijah figure uses none of the supernatural instruments that folklore has so generously assigned to him. There are no tricks or miracles. A great change in the shamash is indeed effected, but it is brought about solely through words, the emotions that accompany them, and the aura they leave behind. It is essential to the dramatic structure of "Until Elijah Comes" that the transformation of the shamash begins to take place only *after* the vagrant has gone off to a neighboring village. During the exchange with the shamash in the beit midrash, the latter gives no sign that he has absorbed one wit of the alternate view of the world that has been put before him. It is only later that we understand that all the while the vagrant's affect and utterances have been performing a kind of therapeutic intervention for the soul of the shamash.

Things get worse before they get better. The genial and optimistic nature of the vagrant's spirit serves only to provoke the shamash into revealing how mean and impoverished his spirit has become. The minute the vagrant walks in the door, he brazenly taps the shamash on the shoulder and confronts him:

> Why, my beloved Jew, are you distressed? We are Jews, blessed be God, and it is good for a Jew to be happy at all seasons, having the merit to be a Jew. But you, my beloved Jew, show a darkened countenance. God forbid that you have forgotten that you are a Jew!

> The shamash looked angrily at the vagrant. He wanted to grab him by the neck and throw him bodily out of the beit midrash. But his heart said to him: Slow down; sometimes, deliverance can come from a person such as this.

> The shamash made his angry face vanish and stretched out his right hand to greet him, as one greets a guest. (p. *59*, 61)

The shamash's distress is real, even if it is of his own making; and it is hardly unnatural for someone in this state to react with rage when told, with no preliminaries and by a vagrant no less, to be happy just because he is a Jew. What the reader knows that the shamash does not is that the beggar who addresses him is *not* natural, and his seemingly-glib wisdom is not shaped by human experience. His ability to address the other as *yehudi ahuvi* (my beloved Jew) is not an affectation, nor is his conviction that the very fact of being a Jew must necessarily confer a profound sense of joy. Not only is the shamash incapable of assimilating the "good news" the vagrant announces, but he mobilizes himself to undertake a plan of expedient insincerity in dealing with him. He counsels himself to suppress his rage and keep his mind on the prize. When he encourages himself by saying that "sometimes deliverance can come from a person such as this," we cannot help being amused because we know that announcing the deliverance in the grand sense of the Redemption is exactly Elijah's line of work.

Yet by embarking on his tactic of ingratiation, the shamash digs himself into a deeper hole. Each time he offers the vagrant some blandishment, not only is it rejected as unnecessary, but the shamash ends up revealing his own obsessive preoccupation with status and wealth. For example, when he attempts to flatter the vagrant by bidding him sit down on the bench reserved for the well-to-do, he cannot help rattling on about "those who have means, the esteemed rich, who have hundreds of gold coins hidden in their cellar cupboards. You and I, my friend, would be happy if we only had as many pickled cucumbers!" (p. 59, 61–62). When the vagrant declines the shamash's offer of food and money—he has no need for money and he has brought his own food with him—he does so not out of self-denial but self-sufficiency. The vagrant's answers serve only to mystify, confuse, and frustrate the shamash because his own deprivation makes it impossible for him to imagine a life lived outside the vicious circle of want and envy.

The sharpest contest concerns the reading of the Curses. The first thing the vagrant does upon entering the beit midrash is to remark upon the shamash's visible distress. In return, the shamash simply describes his predicament. Although he does not reveal the exigent sources of his anxiety, he admits that if he does not find a replacement, he will have to ascend to the Torah for the reading of the Curses. In his eyes, the reason why this should be avoided is self-explanatory and taken for granted by any sensible person. For the vagrant it is quite otherwise.

> The vagrant fixed him in his gaze and said, My beloved Jew, what nonsense are you speaking? Can there be a Jew who is distressed to be given the honor of blessing the Torah? Everyone who merits such an honor should be glad and, what's more, give charity. But you, my beloved Jew, are afraid lest you be called up to bless the Torah? Do not think ill of me if I tell you I am not such a fool as to believe that? If your beard and your side-locks did not testify that you are a man of standing, I might think you a professional jester. (p. 59, 62)

It's worth recalling that it was the heads of the congregations who made the matter of the Curses a provision in the shamash's contract in the first place. The discomfort surrounding the reading of the Curses was an accepted tenet of popular belief rather than a bauble of superstition. Yet what is axiomatic in the popular mind—and in the shamash's—in one direction, is equally axiomatic in the vagrant's mind in the opposite direction. There is no meeting place between the two positions. For the vagrant, the fear is so far beyond the borne as to be tenable only by fools or jesters.

One of the cruxes in interpreting "Until Elijah Comes" is how the shamash's encounter with the vagrant brings about his later transformation. During the exchange between them in the beit midrash, not only does the shamash remain insensible to the vagrant's alternative perspective, but he contorts himself into ever more unctuous displays of dissimulation. The answer, I think, lies in aspects of the vagrant's manner not directly connected to the content of what is said. In the first words of the passage above, the Hebrew reads *hekifo hahelekh leshamash be'einav*, which can be rendered more literally "The vagrant encompassed the shamash with his eyes." The vagrant is taking the shamash in, comprehending him, and orienting himself toward him. He is making his presence available to him and in alignment with him. Furthermore, the epithet he uses to address the shamash, "my beloved Jew" (yehudi ahuvi), is something more than a pietistic appellation. It is an affirmation of an unconditional core of worthiness the shamash possesses despite the distasteful behaviors he displays. It is this mode of relatedness and the aura of presence that attaches to a deeper part of the shamash's self and does its work during the vagrant's absence over the next several days.

Redemption, Upper Case and Lower Case

The remainder of the exchange between the two men takes places under the sign of another fraught Hebrew verb. The fourth section of the story, which describes the shamash's efforts to cajole the vagrant into taking his place at the reading of the Curses, opens thus: "The shamash began to play the innocent with the vagrant" (hithil metamem 'im hahelekh, p. 60, 63 [where metamem is rendered as "to chat"]). Metamem means to play the role of an innocent or a rube (*tam*) for ulterior purposes. Tam partakes in some of the same duality possessed by the term "innocent." A tam can be either a person of unblemished purity or a simpleton. The two men play out these roles in amusing ways. The one who thinks he is running the show turns out to be clueless, while the one who seems to be witless and naïve is the embodiment of profound faith. The encounter comes to a comic crescendo—at least from the reader's privileged vantage point—when the vagrant finally takes his leave to attend a circumcision ceremony in a neighboring village. He has tried several times unsuccessfully to interrupt the shamash's nonstop flow of prying questions and fawning inducements. When he begs leave to set off for the village, the shamash, in a campaign to keep him tethered close to home, launches into a diatribe denigrating village life and the paltriness of their fare when compared with the glories of a city like Buczacz and its famed comestibles. He punctuates his argument with the declaration that even Elijah, who is supposed to attend all circumcisions, wouldn't be caught dead there. All the vagrant can do in response is to smile and keep silent, and so do we.

There is Redemption and there is redemption. Redemption means breaking the yoke of the nations and delivering the Jews from exile; redemption, in the lower-case mode, describes this-worldly shifts in the character of individuals and society that, concerted and amplified, contribute to the possibility of a transcendent deliverance. The title of Agnon's story, "Until Elijah Comes," plays on this difference. Elijah is the precursor of the Redemption, but *until* Elijah comes, in the duration of exilic reality in which our lives take place, we are sometimes given the opportunity to experience moments of transformation. Agnon's story gently mocks the grandiose expectations surrounding the Elijah figure in Jewish folklore, whose mainstay is the premise of "if only. . . ." If only the shamash had realized the vagrant was Elijah, then surely the Redemption would have come! Agnon points us instead to the transformative impact of the Elijah figure on the here-and-now in the form of a shift in the being of a miserable synagogue functionary.

The dramatization of that shift is the business of the second half of the story. Redemption can be experienced as an epiphany, a sudden moment of breakthrough, or it can be experienced as a gradual process that spreads and takes root. These two possibilities correspond to the two stages of the shamash's change in this second half. In the first, the shamash is faced with coping with the vagrant's absence. He has left Buczacz but promised to return for the Sabbath, and the shamash has interpreted his assurance as agreement to stand up for him when the Curses are read in the synagogue.

The test to which the shamash is put begins when the vagrant fails to appear in the synagogue at sundown on Friday, and it continues the next morning when the service has already advanced to the removal of the Torah scroll from the ark and the commencement of the reading and there is still no vagrant in sight. As the narrator admits us to the shamash's inner thoughts during this interval, we see a man who is trying to overmaster his feelings of panic and not succumb to despair. At the same time he is experiencing feelings new to him. "In all his days, he had never so yearned for a person as on that night; in all his days, he had never been as angry with a person as on that night" (p. 63, 68). When the vagrant suddenly and mysteriously appears by the door of the synagogue, the shamash is still undergoing an ordeal of faith that takes him through several steps of moral and theological reasoning. He recognizes in the vagrant's face the qualities of integrity and innocence (temimut), and he recalls the Torah's injunction concerning the payment of vows ("The words of your mouth you must honor," Deut. 23:24), and he assures himself that if there is anyone who will keep his promises it is this man. The shamash then makes a leap to another level of understanding: "In this way, a person's faithfulness grows stronger, seeing that other people rely on him to stand by his word. And just as Israel behaves here below, so it is done for them in the world above; all the promises that have been made to us will be fulfilled" (p. 64, 69). In his own way he has done nothing less than intuit the relationship between redemption and Redemption.

But there are no easy steps for our shamash and, again, the joke is on him. As he spurs himself on to keep the faith, what he is trusting in all the while is the prospect of his being shielded from exposure to the Curses. The vagrant's appearance in the eleventh hour justifies his faith. With calm triumph he descends the dais into the congregation to call the vagrant up to the Torah. The weekly portion is divided into seven sections (*aliyot*), and the section with the Curses is the sixth. With gracious formality the shamash goes through the etiquette of obtaining the vagrant's full Hebrew name and offering him the honor of the sixth aliyah. With equal graciousness, the vagrant responds that nothing would have given him greater pleasure if the honor had been offered earlier. But because he is a kohen, a priest, and kohanim are called to the Torah only for the first aliyah, it is too late for him to accept. There is nothing for it; the congregation is already grumbling over the delay. The shamash must himself take the aliyah and face the consequences.

This is when the breakthrough takes place. What begins in buffo comedy when the balloon of the shamash's expectations is pricked ends in an unexpected moment of an entirely different sort. The vagrant turns his encompassing and loving gaze upon the shamash, addresses him as "my beloved Jew," and urges him to remove anger from his heart and recall that all the sections of the Torah are holy. The anger drains from the shamash and is replaced by love, which in turn makes room for joy. The joy becomes infectious: "From the power of his joy, the whole beit midrash was filled with joy, and from the joy of the congregation, the joy of Yoel Yonah was multiplied. This is the power of transcendent joy—joy that brings joy that brings more joy," (p. 65, 70).

Yoel Yonah. Did we know that the shamash had a name? For the first half of the story we did not. Ordinary narratorial practice would have assigned him a proper name at the outset. But the name is conspicuously withheld and, when we first meet him, the crabbed and crafty soul of the shamash seems wholly coterminous with the occupations he performs on behalf of the synagogue as well as with the private employments he takes on to make ends meet. Because there is no space between function and identity, there is no need for a proper name. But now, as that space is widened and an inner life emerges, the shamash becomes known to us Yoel Yonah.

What follows the moment of joyful exhilaration? After ascending to the Torah and the beatitude he experiences there, Yoel Yonah must now descend into the flow of life and attempt to hold onto the power of the event. In the shamash's mind, that power is directly connected to the vagrant, and at the conclusion of the service the shamash looks for him to invite him home for the midday Sabbath meal. But he is nowhere to be found, and that remains the case at the Minḥah service later in the day. In the persisting absence of the vagrant, the shamash must come to terms with how his life has changed and how that change can be sustained. It is during this penultimate section of the story that the narrator allows us to eavesdrop on the rationalizations, mood swings, and self-assurances animating the shamash's newly active inner life. There is perhaps no better example in the whole of *A City in Its Fullness* of Agnon's modernist-realist way with stories set in traditional life. This is not to say that a figure such as the shamash could not have these thoughts and feelings at this time and in this place; far from it. But it is only through Agnon's imagining this inner life and giving it articulation through the techniques of modern literary representation that it can, belatedly and retrospectively, come into being.

At home with his wife, Yoel Yonah remains flush from his spiritual reversal of fortune, despite the vagrant's absence at their table. He soothes his disappointment by repeating to himself the counsel the vagrant had urged on him in the face of his anger earlier in the morning: "Do not bring distress to your Sabbath rest, my beloved Jew" (p. 65, 70). To his wife he declares aloud, "A vagabond visitor has arrived and transformed my spirit," and he goes on to rue the years of unnecessary vexation and anxiety he put himself through in avoiding being called up to the Torah for the Curses. To himself he silently tries to sort out the transformation that has overcome him.

> Yoel Yonah sat in wonderment. A vagrant, possessed only of his poverty, yet my heart is drawn to him. And even if it is in human nature to sometimes yearn for one another, we don't know the cause of such yearning. If it is because of the man himself, why did I not yearn for him earlier? Now that I know him, I see that the change resides in me, not in him. If this is so, why did it happen now and not earlier? In any case, it makes no sense to waste time in such musings when Sabbath delicacies lie before you. (p. 65, 71)

The wonderment comes from several sources. Yearnings for another human being are a new experience for the shamash, whose world has until now been shaped by the scramble for survival and the sizing up of others in terms of their utility to the pursuit of that goal. Even if he can imagine the existence of such yearnings, his status-bound view of the world can scarcely accommodate the notion that a destitute pauper could elicit those feelings. Because the yearnings are new to him and because he knows that the vagrant has not changed, he works through to the conclusion that it must be he who has done the changing. This turns out to be a line of inquiry too disruptive and perplexing to pursue, and Yoel Yonah, a man perpetually hungry, breaks off his ruminations and turns to the dishes before him.

The pivot to food is far from a trivial move. The shamash thinks and dreams about food, and it would not be an exaggeration to say that it is the system of signification through which he sees the world. He is far from being a glutton after the manner of the well-to-do Fishel Karp, the corpulent hero of the story "Pisces." Yoel Yonah comes by his preoccupation with food honestly: he is poor and perpetually hungry. He is not destitute, however. The conditions of his subsistence are such that his family gets by with meager fare during the week and enjoys a modest satiety on the Sabbath. So when he considers how to extend his contact with the vagrant, it is only natural that he should think of inviting him to his home for a Sabbath meal. It is the only reciprocation he can imagine. The vagrant's disappearance, alas, makes this plan impossible; and as each meal goes by, and the lost opportunity it represents, the shamash clings more and more to a fantasy in which the poor man is a guest at his table eating his wife's dishes. It is a fantasy of donation; the shamash imagines himself in possession of something that the vagrant should naturally be grateful to be given. He thinks, not unreasonably, that as a poor man himself he is in a better position to make his hospitality truly satisfying to the vagrant. If he were a guest at the table of a rich man, the vagrant would end up consuming little because his host, accustomed to rich dishes on a daily basis, would moderate himself because of the presence of a poor man. At the shamash's table, by contrast, there would be no such inhibitions, and the vagrant could partake to his heart's content.

That the language of food is the language of love for the shamash is demonstrated in his changed attitude toward his wife, Brakhah Gitl. We already know about his yearnings for the vagrant; evidence for the fact that the change in him is real and not restricted to this one channel of desire comes from the ready praise he offers Brakhah Gitl's cooking. Although we have not been shown the husband and wife together at home previously, the generosity of spirit that Yoel Yonah shows toward her culinary handiwork during the midday meal feels new and unprecedented. As he lies down for his afternoon nap, he marvels with sincere appreciation at his wife's capacity to "transform a pile of bones into a meaty dish" and as he falls asleep, the "Master of Dreams" takes over and transforms Brakhah Gitl's modest dish into "a royal banquet. A bone that did not hold even an olive-size morsel of meat became roasted doves. Yoel Yonah licked his lips as he murmured, Doves, doves" (p. *66, 73*). Yoel Yonah is then awakened by the sound of doves outside his window. Because *yonah* is the Hebrew word for dove, the dreamer first disappears into the culinary consummation his unconscious wishes have conjured up and then is roused to reality by a live version of the same creatures.

The failure of the vagrant to appear at either the afternoon or evening service presents a challenge to the durability of the shamash's change. He repeats to himself the vagrant's exhortation about not allowing his Sabbath to be ruined, but what was said to him with such joyous conviction he can now recirculate to himself only half-heartedly. He faces the prospect that the vagrant may indeed be an *oreaḥ poreaḥ*, a familiar pair of rhyming words that designate a visitor who is here today and gone tomorrow. The man who had elicited the kind of feelings of attachment the shamash had never before experienced now seems likely to disappear. What comes next gives evidence of a genuine change in the shamash, even if it is not the momentous transformation he thought it was.

Rather than giving way to despair or denying his feelings, he tries to reconcile himself to the loss he is experiencing and he begins to mourn. When he returns home at the conclusion of the Sabbath and recites the Havdalah prayer, the narrator reminds us that Yoel Yonah remains clueless as to the vagrant's true identity: "Even when he mentioned Elijah, whom all Israel mentions joyously, with longing and with the hope that he will come quickly with Messiah, son of David, his voice did not change in the slightest because of his heart's sorrow that the vagrant had not returned" (p. *68*, 74). Yet whereas this disjunction was used to prod us to laugh at the shamash in the first part of the story, here we are urged to respond with empathy rather than ridicule.

The shamash rises very early the next morning and reenters his workaday world, which is the world of ritualized bereavement and commodified memorialization. He presides over the many recitations of the Kaddish by orphans and by men marking the anniversary of a parent's death; he himself joins the chorus because he has hired himself out to a number of widows to recite the memorial prayer for their departed husbands. He devotes himself to making sure the memorial lamps have enough oil lest one burns out when the congregant who paid for it happens by the synagogue. "The world is filled with complaint. No matter how careful you are, you still may not have fulfilled your duty," (p. *68*, 75). The shamash performs his duties with industry and responsibility, and if he has not been turned into a cheerful and selfless servant, he has certainly extricated himself from the shirking and evasion in which he was mired at the outset of the story. When there is a lull in his work, his mind returns to the vagrant, and he wonders over the anomaly he presents to someone like himself whose occupational expertise lies in taking the measure of the itinerant poor. Resigned to the vagrant's disappearance, he is drawn to inspect the chest he has left behind.

The term used for the vagrant's chest, teivah, is the same one used for the ark in the synagogue that contains the Torah scrolls. This was the central term used in the three stories about ḥazzanim in Chapter 3, where the teivah was represented as a source of dangerous holiness for those whose calling regularly drew them close to it. In a more quotidian context, the teivah appears in our story a paragraph earlier as the place around which all those who recited Kaddish gather. The vagrant's teivah is only a rude box, but the name itself augments its mystery, and it is no wonder that the shamash is drawn to see what is inside. If the vagrant is a homeless wanderer who possesses nothing but his own poverty, what, after all, can he be leaving in this receptacle?

When the shamash is about to open the lid, the vagrant suddenly materializes; he takes something that looks like a shofar and places it in the chest. The shamash notices that the vagrant no longer has his shoes hanging by their straps from his arms, and, still clueless, he feels sorry for him, imagining that they were either pawned for food or taken by force. In fact, the narrator informs the reader, the shoes were given to a pauper who needed them more than the vagrant. Yoel Yonah "cannot contain himself" and yearns to speak with the vagrant, but he is dumbstruck. The vagrant sees that he is burning to address him and urges him, "Speak up, beloved Jew, speak up," but he is frozen until God graciously returns the faculty of speech to him. Of the many crucial subjects he could have broached when his speech is restored, the shamash seizes on the one that is seemingly the most trivial.

> Yoel Yonah said to the vagrant, You left your trunk.
> The vagrant waved to him with his right hand and said, Let it rest where it is.
> The shamash replied, For how long?
> The vagrant took him in his gaze, smiled, and said to him, Until Elijah comes.
> The eyes of Yoel Yonah were opened, and he shouted, But you are Elijah!
> The vagrant smiled and vanished. (p. 69, 76–77)

And so the shamash makes the great discovery that we the readers have been privy to all along.

Botching the chance to recognize Elijah and thus to hasten the coming of the Messiah is the *point* of all the folktales of this familiar genre. Yet, in "Until Elijah Comes," this moment is rendered anticlimactic and manifestly not the point of the story. Agnon is working in the aftermath of Y. L. Peretz and other modernist writers who use the folktale as an armature for contemporary concerns. But rather than filling up these miraculous containers with humanistic content, Agnon is advancing a perspective that, even though it is revisionary, remains theological. It turns on the distinction raised earlier between Redemption and redemption. Bungling the encounter with the disguised Elijah means missing the Big Chance, the Redemption in which the subjection of Israel to the nations will be brought to an end. But the encounter with Elijah, as we have seen, possesses the potential to lead to a moral reeducation that betters the world, and this takes place within the historical time in which the life of society is lived. In this non-apocalyptic view of redemption, which is aligned with one of the strong currents in normative rabbinic theology, the Redemption will come when Israel returns to the Torah, and that great moment can be accelerated only by smaller and more local processes of redemption.

Even within a this-worldly phenomenon of redemption, there is both process and event. At the end of the story, the shamash is changed but not transformed. The experience of joy that flows from him to the congregation when he ascends to the Torah is indeed a moment of transcendent grace, but it does not last. He must struggle through the dejection that follows to wrest something lesser but more durable from his encounter with the vagrant. It is this small success that counts, and it places a deposit in the account of the Redemption, which will one day be full.

The material embodiment of the deposit is the humble trunk in the passageway between the old beit midrash and the new one. When the shamash queries the vagrant about the trunk, the latter says, "Let it rest where it is." The dimensions of time and space in this laconic reply are both crucial. The vagrant's words, as well as his manner altogether, express a serene and joyful conviction that the Redemption, though it may tarry, will surely come. As for the place where the trunk now rests, there is no doubt in the narrator's mind that its location in Buczacz between its old and new study houses is not accidental. At the outset of "Until Elijah Comes" the rationale for telling the story altogether, like so many of the stories in the first part of *A City in Its Fullness*, derives from an anomaly encountered in the guided tour of the city. For centuries, an old chest has remained undisturbed between the study houses. Given the narrator's endearing and unapologetic pride in his city, is it any wonder that it is with the shofar that Elijah placed in this particular chest that the footsteps of the Messiah may one day be announced?

In a Single Moment

"Until Elijah Comes" is not set in a recognizable time period. It belongs to the days "when Buczacz was Buczacz," as the narrator frequently calls it throughout *A City in Its Fullness*. Although this is not an idealized time, as evidenced by the suspect behavior of the shamash, it does unfold under the sway of rabbinic and communal authority as well as within a world of belief that would understand a visitation by the prophet Elijah as miraculous but not at all unbelievable. Very different is the world in which the story "In a Single Moment" takes place.[8] We know what time it is. The story invokes a significant historical event: the great fire of 1865 that devastated Buczacz and caused its rabbi to leave the city for an extended period. This is the furthest historical pole of *A City in Its Fullness*. True, there may be few of the kind of specific references to the Austrian regime so crucial to the plot of "Disappeared." But "In a Single Moment" describes a world shaped by these new historical forces, and the focus is on precisely their impact on those values that the narrator of *A City in Its Fullness* holds so dear: the centrality of Torah learning, or at least the respect for it, in the lives of all the Jewish folk of Buczacz, whether artisans, householders, or scholars. Buczacz may be a community of modest means but when it comes to Torah, its star is fixed in the firmament.

Until that ceases to be true. In no other story in *A City in Its Fullness* except "In a Single Moment" is the narrator's love for his city so palpable and in few other stories is this love confronted by evidence that is so starkly challenging. The painful reality is that boorish Jews with money are everywhere asserting themselves, the great scholarly rabbis for whom Buczacz is renowned have been pushed to the sidelines, and fewer and fewer young men dedicate themselves to Torah study. What is the narrator to do with his love in the face of such evidence? He does what disappointed lovers often do: he denies the gross signs of betrayal, redoubles his belief in the worthiness of the beloved, and hopes for a miracle. But denial has its price. Refuting reality inevitably requires of the narrator exaggerations and idealizations whose strained reasoning becomes obvious to the reader. And because the narrator is an inveterate storyteller, the digressions and stories-within-stories that he allows his characters to tell serve to undermine his defense of Buczacz and to betray the depths of his anxiety.

The full weight of this contradiction comes to rest on the institution of marriage, the overriding preoccupation of the narrator and the characters of "In a Single Moment." In the days of Buczacz's glory, "every father would marry off his sons and daughters by means of the Torah" (p. 561, 459), the narrator proudly generalizes; and he then proceeds to elaborate how fathers, each according to his station in life, would seek bridegrooms who distinguished themselves in Torah study. The marriage system was even equipped with a safety net. If a father "was poor and lived off charity, pious women would marry off his daughters, for in every town there was a fund to assist poor brides, and not even the poorest girl would go unmarried" (p. 561, 459). The narrator, however, is compelled to admit that times have changed.

> But over the generations, as people became corrupt and began to think about money, they came to attach a monetary motive to every religious act, until such acts were completely subordinated to financial considerations. There was a proliferation of matchmakers of the kind who do not think about whether a particular girl is suited to a particular boy but rather about how much money the girl's father will allocate to her and how large a fee he himself can get for his matchmaking services. (p. 561, 460)[9]

The phenomenon, alas, is all too familiar. The commercializing and commodifying of marriage is a conspicuous theme in the writings of the Haskalah, the Jewish enlightenment, and especially in the works of the greatest nineteenth-century Yiddish and Hebrew writer Shalom Abramovitch (*Mendele Moykher-Sforim*). Although Agnon is writing almost a century after Abramovitch, the time of the action—the beginning of the second half of the nineteenth century—is the same. Yet there is a key difference in the treatment these two great writers give to this theme. Abramovitch takes the perversion of marriage as an inevitable and foregone sign of the corruption of East European Jewry as a totality. Agnon's narrator, on the other hand, while forced to acknowledge the prevailing debasement of the institution, not only refuses to admit its inevitability but assumes a stance of active resistance, and he throws himself into a wager about the reversibility of this trend.

The wager takes the form of a suspenseful drama surrounding the matrimonial fate of a fifteen-year-old young man named Menaḥem. He is an astonishingly accomplished Talmud student who is devout and deeply respectful of his parents. According to the social practices of his class, a boy of Menaḥem's achievement should have found a match in the daughter of a wealthy man already two years earlier, at the time of his becoming a bar mitzvah.[10] But Menaḥem remains unmarried, and his unmarried state is positioned to be the telling symptom of the broad crisis that threatens to be the unmaking of Buczacz as the holy community, which these stories have endeavored so intently to construct. Is it within the realm of the possible for these forces of disintegration to be confounded by a single, individual act of restitution?

By placing marriage at the center of "In a Single Moment," Agnon is invoking one of the grandest and most layered of themes in Western literature. And if the pious narrator can be fairly acquitted of familiarity with this hoary trope, *his* creator, Agnon, certainly cannot. From the comedies of Shakespeare to the novels of Jane Austen and Anthony Trollope, marriage functions as a way to bring complex works of art to closure as well as to explore the negotiations between the needs of the heart and the interests of society. Within the canon of his own works, Agnon exploited the capaciousness of the marriage plot by making it central to two novels that could not be more different from each other: *Hakhnasat kallah* [*The Bridal Canopy*, 1931] and *Sippur pashut* [*A Simple Story*, 1935]. The former is set within the world of Galician Hasidism at the beginning of the nineteenth century and tells the story of Reb Yudl, a pious but penniless scholar who undertakes a quest to collect charitable donations for the dowries of his unwed daughters. The discovery of a hidden treasure crowns Reb Yudl's quest with success and enables the novel to conclude with a glorious wedding. The reader is aware, however, that the marriage hangs on a miracle and that its successful achievement is far less important than the opportunity it provides Reb Yudl for telling stories and stories-within-stories about traditional life in Galicia. *A Simple Story* is set in Buczacz nearly a century later, in the years before World War One, and it is written in the mode of European realism. In this case, the marriage comes toward the beginning of the novel. Hershel, the only son of successful shopkeepers, is dissuaded from following a romantic attraction to a poor cousin in favor of a socially advantageous match. The novel traces the mental breakdown he suffers as a result of the repression of his feelings and the cure he achieves at the hands of a wise doctor that allows him to accept his role as husband and father.

Unlike *A Simple Story*, "In a Single Moment" is not concerned with the experience of marriage but only with the making of the match that initiates the union. And unlike *The Bridal Canopy*, the world of the story is not one in which matches are the work of Providence and executed through miraculous means. Fifty years later, in a chronological midpoint between the two novels, the Buczacz of "In a Single Moment" is still a town of believers, but it is clear that bringing off the marriage of Menaḥem will have to rely entirely on human agency.

The biggest departure and the biggest gamble Agnon takes is the choice of genre. Whether it is the marital fate of Elizabeth Bennett in *Pride and Prejudice* or the quest of Reb Yudl on behalf of his daughters in *The Bridal Canopy*, there is a whole novel to accommodate all the missteps and misapprehensions and their corrections necessary to arrive at a fortuitous union. To do this in a short story, even a relatively long short story like "In a Single Moment," means to submit the quest to a violent compression. The wished-for outcome, if it is achieved at all, has to be produced in short order; and, indeed, the action of the story takes place during the course of a single day. Agnon's gamble can therefore be summarized thus: he places the whole weight of the imperiled culture of Torah in Buczacz upon the making of this match, and he creates a dramatic situation in which that must happen, literally, in a single moment.

The Narrator as Heartsick Patriot

The story is as much about the narrator as it is about Menaḥem and his parents. Nowhere else in the Buczacz stories does the narrator's tongue wag so garrulously and nowhere else does he wear his feelings for his town on his sleeve so openly. To be sure, the narrator shapes and conveys all the narrative events in *A City in Its Fullness*, but in "In a Single Moment" this mediation is palpable in a way that makes a reckoning with it unavoidable. The reader cannot hope to get at the meaning of the plot events without first disentangling the convictions and biases through which the story is presented. The reader must therefore first learn to read the narrator and take his measure.

The opening paragraph of the story gives us a window onto the narrator's sensibility and the concerns that preoccupy him.

> In the town of Buczacz, where all fine, upstanding Buczaczers come from, there lived a certain man by the name of Avraham David. Avraham David did not stand out among his fellow townspeople. He was like all the other people of Buczacz. He would go to the beit midrash every morning and evening and say all his prayers with the congregation. And if he happened to be among the first ten men needed to make a minyan, he would be pleased with himself all day long, for however early in the morning one gets up to pray, ten others always seem to have preceded him. Like everyone, he would recite, each day, a chapter of the Mishnah, study a page of the Gemara, and read two or three chapters of Scripture. Should he come across a verse he did not understand, he would consult the commentary of Rashi, may his memory be a blessing, or those of the *Metzudot*, or sometimes even the *Mikraot Gedolot*, to see what the great scholars had to say. After completing his morning Torah study, he would turn to works of edification, such as the books of moral instruction that set a person on the right path. If he chanced upon a virtue that was within his grasp, he would embrace it and add it to his other virtues. When it came to charity, if he found a penny in his pocket, he would give it away; and if he did not find one, he would borrow one from his neighbor and contribute, the way his neighbor would, when necessary, borrow from him in order to contribute. (p. 558, 455)

Avraham David is the father of Menaḥem, the erstwhile bridegroom without a bride, and the narrator's purpose in this opening paragraph is to present him to us as a typical citizen of Buczacz. Yet from the very first line we become increasingly aware of a desperate rhetoric of persuasion and over-argument. It is tautological to say that "all the fine, upstanding Buczaczers" come from Buczacz. Well, of course they do. We put this down to the narrator's jejune enthusiasm for his city and his unstoppable pride in being himself a man of Buczacz. Yet at the same time, the overstatement produced by his eagerness suggests an unconscious anxiety. There must therefore be Buczaczers who are *not* fine and upstanding. As the story unfolds and the vapors of the narrator's boosterism dissipate; the encroachment of dark forces within the city cannot be ignored.

The strain beneath the blithe confidence is evident in the insistence on typicality. Throughout the opening pages of the story, the narrator makes it his business to convince us that in their piety and good works Avraham David and his wife Sarah are wholly unremarkable and are in fact interchangeable with any of the other citizens of Buczacz. The argument for typicality is based on the fact that Avraham David is not one of the lomdim, the scholars who spend most of their days in the beit midrash studying at an advanced level of mastery. It is precisely because he is *only* a shopkeeper and a householder that his morning curriculum is relevant. This is what the ordinary folk of Buczacz do. They rise early for prayers and then sit down to study daily portions of the major layers of the sacred textual tradition: Scripture with medieval commentaries, Mishnah, Gemara, and then works of moral instruction. All this before the workday begins.

What is true of the husband is true of the wife, and the narrator makes a point of devoting equal space to Sarah's typical exemplariness. She makes sure there is sustaining, seasonal fare on her table; she does not miss saying *her* prayers when she opens the shop in the morning and adds as many Psalms as time permits. By the light of the candle at night, while her husband and son study Torah, she devotes herself to mending clothes so that all the members of the family can remain presentable without the expense or show of new garments.

Can the reader be blamed for wondering whether all this perfection can be true? Has the lily been gilded? The answer turns on the distinction between typicality and normativity. As we see throughout *A City in Its Fullness*, Agnon—through his narrator—reimagines Buczacz as founded upon the twin pillars of worship and study. These norms define the distinctive identity of Buczacz as a kehilah kedoshah, a holy community; they are principles of value that order and organize this imagined polity. Yet, as almost all the stories testify, the rule of human behavior is deviance rather than compliance. The existence of the norms is necessary to understand that these behaviors are breaches of a code and not simply expressions of human nature. Either dialectically or paradoxically—as one may view it—it is only in the deviations from the norm that Agnon finds the true and necessary fuel for storytelling. In "In a Single Moment," the narrator's rhetoric continually seeks to collapse the difference between the typical and the normative. From reading the others stories in this volume, especially the later ones that take place after the Partition (of which this is one), we know that the lily of Buczacz has indeed been gilded. The city is no longer—if it ever was—a community wholly devoted to the consummate ideals of worship and study, and people like Avraham David and Sarah are paragons rather than representative types.

We learn soon enough that the narrator is not a liar but a lover. He is a patriot in the root sense of being a lover of his patria. His purpose is not to deceive but to persuade us that this shopkeeper and his wife are instantiations of the ideals of Buczacz. And in truth they are. The dissimulation lies not in the portrayal of them as good—they are very good, although not without fault—but in the claim that they represent the whole. The narrator betrays himself in two ways. The repetition of the claim engenders doubt. How many times can we be told that Avraham David is "one of us neither better nor worse than the rest; cut from the Buczacz mold; a Buczaczer like all Buczaczers" before we begin to wonder (p. 558, 456)?

The second way is more subtle. Garrulous by nature in this story as he is in others, the narrator is wont to make a series of small digressions, explanations, and dilations. At first blush, these seem merely signs of narrative exuberance; out of love for his subject the narrator tells us too much. Upon closer inspection, however, we can discern in each of these instances something that chips away at the idealization of Buczacz as well as alerting us to problem areas that lie ahead in the story. In the (unnecessary) explanation of Sarah's second name—her full name is Sarah Raḥel—the narrator informs us that the name is a memorial tribute to a saintly Raḥel who devoted herself to aiding poor brides. Besides introducing us to a figure, who will play an important role later in the story, the reference opens a small window upon the large social problem of women who cannot wed because of their poverty. In a similar vein, the narrator makes the, again, unnecessary point of informing us that Avraham David is *not*, as might naturally be assumed, named after Rabbi Avraham David Wahrman, the former rabbi of Buczacz because he was born while the rabbi was still alive.

Precisely because the narrator is a partisan of Buczacz he is disheartened and unsettled by the fact that Menaḥem remains unmarried. He experiences Menaḥem's situation as a fundamental fissure in the ideal of Buczacz, with which he is so deeply and ardently identified; and it becomes the irritant and point of departure for the story's plotline. Why a fifteen-year-old boy's unmarried state should be so troubling calls for explanation and if not for the narrator's contemporaneous audience, then certainly for the author's modern-day audience. Unstated but taken for granted is the assumption that in traditional East European society the worth of a scholarly boy is measured in part by the proximity of his marriage to his coming of age at thirteen. The greater his achievement and promise the greater the chance that the donning of the talit, which follows upon becoming a bridegroom, will be simultaneous to the donning of tefillin, which follows upon becoming a bar mitzvah. The contradiction is sharpened by the narrator's insistence on Menaḥem's excellence. "Even in Buczacz—a place where Torah reigned supreme, a town that produced Torah scholars renowned throughout the country, such that the great rabbis of Lviv would all hire tutors from there for their sons, who, in turn, then became sages by virtue of the Torah scholarship of Buczacz—even in Buczacz, Menaḥem stood out" (p. 560, 458). The boy is simply the best of the best, yet two long years have elapsed without his finding a match.

The Marriage Plot

Who is at fault? For the narrator, there is not a shadow of a doubt that the blame lies at the feet of unscrupulous matchmakers. Yet, as we have seen before, the stridency of his insistence draws attention away from the existence of other explanations. When it comes to the making of matches, the narrator, unsurprisingly, has a clear vision of the norm that should be respected. This is the norm that once held sway: "At one time, every father would marry off his sons and daughters by means of the Torah" (p. *561*, 459). Up and down the social scale, literacy and erudition in the study of Torah governed the principle of selection. A father sought a son-in-law as learned as his means would allow. But then, alas, is not now. The classical marriage system has been corrupted by greed. Boys of unique genius and accomplishment, rarer now than ever, are extremely valuable commodities. It is in the interests of the matchmakers, who receive a percentage of the dowry, to inflate the expectations of the bridegroom's family, to stimulate a bidding war for the most prized boys and to make dowry size the dominant criterion of choice. Greed infects the parents as well: "So powerful is greed that even those who devote themselves to Torah study use it as a device to marry off their sons for money" (p. *561*, 459). Money attracts flattery, and a father and his marriageable son become vain and high-and-mighty when they begin to believe all the exaggerations made on their behalf. The narrator is so worked up by his indignation that he cannot restrain himself and can only rationalize his screed: "The commandment to be truthful applies everywhere, at all times, in all matters" (p. *561*, 459).

There may indeed be a great deal to decry in the practices of the time, but the narrator's fulsome moralizing camouflages factors that lie closer to home. Menaḥem is Avraham David and Sarah's first-born child, and, after the deaths of the children born after him, their only surviving child. Because six days a week the boy spends the entire day in the beit midrash, his mother hardly sees him, and she does her best to accept his excelling in his studies as a compensation for his absence. When Menaḥem marries, he will leave their home and, according to standard practice, go to live with his new in-laws. To be sure, Avraham David and Sarah are acutely disconcerted by their son's unmarried state, but it does not take a forced psychological understanding to see that they are also ambivalent, and their mixed feelings contribute, however unwittingly, to the delay.

The narrator's screed draws attention away from an even more unsettling possibility—all the fault cannot be with the matchmakers. Despite their

goodness and piety, Avraham David and Sarah have not been wholly imper-
vious to the extravagant qualities attributed to their son in hopes of inflating
his value on the marriage market. They have been dazzled by the prospects
paraded before them; their judgment has become confused and their capacity for action neutralized. Menaḥem is a prize, and if their focus had been
wholly single-minded, he would have long ago become a bridegroom.

The question the story poses is how the family can move beyond this
impasse. For the parents and the son, separately and together, the issue of
agency stands at the center. Enmeshed in the machinations of the marriage
system, the parents have abdicated taking charge of moving their son to this
next, most crucial stage in his life. They are stuck and don't know how to
rectify the situation.

When it comes to Menaḥem, the issue is even more acute. The boy is, of
course, not expected to see to the arranging of his own marriage, but a def-
inite quotient of self-awareness and self-will is expected of him. He has to
be able to assent to a match in such a way that his assent means something.
Yet when we first meet him, he is a cipher, a mere Talmudic automaton. He
is so much a denizen of the beit midrash that his life barely exists outside
it. He may indeed be a prodigy who has mastered impressive swaths of the
Talmud, but the Talmud remains his only source of knowledge about the
world. He embodies the kind of medieval scholasticism that sees the world
as a reflection of the text. His ability to marry, the story implies, depends
upon his ability to *choose* to be married rather than remaining the compliant paragon he is when we first meet him. And his ability to choose, it is
further suggested, depends on his undertaking a journey beyond the beit
midrash, even if it is only to return to it.

The necessary journey takes the form of a walk during which Avraham
David accompanies his son from the beit midrash in the center of Buczacz
across the Strypa to a Ukrainian farmstead and then back. It is the central
action of the story, aside from the climatic wedding at the end, and it is in
every sense a voyage of discovery. The idea for the outing is Sarah's. It has
been months—since Shavuot—that Menaḥem has had any fresh air or exercise beyond walking back and forth from the beit midrash. But it is clear

that the suggestion represents something more than a mother's solicitude for her son's wellbeing. Although she would never question the value of her son's devotion to his studies, she intuitively grasps the fact that his immersion is also a kind of confinement and that the possibility of his marrying depends on the walls of the beit midrash being breached, if only for a moment. Her suggestion meets resistance from her husband at first. As a shopkeeper who is not a scholar—despite the elaborate round of morning studies with which the story opens—Avraham David deeply identifies with the old beit midrash of Buczacz and all it represents. Menaḥem is his proxy in this revered world, and he is reluctant to take any step that might interfere with his studies. But in the end he submits to his wife's will because of the special nature of the day.

What is special about this day? Agnon has configured his story is such a way that the day on which the action takes place—the duration is no more than twelve hours—is both Menaḥem's birthday and an ancient holiday called Tu Be'av.[11] Tu Be'av is the fifteenth day of the month of Av, which falls during the late summer. During Second Temple times, it was known as *yom korban 'eitsim*, the day of the wood offering.[12] During the year, various families throughout the Land of Israel brought lumber to contribute to the Temple. Tu Be'av was the day in which the entire people brought wood offerings. This popular festival, held in the fields surrounding Jerusalem, was the occasion for a round of matchmaking, which is described in the mishnah that concludes the tractate of Ta'anit (4:8):

> Rabban Shimon ben Gamliel says: Never were there better days for Israel than the fifteenth of Av and Yom Kippur, for on those days the maidens of Jerusalem would go out in white dresses, borrowed in order not to cause shame to those who had none of their own, . . . and dance in the vineyards. And what would they say? Young man, look and observe well whom you are about to choose. Regard not beauty alone but look to a virtuous family, for *Charm is deceptive, and beauty is fleeting; but a woman who fears the Lord is to be praised* (Prov. 31:30).

The many motifs that resonate in this brief text make it the inner spring of the story. The celebration requires leaving the city for the countryside. The practice of wearing borrowed dresses is a measure that acknowledges and attempts to mitigate class differences and the special challenge of finding matches for poor girls. The dancing of the women anticipates the joyous conclusion of the story. The urging of the maidens that their prospective matches pay more attention to descent and piety than to mere beauty and wealth prefigures the story's climactic "single moment."

Within the cycle of Jewish time, the fifteenth of Av dispels the gloom of the ninth of Av, the solemn fast day that commemorates the destruction of the two Jerusalem temples as well as other calamities. The heat of the summer is broken and the days begin to get shorter. For Buczacz, as for all Jewish communities, the greatest change is the celebration of weddings. For the three weeks before the ninth of Av, weddings are forbidden. With the passing of the fast and the approach of the fifteenth of Av, there is a spurt of weddings and the instrumental music that accompanies them. By making the fifteenth of Av Menaḥem's birthday, Agnon trains a glaring light on the ironic gap between the boy's unmarried state and the jubilant expectations associated with the day and thereby ups the ante of the plot. This is the Jewish equivalent to being born on Valentine's Day. Will this day of matches and weddings, ancient and modern, deliver on its promise of a nuptial consummation? The intersection of a significant date in the Jewish calendar—not to mention the month of Av—with a date of birth, is far from unfamiliar to Agnon's readers. Agnon himself promulgated the fact that he was born on the ninth of Av, the day not only of the great destructions but also, according to tradition, the birth of the Messiah. The factual inaccuracy of this claim takes little away from its power as a grand act of self-mythologizing. He has made young Menaḥem the bearer of such a twinned destiny, and the question remains whether he will succeed in delivering on the promise.[13]

Yet it is upon the shoulders of the father that the main dramatic burden of "In a Single Moment" rests. By the end of the story, Menaḥem has managed to achieve just enough consciousness and agency to make his assent to his father's grand gesture meaningful. His inner voice is too inchoate to warrant much articulation by the narrator. Most of the talking, and there is a great deal of it, comes from the mouth of Avraham David, and, because he possesses little self-awareness, the reader is faced with the challenge of grasping the character behind and within the abundance of vignettes, digressions, and moralistic advice he is constantly producing. So, for example, when Avraham David enters the beit midrash to take his son on the walk, he discovers that the boy is not learning new material but reviewing the tractate he has recently completed. This becomes an occasion for the father to expound on the theme that the "Torah is acquired not only by adding to one's knowledge but also by reviewing things one already knows" (pp. 564–65, 464–65); he then proceeds to tell a story about an elderly scholar who completed the vast corpus of the Talmud multiple times and who turns out to be none other than Avraham David's father and Menaḥem's grandfather.

Because the boy is *already* putting the moral of the story into practice on his own and thus rendering the story unnecessary, the telling of it reflects back on the needs of the teller rather than the listener. What Avraham David needs is to be important in his son's eyes and to present himself as the spokesman for the great culture of learning in which the boy has the prospects to become a real participant. The father is a fan and advocate and booster of that elite culture, in which the greatness of his beloved Buczacz is embodied in his eyes, but he himself can be neither a member nor a player. It is his anxiety for his city that pushes him to tell stories about it; it is all he can offer. Except, that is, for his son, whom he will soon make into a pure sacrificial offering.

Avraham David cannot rouse himself from his ambivalence on his own; it takes a prick of conscience from the textual tradition he reveres. He can't take action because, even though he is pained by the reminder of his son's unmarried state on this his birthday, he denies responsibility. When it comes to thinking about how this state of affairs has come about, he says to himself, "The reason doesn't matter. It was something that should have been done and had not been," (p. 564, 464). What rouses him to approach his son is a carefully arranged concatenation of circumstances.

Etiquette demands that a man take a book in hand and study for a little while before proceeding with the business for which he has entered the beit midrash. The volume he pulls off the shelf to satisfy this requirement just happens to be the Talmudic tractate of *Taʿanit*. He chooses this tractate because he had been studying it before the ninth of Av, when it is the custom to circumvent the ban on eating meat during the nine days before the fast by concluding the study of a tractate, which necessitates a celebration that, in turn, trumps the prohibition. But Avraham David left off studying the tractate before the end because, as a man of feeling it did not feel right to him to have his sadness over the destruction of the Temple circumvented by a legal mechanism.

Now, six days after the fast, he finishes the tractate as he waits to collect his son, and, low and behold, he comes smack up against the description of the maidens of Jerusalem dancing in the vineyards on the fifteenth of Av and addressing potential bridegrooms with the words, "Young man, look and observe well whom you are about to choose." He puts this together with the fact that the tractate his son has been reviewing is *Kiddushin*, which concerns the laws of betrothal, and he suddenly fathoms that he has been given a sign. His duty has now come into focus, even though this is the precise mission his wife had sent him on. He overcomes the stasis in which he has been mired and confidently engages Menaḥem in the journey beyond the beit midrash.

The Journey Outward

The world outside the beit midrash for Menaḥem is truly a terra incognita full of new phenomena, and as he encounters each one we gain a glimpse into the way his mind works. Impressionable though he may be, his mind is not a blank slate. Epistemologically, the reality of each new experience must first be vetted through the knowledge base of the Gemara, and, if a search of his near-encyclopedic grasp of rabbinic literature fails to return a match, he feels uneasy and unmoored. So, for example, when father and son set forth from the beit midrash, they immediately come upon two of the community's shamashim returning the poles and the canopy of the ḥuppah to the synagogue. Menaḥem observes this and assumes that the day's weddings are over, but his father hastens to correct him and explains that the ḥuppah is returned to the synagogue after each marriage ceremony and then brought back again for the next.[14] The reason for this is so "that the celebrations are not clustered together, prompting Satan to say, 'Jerusalem has been destroyed, but they are still celebrating without letup!'" (p. 566, 467). The custom reflects the sensitivity about the close proximity between the mournfulness of the ninth of Av and the gaiety of the fifteenth. In the midst of his explanation, Avraham David notices that Menaḥem has suddenly stopped walking, and when asked about it, the boy reports, "I was trying to think of a support in the Talmud for what you said, and I did not notice that I had stopped." He has not found support for the custom in question because it is not a rabbinically enacted law but a minhag, a practice the community has voluntarily adopted in response to a felt but unmandated need. Menaḥem is undoubtedly familiar with the distinction and accepts its validity, but his inability to match this experiential praxis with the body of textual theory he has mastered temporarily disrupts him and arrests his forward movement.

The air of Buczacz is thick with the smells of wedding feasts being prepared and the sounds of musical instruments being tuned. Father and son can turn nowhere without being reminded of marriages and weddings. This is even the case in the friendly gossip about the sages of Buczacz that Avraham David exchanges with the shamashim in the next section of the story (pp. 565–69, 467–70). Every topic in this casual conversation comes around to the phenomenon of early marriage for Talmud prodigies and indirectly confronts the father with the consequences of his inaction.

One topic, which occurs to the shamash because it is two years to the day of Menaḥem's bar mitzvah, is the scholarly controversy that raged a generation earlier concerning the propriety of reciting a kabbalistic formula before putting on tefillin.[15] Another focuses on the early history of R. Yekele, who is performing many of the pastoral functions of R. Avraham Teomim, the rabbi of Buczacz, who has withdrawn from public life. R. Yekele served as the private tutor to the son of the distinguished rabbi of Lviv, the Yeshu'ot Ya'akov, until the boy became a bar mitzvah. After a meandering tale, the shamash says, "Here I come to the end of the story. The day he began to don tefillin was also the day he first donned a prayer shawl, and that is not done until one marries" (p. *568*, 469). It all comes back to the same thing. Apparently unaware of the anxiety the family is experiencing, he gently jests with Menaḥem concerning the beloved old ḥazzan, who is about to leave Buczacz and who will make an appearance toward the end of the story. "If your father makes haste and marries you off," he tells the boy, "you can enjoy hearing the old cantor's voice again before he emigrates to the Land of Israel" (p. *568*, 470).

As if to deflect the spotlight from his son's situation, Avraham David asks the shamash about the identity of the couple about to be married. The answer gives Agnon the chance to prepare for the climactic ending of the story as well as to expatiate on the fallen fortunes of Buczacz. The fire that recently devastated the town and wiped out the wealth of prominent Buczacz families has made it easy for strangers to purchase real estate on the cheap. The bridegroom, a widower with children to take care of, is one of those outsiders who prospered from the city's distress. The bride is another story altogether. She is the granddaughter of Raḥel Leah, the saintly woman who busied herself with finding matches for poor brides and in whose memory Sarah was given her second name. The bride's father is a Buczaczer like Avraham David himself, "a God-fearing man, devoted to Torah, who lacks nothing but a bit of luck" (p. *568*, 470).

We are meant to understand that if his luck had been better he would not be forced to marry off his daughter to this parvenu. It is this same parvenu who, later that same day, will withdraw from the wedding and leave the bride-to-be prostrate because her father could not make good on the full dowry promised.

The journey beyond the precincts of Buczacz loosens Avraham David's tongue about his love for his city. He is very close indeed to the attitudes of the narrator both in his pride in Buczacz and in his conviction that the glory of the city rests principally on the fame of its scholars. This love and pride determines a standard against which even the venerable rabbi of Buczacz, R. Avraham Teomim, the Ḥesed Le'Avraham, must be held accountable. After the great fire, the rabbi allowed himself to be persuaded by a delegation from Kamenets-Podolsk to leave Buczacz and accept the rabbinate there. But all the time he was there, he and his wife were homesick for Buczacz and longed to return there, which they eventually did. Their unhappiness, the story implies, was payment for abandoning Buczacz. Avraham David goes on to regale the boy with tales of other great scholars who hailed from Buczacz, but not without an undercurrent of wounded pride; for many of them, although born, raised, and educated in Buczacz, were drawn to rabbinic posts in more prosperous cities and came to be known in the larger world, unfairly in his eyes, according to the cities in which they served rather than the true source of their formation.

Father and son finally arrive at the farm house of Heretzki. Avraham David deals in leather goods, and he has brought the Ruthenian farmer a bundle of roots to be used as a softening agent in the tanning of sheep skins. The narrator uses the occasion to correct the common misconception that the Jews served as the agents of the Poles in the oppression of the Ruthenians. "Being a Ruthenian," we are told, "[Heretzki] was treated by the Poles like an animal, whereas the Jews treated him like a human being and did not humiliate him gratuitously" (p. 571, 473–74). The cordial reception accorded to the Jewish shopkeeper and his son as well as the Ruthenian's unspoken resistance to instructions given him, paint a nuanced picture of the relations between these two groups.[16]

Yet, as piquant as this portrayal of intergroup relations is, it is decidedly secondary to the main function of the visit: to accelerate Menaḥem's education as a human being. The boy is a textual automaton who is incapable of perceiving the world around him without the mediation of scholastic learning. Within the condensed bounds of a plot that must reach its climax within the course of one day, this outing into the countryside has to provide a significant return on the investment made in it. While his father and the farmer conduct their business, Menaḥem is seated on a bench in the shade of an apple tree—to protect his delicate constitution—and left to his own devices.

What happens under the apple tree is quite extraordinary. As is his wont, Menaḥem begins by conducting a mental review of the statements made by the Sages about apples and apple trees. But he is put off his game by the sudden assault on his senses of the aroma of the ripening late-summer fruit and the surrounding grasses and shrubs. This fragrance triggers a more powerful experience: "a profusion of sights so lovely that no description could come close to doing them justice" (p. 572, 474). Menaḥem is seeing the manifest world of creation for the first time, yet, surprisingly, there is no religious language employed in the description, nothing at all from the Psalms or the liturgy that would naturally come to the boy's mind. It is a direct encounter between his sensorium and nature, with no texts intervening. He is content to assume a stance of amazement without the need to find categories through which to make sense of his experience. And rather than feeling agitated and destabilized, he is rewarded with a feeling of peace and tranquility. The experience is vital and dynamic: "From one moment to the next, each of these, the air and the light, each dancing and setting the rest to dancing, would intertwine, pull apart, come back together, and merge, continuously yielding new and unprecedented forms of light and air" (p. 572, 474).

The world has suddenly grown larger for Menaḥem because the faculty of his senses that until this very moment has lain dormant, has not only been brought to life but given a powerful infusion of beauty. The epiphany he has been vouchsafed belongs squarely to the poetry of Wordsworth and European Romanticism, literary territory foreign to the narrator but not unfamiliar to the author. When it is time to go and the boy disengages himself, with difficulty, from the reverie, the mechanisms of rationalization return. "Such worldly pleasures as the sight of gardens and fields may not be sinful," Menaḥem reasons, "but they can take over one's mind" (p. 573, 475). The boy is not wrong, and he successfully resists being taken over, but what he has undergone has left an ineradicable imprint.

Buczacz Desolata

Menaḥem's extramural education continues on the trip back to Buczacz, which is very different from the trip out. On the way there, the minds of father and son were delightfully preoccupied with tales of the great scholars of Buczacz, and the time had sped by. The road back is much more extensive and difficult because it graphically documents the devastation wrought by the fire, as well as the deepening fissures in the moral life of the community. Because of the emphasis on worship and learning, so many of the stories in *A City in Its Fullness* unfold within the communal core of the city, a space tightly bounded by the Great Synagogue, the batei midrash, and the marketplace. In the second half of "In a Single Moment," this knot is undone and the city is unspooled before us, as we are taken on a journey from the periphery back to the center. Close attention, to begin with, is given to the habitations of the Ruthenians and the Jews. In the fields where the city meets the countryside, Avraham David first points out to his son the low clay hovels of the peasants, and a significant detail about their structure suggests the relationship between the two groups: "Originally, there had been no glass in the windows, only pig bladders stretched across them that admitted light. After the fire, they found panes of glass in the town dump, which they took and put in their windows," (p. 573, 477). The next closer ring of settlement contains the modest homes of poor Jews. On the earthen porches of these cottages sit old men, dozing off and occasionally reminiscing about the glories of Buczacz's previous rabbi, the Neta Sha'ashu'im. Closer to the center, where the fire has done the most damage, are the ruins of the more substantial homes of the well-to-do householders as well as the few mansions of the wealthy tax collectors. It is from here that Avraham David and Menaḥem will soon hear the outcries and mayhem emanating from synagogue courtyard.

With Avraham David as guide, the journey into Buczacz becomes a series of lessons on the eclipse of civility and the general decline in the moral and material fortunes of the community. For a man so in love with his city, or at least with its idealized image, these are painful admissions to make. The father points out to his son the ruins of two homes that emblematize the deterioration. The first belonged to Ya'akov Yehoshu'a, who as a boy in ḥeder had shared a bench with Avraham David. Ya'akov Yehoshu'a was a quick student with a photographic mind; to the astonishment of his classmates, he could recite a page of Gemara word-for-word just after reading it. His family was poor, and one day he was brazenly humiliated on account of his poverty in the presence of his fellows—who kept quiet—by another boy, who was the grandson of the same Feivush, the wealthy collector of the candle tax, whose depravity was described in the preceding chapter. Ya'akov Yehoshu'a articled himself to a milkman and never returned to school.

The second ruin belonged to Raḥel Leah the Pious, the same woman that Avraham David's wife Sarah Raḥel is named for. Despite that fact that Raḥel Leah was blind, her home was called the House of Light because poor women with few prospects for marriage would emerge from meeting with her with radiant faces. The father tells the story of a group of irreverent young men who used to meet Saturday nights in a burnt-out old synagogue and hatch plans to play practical jokes on various people in the town. Goaded on by his fellows, one prankster, who was engaged to the daughter of a wealthy family, decided to play such a joke on Raḥel Leah by coming to her door and, in a girl's voice, asking for help finding a mate. He was punished by his hair turning white overnight. His engagement was cancelled, and eventually the only mate he could find was a crippled orphan provided for him by Raḥel Leah herself.

The point of these vignettes is to demonstrate the social forces that have made it so difficult for Buczacz to remain a community of kindness and learning. The miscreants in both stories are emboldened by the positions their families have acquired through wealth—in one case the unsavory business of tax collecting—and in both the insult and abuse they commit are wholly gratuitous. And lest we think that these are merely evil seeds, we are told about the silent complicity of the others around them. As Avraham David's discourse to his son on the road back to Buczacz gathers momentum, it becomes clear that the problems go deeper than the corruption and insolence of the newly moneyed classes. The earth they are treading on is strewn with the rubble and detritus from the fire, which is described with what is for Agnon unusual concreteness and materiality. It is a natural leap from these scenes of destruction to the archetypal, mythic destruction of the Jerusalem temples mourned in the liturgy of the preceding week. Through Avraham David's words, the narrator builds a multivalent analogy between the Destruction and the fire in Buczacz. Within the narrator's traditionalist mind, there is no calamity that is not a punishment; and the fire is understood as retribution for social corruption and dishonor of the Torah.

Yet despite this theological rationale, much remains inexplicable. As in the biblical book of Lamentations and the rabbinic midrash that expounds it, there remain the disturbing examples of the suffering of the innocent and the righteous. Standing over the ruins of Raḥel Leah's house, Avraham David sighs, "Since the day the Temple was destroyed, there has been a harsh decree that the houses of the righteous, too, shall be destroyed" (p. 575, 479). Observing the ruin of another house, which belonged to a man renowned for his scrupulous observance of the Sabbath, he can only opine that this righteous man must have become "entangled in his neighbors' sins" (p. 577, 482). He makes a feeble attempt to explain why a beit midrash they come upon was burned to the ground by pointing to the sin of levity committed by the children of the men who learned there; but his heart is with the learned and unblemished fathers, who, like the once-noble sufferers in Lamentations, now "have embraced refuse heaps." "Overnight, they lost everything they had and were reduced to poverty, may God have mercy on us all" (p. 577, 483).

It is no coincidence that it is this discourse about destruction that is suddenly interrupted by the ear-splitting clamor originating from the synagogue courtyard. The downward cycle reaches its nadir now in section 9 as the news of the rebuffed and abandoned bride is conveyed just as an upward cycle is initiated at the beginning of section 10 with Avraham David making his first announcement of the grand, redemptive gesture to come. The narrator has given away the game, and the reader knows at this point that the story is now moving unstoppably toward a joyous ending. In clock time, that consummation is soon, perhaps no more than an hour or two off, and the father's exhortations are delivered in a frantic, headlong tone, as if every minute of delay is a matter of life and death.

Yet it is precisely at this point that Agnon puts a break on the story's narrative momentum and introduces a series of digressions and scenes that serve to retard the narrative flow. To begin with, he switches venues to the family shop and tracks Sarah's growing bewilderment as she hears the tumult from afar and wonders what to make of it. And just as she is grasping the good news and joining the celebration at the end of section 11, the scene changes and we are brought into the home of our Master, R. Avraham Teomim, the rabbi of Buczacz, who has recently returned from his long sojourn away from Buczacz. The review of the rabbi's recent travails, the visit of R. Natanel, the veteran ḥazzan who is about to settle in the Holy Land, the leisurely discussion of halakhic issues surrounding the kashrut of a new species of bird that had recently appeared in the Holy Land and was the subject of a letter from the rabbis of Safed—there is nothing about this extended scene that yields an inch to the reader's natural desire that the narrator get him to the wedding on time.

Yet, do you think the narrator will own up to all this delaying and postponing? Not a bit of it! He is at his most coy in continually protesting that he is curbing his natural propensity for expansiveness and doing all in his power to move things along. Thus in describing Sarah's state of mind, he tells us, "I am leaving aside thoughts and reflections that would slow down the story in favor of recounting the events and circumstances in full detail" (p. 584, 491). In the midst of the discussion of the strange fowl that has appeared in the skies of the Holy Land, the narrator admits, "This is not the place to dwell on such things" (p. 586, 494). Most playfully of all: "I could tell you a lot about the rabbi's cane, but since our Master did not like to take time for stories that have no halakhic import, I shall not take time for them either" (p. 587, 495). Indeed.

It is as if Agnon the author has implemented a strategic decision to slow things down while his narrator refuses to take the blame. Surely we have a right to ask what game Agnon is playing. Although Agnon is certainly not above a measure of craftiness in his relations with his readers, in the present case, I would argue, his ends are more honest. The conclusion of "In a Single Moment," as will be described shortly, is portrayed as one in which the entire community of Buczacz is seized by a special kind of joy that, in a single stroke and for a single moment, dispels the pall that has settled upon the city. Precisely because of its rarity and evanescence, this is a moment that must be prepared for and built up to. It must accumulate meaning and

substance as it forms and gathers together the various strands of narrative
into a single knot. Such profound joy cannot be truly experienced without
waiting and anticipation. Echoing the Song of Songs (3:5), Agnon is telling
us, "Do not arouse or awaken love until it so desires."

The story also must find time to endow the grandeur of the grand gesture
with the substance it deserves. The news of the scandal of the abandoned
bride is reported to Avraham David and Menaḥem—and the reader—not
directly by the narrator but haltingly by one Yonah, the nephew of one of
the shamashim. His breathless and agitated account of the outrage focuses
on the groom's status as an outsider to Buczacz. No native of the city would
have the effrontery to shout, "I shall not go under the canopy until the entire dowry promised by the bride's father has been deposited in my hand,
every last penny of it, every last cent!" (p. 579, 484).

The issue is not manners and civility but trust. Moshe Ta'anit, the
bride's father, had indeed promised a dowry of a certain amount, but at
the moment he doesn't have the money. If the bridegroom were a member of the Buczacz community, he would know without a shadow of a
doubt that the debt would be made good as soon as the father was back
in funds. But the bridegroom is among those outsiders who have shame-
fully scooped up Buczacz real estate on the cheap after the fire, and he
does not recognize or participate in the covenantal bonds of trust that
hold the community together. It is only by going outside the community
and threatening him with army conscription that there is a hope of getting him to relent and return to the ḥuppah. But this new man turns out
himself to be connected to the authorities, and when he retaliates with the
promise of sending the sons of those who threaten him to the army, there
is a general backing off and a throwing up of hands. He is gone for good.
And in the meantime, the bride has fainted from shock and lies lifeless on
the ground of the synagogue courtyard.

It is at this point, immediately after the gruesome news has been delivered, that Avraham David turns to his son and bids him replace the vanished
bridegroom under the ḥuppah. This is a stunning proposal on all counts. It
comes out of the blue without a shred of deliberation or forethought. From

the point of view of Menaḥem's life, such a marriage would have enormous consequences. In one stroke, he would be confounding the machinations of all the matchmakers and giving up his only chance for the kind of wealth and support that could underwrite his career as a great scholar. For years Menaḥem's parents have been embroiled in dilemmas about how to manage the potentially brilliant prospects of their sole surviving child. Avraham David and Sarah have faced this challenge together; their bond is deep and their relationship collaborative. And now Avraham David proposes to take this bold and consequential step unilaterally? This contradiction is not lost on Menaḥem. Always the respectful child, he utters at this juncture the funniest line in the story: "Perhaps we should tell Mother?" (p. 580, 486).

The father's response is to blanket the son with fervent sayings about the exalted status of saving even a single life and to tell a story about a girl who died because her father ignored her pleas for a drink of water. (Menaḥem annoys his father by citing the source for the story in the Jerusalem Talmud and thus adding to the delay in responding to the emergency.) Operating on the basis of only one hearsay report, Avraham David presents a picture of the bride as not merely having fainted but as being near death. His compulsion to act is so precipitous and peremptory that he is willing to forego consulting his marital partner on a decision that has endlessly preoccupied them as a couple and, further, to ignore calculating the long-term consequences for his son's life. Granting that Avraham David is a sensitive man who would sooner not see a victimized young woman continue to suffer, we are nonetheless left without an adequate explanation for his frenzied urgency.

We can make sense of his behavior only by reviewing what we know about Avraham David. In the long, garrulous speeches the narrator has indulgently allowed Avraham David, we hear a man who is wholly identified with the fortunes of his native town and who feels powerless to prevent its degradation. The distance between the narrator and his character, we have seen, is slight. From the opening sentence of the story, Avraham David's devotion to learning and acts of kindness is presented, with no small measure of pride and triumphalism, as typical of Buczacz at its best. Avraham David himself is deeply invested in an ideal of Buczacz as a city of modest economic means with an outsized and deserved reputation for producing outstanding scholars. He is also closely aligned with a now disused conception of marital choice based on spiritual-intellectual rather than material capital. Because of the value of his son on the marriage market, he feels an unconscious sense of being complicit in the forces that are undermining the integrity of his beloved city. Raḥel Leah the Pious was the exemplar of this lost order, and witnessing the ill-treatment of her granddaughter is more than he can bear. Rescuing the girl is tantamount to rescuing Buczacz from the threats that have beset it. A great chance has come his way, and he will not squander it no matter what.

But can he truly believe that a reversal of fortune can be achieved by a single intervention? Avraham David's inability *not* to act is fueled by another unacknowledged source: a desire to overcome his own unimportance. Between his father, who famously completed the entire Talmud eight times, and his prodigy son, who is poised to join the ranks of the great scholars, he finds himself a shopkeeper who can at most embody the ideals of the laity.

The anecdotes he tells his son about the renowned scholars whose formation took place in the city's institutions of learning and the long colloquy with the shamashim about the city's rabbis all breathe a pronounced sense of vicariousness. Vicarious also is his one opportunity to participate in this admired world through the placement of his son in a successful (read: wealthy) marriage. Such a marriage, however, could never be a vehicle for the salvation of more than his family. In renouncing riches and rescuing the abandoned bride, he is undertaking an act that—in his own mind and in the symbolic code of the story—leverages an individual rescue on behalf of the entire polity. And because it is Avraham David who initiates and orchestrates the improvised match, it is he who emerges from the margins and saves the day.

The father's coup, it hardly needs pointing out, can be realized only through the son. The triumph is diminished if it is coerced. Hence the care the story has taken, through several stages, to move Menaḥem from being a textual robot to becoming a young man who has some channel of experience beyond the walls of the beit midrash. It is perforce a limited transformation; the boy has not abandoned his habit of cross-referencing life experience with citations from the Talmud; but he has learned that occurrences in the world possess their own epistemological status rather than existing solely as a reflection of learned texts. Therefore, when he gives his implicit consent to his father's proposal with his affectingly understated "Perhaps we should tell Mother," he is no longer speaking simply as an extension of his parents' will but as a moral actor himself.

To his father, the glorious and redemptive meaning of the act is revealed in a flash, but it is not so clear what it means to Menahem. In a single moment, as it were, his conventional prospects, his great expectations, disappear. Although the *mitsvah* he is being enlisted to perform may indeed be spiritually exalted, its fulfillment ineluctably requires a form of (self-)sacrifice. The multivalent status of the story's climactic gesture is illuminated by the title Agnon chose for the story. "In a Single Moment" is a good equivalent for the Hebrew title "Besha'ah ahat," but it does not, understandably, toll the bell of allusion in a way that is evident to the literate Hebrew reader.

When Avraham David first broaches the idea of the substitute marriage, he points directly to the text alluded to when he states, "The Talmud teaches that 'one may win a place in eternity in a single moment'" (p. *580*, *487*). He is evoking the passage in *Avodah Zarah* 18b (also 10b and 17a) that describes the martyrdom of R. Hanina ben Teradion during the Hadrianic persecutions at the beginning of the second century of the Common Era. As a punishment for teaching the Torah in public, Hanina was burnt alive wrapped in a Torah scroll. Wet wool was placed around his heart to extend the agony of his death. His executioner was persuaded to remove the wool and hasten the execution in exchange for a promise of eternal life, whereupon he jumped into the pyre and was consumed. At this point

> A *bat kol* [a heavenly voice] exclaimed: R. Hanina b. Teradion and the Executioner have been assigned to the World to Come. When Rabbi heard it he wept and said: One person may acquire eternal life in a single moment, another after many years.

The narrative in the Talmud has its complexities, but its martyrological core is clear. Having been warned by his colleagues in an earlier passage to refrain from his public teaching of Torah, Hanina triggers his own death by his persistence in doing so. His martyrdom is self-sacrifice as well as a sacrifice, and one that elicits divine approval in the form of the bat kol that confirms his place in the world to come. "Rabbi" above is R. Judah the Prince, the greatest Sage of the time and the compiler of the Mishnah, and he interprets and generalizes the meaning of the divine voice. For the generality of the righteous, Rabbi concludes, it usually takes many years of meritorious deeds to secure a place in the world to come; but there does exist the possibility, exemplified by R. Hanina's martyrdom, of winning that place on the strength of a single act. Over the centuries, besha'ah ahat, "in a single moment," came to mean salvation or fame acquired by a single accomplishment. And thus the contemporary Hebrew reader would likely understand the title of the story. But Avraham David's referral to the Talmudic source returns us to the sacrificial origin of the term.

Two different conceptions of sacrifice are invoked in "A Single Moment." There is the sacrifice of innocence in the case of the abandoned bride. Rendered vulnerable by her poverty despite her respectable lineage, she fell victim to the cruelty and self-interest of the new moneyed class, free of covenantal bonds to Buczacz. Her sacrifice is involuntary and leads to collapse and suffering. Agnon need not elaborate on her ordeal because his story comes at the end of a long and lachrymose tradition in Yiddish and Hebrew literature, especially in poetry, of portraying the unenviable fate of a young girl who is essentially sold into the service of an older man to serve his needs and take care of his children from a previous marriage. Her situation is tragically inevitable because as a young girl from a family of reduced circumstances—the bride here is probably no more than fourteen—she has no agency of her own and she has no place she can respectably exist on her own between her father's household and that of a husband.

The sacrifice made by Menahem and his parents is very different. It too requires giving up something valuable, but the renunciation is voluntary, and the sacrifice is made for good purposes. It is an offering rather than victimization; and, although it entails material loss, it leads to a personal redemption that spreads to the collective. The *akedah*, Abraham's near-sacrifice of Isaac in Genesis 22 is not referred to explicitly in the story, yet the power of this archetypal topos cannot be avoided when the following components are conspicuously present: parents named Avraham and Sarah and a father and son walking together on a journey while the mother waits at home, clueless as to the son's impending sacrifice. In the biblical account and its rabbinic elaborations, as in this story, there is ambiguity about whether the participation of the Isaac-figure is passive or active, whether he is old enough to willingly offer himself. Here, too, a father is tested and makes a sudden, on-the-spot decision of fateful proportions.

For this Avraham, the test is especially necessary to give him and his wife the chance to dissipate—and make amend for—their unconscious ambivalence in finding a worthy mate for their son. Yet despite these similarities, the reason the presence of the akedah is muted is because the dénouement of "In a Single Moment" is caught up in joy, and that makes the story a kind of anti-akedah, an akedah turned on its head. There is no joy at the end of the akedah, only relief that a human sacrifice has been avoided and God appeased and then the abiding sadness that Sarah does not survive the trauma.

Joy, *simḥah*, is the keynote of the story's conclusion. The narrator of "In a Single Moment" joins the narrator of "Until Elijah Comes" in asserting that the joy that is unleashed by the performance of a righteous act has special infectious and self-propagating properties. When the shamash steps up to accept the aliyah of the Curses, a wave of joy seizes the entire synagogue. A similar phenomenon is described in "In a Single Moment" but on a grander, more sustained, and even more insistent level. News of the blessed marriage spreads with lightning speed throughout Buczacz and triggers an eruption of dancing on the part of the town's women. Sarah, who has been sitting in the recesses of her shop, hears the dancing and leaves the shop to join in. She is swept up in the rejoicing even though at this point she remains ignorant of its cause.

> When the other women saw what the two were doing, they, too, got up, put their hands on their hips, and danced, until the very ground under their feet was dancing. Do you think I am exaggerating when I say the ground

danced? No, it actually did. Do you think it danced more easily because it was denuded of houses? In fact, there were still the ruins of houses there, and these, too, danced. And those women who had forgotten how to dance with their feet did so with their hands, tapping their fingers so as to enliven the dancing. Do you think Sarah was unhappy because everyone was rejoicing and she did not know the reason? On the contrary, she was as happy as any of them. That is the power of true joy. Fortunate is he who is privileged to experience it; even without knowing what it is about, he can rejoice. So great is the power of joy, you see, that since the day Buczacz was founded there had never been a mother who went to her son's wedding in everyday clothes, but Sarah went in her shop clothes, and in spite of this her joy was uninterrupted and undiminished [. . . .]" (p. 584, 491–92)

The dancing described in this passage, it is important to note, takes place *before* the wedding ceremony. It is a spontaneous expression that erupts at the very news of Menahem's resolve to stand under the huppah with the abused bride. The narrator works very hard to persuade us that the dancing was so joyous that it turns hyperboles into literal truths and passes from the human realm to the surrounding physical world. The ground dances, and even the ruins, reminders of the town's calamity, are compelled to surrender to the exaltation. Can there be no greater testament to the power of true joy, the narrator sagely conjectures, than a mother's willingness to attend her son's wedding in her everyday clothes?

As the women shake the earth with their dancing, the scene switches to the male arena. The leisurely visit of the old hazzan R. Netanel to the rabbi is interrupted by the joyous clamor and then by the entrance of the shamash Mikhl Ber, who urges the rabbi to join the wedding party.[17] Doing so would be no small thing for the rabbi, who has not been seen in public since his return from Kamenets. But out of love for Buczacz he assents. Attired in his special rabbinic coat and his shtreimel and with his fabled walking stick in hand, he sets forth accompanied on his right by R. Netanel and on his left by Mikhl Ber. The composition of his retinue is not accidental. The hazzan, who is about to depart for the Land of Israel, represents the dialectical linkage between Buczacz and Zion, and the elderly shamash is valued by the rabbi as a font of anecdotes about his esteemed predecessors in the town's rabbinate. As they stride toward the courtyard of the Great Synagogue, they are thronged by old men and boys, "all wishing to welcome him back from Russia." The men join the women as the entire Jewish population of the city turns out to celebrate the wedding. This indeed is the city in its fullness.

That fullness is endowed with theological overtones. To be sure, Buczacz as a community deserves credit for returning to the true goodness of its former ways. The surprise betrothal is so discordant with the way of the world that people first are tempted to think that Mehaḥem's gesture is a means to further ridicule the bride. But "Buczacz being Buczacz, no native of the city could joke about one of their own who had fallen on hard times" (p. 581, 487). But the return to their former good ways is also accompanied by the return of God's grace: "The Eternal took pity on Buczacz, preventing improper outsiders from latching onto the daughters of the town" (p. 581 487). The epithet for God in the sentence is *Hamakom*, literally, the Place, and the relevance to Buczacz as a potentially holy space is clear. The concept that hovers over these sections is ḥesed—grace or good fortune—given above and beyond what is deserved. This is the epitome of the decision to wed the humiliated bride, of course. But who would have known that she is also beautiful? "She opened her lovely eyes and looked around. They shone radiantly, and everyone saw how lovely and fair she was" (p. 582, 488). Upon the scene as a whole shines down "the sweet sun," a sign throughout Agnon's work for God's grace.[18]

And so "In a Single Moment" ends in a grand consummation. The beloved but errant rabbi is reunited with his flock; a promising young scholar finds a true match based on kindness rather than greed, the anxiety of his parents allayed; a vulnerable young woman is rescued from an exploitative union; the life's work of a saintly woman is rewarded through the marriage of her granddaughter; the integrity of the marriage system is restored; and the dark forces of disintegration are held at bay. The gathering together of all these strands unleashes an explosion of joy that engulfs the entire community. Buczacz, for one shining moment, has again become Buczacz.

The transcendence and totality that conclude the story are real—real in the sense of being presented without irony—but their realness depends on a crucial condition: the redemption embodied in this fruition is, by its nature, evanescent. It is a moment of redemption, not Redemption itself. Here again the multivalence of the story's title serves both to expand and to constrict our hope. A single, sacrificial act of courageous kindness performed at the right time has the power to purchase an everlasting portion in the world to come. But in this world the duration of that redemption, no matter how illuminating its intensity is, can only be a moment. It is surely a moment that points in the direction of the everlasting Redemption, but it remains contained. And yet, as in the case of the shamash and Elijah, this is not nothing.

The narrator looks ahead to the future progeny of the auspicious match that has just been solemnized under the huppah:

> Thus it was that all the sons and grandsons of Menaḥem, son of Avraham David, were devoted to the study of Torah and obedient to the Torah, among them scholars of halakhah, *well-known in the gates*[19]—until the enemy came and wiped them all out. They were wiped out, but the mercies of Him who is to be blessed were not. Every good deed bears fruit, which, in turn, bears more fruit. And if the Almighty grants me life and strength and tranquility, I shall relate some of the good deeds that the good among the people of Israel did when the Holy One, blessed be He, was good to Israel, and Israel was beloved of the Holy One (p. *588, 497*).

Many of the stories in *A City in Its Fullness* end with this pattern: generation upon generation continued the way of life of the Jewish community of Buczacz until its sudden annihilation by the Nazis. Lacking in this instance are the epithets of revulsion and denunciation that usually accompany these closing references to the enemy. The reason for this austerity is likely connected to the turn toward God's mercies in the next line and a disinclination to position rhetoric of perfidy in proximity of God's name. The juxtaposition itself between absolute evil and absolute good requires linguistic finesse. Agnon takes the root *k.l.h.* and exploits the difference in its meaning between its transitive sense (to wipe out) and its intransitive sense (to cease to be, to be exhausted). The Nazis wiped out the Jews, who ceased to exist as the community of Buczacz as a result, but God's mercies have not been exhausted.

In the closing paragraph, the voice of the narrator collapses into that of Agnon, the author and magister of the entire project of the Buczacz stories.

The idea that good deeds bear fruit that in turn produce more fruit is central to "In a Single Moment." Joy propagates more joy, and a marriage founded on an act of kindness is destined to produce learned and God-fearing progeny. Yet, by a barely perceptible sleight of hand, this notion is transposed from the representational plane of Buczacz and the stories about it to the vocation of the writer. The process of propagation and bearing fruit now takes place, or continues to take place, not in the good deeds themselves but in the writing about them. The potential recipient of God's grace ("if the Almighty grants me life and strength and tranquility") is the writer himself. Unspoken is the failure of God's grace to avail the Jews of Buczacz, whose ancestors are the subject the writer takes for himself. Agnon's intentionality reverberates strongly in these closing lines. The death of his city will not be his theme but its life; yet, in the aftermath of his city's destruction, that life will be known only through his stories.

Epilogue

In "The Sign," the consecration story that initiates the writing of the Buczacz tales, the narrator sits in a small synagogue in the Talpiyot neighborhood of Jerusalem on the night of the Shavuot holiday. Earlier that day, news had reached him of the final murder of the Jews of Buczacz, his Galician home town, and he is repressing his grief. Sitting alone, he undergoes two experiences. In his mind's eye, he returns to Buczacz and repopulates the city—placing each Jewish male in his customary seat in the synagogue. Then he falls asleep and dreams he is back in Buczacz conversing with two ghosts, who describe the city's decimation in the "first destruction" during World War One and its utter destruction during World War Two. The narrator is caught between nostalgia and nightmare, the two modalities—identified by Arnold Band—which Agnon used to deal with the past. But suddenly the great medieval poet Solomon Ibn Gabirol reveals himself to the narrator and presents another option. He composes a sacred song, a piyyut, so the community of Buczacz will not be forgotten. His gesture invites the Agnon-like narrator, who has had a special connection to liturgical poetry throughout his life, to follow suit. Unlike nostalgia and nightmare that visit themselves upon the vacant mind of the narrator, Ibn Gabirol models a willed act of memorialization.

Thus Agnon heeds the call to build a city in its fullness, an undertaking that occupies the last fifteen years of his life. He does so on his own terms as a modern master who purposefully camouflages his modernism to immerse himself in the premodern world and move about freely within it. He invents a talkative, semi-reliable narrator whose values and beliefs reflect the time "when Buczacz was Buczacz." He cannily exploits the digressions and excursus of traditional storytelling to infuse the narratives with ironic insight. In this way he fashions stories that communicate simultaneously to the implied audience of the traditional narrator two centuries ago in Buczacz as well as to contemporary readers of Hebrew literature in Israel.

To represent the world of his ancestors, Agnon sought a literary form that could impose a loose unity upon varied acts of imagination. *A City in Its Fullness*, the volume edited by Agnon's daughter according to his guidelines, is a story cycle. It is neither a novel nor merely a collection of stories. The short story is undoubtedly Agnon's métier, yet all his life he pursued the prestige of the novel. What Agnon accomplished in *A City in Its Fullness* represents a hard-won wisdom, a late-in-life accommodation between his gifts and his desires. In the end, he found a way to have his cake and eat it too. He hit upon an epic novel-like sequence of individual stories, and this coherent yet loose design gave Agnon the freedom to vary the fictional formats and make adjustments in the voice and persona of the narrator in the major stories. Variations could be made as well in the narrator's reliability as an informant and in the degree of criticalness and sympathy with which he relates the behavior of the characters.

What about Agnon's own reliability in recreating the world of Polish Jewry in earlier centuries? The studies in this volume reveal a complex relationship to the historical record, which moves along a gradient from verisimilitude to creative freedom. To begin with, Agnon sought to supply his readers with an abundance of information about the Buczacz Jewish community between the middle of the seventeenth century and the middle of the nineteenth. Like a responsible ethnographer, he works into the stories information about the community's institutions and occupations, its geography and city plan, its customs and folklore. Agnon is all the while engaged in an implicit dialogue with his Israeli readers aimed at revising the received image of the shtetl in the Zionist imagination. By contrast, Buczacz is presented, in the best of times at least, as a self-governing city-state that creatively negotiated its proud existence under a succession of gentile regimes.

At the same time, Agnon has no interest in giving us merely a flattened, objective, and historically accurate Buczacz. Every strong artistic representation contains a bias and an angle of vision. In these stories, Agnon makes no apology for giving us his version of Buczacz by recouping the city under the sign of study and worship, *torah ve'avodah*, and proceeding to organize his fictional universe around these two values. Yet, as a great imaginative writer, Agnon also knows that the stuff of good stories lies not in the norms but in the deviations from norms. A young mother, endowed with a great gift for sacred music, wastes away because she was not born a man. A prayer leader with a seraphic voice cannot pull back from destroying himself in his quest to draw close to the holy. Buczacz loses out on the chance to be served by one of the great scholars of the generation because of his refusal to mix theoretical studies with communal leadership. In *A City in Its Fullness*, Buczacz is constituted in the space between the aspirations toward these ideals and the realities of human nature and political existence.

At his freest, Agnon does not hold back from subverting the historical record altogether. At the level of background, texture, and detail, all the stories loyally hew to their time and place. But in some large matters Agnon intervenes and reverses the oracles. Although the Jews of Buczacz and the lands that became Galicia faithfully served the interests of their noble Polish masters, they remained merely tolerated and more often than not despised and ill treated. And this was despite the broad literacy of the Jews, the discipline and self-sufficiency of their families and communities, and the flowering of a high scholarly culture. This deeper truth could be conveyed by making use of the imaginative freedom afforded by storytelling. Agnon could rewrite the master-slave paradigm of Polish-Jewish relations by constructing one narrative in which a great Polish prince is rescued from death by a Jewish mead merchant whose worldly wisdom is acknowledged or another in which Count Potocki, the fearsome owner of Buczacz, is saved by a humble Jewish charcoal maker, who leverages the count's gratitude to obtain a permanent place for his family in the town's great city hall. Agnon knew that it would be through his stories that future generations of readers would understand the experience of Polish Jewry, and he thus sought to draw out its deeper meaning, the meaning concealed behind the gross facts of historical arrangements. His stories were performing a necessary act of correction, a gesture of tikkun.

Alas, at a midpoint in *A City in Its Fullness*, the worthiness of Buczacz and what it represents are put in question. We know very little about the order in which Agnon wrote the stories included in the work, but we do know that he wanted the volume to be laid out in a clear historical progression moving from the centuries of Polish rule to the advent of the Austrian regime. The idealization of Buczacz as a thriving holy community is centered on the period before the Partition and concentrated in books 1 and 2 in *A City in Its Fullness*. Something fundamental happens between the book's dedication, with its pious encomia in praise of the destroyed holy community of Buczacz, and the degraded state of communal leadership that is depicted in the Austrian stories. It is as if Agnon threw himself into the project of bringing Buczacz back to life without realizing where this imaginative journey might take him. We can be only grateful that Agnon's allegiance to the truth yielded a many-faced Buczacz, all the dearer for its fragility.

East European Jewry, the great cradle of the modern Jewish people, is almost unknowable in its vast spread over many lands and many centuries. Agnon's great coup is to choose one place, no matter how middling its importance, and drill down into its bedrock. This is Agnon's modernity rather than his nostalgia. He knows that it is only through the radical particularity of one community do we gain the chance to fathom the soul of a people. His narrator seeks to make us into honorary or virtual Buczaczers, and we have no reason to resist. We realize that we are witnessing a unique cultural gesture: a great modernist writer turning toward the Jewish past and deploying his gifts to bring it back to life on his own terms. We cannot know whether future writers—according to their own lights, of course—will follow Agnon's lead and provide us with imaginative engagements with the lost ancestral world. For the time being, it has been no small thing to tread the soil of Buczacz.

Notes

Introduction

1. Lilian Dabi-Guri, *Kurzweil-Agnon-Atsag: Ḥilufei Iggarot* [Kurzweil-Agnon-Uri Zvi Greenberg: Correspondence] (Ramat Gan: Bar Ilan University Press, 1987), 56.

2. *Moznayim* 18, no. 2 (1942): 103–4; the full version appeared in *Ha'esh veha'etsim* (Tel Aviv and Jerusalem: Schocken, 1962), 263–315. The one-page kernel from 1944 describes the revelation of Ibn Gabirol's presence. Despite its literary artifice, the story insists on a true mystical experience as its generating core, and an early, fragmentary record of this event strengthens the claim. For the translation by Arthur Green, see Alan Mintz and Jeffrey Saks, eds., *A City in Its Fullness* (New Milford, CT: Toby Press, 2016), 1–30.

3. Translation by Arthur Green. For the text of the story and interpretive approaches to it, see Alan Mintz, ed., *Reading Hebrew Literature: Critical Discussions of Six Modern Texts* (Hanover, NH: Brandeis University Press, 2003), 103–4.

4. Yisrael Cohen, ed., *Sefer Buczacz* (Tel Aviv: Am Over, 1957). The volume and an English translation of its contents is at http://www.buchach.org/book/index.htm.

5. Yisrael Cohen, *Ḥilufei mikhtavim bein Shai Agnon veDavid Ben-Gurion* [Correspondence between Shai Agnon and David Ben-Gurion], ed. Nurit Govrin (Tel Aviv: Eked, 1985), 20–82. The prospect for the volume can be found on pp. 23–25.

6. Ka-Tsetnik, *Beit habubot* (Tel Aviv: Dvir, 1953); Ka-Tsetnik, *House of Dolls,* trans. Moshe M. Kohn (New York: Lion Library, 1956).

7. Alan Mintz, *Ḥurban: Responses to Catastrophe in Hebrew Literature* (New York: Columbia University Press, 1984).

8. On the Holocaust in Agnon's work, see Sidra DeKoven Ezrahi, "Agnon Before and After," *Prooftexts: A Journal of Jewish Literary History* 2, no. 1 (1982): 78–94; and Dan Laor, "Did Agnon Write about the Holocaust?" *Yad Vashem Studies* 22 (1992): 17–63.

9. *Ḥurban,* 2–3.

10. For a general account of the representations of the shtetl, see Dan Miron, *The Image of the Shtetl and Other Studies of Modern Jewish Literary Imagination* (Syracuse: Syracuse University Press, 2001). It is important to note that Agnon himself never used the term *shtetl* or its Hebrew equivalent *'ayyarah.* Throughout *A City in Its Fullness,* he refers to Buczacz as *'iri,* my city. Hebrew has a separate term, *krakh,* for a metropolis, and this was reserved for a city like Lviv.

11. Yehudah Friedlander, "Masekhet shivah ufreidah" [Return and leave taking], *Haaretz*, June 1, 1973; and "A City and the Fullness Thereof," *Hebrew Book Review* (Autumn, 1973): 3–6; Hillel Barzel, "*Ir umeloah*: uvdah uvedayah" [*A City in Its Fullness*: Fact and invention], *Yediyot Aḥaronot*, September 26, 1973; Yaakov Rabi, "Hatorah, ha'emunah, vemirmat hatsedakah" [Torah, belief, and the dishonesty of charity], *Al Hamishmar*, October 12, 1973; Yisrael Cohen, "Haḥavayah ha'arkhitipit shel *Ir umeloah*" [The archetypal world of *A City in Its Fullness*], *Moznayim* 28, nos. 1–2 (Dec.–Jan., 1973–74), 61–73; A. Y. Brawer, "*Ir umeloah*: 'Olam shene'lam" [*Ir umeloah*: A world that disappeared], *Ha'umah* (April, 1974): 246–53.

12. I discussed these changes in *Ḥurban*.

13. Shmuel Werses, *Shai Agnon kifshuto: Keri'ah bikhtavav* [*S. Y. Agnon Literally: Studies in His Writings*] (Jerusalem: Mossad Bialik, 2000); and *Relations between Poles and Jews in S. Y. Agnon's Work* (Jerusalem: Magnes Press of the Hebrew University, 1994).

14. Roman Katsman, *Keinut veretorikah beIr Umeloah leShai Agnon* [Sincerity and rhetoric in *A City in Its Fullness* by S. Y. Agnon] (Ramat Gan: Bar-Ilan University Press, 2013).

15. Cambridge, UK: Cambridge Scholars, 2013.

16. Jerusalem and Tel Aviv: Schocken, 2002.

17. Michal Arbell, *Katuv 'al 'oro shel kelev: Tefisat hayetsirah etsel Shai Agnon* [Written on a dog's skin: The conception of creation in Shai Agnon] (Be'er Sheva and Tel Aviv: Ben-Gurion University and Keter, 2008); "The Melancholic Ḥazzanit Miriam Devorah and Other Ḥazzanim in Agnon's Stories: 'Hahazzanim' and 'Lefi hatsa'ar hasekhar'" [in Hebrew], *Ayin Gimel: Ketav eit leḥequer yetsirat Agnon* 2 (2012): 108–30, http://www .biu.ac.il/js/li/aj/images_ag_eng/second_issue_eng.html; and "R. Amnon of Mainz as Paragon: The Development of a Cultural Icon in the Works of Agnon" [in Hebrew] in *Studies in Jewish Narrative* vol. 2, ed. Avidov Lipsker and Rella Kushelevsky (Ramat Gan: Bar-Ilan University Press, 2009).

18. "Providence and Redemption in the Fish's [Whale's] Belly: Part 1: The Book of Jonah, the Midrashic Versions, Jakob Steinhardt's Illustrated Edition" [in Hebrew], 46–68; and "'Mazal Dagim (Pisces)' by S. Y. Agnon: The Disgust from the Real and the Despair of the Representative, Yosl Bergner's Illustrated Edition" [in Hebrew], 69–82, in *Ayin Gimel: A Journal of Agnon Studies,* http://www.biu.ac.il/js/li/aj/index.html.

19. New York: Simon and Schuster, forthcoming.

20. In her memoirs, she provides a broader picture of her work on the many posthumous volumes of her father's work. Emunah Yaron, *Pirkei ḥayyai* [Memoirs] (Jerusalem and Tel Aviv: Schocken, 2005). See, esp., pp. 197–223.

21. Page 717, quoting from David Knaani, *Shai Agnon be'al peh* [S. Y. Agnon in his own words] (Tel Aviv: Hakibbutz Hameuchad, 1971), 50. The passage, in a fuller form, is returned to in Chapter 2.

22. Yisrael Cohen, "The Reflection of One City," *Moznayim* 3–4 (1940–41): 265–70.

23. A. Y. Brawer, "Agnon's Buczacz," *Moznayim* (April–May 1970): 422–30.

24. Avraham Holtz, *Mar'ot umekorot: Mahadurah mu'eret umeyu'eret shel Hakhnasat kalah leShai Agnon* [Sights and sources: An annotated and illustrated edition of S. Y. Agnon's *Hakhnasat kalah*] (Jerusalem and Tel Aviv: Schocken, 1995).

Chapter 1

1. S. Y. Agnon, *A City in Its Fullness*, ed. Alan Mintz and Jeffrey Saks (New Milford, CT: Toby Press, 2016), 10; the extract comes from the translation by Raymond P. Scheindlin that first appeared in *A Book That Was Lost and Other Stories by S. Y. Agnon* (New York: Schocken, 1996), 233–39.

2. Translation by Raymond P. Scheindlin.

3. Nevertheless, Buczacz is itself portrayed as drawing some of its natural charm from the Land of Israel. In the text that immediately follows "Buczacz," the narrator states that "the Holy One Blessed Be He, as it were, borrowed from the majesty of His land and loaned it to our city" (p. *14*).

4. Mikołaj Potocki was one of the wealthiest of the Potocki clan. His annual income was calculated to be about 50,000 ducats. (This amount is equal to 900,000 zloties. The monthly wage of a carpenter before 1772 was 20 zloties, enough to support a small family. My thanks to Gershon Hundert for this information.) His primary title was Starosta of Kaniow, the administrator and tenant for life of a major crown estate on the Dnieper. In addition to owning Buczacz, he had major estates in Potok, Horodenka, and Gologor. He maintained a private army of up to three thousand men, and he was known for terrorizing large swathes of Polish Rus, especially Lviv, on drunken, debauched, and destructive binges. Out of remorse for the misdeeds of his youth, he later undertook large acts of philanthropy and gave major endowments to the Catholic Church (both Roman and Greek Catholic [i.e., Uniate]); he was also a patron of the arts as evinced by the commission to Bernardo Meretti to design the rococo town hall in Buczacz. Later in life he converted to the Greek Catholic Church and took up residence in the monastery of the Basilian Brothers in Buczacz. (My thanks to Professor George Lukowski.)

5. See Larry Wolff, *The Idea of Galicia: History and Fantasy in Habsburg Political Culture* (Stanford: Stanford University Press, 2010).

6. Agnon allows his narrator to minimize the importance of Hasidism in Buczacz. Because the book showcases the city before the second half of the nineteenth century, after which Hasidic prayer houses were more firmly established, the Hasidic presence can be kept to the margins. Nonetheless, Buczacz remained less hospitable than other cities in Galicia.

7. For a general picture of the "destruction of Galician Jewry" during World War One, see S. Ansky, *The Enemy at His Pleasure: A Journey through the Pale of Settlement during World War I,* trans. J. Neugroschel (New York: Metropolitan, 2002).

8. I use the term focus because there are mentions of later developments in the last section of book 3 of *A City in Its Fullness.* The more crucial question pertains to Agnon's intentions as to the later boundaries of his project. In one of his few remarks about the project, as reported by Canaani (*S. Y. Agnon Ba'al Peh* [Merhaviah: Hakibbutz Hameuchad Publishing, 1971], 52), Agnon declared that the final book within the volume would deal with modern times and the spread of Zionism and socialism in Buczacz. Was Agnon prevented from accomplishing this goal by his death, or did he change his plans in the course of writing the earlier sections and decide not to bring the narrative into the World War One period? I would argue for the latter option in

light of the internal evidence of the book itself and the author's repeated insistence that he wishes to deal with the history of this town "when Buczacz was Buczacz," that is when it was governed internally by the rule of Torah.

9. Quoted in Dan Laor, *Hayyei Agnon* [S.Y. Agnon, a biography] (Jerusalem and Tel Aviv: Schocken, 1998), 485, 693.

10. I am using the term "pre-modern" here to resonate with the sense of time that Agnon creates; today, historians describe this period as "early modern."

11. The diversity and complexity of the issues surrounding the role of minhag in Jewish practice are surveyed in Moshe David Herr and Menachem Elon, s.v. "Minhag," *Encyclopaedia Judaica,* ed. Michael Berenbaum and Fred Skolnik, 2nd ed., vol. 14 (Detroit: Macmillan Reference USA, 2007), 265–78. Accessed Dec. 13, 2012 from the *Gale Virtual Reference Library.*

12. The narrator is aware that his readers may find his preoccupation with minhagim excessive, and he thus moved to offer a justification whose overladen rhetoric speaks for itself: "It is because of the love I feel for the minhagim of the Jewish people with which the holy sages have distinguished ('itru) us—whom in turn the Holy One has distinguished with the Torah—that I have rendered a detail-by-detail account and explained to you each minhag; for if the matter is trivial in your eyes, it was significant in the eyes of our ancestors (p.42)."

13. The translation of this story has been published separately as *The Parable and Its Lesson,* trans. James S. Diamond (with a critical essay by Alan Mintz) (Stanford: Stanford University Press, 2014).

14. The narrator, slipping back into the role of the modern author, testifies that when he was growing up in Buczacz the urgency of 20 Sivan had so waned that there was only one minyan of worshipers, of which he was one, who still observed the fast (pp. *38–39*).

15. Two explanations are given for the origin of this prayer. In this context (p. *21*), we are told that it was brought to Buczacz from Ashkenaz by the ancient founders of the city. In "The Parable and Its Lesson" it is ascribed to the revivalist response of the community to hearing the shamash's account of his journey to Gehinnom (p. *436*).

16. *Perlnik* is presumably a Polish word for beating laundry. (Thanks to Avraham Holtz and David Roskies for this reference.)

17. See Chapter 7.

18. See the fruitful interpretation of the gabbaiim stories in Roman Katsman, "Sh. Y. Agnon's Community Rhetoric: The Heroism and Crisis of Power in Two Tales of the Gabbais (Treasurers) from Ir U-Meloah (The City and All It Has in It)," *Hebrew Studies* 52 (2011): 363–78.

19. Agnon came the closest to a representation in the story "Shenei talmidei hakhamim shehayu be'ireinu" [Two scholars who lived in our town]. The story first appeared in *Luah Haaretz* in 1957; it was included in volume 6 of Agnon's collected stories *Samukh venir'eh* (Jerusalem and Tel Aviv: Schocken, 1962), 5–53. Translated by Paul Pinchas Bashan and Rhonna Wever Rogol, the story can be found in S.Y. Agnon, *Two Scholars Who Were in Our Town* (New Milford, CT: Toby Press, 2014). I regard the story as belonging to the materials of the corpus of *A City in Its Fullness.* The reason it was not

included in the book was because it had already been published in an earlier volume, and Agnon appears to have been insistent that *A City in Its Fullness* contain only material that had not previously appeared in book form.

20. Following the stories about Yeraḥmiel the grandfather and Yeraḥmiel the grandson on pages *195–205*, there are a series of vignettes that underscore and illustrate the centrality of Torah study in Buczacz. One concerns the famous scholar R. Yaakov Yehoshua Falk, the Penei Yehoshua, who found the town a hospitable place to settle when he had to flee Lviv after being dismissed as the rabbi of the city by the rulers. Another tells of his intransigent son whom only the learned air of Buczacz could turn toward the study of Torah. Another tells the story of R. Meshulam Igra, who grew up as a prodigy within the beit midrash of Buczacz and became the rabbi of Tisminitz before going on to Pressburg. Still another describes the famous rabbi of Lviv, the Turei Zahav, in disguise overhearing the give and take between two porters in Buczacz, a father and a son, as they critically evaluate his work.

21. A survey of the spaces of Buczacz would not be complete without mentioning the netherworld, i.e., Gehinnom, which can be accessed, as the astonished Jews of Buczacz learn in the story "The Parable and Its Lesson," from a portal not far from the town. When it comes to the construction of space, this one exists, it need hardly be said, at a different level altogether.

22. One wonders whether Agnon's story has its origins in a kind of back formation or midrash on the curious, longstanding name of the place as the Fedor Hill.

Chapter 2

1. James S. Diamond, trans., *The Parable and Its Lesson* (Stanford: Stanford University Press, 2014), pp. 67–68.

2. The passage is remarkable because it lays out a kind of chain of loss. The Strypa overflows its banks and washes away the boy's tombstone; one of the great periodic fires damages the pinkas; and finally the Nazis destroyed it utterly. The narrator points to the loss of the pinkas as a rationale for his preoccupation with the details of Buczacz life: "Therefore be not astonished that each time I mention our city I go on in great detail; for if these details are not important in your eyes, they are important in the eyes of all those who saw the city in its greatness and mourn for its loss from the world" (p. *186*).

3. For an excellent summary of the significance of the pinkas, see Israel Bartal, *Letaken 'am: Ne'orut ule'umiyut be mizraḥ eiropah* [To Redeem a People: Jewish Nationalism and Enlightenment in Eastern Europe] (Jerusalem: Carmel, 2013), 1–33.

4. Ariel Hirschfeld, *Likro' et Shai Agnon* [Reading Shai Agnon] (Tel Aviv: Ahuzat Bayit, 2011), 217–38. Hirschfeld's readings focus on the stories "Sefer takhlit hama'asim," "Hadom vekise," and "Le'aḥar hase'udah." See also Edward Said, *On Late Style: Music and Literature against the Grain* (New York: Vintage, 2007).

5. Arnold Band, *Nostalgia and Nightmare: A Study in the Fiction of S.Y. Agnon* (Berkeley and Los Angeles: University of California Press, 1968), 330–65.

6. A qualification is in order here. This kind of renunciation is not unprecedented in Agnon's work. Some major stories that deal with the ancestral world of Buczacz also display this quality. These include "The Crooked Shall Be Made Straight" [Vehayah

he'akov lemishor], "The Outcast" [Hanidaḥ], and "Two Scholars Who Were in Our City" [Shenai talmidei ḥakhamim shehayu be'ireinu]. (It is no coincidence that all these works deal with the classical world of Buczacz or Galicia.) The first two are very early works, and the last one was written close to the time of the composition of the Buczacz stories. This makes a case for Agnon reaching back to modes of narration in his repertoire to fix a standard for the larger, later project.

7. A translation of the story, by Amiel Gut, appears in *A Book That Was Lost and Other Stories by S.Y. Agnon,* ed. Alan Mintz and Anne Golumb Hoffman (New York: Schocken, 1995), 128–35.

8. The book, whose authorship is anonymous, was first printed in Izmir in 1732–33. Much scholarly controversy surrounds the question of the volume's Sabbatean roots. It is an important source for our knowledge of kabbalistic practices, and it documents the revival of the celebration of Tu Bishvat and the innovation of the tikkun leil Shavuot, the all-night study vigil on the first day of Shavuot.

9. The narrator goes on to explain that this girl married a grain merchant named Feivush Ringelblum and that their son was none other than Emanuel Ringelblum, the organizer of the Oyneg Shabbes archive in the Warsaw Ghetto.

10. For an additional example, see the last paragraph of the story "The Ḥazzanim, Continued," *122,* 152–53 in which the narrator, while a student in the beit midrash during his adolescence, recalls showing his own poems to the then ḥazzan of Buczacz, who set some of them to melodies.

11. A good example of slight but crucial differences can be seen in comparing "Feivush Gazlan" with "Disappeared." Both stories are part of the cycle of tales relating to communal corruption brought by Austrian rule. The narrator of "Feivush" is intent on denying the regrettable behavior of the townspeople of Buczacz, whereas the narrator of "Disappeared" takes a much more critical, if resigned, attitude to similar conduct.

12. See note 1 above.

13. I have described how the story plays with received ideas of postmortem existence in the introduction to S.Y. Agnon, *A Parable and Its Lesson* (Stanford: Stanford University Press, 2014).

14. *Parable,* 9.

15. *Parable,* 1–2.

16. See the genealogy of art and writing enunciated by the narrator of Agnon's 1937 story "Ḥush hareaḥ" [A sense of smell] in *Elu ve'elu* (Tel Aviv: Schocken, 1962), 296–302. See the discussion above in the Introduction and in Alan Mintz, ed., *Reading Hebrew Literature: Critical Discussions of Six Modern Texts* (Hanover, NH: Brandeis University Press, 2003), 103–4.

17. See the histrionic protestations of the narrator in the opening paragraph of "Pisces" that bring this theme to a comic consummation.

18. This discussion is focused on the hermeneutic situation of *A City in Its Fullness* when the stories were published and later collected in the 1973 volume. Put aside for the moment is the question of a later audience, such as ourselves in the present moment, and future readers of Agnon. It is an issue that I reflect upon from time to time in the course of this study.

19. On audiences and narratees, see Peter J. Rabinowitz, "Truth in Fiction: A Reexamination of Audiences," *Critical Inquiry* 4, no. 1 (Autumn 1977): 121–41; James Phelan, *Narrative as Rhetoric: Technique, Audiences, Ethics, Ideology* (Columbus: Ohio State University Press, 1996), 135–53; Susan Sniader Lanser, *The Narrative Act: Point of View in Prose Fiction* (Princeton, NJ: Princeton University Press, 1981) 130–48.

20. This aspect of the story is analyzed in my "Reading 'Haḥazzanim,'" *Ayin Gimmel: A Journal of Agnon Studies* 2 (2012): 93–107, http://www.biu.ac.il/js/li/aj/images_ag_eng/second_issue_eng.html.

21. This is the famous gap between *fabula* and *sujet*; I prefer to use the terms proposed by Shlomit Rimmon-Kenan: *story*, which denotes the "raw" chronological sequence of events within the work's fictional world, and *text,* the order in which these events are narrated or released into the knowledge of the reader. See Shlomit Rimmon-Kenan, *Narrative Fictions: Contemporary Poetics,* 2nd ed. (London: Rutledge, 2002), 7–30, 45–60.

22. "A Parable and Its Lesson" is a complex work, in part because the main narrator hands the story over to another narrator, and in part because the events surrounding the journey to Gehinnom took place more than a half century before the present time of the narration. For a fuller discussion of the story, see *Parable*, 79–155.

23. Translation by Jeffrey Green.

Chapter 3

1. "The Sign" ["Hasiman"], trans. Arthur Green in *A Book That Was Lost and Other Stories by S. Y. Agnon*, ed. Alan Mintz and Anne G. Hoffman (New Milford, CT: Toby Press, 2008), 397–429; and in Alan Mintz, ed., *City*, 1–29.

2. On the subject generally, see the important early essay by Hillel Weiss, "Stories about Ḥazzanim by Agnon," *Maariv*, April 8, 1977.

3. See the illuminating essay by Ze'ev Weiss, "When Did They Begin to Lower the Prayer Leader before the Teivah?" [in Hebrew] *Cathedra* 55 (1990): 8–21; also Raphael Loewe, "Ark, Archaism and Misappropriation" in *Biblical Hebrews, Biblical Texts: Essay in Memory of Michael P. Weitzman,* ed. Ada Rapoport-Albert and Gillian Greenberg (Sheffield: Sheffield Academic, 2001).

4. Ezra Fleischer, *Shirat haqodesh bimei habeinayim* [Hebrew liturgical poetry in the middle ages] (Jerusalem: Keter, 1975), 23–39.

5. The experience described probably refers to the kind of fervent ecstatic prayer that renders worshipers oblivious to the world around them.

6. The animation or anthropomorphism of the teivah has a parallel in the treatment of the altar, the mizbeaḥ, in the Temple, which it replaced. There are numerous mentions in the midrash of the altar mourning and shedding tears over the exile of the Shekhinah.

7. Agnon returned to reinforce his descent from the Levites and his relationship to song in his Nobel Prize acceptance speech. See http://www.nobelprize.org/nobel_prizes/literature/laureates/1966/agnon-speech.html. This connection was discussed in the Introduction.

8. For an expansion of this idea, see Michal Arbell, "The Sad Ḥazzanit Miriam

Devorah and Other Ḥazzanim in Agnon's Stories 'Haḥazzanim' and 'Lefi hatsaʻar hasekhar'" [in Hebrew], *Ayin Gimel: Ketav eit leḥequer yestirat Agnon* no. 2 (2012): 108–30, http://www.biu.ac.il/js/li/aj/images_ag_eng/second_issue_eng.html.

9. The verb *lenagen*, which today refers to playing an instrument, also meant to sing in earlier Hebrew.

10. *City*, 716; *Book That Was Lost*, 429.

11. Translation by Saul Zaritt.

12. The 20th of Sivan, which falls in the late spring, was a fast day that memorialized the martyrs of the 1648 massacres. It is described at length in James S. Diamond, trans., *The Parable and Its Lesson*, (Stanford: Stanford University Press, 2014).

13. On this story, see Roman Katsman, "'The Cantors' Unrealizable: The Communal Rhetoric of S. Y. Agnon" [in Hebrew], *Ayin Gimel: Ketav eit leḥequer yestirat Agnon* no. 2 (2012): 131–37 (http://www.biu.ac.il/js/li/aj/images_ag_eng/second_issue_eng .html). The biblical prototype for the name Miriam was both a prophetess and singer of songs. The biblical Devorah, in addition to being a warrior leader, was the author of an epic song.

14. The chronology here seems fanciful. If the figure of the narrator correlates with Agnon, who was a boy in the beit midrash of Buczacz at the end of the nineteenth century, there are a number of generations to be accounted for between him and Miriam Devorah at the end of the seventeenth.

15. For a good overview see the Hebrew Wikipedia site under "qol ishah ʻervah."

16. The term for melancholy in the story is *marah sheḥorah*. The description of the progress of the symptoms toward death given on p. *76* (86) of the story coincides remarkably with clinical accounts of melancholy.

17. A significant digression within R. Mikhl's story concerns his second wife Mindl. A famous song about Count Potocki terrorizing a poor Jew on his way to synagogue Friday evening is supposedly based on incidents in her father's life, and the narrator goes so far as to translate a stanza of the song from Polish. This is yet another instance of poetry and songs being based upon persecution. Mindl herself is an additional example of a good woman dependent upon an unreliable man. The infestation of bed bugs, which torment the new bride, took root in the two months of household neglect between the death of his wife and his remarriage.

18. This was a work that was thought to have been written under Sabbatean influence. On this matter, see Tzahi Weiss, "'Things That Are Better Concealed Than Revealed': An Historical-Biographical Study of S. Y. Agnon's Attitude toward the Sabbatean Movement and the Traditional Jewish World," *AJS Review* 36:1 (April 2012): 104, n. 4. Agnon's attitude toward the book seems to have shifted from early enthusiasm to later ambivalence.

19. The story's final paragraph coyly hints at a channel of lineal influence that cannot be stopped up. Miriam Devorah's youngest son Elḥanan, although married into a shopkeeping life, is a dreamy poet whose mind cannot cease composing Hebrew verse.

20. September 26 and 29 and October 10.

21. Translation by Raymond Scheindlin.

22. Ezekiel 9:4, 6; and Daniel 8:16 and 9:21. For a survey of these sources, see Mal-

kah Poni, "'The Man Clad in Linen': Tradition and Innovation in the Development of a Literary Theme" [in Hebrew], *Meḥqerei Givʿah* (1988–89): 47–99. The high priest is also referred by the epithet *levush habadim* (dressed in linen), according to Goldschmidt, referring to the Yerushalmi. See E. D. Goldschmidt, *Maḥzor layamim hanora'im* (Jerusalem: Koren, 1970), 455. There is perceptible difference between the Yiddish moniker (the linen man), which pertains to an economic occupation and the Hebrew term (the man dressed in linen), with its supernal textual resonances. I use "the linen man" simply for its convenient concision.

23. It is worth pointing out that the coins are taken out of a strongbox called *teivat hashulḥan*, and teivah is also the word used later in the story when Gavriel's wife produces coins from a container. The term teivah in the sacramental sense we have been using it derives, of course, from the fact that it was a box that contained the fragments of the Tablets of the Law and then the Torah scrolls. Yet the contrast between these two uses of the term remains intriguing. In another intriguing connection, teivah is also a Hebrew term for a word.

24. On the tragic dimension in Agnon, see Ariel Hirschfeld, *Likro et Shai Agnon* [reading Agnon] (Tel Aviv: Ahuzat Bayit, 2011).

25. The martyrological dimensions of the term *ʿolah* are clear. This is the one sacrifice in Leviticus that is wholly consumed by fire. See the piyyut "Lemi Oy" by Ephraim of Bonn, with its refrain *zot torat haʿolah hi haʿolah ʿal mokdah* ("This is the ritual of the olah sacrifice performed on the pyre"). The piyyut can be found in A. M. Habermann, *Gezeirot Ashkenaz veTsarfat* (Jerusalem, 1946), 133–36, 257–58. My thanks to Menahem Schmelzer for this reference.

26. In the Apocrypha, Sira 3:21.

27. On the image of R. Amnon, see the important article by Michal Arbell, "R. Amnon of Mainz as Paragon: The Development of a Cultural Icon in the Works of Agnon" [in Hebrew] in *Studies in Jewish Narrative*, vol. 2, ed. Avidov Lipsker and Rella Kushelevsky (Ramat Gan: Bar-Ilan University Press, 2009), 325–59.

28. Isserles's fame was based in part on his interpolations in Joseph Karo's *Shulḥan ʿarukh* that reconcile that law code with practice in European communities.

29. The sacrifices and substitutions abound in the story and create a complex analogical set of equivalences. The true, material sacrifice offered in the Temple has been replaced by verbal prayer. Within the telling of the story, the willing sacrifice of the first Gavriel is replaced by the verbal narrative of his grandson.

30. The narrator may be encouraging a supernatural conception of Gavriel, as if he were an angelic being that must return home by daybreak.

31. On the role of Satan, see Aryeh Wineman, "Agnon's 'Linen Man': Abraham and Satan in the Land of Ambiguity," *Prooftexts* 7, no. 1 (1987): 65–71.

32. For an elaboration of this idea, see my *Ḥurban: Responses to Catastrophe in Hebrew Literature* (Syracuse, NY: Syracuse University Press, 1996), 84–105.

33. R. Amnon is the great figure of legend and the composer of one of the most famous prayers in the liturgy. But when compared with Gavriel, it is the latter who never waivered in his faith and who endured sufferings that last two and half years rather than a few days.

34. Translation by Wendy Zierler.

35. Benyamin Luken, http://www.yivoencyclopedia.org/article.aspx/Kamianets -Podilskyi (Pol., Kamieniec Podolski; Rus., Kamenets Podolski). Despite the later size and fame of this fortress city, in the first half of the eighteenth century, when this story takes place, the city had a small Jewish population, having undergone Turkish conquest, an expulsion, and coerced theological disputations. It is no wonder then that Gavriel would be interested in relocating in Buczacz. How the small Jewish population could have sustained a choir in addition to a ḥazzan is less clear.

36. The nameless Russian ḥazzan, a man of estimable qualities, would seem to present a refutation to the argument that it is impossible to overcome the dangers of standing before the teivah. The explanation, I would offer, is lodged in the question of the period. The term of his service lies beyond the vague cut-off after which Agnon declines to follow the fortunes of worship and study in Buczacz precisely because those institutions have lost their numinous power. Therefore the space before the teivah is not charged with dangerous uncertainty.

Chapter 4

1. The meaning of the Hebrew in Isa. 18:2, *memushakh umorat*, is obscure.

2. On the relationship between the magnates and Jewish communities, see Gershon David Hundert, *Jews in Poland-Lithuania in the Eighteenth Century: A Genealogy of Modernity* (Berkeley and Los Angeles: University of California Press, 2004), 84–86, 108–9, 112–17; and Moshe Rosman, *The Lord's Jews: Magnate-Jewish Relations in the Polish-Lithuanian Commonwealth during the Eighteenth Century* (Cambridge, MA: Harvard University Press, 1990), 106–42.

3. Adam Teller, "Tradition and Crisis? Eighteenth-Century Critiques of the Polish-Lithuanian Rabbinate," *Jewish Social Studies: History, Culture, Society*, n.s., 17, no. 3 (Spring/Summer 2011): 1–3.

4. On the state of the rabbinate in this period, see Adam Teller, "Rabbis without a Function? The Polish Rabbinate and the Council of the Four Lands" in *Jewish Religious Leadership: Image and Reality*, ed. Jack Wertheimer, 371–401 (New York: Jewish Theological Seminary, 2004); and Simon Schwarzfuchs, *A Concise History of the Rabbinate* (Oxford: Blackwell, 1993), 50–63.

5. It cannot be accidental that R. Moshe is a fictional character, as opposed to the three later rabbis.

6. "The Parable and Its Lesson" is one of most impressive narratives in *A City in Its Fullness*. I do not discuss the story at length in this study because it is treated in my introduction and essay to S.Y. Agnon, *The Parable and Its Lesson*, trans. James S. Diamond (Stanford: Stanford University Press, 2013).

7. Translation by Jeffrey Green.

8. See also the recent study by Roman Katsman, *Literature, History, Choice: The Principle of Alternative History in Literature (S.Y. Agnon, The City with All That Is Therein* [Newcastle upon Tyne: Cambridge Scholars, 2013), 236–90]). In *'Ir, mishpat, sippur* [City, law, story] (Tel Aviv: Schocken, 2002), Shulamit Almog approaches the story through the lens of law and jurisprudence. She argues that Buczacz, like Zabno and all human

communities that wish to live in civil accord, is faced with the necessity of legal adjudication because of the imperfect makeup of human nature. The search for a rabbi is motivated not only by civic pride but by the real need for an authority who can secure the rule of law. Almog productively calls our attention to the many instances of legal procedures in the novella, almost all of which remain unresolved or whose resolutions are not reported to the reader.

9. This applies only to non-hasidic rabbinic leadership. The notion of the rabbi as a tsaddik was a revolutionary change, but it has little resonance in the mitnagdic world of Buczacz.

10. Auerbach was a historical figure. He left Buczacz in 1740 and died in 1750.

11. The issue recurs in variations twice in this, the first section of the story. After the intensity of their frequent nighttime study sessions, R. Mordekhai announces to R. Avraham that he is moving with his family to Buczacz, and the question then arises of how the two will take leave of each other. The Talmud instructs two parting scholars to exchange a *devar halakhah*, a legal teaching. Another tradition enjoins the departing person to ensure that his debts have been paid, and R. Mordekhai has repeatedly deferred fulfilling the promise he made to relate the story of how he acquired his prodigious knowledge. Here again the dilemma presents itself as a choice between teaching and story, and, again, a rationale is produced to authorize the recourse to the latter (pp. *327–28, 280–81*). Immediately following that passage, R. Avraham interrupts his monologue as dawn is breaking and observes that a whole night has passed without words of Torah learning having been exchanged. R. Ber hastens to put his mind at ease with an anecdote about how his rabbinical sons-in-law once spent a whole evening discussing the ordeals brought on the Jews by Khmelnytskyi, Shabetai Tsevi, and Jacob Frank without exchanging words of Torah. They did so without compunction based on the principle that *maʿaseihem shel yisrael torah*, the act of recounting the tribulations of Israel is itself Torah, a position buttressed by a subtle exegesis of Num. 21:14 ("The Book of the Wars of the Lord") offered by his colleague R. Yeruḥam (p. *329*, 282). In staging these various rationales, is not Agnon in the end conveying to us something fundamental about his own master choice to represent the lost world of Buczacz through story rather than teaching?

12. Except for dialogue and the representation of inner thoughts, the only way we can hear the sustained voice of the characters who populate the stories is for the narrator temporarily to relinquish his monopoly and hand over the baton to one of them. This is precisely what happens at three critical junctures in the volume in which the poetics of the monologue are leveraged to create extraordinarily vivid figures embodied in their voices. Gavriel, the grandson, recounts the martyrdom of his grandfather in "The Man Dressed in Linen"; R. Avraham describes his relationship with the mysterious R. Mordekhai in the story before us now; and the shamash in "The Parable and Its Lesson" recalls the journey to Gehinnom taken a half century earlier. Each of these guest narrators differs from the master narrator in his own way. But they are joined in one thing: unlike the narrator, none is a storyteller, and each story is the great moment in each one's life, a one-time event that has been provoked by a crisis. Each is importuned by an inquisitive audience, but, rather than resisting, each takes the encounter as a

providential opportunity to disburden of a story that has been repressed at some emotional cost. Although the monologist is telling a story about another (R. Gavriel, the linen man, R. Mordekhai, or R. Moshe and his journey to the Netherworld), the true revelation is reflexive. The teller exposes himself in the telling and because the disclosures are inadvertent, they often are found not in the main narrative but in digressions, repetitions, and obiter dicta.

13. Given the fact that Maharam Schiff is a shade—he will return to the Heavenly Academy by first light the next morning—the question is asked whether he should be separated from others by a partition, a *meḥitsah*, during prayer in the way that would be done in the presence of a dead body? (Agnon must surely have appreciated how droll this would strike his contemporary readers.) On this halakhic question R. Avraham happens to have a "huge pilpul" to offer, and he appears poised to present it, remaining, as he does, supremely unaware of the recent blow to the value of his intellectual property in the marketplace of learning. But he refrains from doing so to keep this golden insight on hand "to recite before the saints in Gan Eden" when his time comes.

14. On this notion, see the statement of R. Hiyya bar Abba in Kiddushin 30b and the exegesis of Num. 21:14.

15. Almog points out that despite his flaws and inner struggles, R. Avraham manages to negotiate the dual roles of community rabbi and disinterested Torah sage. Having been taught well by his teacher, R. Mordekhai rejects this path out of hand; but his purism leaves the messy matter of justice for others to handle. Almog, following Dan Laor, proposes a real-life model for R. Mordekhai in the person of R. Shmuel Byalovlosky, an independent rabbinic scholar Agnon admired and consulted in his rabbinic anthologies (*'Ir, mishpat, sippur,* 143–46).

16. The contradictory fact that R. Avraham chooses to stay in Zabno because the Jewish-gentile relations there are superior to those in Buczacz is not addressed.

17. There is a break of several pages to accommodate a return to the present time of the narrative. When the monologue resumes the next morning after prayers, it is worth noting a change in the setting. Now the audience for R. Avraham's narration includes not just the visitors from Buczacz but also the elders of Zabno, who crowd into the rabbi's study. This represents a more extreme, public layer of the rabbi's "outing" of R. Mordekhai.

18. R. Avraham, the narrator here, insists on calling the boy "Rabbi Mordekhai" out of respect for his later learning.

19. Jonathan D. Spence, *The Memory Palace of Matteo Ricci* (New York: Viking Penguin, 1984).

20. Reuven and Shimon, the older sons of Jacob in Genesis, are generic names commonly used in legal discussions of the sort, "If Reuven lent Shimon ten dinars, then. . . ." Not surprisingly no last names or other monikers are given.

21. Such an enormous number would seem like a hyperbole, but there did exist in Poland several noble families whose holdings would come close.

22. The conspicuousness of the biblical allusion draws attention to the fact that God as an actor or a presence is not mentioned throughout the Reuven and Shimon story. Nature is left to act on its own, and the flood becomes a cosmic judgment on the affairs of men.

23. Shimon consistently uses his religious knowledge as an instrument of realpolitik. He learns mishnayot for the repose of the first husband's soul to appropriate his privileges in the mind of the Duke, and he performs a strange kabbalistic ceremony called *tikkun 'almanah*, which he adapts for his own good rather his wife's (pp. *374–75, 341–342*).

24. It is not clear whether this figure is the Polish magnate who owns the city or his administrator, or whether this is the Austrian official who now administers the city as a provincial appointment. Earlier in the story, at the point when Mordekhai's father set up his inn, it was made clear that the Austrians had taken control. But Agnon leaves the historical situation fuzzy, perhaps to suggest, at least in this context, the generic nature of gentile rule.

25. The language describing his reaction is much more colorful: *nitkarkemu panav shel R. Mordekhai venehefkhu keshulei kedeirah* (his face turned green-yellow with consternation and black like the inside of a pot). The idioms are based on *Bereishit Rabbah* 20 and *Shabbat* 30a, respectively.

26. The majority of the novella was published in Agnon's lifetime in *Ha'aretz* (Sept. 21, Oct. 5, and Oct. 12, 1960; and March 2, 1961) and was of course reviewed and vetted by the author. The last sections (pp. *377–93, 345–68*), beginning with the rabbinic jurist who invalidates the participation of merchants who are not scholars) appeared only in *A City in Its Fullness*, and they did not benefit from his revision.

Chapter 5

1. Translation by Jules Harlow.
2. On Mikołaj Potocki, see Chapter 1, note 3.
3. The incident is recounted in the story "Beit hamo'eitsot hakatan," p. *256*.
4. This general picture of Jews and Poles in the region is synthesized from the following works: Gershon Hundert, *Jews in a Polish Private Town: The Case of Opatow in the Eighteenth Century* (Baltimore: Johns Hopkins University Press, 1992); Jerzy Lukowski, *Disorderly Liberty: The Political Culture of the Polish-Lithuanian Commonwealth in the Eighteenth Century* (London: Continuum, 2010); Moshe Rosman, *The Lord's Jews: Magnate-Jewish Relations in the Polish-Lithuanian Commonwealth During the 18th Century* (Cambridge, MA: Harvard University Press, 1990); Omer Bartov, *The Voice of Your Brother's Blood: Buczacz, Biography of a Town* (New York: Simon and Schuster, forthcoming).
5. These numbers represent estimates from latter part of 20th century. Earlier in the century, Jewish historians believed the number to be much greater, well over 100,000, and Agnon was likely basing himself on this understanding.
6. I am dealing here with the representation of Jewish-Polish relations *only* within *A City in Its Fullness*. The topic in the whole of Agnon's fiction is obviously much larger, and fortunately it has been surveyed with characteristic virtuosity by Shmuel Werses in "Between Historical Reality and Fictional Description: The Relations Between Jews and Poles in the Writings of S.Y. Agnon" [in Hebrew] in his *Shai Agnon kefeshuto: keri'ah bikhtavav* [S.Y. Agnon, literally: studies of his writings] (Jerusalem: Mossad Bialik, 2000), 215–63. See also his *Relations between Jews and Poles in S. Y. Agnon's Work* (Jerusalem: Magnes Press, 1994). Agnon was preoccupied with the larger meaning of the Polish-

Jewish experience from early in his career, as evinced by the stories in the cycle *Polin*, that were begun in 1917 and later included in the volume of his collected stories *Eilu ve'eilu*. See Nitza Bendov's insightful analysis of one of the earliest of these stories, "The Story 'Bimetsulot' as a Paradigm for the Relations between Jews and Poles" [in Hebrew] in *Ayin Gimel: ketav 'eit leheqer yetsirat 'Agnon* no. 2 (2012), http://www.biu.ac.il/js/li/aj/images_ag_eng/second_issue_eng.html.

7. See p. 308, the introduction to the stories in book 2.

8. This fact helps to fix the time of the story's action as the beginning of the 18th century. The narrator is disinclined to provide overt historical markers to enable the archetypal nature of the tale to dominate.

9. Translation by Jules Harlow.

10. The Rabbi of Yaslowitz is probably R. Zvi Hirsch Margolies.

11. It is not easy to be precise in identifying the cuts and fabrics the passage describes. My thanks to Avraham Holtz in helping me to reach viable approximations.

12. See the entry in the Jewish Encyclopedia s.v. "head dress." Agnon uses the term *mitsnefet* elsewhere to indicate the fabric head wrap worn by a married woman whose head has been shaven.

13. R. Moshe Aharon is childless. His will leaves a third of this estate to his wife, a third to the synagogue, and a third to the community, despite the ill will of his poor brothers and other relatives (p. *141*, 173).

14. See Eliezer Ben-Yehudah, *Milon halashon ha'ivrit,* vol. 8 (New York and Jerusalem: Thomas Yoseloff, 1958), 7503–5.

15. One arrangement that is especially apposite to the themes of the story is given in the name of Reish Lakish, Yerushalmi Ta'anit 2:6, "[The Holy One says,] if I left Israel to their own devices, they would be swallowed up by the idolatrous nations; therefore, I am associating [*meshatef*] my great name with them so they will live."

16. "Beit hamo'atsot hagadol" ["The Great Town Hall"], *233–38*, 192–200.

17. In the corpus of Agnon's Buczacz stories, there is much less attention given to the Jews' relations with the Ruthenian peasants than their relations with the Polish rulers. Describing a peasant farmer in a later story, the narrator observes, "Being a Ruthenian, he was treated by the Poles like an animal, whereas the Jews treated him like a human being and did not humiliate him gratuitously" ("Besha'ah ahat" [In a Single Moment, p. *571*, 473–74]. The interaction between the elderly charcoal maker and the dispossessed tavern keeper in our story is even more positive. See also the story that immediately follows "The Partners," titled "The Little Town Hall" ["Beit hamo'atsot hakatan," pp. *255–69*], which describes the murderous rampage of a headstrong young peasant who means to conduct his own courtship of a maiden in flagrant disregard for the practices of Ruthenian society. It should be noted in our story that Nahum Ze'ev and his wife seem to dwell in harmony with their gentile, peasant neighbors, and they have no difficulty in borrowing a horse and wagon from them to bring the count home (p. *244*, 207–8).

18. Praying with the community is not just a matter of solidarity. Without a quorum of ten men, the Torah cannot be read, and several important elements of the liturgy cannot be recited.

19. Roman Katsman argues that both charcoal making and yeast manufacture are charged occupations that link to other stories, such as "The Hidden Tsaddik" (pp. *220–28*), in which the promotion of domestic happiness takes on a holy and mystical importance. See Roman Katsman, *Nevu'ah ketanah: Kenut veretorikah be'ir umelo'ah le Shai Agnon* [A modest prophecy: sincerity and rhetoric in *A City in Its Fullness*] (Ramat Gan: Bar-Ilan University, 2014).

20. Translation by Arthur Green in *Book That Was Lost*, 429. In *City*, 716.

21. See the Introduction for a discussion of Roman Katsman's *Literature, History, Choice: The Principle of Alternative History* in *Literature* (S. Y. Agnon, *The City with All That Is Therein, Book Two*) (Cambridge, UK: Cambridge Scholars, 2013) and his comprehensive discussion of alternative history.

Chapter 6

1. "The Jewish Question in Galicia: The Reforms of Maria Theresa and Joseph II, 1772–1790" in *POLIN: Studies in Polish Jewry*, vol. 12, ed. Israel Bartal and Antony Polonsky, 70 (London and Portland, OR: The Littman Library of Jewish Civilization, 1999).

2. Gazlan is Hebrew for robber. Here it denotes a thug or a gangster.

3. James S. Diamond is the translator of all four of these stories.

4. *Continuatio edictorum et mandatorum universalium in Regnis Galiciae et Lodomeriae (1776)*: 76–121, esp. §1, 88; and Michael Stöger, *Darstellung der gesetzlichen Verfassung der galizischen Judenschaft*, 1 (Lemberg, 1833), vol. 2, §59, p. 95. My thanks to Rachel Manekin for her help with these sources.

5. The name Feivush or Feivel is thought to derive from Phoebus, the Latin name for Apollo, the god of light. It is often paired with the name of Shraga, Aramaic for fire. The connection to Feivush's duties is obvious.

6. This is the kind of staged intersection often found in these stories. In "The Sign," the news about the destruction of Buczacz by the Nazis is made to arrive in the afternoon preceding the holiday of Shavuot. In the story titled "In a Single Moment," Menaḥem's birthday falls on Tu be'av (the fifteenth of Av), a festival of matchmaking during Second Temple times. And, most importantly is Agnon's decision to make his own birth date the ninth of Av.

7. For the public discourse surrounding the kapo trials and the Kastner trial, see Tom Segev, *The Seventh Million: Israelis and the Holocaust* (New York: Hill and Wang, 1991), 255–75. My thanks to Omer Bartov for discussions on this topic.

8. Like the titles of all the chapters, the title of chapter 4 has a tongue-in-cheek quality. "Menuḥah vesimḥah" ("Relaxation and Peace") is the first half of the opening line of one of the standard table hymns sung at the midday Sabbath meal. The other half continues *or layehudim* (light for the Jews). The theme of light and the extinguishing of light constantly keeps circulating.

9. The midrashic source is Lamentations Rabbah 14 and 15.

10. Note that throughout these chapters, Agnon presents the denizens of the beit midrash and the other Jews who later stream to the site of the so-called fire as one undifferentiated body without names or individual characters. It is only Feivush and Mamtchi who are discernable and deeply realized characters.

11. Menaḥem Mendel Lefin of Satanov (1749–1826) was an early East European maskil and the author of several works of Musar (ethical) literature. See Nancy Sinkoff, *Tradition and Transition: Mendel Lefin of Satanow and the Beginnings of Jewish Enlightenment in Eastern Europe, 1749–1826* (PhD diss., Columbia University, 1996).

12. Although Maimonides recommends remaining at rest immediately after eating (*Hilkhot De'ot* 4:3), he does not explicitly advise sleep.

13. Philip Birnbaum, ed. and trans., *High Holiday Prayer Book* (New York: Hebrew Publishing, 2000), p. 33.

14. Rabbi Zvi Hirsch Kra (the Neta Sha'ashu'im) served from 1794 to 1814, and Rabbi Avraham David Wahrman (the Da'at Kedoshim) from 1814 to 1840.

15. For the attitude that *A City in Its Fullness* has concerning Hasidism, see "Hasidim harishonim," *526–30, 453–454.* Also, see Chapter 1. It is important to note that the volume's implicit bias leads to a kind of underreporting of the importance of Hasidism in Buczacz. The historical period is an additional factor. In the mid-nineteenth century, Galicia had the greatest number of Hasidic institutions in Eastern Europe. But this was not yet the case at the end of the eighteenth century and the turn of the nineteenth. The Hasidic dynasty centered in and named for the town of Chertikov, close to Buczacz, was later prominently represented in Buczacz, and Agnon's grandparents were affiliated with Chertikov Hasidism. By the end of the nineteenth century these distinctions exerted far less force.

16. The allure of this book also conquered R. Elya in the story "Haḥazzanim." See Chapter 3, note 18.

17. See Mishnah *Yevamot* 6:6.

18. See Shmuel Shiloh, *Dina dimalkhuta dina* [The law of the land is the law] (Jerusalem: Academic, 1976).

19. The general communal opinion pauses for a moment to register the fact that "a woman's testimony is not accepted according to Jewish law," but then goes on to say, "still the matter needed to be investigated" (p. *515,* 448) and be absorbed in the groundswell to condemn him.

20. In "Yekele One" the agency of R. Yisrael Shlomo is mediated by the active presence of the local governor, who prods the compliant parnas into considering the death sentence. The governor is also given a semi-comic scene in which he bosses his clerk around like a petty tyrant.

21. The ritual is described in the ninth chapter of Mishnah *Sotah.* The ritual was abrogated, we are told in *mishnah 9,* once murders became commonplace. It could also not be performed outside the Land of Israel while the Sanhendrin existed. The actions of the Buczaczers are merely a symbolic expression of their bad conscience and their powerlessness.

Chapter 7

1. The conscription of Jews into the Russian army, which began about twenty-five years later, is a parallel phenomenon with different features and aims. Among them is the age of induction. In the Austrian army, the age of conscription was supposed to be no lower than eighteen, whereas in Russia, much younger boys were taken and edu-

cated in military schools before being transferred to the regular army. A boy served a 25–year term of service after he reached eighteen. See the entry "Military Service in Russia" by Yohanan Petrovsky-Stern in *The YIVO Encyclopedia,* http://www.yivoency clopedia.org/article.aspx/Military_Service_in_Russia, accessed June 14, 2015.

2. For an excellent overview of the debate, see Michael K. Silber, "From Tolerated Aliens to Citizen-Soldiers: Jewish Military Service in the Era of Joseph II," in *Constructing Nationalities in East Central Europe* [Austrian and Habsburg Studies 6], ed. Pieter M. Judson and Marsha L. Rozenlit, 19–35 (New York: Berghahn, 2004). It is impossible not to see parallels to this debate in the discussions within the Israeli government, from 2010 to the present, in which the army expresses exasperation about integrating ultra-Orthodox Jews into military service and the government, because of popular outcry, urges their inclusion.

3. For some of the original legislation, see *Continuatio edictorum et mandatorum universalium in Regnis Galiciae et Lodomeriae (1788):* 76–121, esp. §65 and (1789): 98–99, esp. §48–51. (Again, my thanks to Rachel Manekin for drawing my attention to these materials.)

4. 'Ir umelo'ah, 448–92; *City,* 369–426.

5. Jews continued to refer to it as the kahal despite the official nomenclature.

6. This is the concept of *ḥitutei shikhvi,* disturbing the repose of the dead. It is based on *Yevamot* 63b, which quotes 1 Sam. 12:15. See Radak ad loc.

7. The narrator is circumspect in making explicit judgments, but he lets us know about his moral discomfort by telling us about the existence in Buczacz of a dissenting view expressed by "those who seek God selflessly and are faithful to His covenant," (*452,* 375–76). The narrator also points to the example of the venerable Buczacz-born-and-raised scholar R. Meshulam Igra, who left his post as rabbi of Tisminitz and moved to Hungary rather than be complicit in the practice. The rabbi went so far as to say that "if his only son, Rabbi Yosef Eliyahu, ever was about to be conscripted, he, Rabbi Meshulam, would let him go and would not redeem him with another Jewish man," (*452,* 375–76).

8. Wheat money (*ma'ot ḥittin*) was disbursed from communal funds to the poor to buy wheat to be ground into flour from which Passover matzah was baked. The custom of distributing such funds goes back to Talmudic times.

9. A *Landesrabbiner* was the head rabbi of a district or a province in the countries of Central Europe.

10. I am grateful to Ariel Hirschfeld for sharpening my awareness of this feature of the story.

11. The metaphor is Hirschfeld's.

12. An exception is the story of the melodramatic elopement of the son of a Jewish miller and the daughter of a Greek-Catholic priest, "Devarim shekisuyam yafeh megiluyam" [Matters better left unsaid], pp. *214–15.*

13. The telling metonym for the mother's abjection is saliva and spittle (*roq*). "So what did that woman live on? What sustained her?" asks the narrator. "If not her suffering, then it was only her saliva that kept her alive as she had told R. Leibush, the parnas, before he took her son from her," (p. *453–54,* 377). *Roq* is a figure for what an abject person possesses when there is nothing else. *Roq* is also the fluid produced in the

mouth from excessive, demonstrative speaking. In both senses, then, this is truly what that woman lived on.

14. The narrator parses the name as "man of hope"; but *hoff* more likely means court. There is abundant irony in both options.

15. See the entry "Brivnshtelers" by Alice Nakhimovsky, and Roberta Newman in the *YIVO Encyclopedia,* http://www.yivoencyclopedia.org/article.aspx/Brivnshtelers#author24, accessed June 24, 2015. The greatest example of the use of the genre in Jewish literature is Sholem Aleichem's epistolary novel *The Letters of Mehahem Mendl.*

16. The second sentence is not in the translation and is added here.

17. On Perl, see Joseph Perl, *Sefer Megale Temirin,* 2 vols., ed. Jonatan Meir (Jerusalem: Mossad Bialik, 2013).

18. The medic who tends to the injuries of Feivush and his wife is interested in similar moral issues. See "Feivush Gazlan," pp. *292–93, 227–52).*

19. There is also an accounting later of ten years altogether, four in the army and six with the noblewoman. See p. *484, 416.*

20. For "diary" Agnon prefers the antique *sefer hayamim* over the common neologism *yoman.* We are using "lady" as a translation for *adonit,* which is already an equivalent for the Polish term for a female member of the gentry.

Chapter 8

1. *A City in Its Fullness* contains close to one hundred pages of additional material, to be sure; but these two texts are the last full-fledged fictional stories. ("Frogs" ["Tsefarde'im," pp. *589–602, 498–517*] intervenes between the two, but it can be considered as a kind of study for "Pisces.") In Emunah Yaron's editing, the volume concludes with "The Sign" ["Hasiman," pp. *695–716, 1–29*], a story of formidable importance but one that was previously published. As I argued in the Introduction, the story is a consecration story that explains Agnon's calling to undertake the writing of the Buczacz stories but does not belong to the project proper.

2. First published in *Davar (Musaf)* 7, no. 33 (July 22, 1932). The story appears in the standard edition in the volume *Eilu ve'eilu,* pp. 256–67.

3. For a useful overview of the different modalities of the Elijah legends, see Beatrice Silverman Weinreich, "Genre and Types of Yiddish Folk Tales about the Prophet Elijah" in *The Field of Yiddish (Second Collection),* ed. Uriel Weinreich (The Hague: Mouton, 1965), 202–25.

4. Translation by Hebert Levine and Reena Spicehandler.

5. The gift of a kerchief from a husband to a wife recalls the story "The Kerchief" mentioned above (see note 2). In that story the kerchief is a richly endowed symbol of the sanctity and purity that inhere in family attachments.

6. Although the story doesn't use the term, what he has done is an instance of *me'ilah,* the appropriation for one's own benefit of resources devoted to holy purposes. It is a cardinal sin for those invested with the community's trust.

7. "Vagrant," with its slight pejorative inflection, is a translation of the Hebrew *helekh,* which comes from the common verb to walk or travel. The Hebrew emphasizes impermanence, sojourning, and movement rather than poverty. The *helekh* is a *homo viator.*

8. "In a Single Moment" first appeared in *Haaretz* on September 16 and 25, 1955. Agnon is reported to have special regard for the story. See David Canaani, *Shai Agnon be'al peh* [S.Y. Agnon in His Own Words] (Merhavia: Kibbutz Hameuchad, 1971), 51–52. In one of the few critical discussions of the story, Shmuel Werses states that Agnon first thought about the plot for the story in 1948. Shmuel Werses, "Intertextual Patterns and Their Function in "In a Single Moment" [in Hebrew] in *Kovets Agnon II,* ed. Emunah Yaron et al., 213–24 (Jerusalem: Magnes Press, 2000). See also S. D. Goitein, "In a Single Moment" [in Hebrew] in *Le'Agnon shai* [A tribute to Agnon, S.Y.] (Jerusalem: The Jewish Agency, 1965), 27–45.

9. Translation by Michael Swirsky.

10. The question of whether such early marriage—and early procreation—is or is not a good thing for the boy and the girl is not dealt with in this story or elsewhere in *A City in Its Fullness.* A severe critique of this practice is one of the themes of the new Hebrew literature that emerges in the nineteenth century. See my *Banished from Their Father's Table: Loss of Faith and Hebrew Autobiography* (Bloomington: Indiana University Press, 1989), ch. 2. On the social background of this practice, see Shaul Stampfer, *Families, Rabbis and Education: Traditional Jewish Society in Nineteenth-Century Eastern Europe* (London: Littman Library, 2014).

11. On the origins of Tu Be'av, see Vered Noam, *Megilat ta'anit* (Jerusalem: Yad Ben Zvi, 2003), 217; and Paul Mandel, "Never Were There Such Good Days for Israel" [in Hebrew], *Te'udah* 11 (1996): 147–48. Through an analysis of the textual witnesses, Mandel argues that the festivity surrounding the offering of the trees preceded the matchmaking.

12. The occasion for the festivity described in the Mishnah is connected directly to trees, and it is under an apple tree that Menaḥem will experience the epiphany that enhances his humanity and makes him ready to be a bridegroom.

13. Dan Laor, *Ḥayyei 'Agnon: Biografiyah* [The life of Agnon: A biography] (Jerusalem and Tel Aviv: Schocken Books, 1998), 19–20.

14. There is the additional halakhic consideration of keeping *mitsvot* separate (*ain 'osin mitsvot ḥavilot*).

15. The issue concerns the recitation of a mystical formula beginning with the words: *leshem yiḥud* [For the sake of the unification]. This is a kabbalistic practice intended to enhance awareness of the commandment's capacity to effect reunification within the Godhead. The controversy reflects the deep penetration of Lurianic Kabbalah into the religious life of Polish Jewry as well as equally deep concerns about the potential sectarian exploitation of these practices.

16. A similarly positive portrayal of relations between Jews and Ruthenians is found in the opening pages of "The Partners."

17. Mikhl Ber is the protagonist of the story "Frogs," which appears directly following "In a Single Moment."

18. The narrator makes a point here of citing the practice instituted in Buczacz by R. Avraham Teomim of uncovering the face of the bride so that the witness could be assured of her identity. The inhabitants of Buczacz took the liberty to see it as an opportunity to endear the bride to the bridegroom.

19. "Well-known in the gates," Prov. 31:23. The husband of a "capable wife" is "well-known in the gates" (gathering places) of the city.

Index

9th of Av, 262, 271
15th of Av. *See* Tu Be'av
20th of Sivan, 57, 121, 170, 218, 404n12

Aaron [young scholar], 89–90, 103, 218
Abramovitch, Shalom, 362
afterlife, 87–88. *See also* Gehinnom
Agnon, S.Y., 1–5, 10–11, 394–96; creative
   choices/principles, 14–20; Holocaust
   literature and, 12–14. *See also* narrative
   authors/narrators
akedah. See sacrifice of Isaac
Almog, Shulamit, 22–23, 406–7n8
alternative history, 22, 30, 250–51
Amnon of Mainz, 138, 147, 405n33
Arendt, Hannah, 265
Ark (Holy Ark; Ark of the Covenant),
   113–14, 240
arrendators, 165, 215. *See also* Reuven
   and Shimon
artists, romantic, 118–19
audience/readership, 93–98, 101, 108. *See
   also* narrative authors/narrators
Austrian Empire: Agnon's view, 293;
   conscription/military service and (*see*
   military service); Jews and, 43–44, 52,
   69, 253–55, 279–81, 295–96, 305–6,
   312; officials, 322–26, 339; Polish
   nobility and (*see* Austrian-Polish relations); on religion, 292
Austrian-Polish relations, 191, 239, 294,
   304, 323–26

Avodah service, 116–17
Avraham David [Menaḥem's father],
   107–8, 342, 365–66, 370–81, 383–88
R. Avraham Moshe (Abush) of Zabno,
   105–6, 166, 168–69, 171–88, 408n13,
   408n15

Band, Arnold, 79, 393
Bartov, Omer, 23, 47–48
batei keneset (sing. *beit keneset*). *See* syna-
   gogues/synagogue worship
batei midrash (sing. *beit midrash*). *See* study
   houses
beit hakeneset hagadol. See Great
   Synagogue
benei torah, 53
the Bible, study of, 194–96. *See also* Torah
   study/chanting
biblical allusions/imagery, 202–3, 408n22;
   creation and flood, 203; Elijah, 340–
   44, 348, 350–52; great town hall and,
   42–43; "Haḥazzanim" and, 404n13;
   Joseph, 331; letter writing and, 314; in
   "R. Moshe Aharon the Mead Merchant," 226; sacrifice of Isaac, 388; in
   "The Man Dressed in Linen," 133; in
   "The Sign," 8
Bilhah, 299, 303–4, 327–28, 330; Dan's
   mother and, 308, 310, 315–16, 321–23;
   management of suffering, 308–10,
   321–23; significance of Dan's letters,
   315–16

STANFORD STUDIES IN JEWISH HISTORY AND CULTURE
Edited by David Biale and Sarah Abrevaya Stein

This series features novel approaches to examining the Jewish past in the form of innovative work that brings the field into productive dialogue with the newest scholarly concepts and methods. Open to a range of disiplinary and interdisciplinary approaches from history to cultural studies, this series publishes exceptional scholarship balanced by an accessible tone that illustrates histories of difference and addresses issues of current urgency. Books in this list push the boundaries of Jewish Studies and speak compellingly to a wide audience of scholars and students.

For a complete listing of titles in this series,
visit the Stanford University Press website, www.sup.org.